REGNUM S

Voices Loud and Clear

Series Preface

Regnum Studies in Mission are born from the lived experience of Christians and Christian communities in mission, especially but not solely in the fast growing churches among the poor of the world. These churches have more to tell than stories of growth. They are making significant impacts on their cultures in the cause of Christ. They are producing 'cultural products' which express the reality of Christian faith, hope and love in their societies.

Regnum Studies in Mission are the fruit often of rigorous research to the highest international standards and always of authentic Christian engagement in the transformation of people and societies. And these are for the world. The formation of Christian theology, missiology and practice in the twenty-first century will depend to a great extent on the active participation of growing churches contributing biblical and culturally appropriate expressions of Christian practice to inform World Christianity.

Series Editors

Marina Behera	Research Tutor, Oxford Centre for Mission Studies
Paul Bendor-Samuel	Director, Oxford Centre for Mission Studies
Michael Biehl	Retired, former Executive Secretary for Mission Studies
Bill Dyrness	Former Dean of the School of theology, Fuller Seminary
Tony Gray	Director, Words by Design
Paul Woods	Asia Graduate School of Theology – Alliance

REGNUM STUDIES IN MISSION

Voices Loud and Clear

Kong Hee, Byron D. Klaus
& Douglas Petersen (eds)

Copyright © Kong Hee, Byron D. Klaus & Douglas Peterson 2024

First published 2024 by Regnum Books International

Regnum is an imprint of the Oxford Centre for Mission Studies
St. Philip and St. James Church
Woodstock Road
Oxford, OX2 6HR, UK
www.regnumbooks.net

The rights of Kong Hee, Byron D. Klaus & Douglas Peterson to be identified
as the editors of this work has been asserted by them
in accordance with the Copyright, Designs and Patents Act 1988.

All rights reserved. No part of this publication may be reproduced, stored in a retrieval system, or transmitted, in any form or by any means, electronic, mechanical, photocopying, recording or otherwise, without the prior permission of the publisher or a license permitting restricted copying. In the UK such licenses are issued by the Copyright Licensing Agency, 90 Tottenham Court Road, London W1P 9HE.

British Library Cataloguing in Publication Data
A catalogue record for this book is available from the British Library

ISBN: 979-8-8898-3871-5
eBook ISBN: 979-8-8898-3872-2

Typeset by Words by Design

Cover images © Matt Botsford www.unsplash.com

Distributed by Fortress Press in the US, Canada, India, and Brazil

Contents

    Editors' Introduction   1
    Words of Wisdom for Global Pentecostals   3

1. Abraham "made his home in the promised land" (Heb. 11:9, NIV)
   Brian Stiller   7
2. Abraham was "A stranger living in tents" (Heb 11:9, NASB)
   Brian Stiller   15
3. Voices Loud and Clear: What Does This Mean?
   A Reflection on Acts 2:1-13
   Paul Bendor-Samuel   23

    Foundational Considerations for Global Pentecostalism
    Kong Hee, Byron D. Klaus, and Douglas Petersen   29

4. From the Atonement to Pentecost:
   An Exegetical and Theological Reflection
   Frank D. Macchia   33
5. Toward Spirit-Empowered Leadership:
   An Old Testament Foundation
   Wonsuk Ma   45
6. The Voice of Truth in the Christian Encounter with World Religions
   Ivan Satyavrata   59
7. The Role of Prayer and its Centrality in Sustaining the
   Effectiveness of Global Christianity
   Young-Hoon Lee   77

    Affirmations for Global Pentecostals
    Kong Hee, Byron D. Klaus, and Douglas Petersen   101

8. The Role of the Church in the Context of Violence
   Juan Angel Castro   109
9. In the Power of the Holy Ghost: Africa and Spirit-Empowered
   Christianity in the Twenty-First Century
   J. Kwabena Asamoah-Gyadu   121
10. Spirit Empowered Women: Why and How the Full
    Participation of Women in Spirit Empowered
    Ministry Strengthens Global Christianity
    Jacqueline Grey   141
11. Unreached People Groups and the Cultural Intelligence Model
    Karl Hargestam and Jennifer Hargestam   151

12	Healing God's Creation: A Contribution of Pentecostal Understanding of Divine Healing to Ecotheology in Response to the Global Ecological Crisis *Gani Wiyono*	165
13	Singapore: The Antioch of Asia? *Kong Hee*	181
	Contemporary Challenges Facing Global Pentecostalism *Kong Hee, Byron D. Klaus, and Douglas Petersen*	205
14	The Challenges of the Church in China in the Next Decade *Kim-Kwong Chan*	211
15	Women's Leadership in Asia and Their Influence on Global Christianity *Julie Ma*	227
16	Spirit-Empowered Global Christianity: The Pathway to Agency for Children at Risk *Mary Mahon*	245
17	Megachurches and Public Life: How Megachurch Congregants See Life as a Whole and Live Out Their Faith in Public Life *Joel Tejedo*	257
18	Digital Pneumatology: Presence and Power of the Holy Spirit in the Metaverse *Guichun Jun*	283
19	Global Christianity and Gen Z: What is the Hope for the Future of Faith? *Antipas Harris*	303
	Contributors	325

Editors' Introduction

Voices Loud and Clear is the result of the Global Pentecostal Summit that took place at City Harvest Church in Singapore, 3rd–6th November 2023. This initiative was conceived through both spiritual discernment and theological conversations between friends who have become siblings in the Lord and colleagues bound together by a deep commitment to the Pentecostal tradition.

The centre of Christianity is most vibrant presently in places where it is most resisted and least accessible. We believe that voices from those challenging locations must be given space to speak to Christianity globally. We also believe that Pentecostal scholarship must serve the Church and not be beholden to academic guilds whose agendas are often self-serving, distancing themselves from the very spiritual communities that need thoroughness in theological reflection.

It was no coincidence that this Summit was hosted by a vibrant local church in Singapore whose resources were stewarded for this particularly unique event. Our hope is that that the intentional location of this event at City Harvest Church and the community of global Pentecostal scholars engaged in significant presentations and conversations will provide the reader with both richness in Pentecostal scholarship and a resource for their own study to serve Christ's Kingdom obediently.

The Global Pentecostal Summit is not unique in bringing together quality Pentecostal scholars from around the world. Significant events held on an increasingly regular basis bring together Pentecostal scholars of global renown. What we *did* try to highlight and reemphasise at the Summit, however, were several key factors not often seen together:

- Our scholarship focused on themes intentionally chosen to serve the contemporary needs of the Majority World Christianity.
- We held this event in a local church, whose effective ministries strive to strengthen their commitment to the Word of God and the empowering presence of the Holy Spirit in a complex world.
- This event was not funded by Western resources; all resources – physical, fiscal, and technological – came from the Majority World.
- The publication of the proceedings of this event – by Regnum Books in both print form and open access format – is being facilitated with the focus on those who could not attend such an event. All sessions from the Summit are available at www.pentecostalsummit.org so that the richness of this significant event can be a resource globally.

This book represents a new relationship that we believe God has graciously granted us. Byron and Doug had previously co-edited two volumes together: *Called and Empowered: Global Mission in Pentecostal Perspective* (Baker Academic, 1991) and *The Globalization of Pentecostalism: A Religion Made to Travel* (Regnum Books, 1999). Our third partner in those endeavours was our forever friend, Murray W. Dempster. We had long hoped to do a third volume together, but Murray's declining health prohibited this. Over the past several years, a wonderful relationship emerged, first between Doug and Kong, and then with Byron joining the new team. We mourn the loss of Murray in December 2023, whose life deeply impacted ours for decades. Doug and Byron have lost our forever friend. His scholarship was renowned, and his joy was infectious. His friendship is simply irreplaceable. But we rejoice in the powerful new relationship that has emerged by the Spirit's direction. Kong Hee is a seasoned pastoral leader in Asia. He and his wife, Sun Ho, founded City Harvest Church in Singapore over thirty years ago, and its powerful ministries are a testimony to the move of the Holy Spirit globally. Together, we believe that this coming season will testify to the goodness of God and the renewing power of the Holy Spirit.

We are grateful to the *Oxford Centre for Mission Studies* (www.ocms.ac.uk). Their partnership in the Global Pentecostal Summit and in the publication of *Voices Loud and Clear* through their publishing arm, Regnum Press, allows this volume to be accessible to Majority World Christian leaders. We are grateful to Paul Bendor-Samuel, executive director of the Oxford Centre for Mission Studies and Regnum for making this volume a reality. We also want to express appreciation to Elizabete Santos and Tony Gray at Regnum Books who worked diligently to make this book available.

We are grateful to a host of people who made the Global Pentecostal Summit happen:

- To Eric Soo, the go-to person for every logistical detail that prepared the City Harvest team for this event and made sure all the presenters actually got to Singapore.
- To Alicia Leo, whose event management and professionalism are a dream for any leader.
- To Dr Bobby Chaw, executive pastor of City Harvest Church, the executive who stands responsible for everything and does it with resolve.
- To the hundreds of City Harvest staff and volunteers who skilfully and joyfully made this a memorable event with their gracious hospitality that no attendee will ever forget.

Thank you also to Dr Lois E. Olena, whose copy-editing skills and commitment to this project made possible an expedited publishing schedule for *Voices Loud and Clear*.

To Sun Ho, Lois, and Myrna who are married to Type A men and whose wisdom keeps us from self-destruction (on a regular basis).

Kong Hee
Byron D. Klaus
Douglas Petersen

Words of Wisdom for Global Pentecostals

Kong Hee, Byron D. Klaus, and Douglas P. Petersen

Each morning of the Global Pentecostal Summit began with worship and the Word. The preachers in these morning sessions were asked to speak candidly to an audience deeply connected to the Pentecostal tradition. Both presenters spoke from the vantage point of long experience with a broad spectrum of Christian traditions. Dr Brian Stiller is Global Ambassador for the World Evangelical Alliance. Dr Paul Bendor-Samuel is the executive director for the Oxford Centre for Mission Studies. The breadth of their experience with global Christianity yielded words of wisdom for all attendees.

Inspiration with poignant warning was reflected in Dr Stiller's exposition of Hebrews 11. His first presentation focused on the phrase in verse 6a, "by faith he made his home in the promised land." Stiller asked the question, what does it mean to "live in the land"? He wonders whether "living in the land" means aligning with political leaders, pastors, or associations so as to gain political advantage, only to lose our prophetic distance? He went on to say that living in the land requires a conscious effort to decipher what in fact it means to live under the reign of Jesus.

Living in the land requires Pentecostals to humbly recognise that we are members of the larger body of Christ. Until Jesus returns, the question remains of whether or not we will be a centre of His flow and empowerment or be "settlers" in the land – consumed and overwhelmed with the details of living comfortably? Stiller asks sternly, what would Jesus make of "living in the land" as it relates to Pentecostals today?

Stiller juxtaposed his first presentation about "living in the land" with a second presentation that focuses on the more agile picture of verse 6b: "like a stranger in a foreign land, he lived in tents." Comparing two kinds of pictures, Stiller comments that Abraham lived in the land but also was alert, not lured into a permanent abode, but ready at a moment's notice to move out. This compares to the description from the classic *City of God*, that we live as citizens in the world, described by St Augustine as "resident aliens" (in Latin, *parengreni*).

Stiller notes the revolutionary nature of the Pentecostal Movement in that it has opened the door to understanding the Trinity in new and clearer ways. The Holy Spirit, often the overshadowed element of the Trinity, has been brought into the light, and global Christianity is the richer for it. Yet history does not stand still, so Pentecostals must not stagnate but move nimbly. Could the imagery of Abraham living in tents offer wisdom to us to think seriously about what it means to be "resident aliens" living in tents?

Stiller pairs this theme of faith with Jesus' prayer in John 17 that focuses on unity among His followers as a picture for "living in the land, but as resident aliens." Unity with others in the body of Christ is an idea that challenges the failure of organisational life, which tends to default to protecting self-interest.

Stiller concludes by admitting what he has suggested is hard work but offers that what the Holy Spirit wants is a resident alien living in the land to remain free and unhindered so the love of Jesus becomes a living reality in all we say and do.

~

Dr Paul Bendor-Samuel offered the final morning exposition, rooting his thoughts in the query of those attendees on the Day of Pentecost recorded in Acts 2:13: "What does this mean?" Comparing the liminal space that the first disciples experienced at Pentecost with the current VUCA world (volatile, uncertain, complex, and filled with ambiguity) that we now experience, Bendor-Samuel posits that liminal spaces need not be limiting, but transformative.

As the Day of Pentecost recorded in Acts is centred in a community praying on their knees in dependence on God, Bendor-Samuel reports that the result of this moment in redemptive history connects the coming of the Spirit with a community gathered from every nation under heaven who break the curse of Babel and now represent an empowered community reflecting Christ's Kingdom rule. However, the human dilemma, in which old habits die hard, reflects the experience of early believers rely on established theological assumptions. The struggle between established theological paradigms and transformative new theological expressions comes to a critical impasse in Acts 15.

Bendor-Samuel then pivots to ask whether the case study of the first theological challenge in the first century could possibly be repeated in the twenty-first century? Simply put, is it still the current tendency to assume that we must maintain our theological presuppositions as the standard by which to judge all others?

He notes that over two hundred years of the Western missionary movement has all too often assumed that their work on theology and mission were to function as normative for all people. Have we rejected the description implicit in the Pentecost event that the global Church is to reflect the mission of God through all the redeemed and transformed cultures and languages?

Bendor-Samuel posits that much work remains to demonstrate what the kingdom of God might look like in varied contexts, cultures, and languages. For example:
- contexts of affluence and poverty;
- contexts of war, displacement, and migration;
- contexts dominated by a particular religion, pluralism, or deep secularism;
- rural and urban contexts;
- contexts in which the church has a long history and those where it is young; and

- contexts where the church is numerous and those where it is still a tiny percentage of the population.

Bendor-Samuel concludes that we should avoid a triumphalist view of Pentecost (and modern Pentecostal history) to focus our attention on the work yet to be attempted. In this conclusion, he mirrors the late Pentecostal mission leader, Loren Triplett, who famously said, "The measure of our success is not calculated by what we have done, but the work yet to be finished!"[1]

Bibliography

Petersen, Douglas D. "The Missionary Manifesto of Loren Triplett." Legacy Lecture Series. Assemblies of God Theological Seminary, Springfield, MO, January 2012.

---

[1] Douglas D. Petersen, "The Missionary Manifesto of Loren Triplett," Legacy Lecture Series, Assemblies of God Theological Seminary, Springfield, MO, January 2012.

1. Abraham "made his home in the promised land" (Heb. 11:9, NIV)[1]

Brian Stiller

In these two mornings together, I want to direct our attention to Hebrews 11:8-10 as we reflect on the contributions of Pentecostals to Kingdom life. We will see two counterposing and interlocking ideas that call us to become not just either, but both. The first idea is about Abraham who "made his home in the promised land" (v. 9). The second idea is that "like a stranger in a foreign country; he lived in tents" (v. 9).

We need to read that biographical comment about Abraham in context. The writer of Hebrews, when laying out in previous chapters the plan of God in Jesus for Jewish readers, describes the absolute superiority of Jesus in all aspects of creation and wraps up the argument with a call to persevere for Christ. Hebrews 10:37-39 states: "For in just a very little while he who is coming will come and will not delay. But my righteous one will live by faith. And if he shrinks back, I will not be pleased with him. But we are not of those who shrink back and are destroyed, but of those who believe and are saved."

With those verses as a prelude, in Chapter 11, the writer launches into an extensive soliloquy on faith. Nothing in Scripture matches this extraordinary painting of a landscape, describing how we interlock with all that the writer has told us about Jesus. It's Jesus and us, connected and made alive by this process called faith.

Growing up in a Pentecostal pastor's home on the Canadian prairies, I heard thousands of sermons, including many on faith. This theme was embedded in our living and thinking. In our small and often struggling church, resilience and planning were fuelled not only by trust in a caring and responsive God but by the faithful actions required of us. For surely, faith is an act. The superb flow of images and actions in Hebrews 11 gives us a descriptive analysis of what faith really is.

To understand faith fully, we could distinguish between the mind, heart, and will. With the mind, I choose to believe; it is this and not that. I can spell it out. This part of faith is cognitive. Meanwhile, the heart lifts me in hope. It frames my life. Third, faith is an act of the will based on trust in God. Faith is what I do. Of course, faith is aligned with belief and hope, but faith is more than that: it is

---

[1] All Scripture quotations, unless otherwise noted, are from the New International Version.

an act made sure by the will. It is the actual outworking of what we do, based on the trust that the God of promise is a God of fulfilment.

Surprisingly, the writer of Hebrews throws us a curve in 11:6, stating that without faith we cannot please the Father. Really? Not by living a holy life or through consistent obedience? Is the writer saying that those things would not also please God? Of course not. But something happens in our relationship with God when we take a risk by faith, and with that, God is pleased.

I define faith as going beyond what I believe I can do, trusting that God will engage by his presence and provision. The story of Joshua crossing into the Promised Land provides an illustration. God's command was, "When the feet of the priest touch the water, then I will stop the water" (Josh. 3:13). I might have countered, "But I have a better idea: you stop the water, then we will walk across." God shakes his head. That's not faith. Faith is taking the risk, knowing that if he doesn't come through, we sink. It is an act based on our trust in his provision.

Abraham left his residence in Ur of the Chaldeans, bringing his family to the land that he was promised which was filled with people from other tribes and nations. In a sense, by making his home in the land, he did something contradictory to the preferred mode of operation for us Pentecostals in our early years. The "soon return of Jesus" theme filled our music, sermons, and reading of world events. John Nelson Darby and his notes on the Bible secured our future, so we decided God was giving up on our world. Fixating on the certainty of his soon return obviated our need to be concerned about our own land at all.

Now, a century later, we see creation undergoing both micro- and macro-level change. A century ago, our eyes were heaven-directed. Heaven was coming soon, so "get me out of here, Lord." However, in time we built churches, developed NGOs, trained pastors, and put systems in place to pay our bills and secure mortgages. Like it or not, we made our home here.

In most places, we Pentecostals are no longer the outliers on the edge of society, and our churches are no longer necessarily nondescript. Now that our enterprises are better financed, I wonder: what did the writer of Hebrews mean when writing that Abraham made his home there? Watch out for the next line: "Like a stranger in a foreign country, he lived in tents" (Heb. 11:9). But that is my second devotional. For now, let's stay with this part of the text: "By faith, he made his home in the promised land" (v. 9).

You and I know the warning: "Be careful – you are so earthly minded that you are of no heavenly use." But in this text – used to illustrate faith – Abraham lives in a place promised to him. It isn't his yet, at least not by possession. That would take many more years. Even so, his act of living there affirmed the promise.

As Pentecostals, what does "living in the land" mean for us? We are now valued members of a global evangelical community. What might our unique and important offering be?

Today, evangelicals and the wider Christian world are increasingly acquainted with the Holy Spirit. That is largely because of us. We gave the Christian world new insight into the person, workings, gifts, and anointing of the Spirit of God. For most of Church history, the Spirit was caught in the shadow of the Father and the Son. As theologian Emil Bruner put it, "The Holy Spirit has always been more or less the stepchild of theology, and the dynamism of the Spirit [has been] a bugbear for theologians."[2]

The Pentecostal Movement opened up a fresh and revitalised understanding of the Trinity and emboldened the people of God in new ways. For centuries, ministry had been placed in the hands of clergy, those trained and approved to administer the grace of faith. All of a sudden, a plumber could invoke prayers for the needy and not have to wait for the approved clergy. Laity were stirred to witness, do missions, and trust God in their lives. Missions became evidence of the influence of this accelerator: the Holy Spirit.

Now the theology of the Spirit has spread across Christians everywhere. No longer is it present just within our Pentecostal tribe. The multiple effects of this understanding have changed the Church. So how, then, might we view this text? It's not that we want to always be different, in front, or on the leading edge. As grateful as we are for what has happened in this past century, we are all members of the body of Christ. We might reflect on this text from Hebrews in a couple ways:

1. It's a metaphor. God's promise to Abraham models Jesus' promise to us. We too have a future "promised land," both timeless and limitless.

2. It's an actual promise. For Abraham, the Promised Land was an actual place for the people of God, situated and designed to bless the nations. It was real geography, not just an idea. It was part of God's strategy to enter humanity, resolve our sins, and carry out his eternal plan for us and in us. This eternal God who crafted us in his image, and whose image is imprinted on us, seeks an unbroken relationship with us.

What is the application of this text today for Pentecostals and the wider Church?

Let me take you to a parallel Old Testament story. It is not a perfect match, but it can help us see what was in God's heart for his people, whether within the Promised Land or on their way to it.

Jeremiah 29 is written to the Jews in exile. Nebuchadnezzar has taken them from Jerusalem to Babylon. There are five takeaways from this text: settle, be productive, raise families, promote peacefulness, and avoid distractions. In short, "be my people wherever you are." Bless the land and the people where you are located.

---

[2] Taken from Emil Brunner, *The Misunderstanding of the Church* (Cambridge UK: The Lutterworth Press, 2002).

Engage the Culture

One phrase we see in many vision statements today is to "engage the culture." Take a brief glance at our history: Evangelicals rose out of a reaction to theological liberalism's spread through much of the Protestant Church in the early twentieth century. Globally, among this conservative response, there was a move to disengage from culture, in contrast to liberal Protestantism's aspiration to be the ruler and designer of culture. In evangelical churches and even more so in Pentecostal communities, being as far away as possible from the general culture was seen as being more spiritual. In part, our spirituality was performance-driven: we were defined by the social sins we did not commit. We saw culture as a place the Spirit did not inhabit, and neither should we.

Today, we perceive a calling to engage culture, aiming to bring it under the rule and dominion of God. The danger is to assume that this engagement means us landing the kingdom of Christ into the world. Chuck Colson, as an aide to US President Richard Nixon, watched clergy sidle up to politicians. Later, as a Christian leader, Chuck Colson said, "Remember, Christ's kingdom does not arrive on Air Force One."[3] Too often, we try to engage culture without a thoughtful analysis of what the Kingdom actually means. We become so enraptured by the glamour and power in our culture as to become seduced, interpreting our increased influence as reflecting God's desires.

In some countries, I see Christians acting as if "living in the land" means aligning with particular political leaders, parties, or associations so as (we think) to gain spiritual advantage, when in fact we are in danger of losing our prophetic distance. When we get too close to power, we lose, by the very nature of our proximity, our ability to say, "Thus says the Lord." Understanding what it means to "live in the land" requires a conscious effort to decipher what in fact it means to live under the reign of Jesus.

Lessons from Abraham

Abraham's taking up residence in the Promised Land offers us substantial lessons.

First, the God of creation owns all land. The implications of this truth are many, not the least of which is our calling to steward this land, which is ours by his creation.

Second, wherever we are, it is God's territory. The sacred-secular divide, while helpful to keep religions from killing each other, sets up a false division of creation.

---

[3] Chuck Colson. A statement attributed to Colson that is oft quoted but is more an example of an oral tradition surrounding Colson rather than explicitly stated in his writings.

Third, whether we are caught in Babylon or have entered the Promised Land, God calls us to bless that land. Recall his words to Abraham: "I will make your name great, and you will be a blessing" (Gen. 12:2).

After over one hundred years as Pentecostals, what have we brought to the land? Our understanding of the Holy Spirit was remarkable in Church history. When writing *From Jerusalem to Timbuktu*, I realised how little the church knew of the person and work of the Holy Spirit.[4] This was a time of modernity when science ruled. As Pentecostals, in a sense, we were postmodern, believing that revelation and inspiration were also legitimate means of perceiving and receiving truth. But now we are the established Church. We are the new normal. And so, I wish to suggest some implications as we seek out a place in God's Kingdom life.

We begin by recognising ourselves as members of the larger body of Christ. The danger of feeling or acting in ways that smack of arrogance is unfitting. Like Peter discovering that the Gentiles were also within God's concern, we must remember that all of us stand on common and level ground before the Cross.

From there, as we reflect on the flow of history and these one hundred-plus years of our giving to the larger Church, we know that this is not the end. In fact, it may not even be the apex of his working among us. Are we living in the end times? Yes, we are, but we've been living in that era for two thousand years. And, until Jesus returns, we are in the centre of his flow and empowerment. However, we are also part of his eternal working. We are called to live in this tension of his possibly coming today, without becoming so brazenly sure of our interpretations that we make time predictions, when even Jesus said he didn't know the time.

It is not surprising that, when we become settlers, we become concerned with the issues of living and occupying in the land. Household management takes over. The writer of Hebrews understood that, as one also living in the time and era of grace, with Jesus as the centre. We are still in that era. What would Jesus make of "living in the land" as it relates to his Church today?

When Jesus spoke to his own chosen race, the people inhabiting that very land God had promised much earlier to Abraham, he used blunt, direct, and unequivocal language. He looked into their faces and said who the actual inheritors of the promise would be. He didn't say, "If your father is Abraham [...]". I'm sure what he said stirred some dust among those listening. Here is what he said: "Blessed are the meek, for they shall inherit the land" (Mt. 5:5).

What does he mean by "meek"? And what does meekness have to do with inheriting the land? We might tend to associate inheriting the land with mischief and deceit, as in Jacob's dealings with Esau, or with Joshua moving his people in and pushing out existing tribes.

---

[4] Brian Stiller, *From Jerusalem to Timbuktu* (Downers Grove: IVP Books, 2018) pp 23-47.

But Jesus has another take on the question. "Meek," we know, doesn't mean "weak". Rather, it refers to a patient, waiting person, looking for an alignment of factors that allow for the inheritance to materialise.

This picture might be helpful. A racehorse is powerful, trained, and determined to be at the front of the pack, but to be great, it must also be meek. Muscles taut, driven by a competitive spirit, it pounds down the racetrack, yet holding its explosive breakout power in check, waiting for the timing of the rider. When the jockey sees circumstances in their favour, a slight touch of the riding stick or a gentle murmur in the horse's ear triggers a release of adrenaline. The racehorse leaps forward in the final leg of the race, now in full stride, pressing for the win. To be meek is to wait for the right time, to hold one's gifts and vision under control, until the signal is given.

Meekness is a state of mind, also shaped and influenced by patience and humility. My prayer for our community is that meekness will characterise our people, churches, and ministry as we wait for the signal of the Spirit. From this flows our inheritance, our dwelling in the land that gives us presence, grace, and wisdom to bless the nations.

If the meek are inheritors of the land, what central and dominating concerns of Jesus might call us to a new season of meekness? For one thing, the teachings of Jesus touch the full spectrum of our lives. The core elements of love, hope, and faith are broad categories, but Jesus doesn't let us get away with only affirming broad categories. He cuts into the heart of who we are, how we think, our prime concerns, and how we live them out daily.

One word that has gone global today is *empower*. Power shapes our understanding of the work of the Holy Spirit. This is biblical and appropriate. But what is meant by power? Is it power to influence the community politically, to ensure that policies are supportive of our witness and value? We need to filter such assumptions through the grid of what Jesus actually said, not only to those who were living in the Promised Land, but to us whose future is truly the eternal promised land. At the core of the role and calling of the Spirit is Jesus. He is the raison d'être of the Spirit.

I suggest we ask ourselves what it means to "make our home" in this land as we are empowered by the Spirit. What is the Spirit's aim or objective in giving us power? And how did Jesus intend this power of the Spirit to be used?

We Pentecostals have been a catalyst for the Church to learn about the Spirit. Those barriers are essentially broken. So now, what is there of the life and presence of Jesus that the Spirit says needs our attention?

We could compile a list of words, stories, and promises of Jesus that apply to what he might want us to understand by "occupying the land" today. I have noted his promise that the meek shall inherit the land. With this in mind, try rereading some of Jesus' stories, such as the Good Samaritan or the Prodigal Son. Go back and scour the Sermon on the Mount, or take a crack at the story about paying taxes to Caesar. In the life of Jesus and in the outworking of his life in the Early Church, we will find striking answers to the questions of what power is and how it is to be used.

When I was leading the Evangelical Alliance in Canada, part of my assignment was to interface with senior political leaders. One day, I was scheduled to meet with the Prime Minister. My committee and I had carefully gone over which issues I would raise with him. I arrived at the Parliament buildings in Ottawa and was ushered to a side room, awaiting my appointed time. As I waited, I opened my Bible to Daniel 11, which I had recently been studying. As I reread the opening verses, I felt an inner nudge to drop my agenda and bless the country's leader. It seemed so contradictory to my reason for being there, but as we sat together and, after some general conversation, he asked what was on my mind, I said, "Mr Prime Minister, I'm not here to ask for anything other than to encourage you." After a few minutes of sharing Bible verses and prayer, my appointment ended. I had no idea whether my behaviour was appropriate.

The next week, while I was boarding a plane, Canada's Minister of Justice saw me and called me over. He asked, "Brian, what happened with you and the Prime Minister last week?" My heart dropped. Had I crossed a line? But he smiled and said, "At our Cabinet meeting, the Prime Minister told us of his meeting with you. He ended by saying that if we ignore the evangelical community, both the government of Canada and the people of Canada are the losers." I discovered then the life-giving impact of a blessing.

Bibliography

Brunner, Emil. *The Misunderstanding of the Church.* Cambridge, UK: The Lutterworth Press, 2003.

Stiller, Brian. *From Jerusalem to Timbuktu.* Downers Grove: IVP Books, 2018.

2. Abraham was "A stranger living in tents" (Heb. 11:9, NASB)

Brian Stiller

In my first devotional, we entered Abraham's life, walking the hallway of faith and reminding ourselves of the stunning portraits of so many who, in the history of the Hebrew people, learned to engage with God in acts of faith.

Abraham was called to leave his homeland, wandering in a new and foreign land. That was his first act of faith. Then he set up home in a land promised by God, the place where he would build a people. This too was an act of faith. He planted his feet and settled his family on territory occupied by others, all based on a promise. Hundreds of years would pass before this land of promise became the land of possession, but Abraham could see with an eye of faith and there he lived, blessing the land.

The parallel for us is that we too are called to take up residence in the land, to be salt and light in the world we occupy. Indeed, our immediate inclination is to set up home and call it ours – to let the issues and demands of our place and time take over. We become immersed in the here and now and what we own, to the extent that eventually it owns us.

Again, we are looking at this biblical text as Pentecostals, more than a century into our sojourn. We are asking for a vision that will keep us from stagnating, as we lift our eyes of faith to prepare ourselves to be in the vanguard of God's ways and plans.

This brings us to the second comment that the writer of Hebrews makes about Abraham. Yes, we know Abraham made his home there, but that is offset by this curious modifier about *how* he lived: "like a stranger in a foreign country; he lived in tents" (Heb. 11:9, NIV).

You get a sense of two kinds of motion. On one hand, Abraham stays put, living in the land; on the other hand, he is on the alert, not locked into a permanent abode but ready to pick up at a moment's notice, move out and move on. Augustine of Hippo, in *The City of God*, describes citizens in the world as the Latin *parengreni*, or *resident aliens*.[1]

---

[1] Augustine, *City of God* (New York: Penguin Books, 2003) For a focused discussion on the Latin *parengreni* – resident alien see Gillian Clark's essay entitled *Rome, Jerusalem and Babylon: Augustine on transient empires and everlasting cities* in Nation, State and Empire: Perspective from The Englesberg Seminar, Axess, 2017 www.engelsbergideas.com.

I was raised in a church where hymns about heaven and the afterlife offered a weekly reminder that this home was temporary. But there is another take on this metaphor of "living in tents." Thinking about heaven is not just to remind us that our location in the here-and-now is temporary or that our time of entry into our eternal home is coming soon. Living in tents also means that our current reality does not define our identity, hopes, and security.

We are in danger of making our homes in the promised land too comfortable. We build secure structures, homes, businesses, educational communities, and civil society, all to make our lives comfortable, secure, and predictable. All that is good. That's how we're made. I love to camp in the wilderness, but I don't want to live there. It is too discomfiting, unpredictable, and exposed to roaming bears and annoying skunks. So, if Abraham saw himself as a resident alien, what might that look like for us?

Pentecostal Revolution

Tom Holland, in his book *Dominion*, puts forward an argument that the gospel changed the world. His amazing research begins with how the gospel brought a halt to the despicable and torturous method of killing by crucifixion. In short, the gospel was revolutionary.[2]

The Pentecostal Movement has also been revolutionary. It opened the door to understanding the Trinity in new ways. The Holy Spirit, so often an overshadowed member of the Trinity, was brought into full light, and the Church has never been the same since.

But history does not stand still. Celebrating that growth does nothing for tomorrow. We are now caught up in wars that we could never have imagined two hundred years ago. We are in discussions about perceptions of sexual identity that boggle my mind as I attempt to decipher the new definitions and acronyms that splash their way across public media. Swirling issues of justice, poverty, new forms of artificial intelligence, capital markets, conflicts and wars, and sabre rattling on many fronts are defining this age.

We have watched spiritual movements through the lens of history, seeing them come and go. We are no different. We too are susceptible to the classic triad – from movement to monument to mausoleum. Spiritual pride could quickly morph our movement into a monument. We have established our offices, churches, missions, foundations, scholars, and heroes. We set up global events, defined by our core beliefs but also celebrating who we have become in both size and influence. The makings of the monument are in place. But what should be next for us? Where is the place that we should occupy?

Our new phase will be different. The Pentecostal revolution has remade the Church. Our message resonates across the many religious boundaries that

---

[2] Tom Holland, *Dominion: How the Christian Revolution Remade the World* (New York: Basic Books, 2019).

previously kept us secluded and shut out from each other. The future for us will be different from the past. The importance of the message doesn't change, but the message may take on a different tone.

As this Pentecostal revolution moves into a new phase, it might be wise for us to think seriously about how Abraham lived while occupying the land that was promised but not yet his. As a resident alien, he lived in tents.

Peter in his first letter to the Christians in Rome, the power centre of the world, addresses them in this way: "To God's elect, strangers in the world scattered {…} who have been chosen." He uses the phrase, "elect sojourners," or "resident aliens" in some translations, to describe those living out the gospel in Rome. (See www.biblegateway.com for comparison of multiple versions of 1 Peter 1:1)

Peter picked up on Abraham's pattern. One could argue that being a resident alien was a defining feature of the people of God even before Abraham was called. Noah too was a resident alien. The people of Israel were resident aliens in Egypt and again in Babylon. Jesus, even as a Jew who lived in a Jewish world and ate and drank from their culture, was an alien too.

In case you are planning to carve up this "resident alien" business and say "I'll be 50 percent resident and the other half alien", it doesn't work that way. We are both 100 percent residents and 100 percent aliens. We do not split ourselves half and half with the logic of creating a whole. In this regard, we are not unlike Jesus who in his Incarnation was both wholly divine and wholly human. The integration does not come about by getting half of each. We are fully residents, living in the land, and also fully alien, living in tents. Neither can we shift from one status to the other when it seems convenient. God calls us to live fully in the land but to do so as aliens living in tents.

What might it mean for us as Pentecostals to be aliens living in tents? I want to consider a proposition that may enable God's Spirit to hold us as an effective tool, rather than allowing this movement to become a monument or mausoleum. This marvellous metaphor of living in tents prompts me to see Abraham as one who was free to respond to God's call to move on.

To develop this argument, I will start by asking, what is central to our life and witness? We agree that it is Christ. Then what would be most critical to that witness? What constitutes the singular and most potent elements of that witness?

- Is there something greater than the gifts of tongues?
- Is there something more important than the power to raise people from beds of sickness?
- Is there something more important than preaching under God's anointing?

Living in tents suggests remaining free from finding identity in where or how I reside. The tension of living in the land and yet living in tents is that pull-push action that helps me keep my responsibility to God in mind.

Of everything Jesus said, is there one call, one request that sums up his deepest aspiration?

I don't want to cherry-pick the answer. I want to carefully understand what he is asking of us and why it matters so much. Of course, we would cite the passage where Jesus says the greatest commandment is to love God fully and to love our neighbours as ourselves. But to me, the text that best describes Jesus' relationship to the Father occurs when he lets us listen to his prayer time. In John 17, we hear his intimate exchange with the God of all creation. That prayer embraces the grand narrative of creation, the majestic arc of him coming down and lifting us from brokenness and putting in place the eternal bond that cements God and his people.

To make sense of what it means to live in tents, we must be attuned to his prayer, so that his deepest desires will define both how we live in the land as residents and how we live in tents as aliens. In John 17, he expresses his explicit hopes and his deepest yearnings. In doing so, he gives us an inside glimpse of his call to us and his Church.

> My prayer is not for them alone. I pray also for those who will believe in me through their message, that all of them may be one, Father just as you are in me and I am in you. May they also be in us so that the world may believe that you have sent me. I have given them the glory that you gave me, that they may be one as we are one: I in them and you in me. May they be brought to complete unity to let the world know that you sent me and have loved them even as you have loved me (Jn 17:20-23, NIV).

The past six decades have seen the Church expand as never before in history. Yet even with this dynamic outreach, division reigns within the evangelical Church. Multiple churches on the same street battle for members and presence, oblivious to others, acting as if they are the only "real" church in town. Political elections pit evangelicals against each other, divided by ideologies and rhetoric. It is a challenge to maintain a thoughtful and Christ-like presence when Christians are oppressed because of their faith, but these challenges are further escalated when certain Christians, due to their political and social preferences, demonise their brothers and sisters in Christ who might hold another view.

What is the global *zeitgeist* today? We see it within families, countries, and regions. Are not division and hostility the common parlance of today?

The strength of our Pentecostal community is our deeply held belief that Jesus is the expressed will of the Father and that the Spirit calls, equips, and empowers us for ministry. Yet, at the same time, as we pursue our calling and work to achieve goals, we end up with multiple denominations, independent churches, hundreds of thousands of ministries and agencies, often living and serving as if they are the only ones God is using.

In a decade of factionalism, what are we to do with the prayer of Jesus to be one as he and the Father are one (Jn 17:22)?

Jesus gave us the litmus test for disciples: "By this everyone will know that you are my disciples, if you love one another" (Jn 13:35, NIV). What a verse to stamp on our foreheads, at a time when loyalty becomes defined in terms of hardened views, often breaking friendships, and pitting believers against another. Where agencies, missions, and ministries too often seek for position and prestige and as gamesmanship becomes our mode of operation, the Spirit is calling us into a special oneness in Jesus.

Chapter 2

Jesus' call for unity was at the top of his wish list. He prayed that we might be one in him. There is power in unity. A husband and wife can handle enormous pressure when they are together in unity. Jesus' prayer is not window dressing. It is not to make life easier or to facilitate operations. Rather, it rises from the essence of the Trinity: where God is, there is unity, for within God, unity affirms loving relationships, acknowledging specific gifts and callings. This in turn generates mutual dependence, underscoring our calling to honour Jesus of Nazareth and make him known.

Could it be that in this very period of Church history, in the middle of unprecedented growth in the evangelical world, when divisions and factions seem too often to be the sign of who we are, the Spirit is calling us to change the narrative, to raise up a new standard of love for each other and a new determination to be one in him?

What does unity look like? Jesus' prayer builds our understanding of the relationship of the Father and the Son, a dynamic he invites us to live out. Indeed, the marker of unity notes what God is doing in our very lives. "My prayer is [...] that all of them may be one, Father, just as you are in me and I am in you. May they also be in us so that the world may believe that you have sent me" (Jn 17:21, NIV).

Unity respects the varieties of people, institutions, and ministries, yet always while reminding us that what we do is for the glory and in celebration of Jesus Christ. We are drawn up into him. He is the centripetal force that mitigates the centrifugal forces of our ideas, personalities, and plans. We affirm that "in him all things hold together" (Col. 1:17, NIV). His gravitational pull works against my tendency to go my own way, to celebrate my tribe's success, to view Kingdom life in terms of God applauding my own country, church, denomination, or theological variety.

Unity with others in the body of Christ is an idea that challenges the natural state of organisational life, which tends to its own self-interest. Unity is what we pray for. It requires discipline of the heart. It is something we should pray for and work to make so.

The idea of unity calls us to consider how we might affirm others in their calling and gifting, to find time to encourage and even promote others. It brings the presence of the Spirit into the varying gifts and strengths of those who choose to live in unity. Rather than going our own way, we acknowledge that the apex of our life, now and into eternity, is in the crowning of King Jesus.

What might the Church become if, in our own worlds, we made unity in Jesus more dominant than other worthy callings such as "engaging the culture"?

- We would be free from our own drive to be successful.
- We would be released from self-congratulatory reminders of how big and influential we are now
- It would break the bondage of trying to deliver the gospel on our own terms.
- We would be freed from our absolutes about what the Bible defines as "Spirit-filled."

How might this change happen? We could imagine Christian leaders in a few countries agreeing to give greater attention to this call. Then, they might bring together other leaders for whom this call resonates, and in prayer and discussion, they would ask the Lord what unity might look like in the towns and cities of their country. From these results, we might anticipate the Spirit enabling a similar hope and prayer to emerge in other places. The influence of the Spirit in making Jesus known through unity has crossed boundaries, overcome downright hatred, and melted hearts.

As we craft our various outreach strategies, along with clever and contemporary styles, we believe those things draw people to Jesus. Yet in John 17, we see Jesus describing this profoundly mystical relationship as that which matters most to him, even more than the polished marketing plans of our contemporary Church. The God of creation reminds us that living in unity is more powerful, enduring, and compelling than our grandest schemes. And in his prayer, Jesus gives a strategic rationale for this emphasis. As others see God's people in close relationships, this will be the best marketing device ever imagined, for in our bonding as his followers, people come to see Jesus in his grand and loving self. We may think that we need to advance compelling apologetics, craft catchy worship tunes, design attractive buildings, format dynamic media, and generate overwhelming presentations to call people to Jesus. What might happen if we made deeper Christian unity the foremost part of our vision instead?

In some countries, there is open warfare: church against church, pastor against pastor, deacon against deacon, taking political sides in verbal wars like I have never before seen. And amidst of all this, the Church seems separated by the same cleavages as the broader society. Divisions become so deeply ingrained that the idea of unity is not even an afterthought.

We know what lack of unity does in a marriage or family. I have looked into the troubled eyes of parents or young people who do not speak to each other, or whose family is broken by abuse or misunderstanding. At the core is a lack of love.

The solution is found in the love of God. Where you and I are his beloved, and when we are brought together within the boundaries of his love, that unity becomes a natural working base.

In this moment of national, regional, and global factions, one side pitted against the other, the solution can be found in Jesus' prayer to the Father that his people would be in unity as he and his Father are. And the gravitational pull that brings about unity again is the powerful, redeeming, transforming presence of his love.

That's a broader solution. How that comes about, I don't know. But I do know that the Spirit wants us, as resident aliens living in this land, to remain free and unhindered so that his love becomes our living reality, and so that the deepest desire of our risen Lord becomes reproduced in all we say and do.

So today, let us seek to settle our hearts in God, and as our hearts are nestled among the Trinity, we will then be positioned to answer the prayer of Jesus and, by so doing, to live as his called ones in the land while residing in tents. Being resident aliens is to live a real life in the enfolding circles of mystery. It is the Pentecostal way.

Bibliography

St. Augustine of Hippo. *City of God.* New York: Penguin Books 2003.
Holland, Tom. *Dominion: How the Christian Revolution Remade the World.* New York: Basic Books, 2019.

3. Voices Loud and Clear: What Does This Mean? A Reflection on Acts 2:1-13

Paul Bendor-Samuel

Over the past few days, as we have enjoyed the shared learning, fellowship, and phenomenal hospitality of City Harvest Church, many of us whose daily environment is the academy have been asking, "What does this mean?" What does it mean when the local church becomes the space for theological education and reflection? What might God be doing among us? Since it is impossible to imagine a global Pentecostal summit without reflection on Acts 2, this devotional serves as an invitation to reflect on a passage in which the startled participants end with the same question, "What does this mean?" (Acts 2:13).

At the dawn of Pentecost, we find the gathered community of disciples, family, and friends of Jesus, around 120, unsure of who they were and of what they were to do. As they watched Jesus ascend, the angels told them Jesus was going to return, but *when*? They had been told to wait in the city and keep the appointment at which they would be "clothed with power from on high" (Lk. 24:49). What could this mean? The disciples found themselves in a liminal space. As in a doorway moving between rooms, they were in transition from one experience of reality to another. This liminal space was a time of waiting. The three years of Jesus' presence had ended, and they stood on the threshold of something new, but what that was they knew not.

We live in a moment of history characterised by change, uncertainty, and instability. It has been described as a VUCA world – volatile, uncertain, complex, and filled with ambiguity. We are so familiar with these changes that we hardly need to rehearse the list of processes and global issues: shifts in global power, the devastating impacts of climate change, unsustainable economic models, unprecedented mobility and migration, the reawakening of fierce nationalisms frequently combined with religious radicalism, unimaginable developments in the field of Artificial Intelligence, and so on. We know that much of the old ways of doing things are passing, and we do not know what the future holds. We find ourselves frequently in liminal spaces.

Yet liminal spaces are not simply transitional; they can be transformational. The disciples were not fully aware yet, but with the coming of Christ, God had launched his Kingdom – one that will not pass away. So, those 120 did the single most important thing they could do: they gathered together constantly and prayed (Acts 1:14). Why? In part, they gathered simply because they were Jews, for whom prayer was a daily practice. But I suggest it was much more than that. For three intense years, they had shadowed their master, picking up his ways, being his disciples. A central feature of Jesus' life centred on seeking silence and solitude, the quiet spaces where he could be with the Father in prayer. They turned to prayer in the upper rooms where they stayed. Indeed, everything that characterised the life of the early Christian community that we see in the Book of Acts – their teaching, breaking of bread, prayer, meeting in temple and homes, fellowship, and radical generosity in which they shared all things in common – the Master had modelled all of this to them during those three years of common life on the road together.

The disciples also did a very natural thing: they tried to sort out their leadership structure, which as the Book of Acts unfolds, becomes slightly amusing as they were about to discover that Jesus, by his Spirit, was still very much their leader, and in any case, God would raise up new leaders from completely unexpected, non-Jewish places.

So, we find them together in one place, praying. In that posture of dependency, the Spirit comes. The coming is not some gentle reassurance that all will be well, of comfort and a call to persevere. That would come at other times but not this day. Today, the Spirit of the risen and ascended Jesus comes with a violent wind and flames of fire. Today is fulfilled a prophecy made through Joel many centuries earlier, a promise of a new era when the Spirit of God comes not just on prophets and spiritual leaders but is poured out on all God's people, never to be removed. Wind and fire indicate the disruptive, powerful in-breaking of the reign of God. The ascended Christ, who now sits at the right hand of the Father and to whom is given all authority in heaven and earth, sends his Spirit on his people.

When Jesus walked the roads of Israel – the same roads currently being torn apart by hatred, violence, and indiscriminate revenge – he announced that the kingdom of God had come. God's reign of justice, peace, favour to humankind, of grace and mercy, of reconciliation and new life – in Christ the kingdom of God had come. As Lesslie Newbigin puts it, "The kingdom of God, his kingly rule, now has a human face and a human name – the name and the face of Jesus from Nazareth."[1] Jesus has ascended, and now, with the outpouring of His Spirit, the people of God have become the human face of that Kingdom. This, of course, has enormous implications for what we understand the mission of the Church to be. Put simply, the scope of the Church's mission is defined by the scope of God's mission as revealed in the life, person, and work of Jesus of Nazareth.

The outpouring of the Spirit is not only manifest in wind and fire but through the transformation of the community. Empowered by the Spirit, a new community forms characterised by boldness, authority, radical generosity within, and openness to those outside the community. The kingdom of God is made visible through those who will come to be known as Christians. This transformation is first expressed through the speaking in other tongues. The

---

[1] J.E. Lesslie Newbigin, *Mission in Christ's Way: Bible Studies* (Geneva: WCC Publications, 1987), 7.

Greek word for other is *heteros*, emphasising difference. It is the word from which in English we get our word *heterogeneity*, which means diversity, in comparison with homogeneity, meaning the same or similar. A homogeneous group whose common language was Aramaic suddenly found themselves speaking a whole array of languages. The text emphasises that this was not because they had learned these various languages, but they spoke them "as the Spirit enabled them" (Acts 2:4).

Now, of all the gifts God would prioritise on the launch of his Kingdom, have you ever considered why God would choose this? Not miracles, healing, raising from the dead, the casting out of demons. Instead, the Spirit reveals the presence of the Kingdom through the gift of diverse languages. The significance of the gift becomes apparent immediately in the text (Acts 2:5-12). Jews and converts to Judaism scattered across the Roman world had gathered for the feast of *Shavout*, fifty days after Passover, to celebrate the first fruits of the wheat harvest and the giving of the Law on Mount Sinai. The text lists fifteen regions across a vast area of the Roman world.

The miracle is that these Jews of diverse languages and cultures hear the wonders of God each in their own language. The significance of this is underlined by the fact that three times in the text we are told that the population is amazed to hear the good news "in their own language" (Acts 2:6, 8, 11). The text, with its statement that those gathered came "from every nation under heaven" (v. 5), is a clear reference back to Genesis 10 and 11.

Genesis 10 provides us with a table of nations. The offspring of Noah are described by their "clans, languages, territories and nations" (Gen. 10:4, 20, 31). We are given a picture of completeness of the nations, indicated by the fact that seventy are mentioned. One of the key themes of the early chapters of Genesis is the oneness of humankind. Genesis chapters 1, 2, and 5 tells us that humankind has descended from one couple, Adam and Eve, and in Genesis 10, all nations trace their origins back to Noah and his sons. The message is clear that, in all our diversity, we are one.

The sense of wholeness and unity is shattered in Genesis 11 with the story of Babel – a story of human pride and sinful exclusivity – when the people say, "Let us make a name for ourselves and not be scattered over the whole earth" (v. 4). The text introduces us to the sin of ethnocentrism and the roots of racism. If Genesis 3 shows us the effect of individual sin, the story of Babel introduces us to systemic sin. The result is the shattering of oneness under the curse of Babel, where language becomes the source of confusion, disunity, and scattering.

Now, at Pentecost, the curse of Babel is reversed, and the nature of the kingdom of God revealed. All nations come together, and in their coming together, their diversity is honoured. How much easier it might have been if the listeners had all been given the ability to understand Aramaic. In building the church, would it not have been more useful if they had all shared a common language and could understand each other? No, the oneness that the Spirit brings does not obliterate the diversity of language and culture.

When the Spirit is poured out on the whole people of God, the result is that representatives of the whole Roman world hear the good news of the Kingdom in their own languages. They feel confused by this unparalleled event and ask, "What does this mean?" (Acts 2:13). What it means is that here, at the birth of the Church, a profound statement is made of huge theological, ecclesiological, and missiological significance. The unity of the Church will not be based on uniformity. You do not need to understand Aramaic to join the community. No one language is normative in the kingdom of heaven: not Latin, Greek, or English. You do not need to abandon your language and culture to join the community. In fact, you must not abandon your language and culture, as that would betray God's intentions as revealed at Pentecost. Unity will be built on the reality that there is no other name by which we may be saved (v. 38), and that unity in Christ will be built in diversity.

Did the apostles understand the significance of the Spirit-given ability to communicate the gospel in the native tongues of the hearers? The story of Acts suggest they did not. Peter, leader of the apostles, had to go on a long journey of personal conversion. His encounter with Cornelius (Acts 10) set him on the way, but reluctantly so. He is almost apologetic when speaking with the other Jerusalem leaders when explaining why he baptised a gentile: "So if God gave them the same gift [Holy Spirit] as he gave us [...] who was I to think I could oppose God?" (11:17). In Acts 15, at the Council of Jerusalem, despite his personal experience and revelation from God that the Gentiles are not unclean, Peter and the other apostles have to be persuaded by Paul and Barnabas that they could be saved while retaining their culture and practices. Even then, Peter's conversion remains incomplete. In the Book of Galatians, Paul explains how when Peter fled from Jerusalem to Antioch, he was happy to eat with Gentiles until hardliners came from James in Jerusalem, at which point he shattered the oneness of table fellowship and withdrew to eat with Jewish converts separately. Paul has to confront Peter, pointing out that such behaviour was contrary to "the truth of the gospel" (Gal. 2:14).

This brings us to why we have gathered here in Singapore for these days. We have come to hear the diverse voices of the global Church that Pentecost embedded in the core DNA of the people of God. The long journey of conversion from the security of homogeneity to richness of heterogeneity is the journey we all must take.

What do I mean?

Put simply, most of us tend to assume that our experience, our perspective, is the normal Christian experience and perspective. Our theology and practice become normative, meaning that our theology, experience, and practice become the standard by which others are judged. The ethnocentrism that first appeared at Babel is alive and well in most of us.

We live at a critical juncture in the growth of the Church globally. For over 200 years, the Western mission movement has been used by God to grow the Church around the world. In the past thirty to forty years, this has become a global mission movement. The churches in Singapore have contributed strongly, especially in Southeast Asia. In the process, unfortunately, the weakness of the Euro-American mission movement has also been absorbed into the newer movements. In particular, Western mission, as developed in a particular Euro-American context, with its own particular Euro-American Church history, assumed that its understanding of theology and mission was normative for all peoples in all contexts. This is evident powerfully in the kind of slogans propagated in the West, including phrases like "10/40 window", "Unreached People Groups", and "Finish the Task".

While we understand that the revelation of God through the Scriptures and in the person of our Lord Jesus Christ is unchanging and normative, every attempt to understand and grasp this revelation is shaped by our context and experience. Thus, the Euro-American context and culture shaped the theology and practice that spread through the mission movement. We see the same assumptions being made in new mission movements such as Korean, Nigerian, and, dare we say it, Singaporean.

The vision of the people of God declared at Pentecost is of a global Church that reflects the face of God through all the redeemed and transformed cultures and languages that are the legacy of Babel. Now, language and culture need no longer exist as barriers that separate and result in confusion and dispersion. Instead, out of our unity in Christ, our language and cultures – when drawn into and redeemed by the Church – can serve as the myriad facets of a diamond that sparkle with the light, grace, and truth of Christ, the true light of the world.

There is work to be done, friends. One of the significant challenges and opportunities before the Church today is how to encourage, nurture, celebrate, and learn from the many faces of Christ and his Kingdom revealed to us through the authentic discipleship of those from diverse cultures and languages. We must first embrace the particularity of our own culture, with its riches, gifts, and weaknesses. Having done this, we will be in a better position to avoid the trap of normalising our culture, theology, and practices as we go into the world in mission. A serious commitment is needed from those who hold power in the church if we are to hear "global voices loud and clear". Much work is needed if we are to help each other demonstrate what the kingdom of God looks like in the varied contexts in which the Church finds itself, including:

- contexts of affluence and poverty;
- contexts of war, displacement, and migration;
- contexts dominated by particular religions, pluralism, or deep secularism;
- rural and urban contexts;
- contexts in which the Church has a long history and those where it is young; and
- contexts where the Church is numerous and those where it is still a tiny percent of the population.

In each place, followers of Jesus Christ, empowered by the Spirit, are called to demonstrate what the kingdom of God is like and to bear witness to God's grace and abundant life in their own language and culture. Then, the glory and honour of the nations will be brought into the heavenly city (Rev. 21:24-27), reflecting for eternity the manifold wisdom and transforming grace of God.

The vision is clear: to see the first fruits represented by those gathered in Act 2 become the global harvest, where the glory and honour of the nations is brought into the heavenly city.

Forget the slogan, "finish the task." We have barely begun.

Foundational Considerations for Global Pentecostalism

Kong Hee, Byron D. Klaus, and Douglas Petersen

When anyone attempts to identify those themes that might be considered as foundational for global Pentecostalism, the list could be quite extensive. The themes identified as foundational in this section do not represent an exhaustive list. However, the themes represented would, arguably, be on most lists of foundational concerns.

The first theme is a theological reflection on Pentecost and more specifically the connection between the Atonement and Pentecost. This chapter is a full biblical-theological engagement, which undergirded the Global Pentecostal Summit and sought to give voice to those whose human experience in liminality need not be repeated in Christ's Kingdom. **Frank Macchia's** work provides the foundation for the theological agency of Majority World Pentecostal Christians

Macchia looks to the picture framed in Revelation 5:9 representing the work of redemption, including those from every tribe and language and people and nation. He asks, what if, in following this text, believers can show that Christ on the Cross follows the Spirit in embracing humanity, in all its diversity, to incorporate them all into his life with that full array of human diversity preserved for all eternity? Further, what if we say that the Spirit is poured out through Christ at Pentecost to give Christ a diverse body that he gave his life for on the Cross?

Macchia posits that the Atonement is that place where Christ represents all of us and the breadth of human diversity just as is seen in Revelation 5:9. This chapter provides an in-depth study of this dynamic connection between the Atonement and Pentecost. After an extensive biblical-theological excursus to develop this connection, Macchia offers several poignant concluding remarks. On the Cross, Christ follows the leading of the Spirit in offering this global array of persons. Christ rises in the fullness of the Spirit to incorporate these people into his risen life. The outpouring of the Spirit on "all flesh" at Pentecost and the many tongues that gave voice to the Spirit at that event is the fruit of the Cross. Again, Macchia looks to the Book of Revelation to demonstrate that the work of Atonement and the empowering of Pentecost yield a multitude who praise the Lamb (7:9) and where the kings of nations bring praises of the Lamb of God in all his splendour and glory (21:22-26).

The second foundational theme in this section focuses on the necessity of leadership, which **Wonsuk Ma** suggests has existed as a critical issue from the inception of the Pentecostal movement. Ma notes that the "charismatic leadership model", usually associated with Max Weber, and indicative of industrial, social, and political sectors, has seemingly been a "natural fit" for Pentecostal leaders. While it may best describe the pioneering, entrepreneurial leadership of many Pentecostal leaders globally, Ma also notes its shadow side as has been displayed in very public moments of disgrace for Pentecostal leaders.

Ma offers an alternative to the charismatic leadership model by moving towards what he terms a Spirit-empowered leadership model. Acknowledging leadership studies among Pentecostal scholars including Truls Åkerlund and Stephen Fogarty, Ma interfaces their work with an initial set of four key characteristics in his proposed Spirit-empowered leadership model from relevant Old Testament evidence.

From Old Testament sources, Ma identifies *calling* as one of those four key characteristics that belongs in a Spirit-empowered leadership model. Exploring this concept in the narratives of OT prophets and kings, he describes calling in terms of the enduring consciousness of divinely initiated purpose that guides a leader's life. The second of his key characteristics is the *alignment of the human and divine elements* of the calling. This process of integration of rationality and spirituality includes the dynamic of the "otherworldly" legitimising the "this worldly." When this process is compromised, the result turns inevitably tragic. Noting that leadership studies usually focus on the interactions between leader and follower (and in many cases organisational structures), Ma offers a third element as the necessity of considering *the leader's relationship with God*. Moving from this focus on personal piety, he continues using OT leadership narratives and identifies the fourth characteristic in his alternative model as the *initiative to empower others within their sphere of influence*.

Ivan Satyavrata offers his work in the third foundational theme for this section by focusing on the Christian encounter with world religions. The missionary impulse of Pentecostalism has provided ample encounters with a broad spate of world religions. Noting that secular prophets of a previous generation expected the demise of religion, Satyavrata observes that we now live in unprecedented multiculturalism and religious plurality with the potential for communal conflict greater than ever before.

Satyavrata's life in South Asia provides him a challenging context in which he notes Christians must live under the prophetic mandate to be the "Voice of Truth" and face all the accompanying missiological challenges as well as existential implications. He identifies the unofficial orthodoxy of religious pluralism as a firmly entrenched ideology in the influential institutions of academia, entertainment, media, and popular culture. He notes *New York Times* columnist, Thomas Friedman, who published a post-9/11 article entitled the "Real War", as an articulate voice of what has become secular "dogma." Satyavrata offers a thorough response to Friedman and the challenge of religious pluralism and subsequently moves to offer an alternative viewpoint rooted in the case study of the Apostle Paul in Athens recorded in Acts 17.

Noting that Pentecostal scholars have not been silent in their theological reflection about world religions, Satyavrata includes a brief interaction with the works of Pentecostal theologians Veli-Matti Kärkkäinen and Amos Yong. He elaborates on his response to these two scholars in the subsequent sections that complete this chapter. In the light of a post-colonial era in which Christian mission is often seen as the continuation of Western imperialistic impulses, Satyavrata offers four features of a Pentecostal spirituality that reveal the deep connection Pentecostals display with respect to their encounters with people of other faiths.

Speaking from an Asian setting, Satyavrata notes that this region has been home to some of most enduring and resilient Christian communities historically and serves as the location of a majority of the world's unreached people groups. He views those seemingly polar realities as sufficient reason to anticipate great evangelistic opportunity in this region. He notes that the challenge to all God's people is to continue to integrate wonders, works, and the Word in a presentation of the gospel that connects with the hopes and aspirations of neighbours of other faiths.

The final chapter in this section is written by **Young-Hoon Lee**, current lead pastor of the Yoido Full Gospel Church in Seoul, South Korea. This chapter focuses on the centrality of prayer in sustaining the effectiveness of Global Christianity. As pastor of the church that many view as the largest Christian congregation in the world and whose renown is regularly linked to prayer, Lee does have a unique perspective. Continuing the legacy of the church's founder, Paul Yonggi Cho, Lee's leadership at Yoido Full Gospel Church provides a powerful case study of the role of prayer in the life of a congregation known globally for its commitment to corporate prayer.

Built on the foundation of his doctoral research at Temple University (USA), Lee surveys prayer in the Old Testament, in the New Testament, and throughout Church history – including early Pentecostal and Charismatic Movements. He continues with the study of prayer movements in Korea in the early part of the twentieth century. An especially insightful focus is an in-depth chronicling of the impact of prayer in the founding of Yoido Full Gospel Church. While this church is commonly connected to the centrality of prayer in its inception and in its growth, Lee provides an extensive look at details not usually reported in the regular references made to this congregation. As such, this chapter reads as a congregational case study that provides both encouragement and reproducible action steps that could undergird congregational life globally.

4. From the Atonement to Pentecost: An Exegetical and Theological Reflection

Frank D. Macchia

Introduction

In rightly cherishing the diversity that constitutes the one people of God, it is common to open our Bibles to Acts Chapter 2. There, we find that the Spirit is poured out on the Day of Pentecost for the sake of all peoples, and the subsequent chorus of various tongues that spring forth from a small band of Christ's Galilean followers signals the future rise of a vastly diverse global Church.

We celebrate what we have learned from Pentecost about the way in which the Spirit cherishes diversity, but all that we say about Christology in the context of the Atonement seems abstract and uniform by comparison. When it comes to the Atonement, or Christ's representation of humanity on the Cross so as to redeem them to God, it feels tempting at that point to turn to abstractions. Christ is said to have died for all "humanity" or "sinners" as an indistinct mass. But what if what happens at Pentecost follows the lead of what Christ does in the Spirit at the Cross?

If we follow Revelation 5:9, we learn that Christ redeemed persons "from every tribe and language and people and nation." What if, in following this text, it can be shown that Christ on the Cross follows the Spirit in embracing humanity in all of its diversity in order to incorporate them all into his life with all of that marvellous diversity preserved for all of eternity? And what if we say, then, that the Spirit is poured out through Christ at Pentecost for the sake of Christ, to give him the diverse body that he gave his life on the cross to have? This is the argument I wish to develop in this chapter taking us all from the Atonement to Pentecost.

The Cross and Human Diversity in Revelation: An Exegetical Foundation

I begin by quoting Revelation 5:9-10:

> And they sang a new song, saying:
> "You are worthy to take the scroll
> and to open its seals,
> because you were slain,
> and with your blood you redeemed for God
> persons from every tribe and language and people and nation.

You have made them to be a kingdom and priests to serve our God,
and they will reign on the earth."[1]

The context of this text describes the lamb, "looking as if it had been slain" (v. 6) approaching him who sits upon the throne so as to take the scroll from his hand, break its seals, and reveal its contents (v. 7). The lamb is worthy to do this because he has redeemed a diverse community of people from "from every tribe and language and people and nation" (v. 9), overlapping terms listed together so as to emphasise the diversity and universality of the people redeemed by the lamb and to whom the message of the scroll was directed. The implication is that the slain and overcoming lamb is the central fulfilment of the scroll's prophecies. The context of this text about the slain and overcoming lamb, however, implicitly reaches all the way back to the Book of Daniel, where Daniel's prophecy was said to be rolled up and sealed into a scroll "until the time of the end" (Dan. 12:4). Part of that prophecy involved a vision of "one like a Son of Man" approaching the Ancient of Days so as to receive sovereign authority to reign over "all peoples of every language" who then respond by worshipping him (Dan. 7:13-14). By way of partial fulfilment, in Revelation 5, the lamb likewise approaches the one who sits on the throne so as to take the scroll from his hand to reveal its meaning and is worshipped as a result (5:1-13), foreshadowing the global fulfilment foretold in Daniel 7:13-14. Following this text, Revelation 5:9 specifically mentions that the Messiah had redeemed for God people from all peoples and languages!

Interestingly, Revelation anchors the globally diverse reach of the Messiah's reign theologically in the Atonement or Christ's death on the Cross to redeem all peoples from slavery to sin and death. Christ's representation of humanity at the Cross is then viewed as all-inclusive and diverse. The explicit mention of "every tribe and language and people and nation" (v. 9) in the context of describing the Atonement is thus significant, but are we not possibly reading too much into Revelation 5:9 at this point? Is not Christology (incarnation and atonement) the victory of the "one" while Pentecost involves the "many?"

Following this distinction, we Pentecostals are especially quick to link the globally diverse reach of the gospel with the outpouring of the Holy Spirit at Pentecost. Luke-Acts is the part of the canon to which Pentecostals typically turn to understand this fulfilment. Our favourite text to describe it is Acts 2:4, where it states that all 120 followers of Jesus "were filled with the Holy Spirit and began to speak in other tongues as the Spirit enabled them". Luke tells us that an audience had gathered involving "God-fearing Jews from every nation under heaven" visiting Jerusalem at that time and that many of them heard their own languages spoken from this group of Jesus' Galilean followers. In Luke's Acts narrative, this event involving speaking in tongues had notable symbolic significance, for it signalled a global witness that would involve both Jews and a diversity of Gentile peoples from diverse backgrounds, all ages, genders, and

---

[1] All Scripture quotations, unless otherwise noted, are from the NIV version.

servants as well (2:17-18). The event of the Spirit overflowed the boundaries of Israel because the Spirit overflowed the body of Israel's Messiah. Put differently, the Spirit was poured forth from the heavenly Father through Israel's Messiah and for his sake, for he redeemed them, making them worthy of the Spirit (Acts 15:8). Christ now reigns as Lord and Head of his Church in all its expanding diversity (2:33-36).

The Acts narrative tells us further on in the story that God had been preparing the nations for their encounter with the gospel of Christ. God provided the peoples of the earth with sustenance and guidance, marking out "their appointed times in history and the boundaries of their lands" (Acts 17:26). This reference to "appointed times" (προστεταγμένους καιροὺς) referred to events rich with potential meaning in the diverse lives and journeys of these various peoples. The use of the term *kairos* arguably has this connotation. God provided for and guided these peoples throughout the *kairos* moments of their unique journeys so they would seek after him, each in their own contextually determined ways (v. 27). The goal was undoubtedly to add their diverse voices to the praises and witness of the people of God begun at Pentecost. The diversity of tongues points to the fact that the Spirit-empowered mission of the Church was the expanding boundary of the Church's diverse inclusivity. All of this is familiar territory for Pentecostals, and so it should be. Luke fills in the valuable pneumatological dimension of a Church that would include persons "from every tribe and language and people and nation" (v. 9).

True, Christ's atonement is the victory of the one, and the granting of the Spirit at Pentecost involves the possibility of receiving this victory among the many. I wish to propose, however, that texts like Revelation 5:9 imply that Christ on the Cross gave his life for the many and in a way that opens space for them in all their particularity and diversity within his risen body, the Church. Thus, the question that the Book of Revelation causes us to ask is how the Atonement anchors the contextually diverse reach of the Spirit depicted at Pentecost in Luke's Acts. How are we to understand the movement at the Atonement from Israel to all peoples?

The following additional points could be made at this point about Revelation 5:9-10. The lamb does indeed overcome to redeem Israel. He is "slain" or "slaughtered" in 5:6 like the paschal lamb of Israel. Yet, this lamb "overcomes" according to 5:5, for the "lion of the tribe of Judah, the root of David, has triumphed". Yet, the fact that the lamb overcomes for all peoples in 5:9 means that the image of the paschal lamb has transcended a Jewish nationalistic notion of atonement. Bear in mind that, according to Daniel 7:13-14, all peoples of the world praise the Son of Man. In his triumph on the Cross and in the Resurrection, the lamb of Revelation 5 has redeemed or purchased for God a people from all the diverse peoples of the world. This phrase "redeemed for God" in Revelation 5:9 literally means "purchased" or "ransomed" for God (ἠγόρασας Θεῷ). As Kevin John O'Brian notes, this term referred in the ancient world to the "redemption" or the purchasing of freedom from slavery: "Herein lies the significance of the lamb. Just as the blood of the paschal lamb signified the deliverance of the people of Israel from slavery and bondage in Egypt, so too the blood of the Lamb signifies the deliverance of God's people from slavery to sin and death."[2] This new Exodus, however, is to involve a global redemption that expands the kingdom of God to include all nations, tribes, and tongues.

The larger context in the Book of Revelation of the deliverance of all peoples through the slain lamb constitutes this new Exodus. As God delivered Israel from bondage in Egypt using plagues, so also does he deliver people from among all nations using plagues in the Book of Revelation (e.g., 16:2-15). In fact, the new Exodus in Revelation now points to the deliverance of all nations who will worship the Messiah King as freed peoples. Note the "song of Moses and of the Lamb" that will be sung to the Messiah by people of all nations in Revelation 15:3-4:

And [they] sang the song of God's servant Moses and of the Lamb:

Great and marvellous are your deeds,
    Lord God Almighty.
Just and true are your ways,
    King of the nations.
Who will not fear you, Lord,
    and bring glory to your name?
For you alone are holy.
All nations will come
    and worship before you,
for your righteous acts have been revealed.

In the evil city of Babylon, according to Revelation, human beings "are sold as slaves" (Rev. 18:13) but in the city of God, the lamb of God will have redeemed all peoples from slavery in every sense of the word. And the power of that deliverance currently sustains them in their battle against the forces of darkness. Indeed, the saints purchased for God by the lamb have no fear of the devil or of death. In the victory and authority of their Messiah, they too triumph over Satan the accuser:

Then I heard a loud voice in heaven say:

Now have come the salvation and the power
    and the kingdom of our God,
    and the authority of his Messiah.
For the accuser of our brothers and sisters,
    who accuses them before our God day and night,
    has been hurled down.
They triumphed over him
    by the blood of the Lamb
    and by the word of their testimony;
they did not love their lives so much
    as to shrink from death (Rev. 12:10-11).

---

[2] Kevin John O'Brian, "Revelation 5:5-14," *Interpretation* 53(2) (April 1999), 178-79.

The diverse inclusivity of all peoples in Christ's representative atonement maintains its significance throughout the Book of Revelation. In Revelation 7:9-10, for example, John sees the inclusively diverse heavenly throng praising God and the lamb for their salvation:

> After this I looked, and there before me was a great multitude that no one could count, from every nation, tribe, people and language, standing before the throne and before the Lamb. They were wearing white robes and were holding palm branches in their hands. And they cried out in a loud voice:
>
> "Salvation belongs to our God,
> who sits on the throne,
> and to the Lamb."

After praising God and the lamb for salvation, they are then led to drink from the "springs of living water" (7:13). Even in heaven, the liberated saints are designated as coming from "every nation, tribe, people, and language". They maintain their connection to their heritages. Passing through the Cross and through the heavenly portal did not dissolve the significance of the diverse paths they took in their journeys towards God.

One may ask at this point, could not Revelation 5 and 7 simply indicate that the redeemed people, although coming from diverse backgrounds, have since left them behind? Significantly, the eschatological fulfilment of the lamb's victory in Revelation 21 does not give us this impression. Note Revelation 21:22-24: "I did not see a temple in the city, because the Lord God Almighty and the Lamb are its temple. The city does not need the sun or the moon to shine on it, for the glory of God gives it light, and the Lamb is its lamp. The nations will walk by its light, and the kings of the earth will bring their splendour into it." Notice that in the heavenly city at the fulfilment of God's salvific plan, the "nations" walk by the light of the lamb and their kings bring the "splendour" of the nations into the city in honour of the lamb. No matter how one interprets this text, it seems clear that its author does not want his readers to conclude that the redeemed enter eschatological fulfilment leaving their diverse cultural identities behind.

A few further points in this text bear noting. First, there is no need for a temple in the heavenly city; the Father is immediately present through the lamb, who is the radiance of the Father's glory (cf., Heb. 1:3). The presence of God permeates the heavenly city making the existence of a temple in the traditional sense of the word unnecessary. God present to us and through us in heavenly communion is the temple. As John Christopher Thomas puts it, "The relationship between God and his people in the holy city Jerusalem represents complete integration of God with his people."[3] In fact, Thomas notes further that the holy city is shaped "as a cube like the holy of holies".[4] The concentration of the light and glory of the

---

[3] John Christopher Thomas and Frank D. Macchia, *Revelation* (Grand Rapids, MI: Eerdmans, 2016), 383.
[4] Thomas and Macchia, *Revelation*, 383.

divine presence in the city functions as a kind of holy of holies for the new creation (Rev. 21).

Second, notice that the nations walk by the light of the lamb, and their kings bring the splendour of their peoples into the heavenly city in honour of the lamb. I agree with Thomas concerning the heavenly city in this text: "There could be little doubt that the hearers would understand this language to mean that the nations who walk in its light are those who have experienced his salvation."[5] No sun or moon is needed because of the light of the glorified Christ (Rev. 21:23), but the nations and their kings walking by this light is not just a physical phenomenon. As Thomas notes, walking by the light in the Johannine tradition is profoundly spiritual in implication.[6] The implication here is that the "splendour" brought before the lamb arises from countless diverse testimonies of praise from the experience of glory radiated through the lamb but experienced concretely and diversely among the populations that inhabit the new earth as well as the heavenly city. Those who bring their splendour into the heavenly city in honour of the lamb have been shaped by him into a "kingdom and priests" to serve God (5:10).

Third, it is the glorified lamb who radiates the beauty, truth, and purity of the Father's glory to transform the nations. This fact harks back to Revelation 5:9, where the lamb who overcomes at the Cross and the Resurrection may be said to represent all peoples in all their diverse paths and contexts. Those diverse peoples who now walk by the light of the lamb were represented by Christ in all of their diversity at the Cross. He rose to glory on their behalf so they may be transformed by this glory and reflect it. The Gospel of John in fact tells us that the Word of the Father who mediated creation on behalf of the Father "was the light of all mankind" (Jn 1:4). John says further that the darkness could not overcome this light (1:5). Indeed! The lamb redeems people unto God from every tribe, language, people, and nation, and the door of hope in the far future remains open! Not only does Revelation 7:9 depict a diverse chorus of people "from every nation, tribe, people and language" praising the lamb in heaven, but in the new creation, the heavenly city's doors remain open to them all as well: "The nations will walk by its light, and the kings of the earth will bring their splendour into it. On no day will its gates ever be shut, for there will be no night there" (Rev. 21:24-25). Obviously, the diverse contexts from which the people of God come are not forgotten, not in heaven nor in the heavenly city.

Fourth, although the lamb in Revelation 5:9 dies to triumph over sin and death for all peoples and nations, the initial response among the nations is not entirely positive! In the very next chapter, the seals broken open by the lamb occasion a massively violent campaign "bent on conquest" (6:2). War, famine, and death follow. "The nations were angry" says 11:18, but God's wrath meets that anger, "destroying those who destroy the earth". Yet, there were obviously rays of hope

---

[5] Thomas and Macchia, *Revelation*, 384.
[6] Thomas and Macchia, *Revelation*, 384.

unleashed by the witness of Christ through the people of God. Let us not forget that a uncountable multitude came out of the Tribulation and now occupy the heavenly chorus of praise to the lamb (7:9-14). Interestingly, Isaiah 60:1-3 speaks prophetically of the rising of glory over the people of Israel and the nations of the earth while the world is still dark, yet this light offers hope for everyone: "nations will come to your light, and kings to the brightness of your dawn" (v. 3). The church fathers saw this rising of the light as fulfilled in the risen Christ and the eventual coming of all the nations to this light as fulfilled in texts like Revelation 21:22-24. Surely, this overcoming of the darkness by the light of Christ who conquers at the Cross for all peoples (Jn 1:4; Rev. 5:9) occurs while the world is still overrun by darkness. The Book of Revelation bears abundant witness to this fact, as does our world today, but the day is coming in which the nations will come to this light and walk by it. That is the hope offered by Revelation 21:22-24.

Does Christ erase differences? I propose that the victory of the lamb's redemptive death in the new creation according to the Book of Revelation does not erase our unique differences as people. I am not saying that, according to Revelation, the old creation remains fundamentally unchanged in the new creation. After all, Christ himself in the Book of Revelation is glorified in ways that go beyond how he looked in the flesh. According to Revelation 1:16, looking at his face resembles gazing at "the sun shining in all its brilliance!" No doubt we will be changed to reflect the brilliance of divine glory as well, perhaps not to that degree, but profoundly, nevertheless. John's depiction of the new creation as involving kings and nations obviously draws raw material from the world as John knew it. My point rather is that our diverse humanity transcends historical fulfilment, because that humanity was taken up into Christ's risen life. In eschatological fulfilment, the diversity of our physical and cultural uniqueness, although purified and glorified, is not erased by union with Christ – not in the Book of Revelation, not at the Cross, not in the life of the Spirit, not in heaven, and not in the new creation.

I do not think the eschatological endurance of our diverse humanity should be ignored because it has profound theological importance – one which is significant to the message of Revelation and to the multi-contextual message of the churches today. According to Revelation 5:9, Christ opens himself on the Cross (and by implication at the Incarnation in uniting to flesh by the Spirit, Luke 1:35) to all the peoples of the world, to "every tribe and language and people and nation" to redeem or to liberate them so they can flourish precisely as God created them, in all their uniqueness, to flourish. Christ annihilates sin and death at the Cross but not the concrete and diversely unique humanity objectively embraced and potentially liberated in that event. This view of the Atonement has profound implications linking it to the outpouring of the Spirit at Pentecost as cherished among Pentecostals.

The Link between Atonement and Pentecost: A Theological Reflection

Most Pentecostals rightly note that the Holy Spirit in Acts does not dissolve human diversity but rather embraces and transforms it into a vehicle of the praise and witness of the people of God. As noted above, the Book of Revelation indicates that this pneumatological embrace of human diversity at Pentecost is rooted in how Christ opens his life to humanity in all its diversity at the Atonement. How must we understand this rootage theologically? With the exegetical insights I have noted above from the Book of Revelation in mind, I will explain here more precisely how the Atonement leads to Pentecost.

I start by focusing on the issue of Christ's representation of humanity at the Cross. Of course, Christ represents God at the Cross "reconciling the world to himself" (2 Cor. 5:19), but Christ also represented humanity by paying our debt to God, or the "ransom" necessary for our freedom (Rev. 5:9). How do we understand more precisely Christ's representation of humanity at the Cross? Regardless of which theory of atonement one highlights, some notion of Christological representation of humanity is involved. Revelation 5:9 has Christ redeeming us by purchasing our salvation by his death. His death was a ransom that secured our freedom, as in Mark 10:45. He represented us by paying our debt to God. The Lord has laid on him the iniquity of us all in Isaiah 53:6. He died for our sins (1 Cor. 15:3) and was delivered up for our transgressions (Rom. 4:25). Christ bore our sin in his body on the Cross (1 Pet. 2:24). In Christ, "one died for all" (2 Cor. 5:14). In representing us, Christ's goal in the Atonement was to overcome sin and death and fulfil justice on our behalf. He did this so as to provide the means by which we can be reconciled to God by faith in him. Indeed, Christ was delivered up for our transgressions but raised for our justification (Rom. 4:25). The Cross also points in the direction of a new way of life. In representing us, Christ also functions as the last Adam who opens up a new path to being human that reflects the way of the crucified Christ, or the love of God given for the world. The saints in Revelation willingly suffered death in their witness to the world, overcoming hostilities by the blood of the lamb poured out for humanity (Rev. 12:11). Paul also writes movingly that he is crucified with Christ so that he may live "by faith in the Son of God, who loved me and gave himself for me" (Gal. 2:20).

Christ represents humanity in its diverse concreteness in many different contexts. Viewing Christological representation as a differentiated reality is due in part to the involvement of the Spirit in Christ's self-giving at the Cross. The Book of Revelation implies as much by referring to the lamb who ransomed people from all nations on the Cross having eyes that are the seven spirits sent by God "into all the earth" (Rev. 5:6). The seven spirits are global! An argument can be made that these seven spirits actually are the "seven-fold Spirit" or the Spirit in his fullness ("seven" may indeed symbolise fullness). This point is shown by the fact that the seven spirits appear at the opening triadic greeting of the Book of Revelation right where the Holy Spirit is expected (1:4-5). Also, Revelation 5:3 insists that no creature in heaven or on earth can look upon the scroll. Only God, only the lamb, can look upon it. And, yet, the lamb's eyes, which are the seven spirits, look upon it! This fact places the seven spirits on the divine side of the God/creature divide. Thus, one could argue that the lamb who ransoms all peoples in Revelation 5:9 bears the seven-fold Spirit or the Spirit in his fullness to be sent throughout the earth! The Spirit in his fullness at the Cross? Yes, for it is by the Spirit that Christ embraces humanity in all its diversity at the Cross. One may also refer here to Hebrews 9:14, where Christ offered himself for us on the cross "by the eternal Spirit". Christ on the Cross followed the leading of the Spirit in his embrace of all peoples in all their diversity. The Spirit in Acts will later follow the lead of the crucified Christ in resting upon all of the diverse peoples of the world that Christ had earlier represented.

There is more to say about Christ's representation of humanity in all its diversity at the Cross. Wolfhart Pannenberg proposes that, at Christ's death, Christ transcends, even dies to, his own particularity as a man of his time and place in order to represent a diverse body from every people and nation as their Lord and Head. Christ transcends his own particularity at the Cross in order to open space for ours! In other words, Christ does not cause us to leave behind our human particularity at the Cross; he leaves behind his in order to open space for ours in his own ecclesial and eschatological body! In this light, Pannenberg opposes a "Christological totalitarianism" that has Christ obliterating the diverse uniqueness of humanity in his act of redemption on the Cross.[7] Christ represents all of humanity in all its historical particularity; he wins the victory for them all, opens his life potentially to them all. As Miroslav Volf writes of Christ at the Cross, "Far from being the assertion of the one against the many, the cross is the self-giving of the one for the many." Of the unity among diverse peoples occasioned by the reconciliation of the Cross, Volf writes further, "Unity here is not the result of 'sacred violence' which obliterates the particularity of 'bodies' but a fruit of Christ's self-sacrifice which breaks down the enmity between them."[8] In Ephesians 2:11-22, the cross thus reconciles Jews and Gentiles into a united diversity, precisely because Christ does not obliterate their diversity by taking their place as their representative. Christ rises as the Head of his Church that will incorporate a variety of peoples and giftings, breaking down the enmity among them to do so. At Pentecost, at the expanding boundary of the Spirit-empowered Church, Christ welcomes them all to incorporate them into his own life with all their wonderful God-given diversity. The tongues of Pentecost signify this.

Some readers may express a degree of hesitation at this point. Does not the gospel call us to deny our former selves in order to identify exclusively with Christ? Didn't Paul write, "I no longer live but Christ lives in me" (Gal. 2:20)?

---

[7] Wolfhart Pannenberg, *Systematic Theology*, vol. 2 (Grand Rapids, MI: Eerdmans, 1994), 432-34.
[8] Miroslav Volf, *Exclusion and Embrace: A Theological Exploration of Identity, Otherness, and Reconciliation* (Nashville, TN: Abingdon, 1996), 47.

Paul thus refers to the "old self" involving a body ruled by sin. Christ died and rose again so this body could be "done away with" or "annulled" (καταργηθῇ) in terms of its claim on us (Rom. 6:6). Paul thus characterised his former life prior to his union with Christ as filled with distinctive privileges of which he boasted as a Jew, but his achievements only led him down the path of grievous and disobedient confidence in his flesh; Paul in his zeal even persecuted the Church. His new-found devotion to Christ, however, caused him to abandon his former life and consider it refuse so as to win Christ (Phil. 3:4-11). The idea that Christ's death and resurrection abolished our unique humanity often emerges in the resistance of some Christians to any cherishing of bodily or cultural diversity in the church. This resistance can take the form of a protest. Doesn't a focus on this diversity emphasise our differences, thus giving rise to division? Are we not at risk of drawing attention away from our unity in Christ? Especially if marginalised peoples seek social justice, the charge of divisiveness can be levelled with even greater intensity. To support such a protest, the idea that our bodily and cultural uniqueness has been abolished in Christ and is replaced by a new self that considers such uniqueness insignificant can be invoked. Who cares what race or sex we are or what unique path our people have taken in history? None of that matters now! It's all been replaced by a Christological identity that supersedes it all!

Some support the above protest by arguing that in passing through the cross towards the life of the Resurrection, we lay our earthly selves down with all of their glories in order to take on the glories of the risen Christ. This proposal requires more careful definition. In point of fact, according to Paul, we lay down our sinful self – that which is driven by pride, under condemnation, and headed for destruction. For example, Paul's reference to the "body ruled by sin" (σῶμα τῆς ἁμαρτίας) that will be done away with has been translated "body of sin" as though we are to regard our bodies as sinful through and through and unredeemable. Based on this understanding of this text, some think it best to give our earthly bodies and particularity no regard, along with everything distinctively connected to it.

In rejecting this viewpoint, the great interpreter of Romans, James Denney, notes that the use of the genitive in σῶμα τῆς ἁμαρτίας (body of sin) is qualitative rather than possessive. The phrase may thus better be paraphrased as, "the body of which sin has taken possession".[9] This rendering implies that our embodied existence can be delivered and renewed after the image of the crucified and risen Christ, the image of the Father's love. When Paul writes in Galatians 2:20, "I no longer live," he means that he no longer lives as a self in isolation. When Christ living in him becomes the decisive source of his new existence, such isolation disappears. His "I" is no longer alone, for he now belongs to another (in life and

---

[9] James Denney, "Romans," in W. Robertson Nicholl (ed), *Apostles, Romans, 1ˢᵗ Corinthians,* vol. 2 of *Expositor's Greek New Testament* (Peabody, MA: Hendrickson, 2002), 633.

in death, Rom. 14:8). He lives now by faith and in conformity to Christ. The Cross does not obliterate the self; rather, it saves it from self-centred isolation, centring it instead on Christ and his cause in the world. This rescue creates space for us to embrace others in all their uniqueness as well.[10] When Paul says in Galatians 3:28 that there is no male nor female, no Jew nor Gentile, in the body of Christ, he is not seeking to have all that is beautiful about such distinctions reduced to insignificance – only the sinful ways of asserting or responding to these distinctives in our fellowship together so they become barriers to our mutual respect and cooperation. We would thus be justified in interpreting this text in our time to mean that one is to reject unjust privileges or distorting stereotypes.

Love fashioned after the Christ of the Cross does not denigrate what God has created – the variety of bodies, languages, and cultures that have blessed this earth and this history we currently occupy. Love does not disrespect the uniquely embodied existence of various peoples. True, flesh and blood cannot inherit the kingdom of God (1 Cor. 15:50). We cannot evolve from this earthly existence to the immortality of the risen Christ! Yet, by representing peoples in all their earthly diversity, Christ rises to glory in a way that incorporates that diversity into his body and does it in a way that grants it eternal significance! Of course, Christ is indeed the supreme goal of all we are and become, both in this life as well as the next. Truly the beauty of which we partake as creatures of God in our current historical contexts does not serve as an end in itself. The unique intercontextual nature of our life in the Spirit is devoted above all else to the cause of Christ, of divine love in the world. Paul was a Jew when he was among the Jews and a Gentile when he was among the Gentiles, not only to enjoy an intercultural experience but also to serve the cause of Christ in all of these diverse contexts (1 Cor. 9:20-22). But this earthly beauty matters. We are not Gnostics. We do not believe that the new creation leaves the old creation entirely behind.

Part of the problem is that we are accustomed to interpreting Christ's representation of us at the Cross entirely in negative terms. Christ takes our place as sinners. He takes on our sin and condemnation; he bears our suffering and death. He takes our place, descends into the pit of our despair so as to rise up and open a door of hope to an entirely new future. And, of course, all of this is marvellously true – but also one-sided. If this was all that we see, we might well conclude that the Cross abolishes us in order to create something entirely new, radically disconnected from our former existence.

However, there is also a positive side to Christ's representation of all peoples, in all of their diversity, on the Cross. Christ takes up into himself not only our sin so as to abolish it, but he also takes up our frustrated and unfulfilled yearning for God so as to fulfil it, a yearning that God put there not only by creating us in his image but also by leading us throughout our unique paths of suffering and hope, paths sustained by divine grace and leading in the direction of the Cross.

---

[10] Volf, *Exclusion and Embrace*, 50-51.

The self, created by God, is abolished in its sinfulness but made new in fulfilment of its graced capacity for God, a capacity that takes many forms just waiting to be unleashed as vehicles of the Spirit. The many tongues of Pentecost in fulfilment of the Cross serve as an example of such vehicles.

Conclusion

The Atonement is that place where Christ represents all of us in all our colourful diversity, just as Revelation 5:9 implies. On the Cross, Christ lays down the limits of his own particularity as a person of a given time and place to open himself to a vast diversity of persons "from every tribe and language and people and nation". On the Cross, he follows the leading of the Spirit in offering this vast diversity of persons his embrace, and he rises in the fullness of the Spirit to incorporate them all into his risen life. He does so in such a way that does not dissolve their diversity but rather cherishes and uses it to bear diverse witness to the glorious love of God in the world. The outpouring of the Spirit for all flesh at Pentecost and the many tongues that give voice to the Spirit at that event is the fruit of the Cross. And that marvellously diverse witness is not forsaken at the heavenly gates, where people of every nation and tongue praise God and the lamb (Rev. 7:9), nor at the gates of the New Jerusalem where the kings of the nations bring the praises of the nations before the lamb of God in all his glory (21:22-26). Indeed, the risen and exalted Christ does not forsake the rich diversity of persons with whom he has come into solidarity, for he has made them all in their uniqueness forever members of his body. He will never dissolve their uniqueness to make room for his image. Indeed, his very image in tandem with the work of the Spirit of Pentecost creates space for otherness and cherishes it, sanctifying and freeing it to be all that God ever intended it to be. Walking in the way of the Cross challenges us to relate to one another in the same way, repenting so that we also open space in our lives for others in all their otherness.

Bibliography

Denney, James. "Romans." In *Apostles, Romans, 1st Corinthians*, edited by W. Robertson Nicholl, Vol. 2 of *Expositor's Greek New Testament*. Peabody, MA: Hendrickson, 2002.

O'Brian, Kevin John. "Revelation 5:5-14." *Interpretation* 53(2), (April 1999), 178-79.

Pannenberg, Wolfhart. *Systematic Theology*. Vol. 2. Grand Rapids, MI: Eerdmans, 1994.

Thomas, John Christopher, and Frank D. Macchia. *Revelation*. Grand Rapids, MI: Eerdmans, 2016.

Volf, Miroslav. *Exclusion and Embrace: A Theological Exploration of Identity, Otherness, and Reconciliation*. Nashville, TN: Abingdon, 1996.

5. Toward Spirit-Empowered Leadership: An Old Testament Foundation

Wonsuk Ma

Introduction

From the beginning of the modern Pentecostal Movement, the crucial role of leaders has generally been acknowledged. Thus, in seeking the best leadership model, charismatic leadership – already prevalent in the industrial, social, and political sectors – has naturally emerged as a viable option. Insiders and observers of Pentecostal Christianity have subsequently adapted this model to analyse and explain the extraordinary leadership capabilities of selected Pentecostal leaders. Also, several unfortunate downfalls of Pentecostal "stars" have prompted scholarly interest in leadership studies. This enduring scar in the Spirit-empowered movement exists not only as a scandal on its claim of extraordinary spirituality but also presents a continuing quest for spiritual and practical solutions.

My inquiry represents this ongoing interest in leadership issues within the movement. In this study, I assess the suitability of the charismatic leadership model for Pentecostal Christianity and propose Spirit-empowered leadership as an alternative. As a first step, I study relevant Old Testament (OT) evidence to elucidate key elements of this leadership model.

Charismatic vs. Spirit-Empowered Leadership

A leadership model should serve as a tool not only to analyse and assess one's leadership abilities but also to enable one to identify the nature of a problem and to point to solutions. Religious leadership studies should look beyond giftedness and performance and also investigate motivation, values, and attitudes.

Charismatic Leadership

Initially popularised by Max Weber[1] and widely adapted for diverse sectors, Christian leadership theorists include charismatic leadership as a Christian leadership type. Applying Weber's leadership theory has had wide implications

---

[1] The first introduction to charismatic leadership is found in Max Weber, *The Protestant Ethic and the Spirit of Capitalism*, trans. Talcott Parsons (Auckland, NZ: Pantianos Classics, 1930) based on the 1904 original.

in economics, politics, and religion.[2] My Google Scholar search on "Max Weber charismatic leadership theory" yielded a large number of academic studies, with "authority" as one frequently appearing keyword. One may then ask: how Christian is this leadership model, especially since Weber first espoused it in the context of Protestantism? He focused on work ethics shaped by the Protestant faith; thus, his theory related to business. The word *charisma*, a biblical term, appears frequently in Pauline literature, referring to spiritual gifts (e.g., 1 Cor. 7:7). Many widely use its derivatives today, for example, the "Charismatic Movement". However, these usages do not make the concept of charismatic leadership biblical.

To play with the fast-emerging generative AI technology, I asked ChatGPT to "compare Max Weber's and a biblical model of charismatic leadership." It lists four areas of similarities: extraordinary qualities, inspiring vision, emotional connection, and transformational influence. It also generates four areas of differences: the source of authority, religious foundation, ethical framework, and succession and stability.[3] Although ChatGPT's accuracy remains a subject of debate, these lists prove illustrative.

Despite the "Christian" language found in Weber's model, it is soon evident that the concept does not adequately describe or serve religious leadership. Picture the leader of a Christian congregation or ministry as I explore the differences between these two models. The first difference has to do with the single focus on gifted leaders in the charismatic model. Their authority comes from their extraordinary ability to perform well, convince followers, and lead an organisation. This presents problems for religious leadership as their mandate and authority come from outside. Thus, their role gets its definition from the one who elects and commissions them. Sometimes, their extraordinary giftedness originated from elsewhere. Structurally, therefore, secular charismatic leadership model is bilateral, a relationship between the leader and followers, while the religious model organises a trilateral relationship: the commissioner, the leader, and the followers. Imagine in a Christian organisation, a leader ignoring God's authority, lordship, and commissioning, but staying solely mindful of his or her followers, e.g., congregants. This makes the charismatic leadership model secular.

The second difference addresses the areas of concern, related to the first. The charismatic model evaluates a leader's effectiveness by personal capabilities and performance, such as a company's board would assess its CEO by organisational

---

[2] See the informative assessment of this book's impact: Mervyn F. Bendle, "Max Weber's *The Protestant Ethic and the 'Spirit' of Capitalism* (1905), A Centennial Essay," *Journal for the Academic Study of Religion* 18(2) (2005), 235-250. Also, for example, M. Rainer Lepsius, "Charismatic Leadership; Max Weber's Model and Its Applicability to the Rule of Hitler," in C.F. Graumann and S. Moscovici (eds), *Changing Conceptions of Leadership* (New York: Springer, 1986), 53-66.

[3] This chat is found at "Charismatic Leadership Characteristics," Chat Open AI, 24th August 2023, https://chat.openai.com/share/c833561b-be24-4aab-abf6-bc8172303ab3.

control and the company's profits. In the political world, we have seen an increasing tendency for voters to prioritise performance over morality. The very nature of charismatic leadership contains an inherent "dark side".[4] The priority of outcome can easily sidestep more fundamental values, such as motivation, ethics, fidelity to the community's identity, etc. One cannot imagine that a local church can evaluate its senior pastor by performance alone, such as annual income, new members added, and new building projects. However, due to the church's nature and mission, the leader's relationship with God, spirituality, ethical life, integrity, and passion for the congregation will prove foundational and, thus, more critical.

Also, this leadership discourse completely assumes individuals as leaders. However, the biblical tradition also expands to include God's people as a "leader". This communal dimension of leadership includes Israel (for example, "my servant," Is. 41:8),[5] the Church, a nation in a given period, and a local church.

Pentecostal Leadership Studies

Naturally, Pentecostal scholars have steadily produced studies on Pentecostal leadership, fully aware of leadership challenges within the movement. Two examples may help. Truls Åkerlund undertook a phenomenological study among Scandinavian Pentecostal leaders and concluded that his respondents identified the following characteristics as essential for Pentecostal leadership: (1) motivated by a sense of higher, divine purpose:; (2) derived leadership (from God); (3) human and divine agency in a seamless interaction between rationality and spirituality; (4) pragmatic and eclectic stance toward the Pentecostal tradition; (5) persuasive communication; (6) dialectic relationship between structure and agency; (7) adaptive to context; and (8) involving a leader's entire life.[6] The charismatic leadership model will not adequately meet this leadership demand by contemporary Spirit-filled Christians.

Stephen Fogarty's study on the dark side of charismatic leadership[7] also sheds some helpful light. Following R.J. House and J.M. Howell, who subdivided

---

[4] For example, K.A. DeCelles and M.D. Pfarrer, "Heroes or Villains? Corruption and the Charismatic Leader," *Journal of Leadership & Organizational Studies* 11(1) (2024), 67-77.
[5] All Scripture quotations, unless otherwise noted, are from the New International Version.
[6] Truls Åkerlund, *A Phenomenology of Pentecostal Leadership* (Eugene, OR: Wipf and Stock, 2018), 95-128.
[7] Stephen G. Fogarty, "The Dark Side of Charismatic Leadership," *Australian Pentecostal Studies* 13 (2010) [Available at: https://aps-journal.com/index.php/APS/article/view/104] [Last accessed: 13th March 2024].

charismatic leadership into personalised and socialised charismatic leadership,[8] Fogarty characterises personalised charismatic leaders as prioritising their personal interests over the organisation's, often exhibiting the need for power, negative life themes, and narcissistic tendencies.[9] The consequences of such a leader's unethical and destructive behaviour without self-regulatory mechanisms can prove detrimental to the self and the organisation.[10] To address this negative leadership potential, Fogarty advocates socialised charismatic leadership, which prioritises the organisation's interests over personal gains. Recognising charismatic leadership's "risky" nature, he also proposes several safeguards for Christian leadership.[11]

"Spirit-Empowered Leadership"

Pentecostal scholars have used several expressions for the full spectrum of the contemporary Spirit movement. Among them are "Pentecostal-Charismatic," "Renewal," "Pentecostal," "Apostolic," "Full Gospel," and others.[12] "Spirit-empowered" has been popularised by the Empowered21 Movement, a global relational network, tracing back to the 2006 Azusa Revival Centenary.[13] Oral Roberts University, which serves as its institutional base, has adopted this expression, for example, in its mission statement: "To develop Holy Spirit empowered leaders through whole-person education to impact the world".

When it comes to leadership, "Spirit-empowered" appears more appropriate over "Spirit-inspired" or "Spirit-motivated," considering the Pentecostal distinctive belief in Spirit-empowerment. Eric Newberg of Oral Roberts University recently published a study on the paradigm of Spirit-empowered leadership, following the five-fold ministry models.[14] He aptly illustrates these

---

[8] R.J. House and J.M. Howell, "Personality and Charismatic Leadership," *The Leadership Quarterly* 3(2) (1992), 81-108 [Available at: https://doi.org/10.1016/1048-9843(92)90028-E] [Last accessed: 13th March 2024].
[9] Fogarty, "Dark Side," 12.
[10] Fogarty, "Dark Side," 12.
[11] Fogarty, "Dark Side," 14-16.
[12] "Have Pentecostals Outgrown Their Name?" *Christianity Today*, 29th May 2020 [Available at: https://www.christianitytoday.com/news/2020/may/holy-spirit-empowered-christian-global-pentecostal-study.html] [Last accessed: 13th March 2024].
[13] Vinson Synan and Billy Wilson, *As the Waters Cover the Sea: The Story of Empowered21 and the Movement It Serves* (Tulsa, OK: Empowered Books, 2021), 59-61.
[14] Eric N. Newberg, "Paradigms of Global Spirit-Empowered Leadership," Spiritus: ORU Journal of Theology 7(2) (2022), 169-98.

paradigms by five case studies of Opoku Onyinah,[15] Pope John Paul II,[16] Jimmy Swaggart,[17] Reinhard Bonnke,[18] and S.B.J. Oschoffa.[19]

My study thus proposes "Spirit-empowered leadership" as an alternative to charismatic leadership. Building upon my descriptive studies of Spirit-empowered leaders in the Old Testament (see below), I identify four key characteristics of ideal Spirit-empowered leadership initially from the Old Testament texts. The New Testament (NT) provides a fuller picture of Spirit-empowered leadership in the life of Jesus and the apostles. Therefore, this serves as a theological study based on closely reading relevant passages.

Cruxes of Spirit-Empowered Leadership in the Old Testament

In elucidating key qualities of Spirit-empowered leaders in the Old Testament, I utilise here findings of two previous studies. My first study examined Samson and Saul as tragic cases of Spirit-empowered leaders,[20] while my subsequent study portrayed the ideal Spirit-filled and empowered leader as "prophet-servant".[21] I also place my studies in conversation with several Pentecostal leadership studies, such as Fogarty's socialised charismatic leadership model and Åkerlund's leadership qualities among contemporary Scandinavian Pentecostals.

Call: Enduring Consciousness

Call narratives are a distinct OT tradition, and many OT characters have details of their call experience. For example, Saul had a surprise but distinct call experience. Unknown to him, Samuel had been instructed by God to anoint him as the first king of Israel. The prophet announced his election to be the leader ("Has not the Lord anointed you ruler over his inheritance?" 1 Sam. 10:1), followed by three signs that subsequently appeared. The last sign was the coming of the Spirit as he was met by a group of prophets (v. 10). Indeed, immediately,

---

[15] David Osei-Nimoh, "Profile of a Spirit-Empowered Leader: Opoku Onyinah, the 'African Paul'," *Spiritus* 7, no. 2 (2022), 199-210.
[16] Tomasz Bialokurec, "John Paul II: A Role Model of Participative, Transformative, and Empowering Leadership," *Spiritus* 7(2) (2022), 211-26.
[17] Robert D. McBain, "Jimmy Swaggart: The Conflict between Spirit-Empowerment and Human Weakness," *Spiritus* 7(2) (2022), 227-41.
[18] Charles Morara Obara, "A Critical Analysis of Reinhard Bonnke's Charismatic Leadership Paradigm," *Spiritus* 7(2) (2022), 243-55.
[19] Samuel Olamiji Akibu, "S.B.J. Oschoffa (1909-85), The Miracle of a Shared Life," *Spiritus* 7(2) (2022), 257-69.
[20] Wonsuk Ma, "Tragedy of Spirit-Empowered Heroes: A Close Look at Samson and Saul," *Spiritus: ORU Journal of Theology* 2(1-2) (2017), 23-38.
[21] Wonsuk Ma, "Prophetic Servant: Ideology of Spirit-Empowered Leaders," *Spiritus: ORU Journal of Theology* 5(2) (Fall 2020), 217-34.

"God changed Saul's heart" (v. 9). Samuel predicted that the Spirit's presence would also turn him "into a different person" (v. 6). These compounding affirmations of God's call upon Saul suggest the life-changing impact of the call experience.

On the other hand, there is only a passing reference to the Prophet Amos' call experience. When confronted by Amaziah, the priest of Bethel, about the legitimacy of his prophetic activity in the northern kingdom, he replies, "I was neither a prophet nor the son of a prophet, but I was a shepherd, and I also took care of sycamore-fig trees. But the Lord took me from tending the flock and said to me, 'Go, prophesy to my people Israel'" (Amos 7:14-15). The call became the very motivation for his courageous prophetic ministry: "Surely the Sovereign Lord does nothing without revealing his plan to his servants the prophets. The lion has roared – who will not fear? The Sovereign LORD has spoken – who can but prophesy?" (3:7-8).

However, the call experience does not ensure the success of the called. Despite the multiple layers of affirmation of God's call and subsequent experience with God's Spirit (1 Sam. 11:6) and splendid "Spirit-empowered" victory, Saul failed miserably, almost immediately. The called must internalise the call, with it affecting every aspect of the receiver's thoughts, words, and actions. This should involve a conscious and repeated decision so that the call becomes an enduring lifestyle. The Prophet Jeremiah, for example, has a distinct call experience, characterised by God's word, "Then the Lord reached out his hand and touched my mouth and said to me, 'I have put my words in your mouth'" (Jer. 1:9). God's call and commission shape his life and ministry. Some time into his ministry, Jeremiah's prophetic utterances invite harsh opposition, ill-treatment, and imprisonment. Amidst the repeated and painful cycle of Jeremiah's obedience and persecution, he complains to God about his "deception" (20:7), and yet pours out his dilemma: "But if I say, 'I will not mention his word or speak anymore in his name,' his word is in my heart like a fire, a fire shut up in my bones. I am weary of holding it in; indeed, I cannot" (v. 9). Only the internalised and enduring awareness of God's call sets the whole life to be consumed by passion. Thus, I argue that the ideal leadership is better reflected by prophets and kings.[22]

Åkerlund's research places more prominence on the "higher and divine purpose" than a call experience per se. Noticing the difference in call experiences among missionaries, the sense of one's call can be subjective: some perceive it by an external authority (that is, God) while others by "obligation to one's authentic self".[23] Regardless of the mode or process, Åkerlund observes that

---

[22] Ma, "Prophetic Servant," 229-31.
[23] Åkerlund, *A Phenomenology of Pentecostal Leadership*, 95.

Pentecostal leaders in Norway are motivated by a sense of God's call.[24] Applying this trait of Spirit-empowered leadership, one can attribute the failure of Samson and Saul to their personalised charismatic leadership, which prioritises personal interests over corporate ones, resulting in unethical leadership behaviour.[25] Thus, the true mark of empowered leadership, in contrast, involves a call or purpose-directed life.

Human and Divine Alignment

My study on the tragic heroes argues that their initial encounters with the Spirit of God were intended as (semi-)private. After Samuel's anointing of him, Saul experienced the Spirit as he met a group of prophets in their Spirit-inspired procession. Then, he experienced inner transformation: "You will be changed into a different person" (1 Sam. 10:6). The core of this internal transformation and the fulfilled signs is an intuitive and complete alignment of his heart or thoughts to God's, and he could "do whatever [his] hand finds to do, for God is with [him]" (v. 8). Although less explicit, Samson's first encounter with God's Spirit also appears personal and thus, intended for an inner realignment with God's purpose and character development.[26]

Isaiah 11 presents the ideal ruler, upon whom rests the abundant presence of the Spirit. That ruler's particular qualities include "the Spirit of wisdom and understanding, the Spirit of counsel and might, and the Spirit of knowledge and the fear of the Lord" (Is. 11:2). With unmistakable wisdom language, the text portrays the ideal king as more of a sage[27] or prophet than a military warrior. The foundation has to do with the king's alignment with God's demand and mission, by submitting to the inner working of his Spirit:

> As the "fear of the Lord/God" sums the characteristics of the ideal king, the Spirit's endowment is predominantly moral and spiritual [...] the "internalisation" of the Spirit's endowment. The Spirit of God works through the recipient's heart and character, resulting in the qualities desired for the ideal king. [...] His righteous and just rule, therefore, is the manifestation of his inner disposition endowed by the Spirit.[28]

The outer demonstration of the Spirit's empowerment is a natural consequence of the internalised Spirit's presence and transformation.

---

[24] Åkerlund, *A Phenomenology of Pentecostal Leadership*, 97, identifies the process "through their relationship with God and an understanding of his purpose [for their lives]".

[25] Fogarty, "The Dark Side," 12.

[26] Ma, "Tragedy of Spirit-Empowered Heroes," 26-27.

[27] Patricia K. Tull, *Isaiah 1-39* (Macon, GA: Smyth & Helwys, 2010), 228.

[28] Ma, "Prophetic Servant," 219. Aubrey R. Johnson, *The One and the Many in the Israelite Conception of God* (Cardiff: University of Wales Press, 1961), 2, refers the Spirit of God to the "undeniable extension of his personality; thus, the presence of God.

Åkerlund ranks "human and divine agency" as the second characteristic of Pentecostal leadership. Although this stresses the critical role of the human leader, he places the primacy on the divine by referring to Grant Wacker's expression, "The otherworldly legitimates the this-worldly."[29] In this one-sided alignment, the human must align to God's will but not the other way around. Naturally, the leader's entire life embodies this close alignment.[30] When the human leader deviates from this relationship, tragedy happens. Under this discussion, Åkerlund also observes a "seamless interaction between rationality and spirituality, against dichotomy between the two".[31] The ideal king possesses both spiritual/moral qualities and rational or executive functions (e.g., "the Spirit of counsel and might"). In leadership studies, related to this is the routinisation of charismata, or the tension between charismatic leadership and institutional structures.[32]

In a biblical reflection of charismatic leaders, Catholic Charismatic scholar, Tomasz Bialokurec, contends that the relational nature of leadership remains essential and is based on the leader's affinity with God.[33] Fogarty also suggests that the Trinity can serve as a model for Christian leadership, especially in the relational nature of the three persons in one.[34] The Spirit-empowered leader must retain the attitude of "God in me and me in Him".

Serving Two Entities

While leadership studies focus on the relationship between the leader and follower, Christian leadership has a third party – God. The two characteristics of Spirit-empowered leadership explore this fundamental layer, the leader's relationship with God. Take Moses' leadership role; God called him, empowered him, and sent him to lead his people out of the bondage of Egyptian slavery. This positioned him as leader between God and the people or nation God sent him to lead. God calls the ideal king in Isaiah 11 to bring just and righteous rule to his people and judgement to the wicked. Similarly, he calls the Spirit-anointed servant in Isaiah 61 to minister to the marginalised: "to proclaim good news to the poor [...] to bind up the broken-hearted, to proclaim freedom to the captives, and release from darkness for the prisoners" (Is. 61:1). Throughout the Old

---

[29] Åkerlund, *A Phenomenology of Pentecostal Leadership*, 101.
[30] Åkerlund, *A Phenomenology of Pentecostal Leadership*, 126-28.
[31] Åkerlund, *A Phenomenology of Pentecostal Leadership*, 101.
[32] The entire book of Margaret M. Poloma, *The Assemblies of God at the Crossroads: Charisma and Institutional Dilemmas* (Knoxville, TN: University of Tennessee Press, 1989) studies the challenge of the historical process of institutionalisation as an expression of "routinisation."
[33] Tomasz Bialokurec, "Charismatic Leadership Redefined: Transformed by Servanthood," *Pentecostal Education* 6(1) (Spring 2021), 16.
[34] Fogarty, "Dark Side," 16-17.

Testament, care for the weak and powerless stands as the hallmark of God's leadership.

However, serving the sender (God) takes priority over those the leader is sent to when interests conflict. The narrative of Ahab's four hundred prophets and the lone prophet Micaiah (1 Kgs. 22) illustrates this dynamic well. God called Micaiah to bring his message to Ahab, confronting the crowd of royal prophets. He resolves to speak "only what the Lord tells [him]" (v. 14) and conveys the message of defeat and death of the king. When Zedekiah, the leader of Ahab's prophets, challenges the source and authenticity of Micaiah's message, Micaiah confidently replies, "You will find out on the day you go to hide in an inner room" (v. 25). This incident demonstrates Micaiah's affinity with God, through which flowed genuine revelation, the ability to discern, and courage to confront the authority. However, the prophet felt motivated by his loyalty to the Lord and his deep concern for the fate of God's people.

In this triad relationship, priorities remain clear: God, the people Micaiah was sent to, and the self; the leader takes the last priority. When this order is not heeded, even an empowered leader fails. Take Saul again. In his first campaign after the public coronation of Saul (1 Sam. 11:12-15), he violates Samuel's specific command to wait for him (13:8). He offers a burnt offering under pressure from his people, even though he is not a priest (v. 9). Samuel harshly condemns him, saying, "You have done a foolish thing" by not keeping the Lord's command (v. 13). As a consequence, Saul's kingdom will not endure, and another man "after [God's] own heart" will replace him (v. 14). The violated priority is quite clear: Saul had placed his own position first, by pleasing the people (second), and taking God as the last priority. The result was deadly: failed Spirit-empowered leadership.

Åkerlund highlights this relational dynamic under "derived leadership".[35] The leader is also a follower of God's call, as much as serving as the leader of those to whom they are called. Åkerlund rightly points out that the unique Pentecostal worldview conditions believers to experience the power of the living God through his Holy Spirit.[36] In this worldview and leadership orientation, Christian leadership centres and integrates "everything around God," who is "the ultimate source of authority".[37] This makes relating with God the leader's priority. Because of this orientation, Spirit-empowerment can exhibit itself in superhuman performance, such as Samson's feat, or sacrificial suffering for others, as in the Suffering Servant (Is. 53).

---

[35] Åkerlund, *A Phenomenology of Pentecostal Leadership*, 97-101.
[36] Åkerlund, *A Phenomenology of Pentecostal Leadership*, 98. Also, Wonsuk Ma, *Mission in the Spirit: Formation, Theology, and Praxis* (Oxford: Regnum, 2023), 94-95.
[37] Karl Inge Tangen, *Ecclesial Identification beyond Late Modern Individualism? A Case Study of Life Strategies in Growing Late Modern Churches* (Leiden: Brill, 2012), 334.

Empowering Others

God elected his servants to guide his people through covenant relationship with him. He called prophets to admonish the people to return to the Lord. In this restored relationship, Israel, God's servant, would experience the flourishing of life: "For I will pour out my Spirit on your offspring and my blessing on your descendants [...] like poplar trees by flowing streams" (Is. 44:3-4). This work of the Lord, in turn, would bring nations to God's reign (v. 5). God's Spirit empowers Israel to empower the nations.

On an individual level, Moses and his seventy elders illustrate the cycle of empowerment. To share his administrative and leadership burden, Moses chose seventy as instructed by God. Then God "took some of the Spirit that was on him [Moses] and put it on the seventy leaders" (Num. 11:25, Complete Jewish Bible). Although Moses played a passive role, his Spirit-empowered experience multiplied in the seventy through the election and empowerment of the same Spirit.[38] They were then to serve the people as well as Moses. In a study on the Spirit in Isaiah, I argue that "the emphasis on power or empowerment [...] has to do with the well-being of God's people."[39] In the first Servant Song, the single mission of this Spirit-empowered leader was to "bring justice to the nations" (Is. 42:1, 3-4). Despite various interpretations of "justice," the outcome of the Servant's mission is for the nations (or "islands") to "put their hope" in the servant's teaching (v. 4).

In the Old Testament, this continuing cycle of empowerment would ultimately result in the Spirit's empowering presence on everyone in God's community. Joel predicts this universalised outpouring: "And afterward, I will pour out my Spirit on all people. Your sons and daughters will prophesy, your old men will dream dreams, your young men will see visions. Even on my servants, both men and women, I will pour out my Spirit in those days" (Joel 2:28-29). This "democratisation" of the Spirit makes everyone in God's community equally empowered, creating an egalitarian community.[40] The Spirit-empowered community then exercises its God-endowed leadership to the nations. As God called Israel to serve as a Spirit-empowered community to empower others, so too has he called the Church.

Closing

The space limitations here do not allow me to explore other key qualities/characteristics of Spirit-empowered leadership, such as moral

---

[38] Bialokurec, "John Paul II," 16-17 contends, "The Spirit-empowered Leader Empowers Others."
[39] Wonsuk Ma, "Isaiah," in Trevor J. Burke and Keith Warrington (eds), *A Biblical Theology of the Holy Spirit* (London: SPCK, 2014), 44.
[40] Fogarty, "Dark Side," 16, stresses egalitarianism as a key characteristic of Christian leadership, based on the Trinitarian relationship.

authority, bold vision, signs and wonders, and a strong appeal to the followers. I hope this initial proposal encourages others to join the conversation to expand the list of Spirit-empowered leadership traits.

As a closing remark, I address a pressing question: if the chosen leader is only good for sacrifice and hard work, do they enjoy anything in life? So far, my discussion may have inadvertently portrayed the Spirit-empowered leader as living a life that all other humans want to avoid as much as possible. However, the chosen ones in Scripture I have described here lived and served with a deep sense of privilege and honour despite a hard life for many. This paradigm runs throughout the Bible, including the very creation of humans.

First, the elect are God's own. The first humans were distinguished from the rest of creation by carrying God's image (Gen. 1:26) and breath (or "Spirit," 2:7). The call experience closely relates to this intimate relationship. Elsewhere, God called these individuals his "treasured possession" (Ex. 19:5), "my son" (Ps. 2:7), "my servant," and "my chosen" (e.g., Is. 42:1). This intimate relationship is also expressed in various declarations and actions. God knew them before they were formed (e.g., Jer. 1:5); he will never leave or forsake his chosen (e.g., Dt. 31:6); and he has written their names on the palm of his hands (Is. 49:15). God's relentless pursuit of his people, despite their rebellion, depicts his commitment to his own.

Second, the presence of the "God matter" in the chosen servants sets them apart. As "image" and "breath/Spirit" in humans distinguish them from the rest of the creation,[41] so did the Spirit upon the leaders separate them from the people. While this affirmed their special relationship with God, as seen above, the Spirit's presence also came with God-given authority and empowerment. God unmistakably upheld Moses' authority as he took "some of the Spirit from upon Moses and placed it on the seventy elders" (Num. 11:25, my translation). The decisive military victory of Gideon over the Midianites through the empowerment of the Spirit set him apart from the whole nation (Jg. 8). The very word *servant* was often used for God's elected leaders to imply God-given authority.

Third, relatability is another special privilege of the elect. Although this closely relates to the previous points, it nonetheless remains significant. Again, reaching out to the creation record, God relates with the humans: when Adam and Eve hid from God who "was walking in the garden in the cool of the day" (Gen. 3:8), the Lord calls to Adam, "Where are you?" (v. 9). This incident indicates God's desire to relate with his image/breath/Spirit bearers. God's reluctance to hide his plan from Abraham reveals this relationship: "Shall I hide

---

[41] I have argued in several places that the "breath" in Genesis 2, often used interchangeably with the Spirit, has a unique role referring to Adam's status in relation to God and the animal world. For example, Julie C. Ma and Wonsuk Ma, *Mission in the Spirit: Towards a Pentecostal/Charismatic Missiology* (Oxford: Regnum, 2010), Chapter 2: "Spirit, Creation Theology, and Mission," especially pp. 21-22.

from Abraham what I am about to do?" (Gen. 18:17). This intimate relatability gave Abraham the boldness to "negotiate" with God over the fate of Lot and his family in Sodom (vv. 23-33). Thus, God identified Abraham as "my friend" (Is. 41:8). Similarly, God spoke to Moses "face to face as a man speaks to his friend" (Ex. 33:11). This ability to relate with God intimately became the highest reward as the psalmist cried out with joy, "the Lord himself is my inheritance, my prize. He is my food and drink, my highest joy!" (Ps. 16:5).

Fourth, the elected servant became God's close partner in fulfilling his plan, primarily due to the calling and the intimate relationship with God. They particularly worked to keep God's people in the covenant relationship. In this process, the Lord revealed his plan unknown to others. This revelatory experience took different forms. One of them is the heavenly court scene: God's chosen servant was invited to view what took place behind the divine curtain. Isaiah saw the Lord in his glory and heard his sermon, "Whom shall I send? And who will go for us?" (Is. 6:18). After this call and God's commission, Isaiah relentlessly warns the nation to turn to the Lord, rebuking the kings when necessary and advising them about how to make godly decisions (e.g., Nathan confronting David, 2 Sam. 12:1-14). In the face of judgement, Isaiah also admonishes the people with the ultimate hope of restoration through the Spirit (e.g., Is. 32:15-18; cf. Ez. 37). Through the revelatory experiences and faithful proclamation of Spirit-empowered servants, the fate of a nation was changed.

This close partnership between God and Spirit-empowered leaders can bring success and fame, but also hardship and even death. However, any rewards in life were insignificant; we remember these leaders as men and women after God's own heart. After all, God is the ultimate reward for his Spirit-empowered servants and leaders.

Bibliography

Åkerlund, Truls. *A Phenomenology of Pentecostal Leadership*. Eugene, OR: Wipf and Stock, 2018.

Bendle, Mervyn F. "Max Weber's *The Protestant Ethic and the 'Spirit' of Capitalism* (1905), A Centennial Essay", *Journal for the Academic Study of Religion* 18(2), (2005), 235-50.

Bialokurec, Tomasz. "Charismatic Leadership Redefined: Transformed by Servanthood", *Pentecostal Education* 6(1), (Spring 2021), 16.

———. "John Paul II: A Role Model of Participative, Transformative, and Empowering Leadership", *Spiritus* 7(2), (2022), 211-26.

"Charismatic Leadership Characteristics." Chat Open AI. 24th August 2023. [Available at: https://chat.openai.com/share/c833561b-be24-4aab-abf6-bc8172303ab3] [Last accessed: 12th March 2024].

DeCelles, K.A. and M.D. Pfarrer. "Heroes or Villains? Corruption and the Charismatic Leader," *Journal of Leadership & Organizational Studies* 11(1), (2024), 67-77.

Fogarty, Stephen G. "The Dark Side of Charismatic Leadership", *Australian Pentecostal Studies* 13 (2010). [Available at: https://aps-journal.com/index.php/APS/article/view/104] [Last accessed: 12th March 2024].

"Have Pentecostals Outgrown Their Name?" *Christianity Today.* 29th May 2020. [Available at: https://www.christianitytoday.com/news/2020/may/holy-spirit-empowered-christian-global-pentecostal-study.html] [Last accessed: 12th March 2024].

House, R.J., and J.M. Howell. "Personality and Charismatic Leadership", *The Leadership Quarterly* 3(2), (1992), 81-108. [Available at: https://doi.org/10.1016/1048-9843(92)90028-E] [Last accessed: 12th March 2024].

Inge Tangen, Karl. *Ecclesial Identification beyond Late Modern Individualism? A Case Study of Life Strategies in Growing Late Modern Churches.* Leiden: Brill, 2012.

Johnson, Aubrey R. *The One and the Many in the Israelite Conception of God.* Cardiff: University of Wales Press, 1961.

Lepsius, M. Rainer. "Charismatic Leadership: Max Weber's Model and Its Applicability to the Rule of Hitler", In C.F. Graumann and S. Moscovici, Eds. *Changing Conceptions of Leadership.* New York: Springer, 1986: 53-66.

Ma, Wonsuk. "Isaiah", In Trevor J. Burke and Keith Warrington, Eds. *A Biblical Theology of the Holy Spirit.* London: SPCK, 2014: 34-45.

——. *Mission in the Spirit: Formation, Theology, and Praxis.* Oxford: Regnum, 2023.

——. "Prophetic Servant: Ideology of Spirit-Empowered Leaders", *Spiritus: ORU Journal of Theology* 5(2), (Fall 2020), 217-34.

——. "Tragedy of Spirit-Empowered Heroes: A Close Look at Samson and Saul", *Spiritus: ORU Journal of Theology* 2(1-2), (2017), 23-38.

McBain, Robert D. "Jimmy Swaggart: The Conflict between Spirit-Empowerment and Human Weakness", *Spiritus* 7(2), (2022), 227-41.

Morara Obara, Charles. "A Critical Analysis of Reinhard Bonnke's Charismatic Leadership Paradigm", *Spiritus* 7(2), (2022), 243-55.

Newberg, Eric N. "Paradigms of Global Spirit-Empowered Leadership", Spiritus 7(2), (2022), 169-98.

Olamiji Akibu, Samuel. "S.B.J. Oschoffa (1909-85), The Miracle of a Shared Life", *Spiritus* 7(2), (2022), 257-69.

Osei-Nimoh, David. "Profile of a Spirit-Empowered Leader: Opoku Onyinah, the 'African Paul'", *Spiritus* 7(2), (2022), 199-210.

Poloma, Margaret M. *The Assemblies of God at the Crossroads: Charisma and Institutional Dilemmas.* Knoxville, TN: University of Tennessee Press, 1989.

Synan, Vinson, and Billy Wilson. *As the Waters Cover the Sea: The Story of Empowered21 and the Movement It Serves.* Tulsa, OK: Empowered Books, 2021.

Tull, Patricia K. *Isaiah 1-39*. Macon, GA: Smyth & Helwys, 2010.
Weber, Max. *The Protestant Ethic and the Spirit of Capitalism*, trans. Talcott Parsons. Auckland, NZ: Pantianos Classics, 1930, based on the 1904 original.

6. The Voice of Truth in the Christian Encounter with World Religions

Ivan Satyavrata

Introduction

The history of the Jesus Movement is a story of ongoing encounter with various pre-existent religious traditions over time across various geographical regions and peoples across the globe. While plurality of religions and cultures have been integral features of life since time immemorial, modernisation and globalisation have brought about a mingling of peoples and cultures without parallel in the history of civilisation. Contrary to the predictions of secular prophets of the previous generation who anticipated the demise of religion, the late twentieth and early twenty-first century have also seen the revival and global expansion of the world's living religions.[1] Life today is marked by unprecedented multiculturalism and religious plurality and, as various religions passionately assert the supremacy of their truth claims, the potential for communal conflict is greater than ever before.

Nowhere is this trend more evident than in the continent of Asia, the cradle of human civilisation with a five-thousand-year history; a rich mosaic of traditions, cultures, and civilisations; home to all the living religions of the world, including Judaism, Islam, Christianity, Hinduism, Buddhism, Jainism, Sikhism, Confucianism, Taoism, Shintoism, and Zoroastrianism. Surrounded by deeply entrenched ancient religious traditions, in many parts of Asia the Church is regarded as a foreign presence and viewed with suspicion as a vestige from the colonial era. Although Asians have, for most of their history, tolerated their neighbours of other faiths, some countries have recently witnessed rising communal tensions and conflict.[2] At a time when nurturing a culture of tolerance remains such a pressing need, Christian missionary activity is seen as needlessly provocative, stoking communal passion and religious conflict by pitting the claims of one faith against another.

---

[1] Gailyn Van Rheenen, "Religionquake: From World Religions to Multiple Spiritualities", in Michael Pocock, Gailyn Van Rheenen, and Douglas McConnell, Eds. *The Changing Face of World Missions: Engaging Contemporary Issues and Trends* (Grand Rapids, MI: Baker Academic, 2005), 79-89; Harold Netland, *Encountering Religious Pluralism* (Downers Grove, IL: InterVarsity Press, 2001), 9-15.
[2] Jehu J. Hanciles, "Migration and Mission: Some Implications for the Twenty-first Century Church", *International Bulletin of Missionary Research* 27(4) (October 2003), 146, https://doi.org/10.1177/239693930302700401 [last accessed 13th August, 2024].

Followers of Christ today thus find themselves on the defensive, having to think afresh and pray through questions that strike at the jugular of the Christian faith: what attitudes should we cultivate towards the diverse faiths of our neighbours amidst the growing multiculturalism of our times? If every religion claims to be the only true one and sees its mission as converting those of other faiths, will that not inevitably intensify religious bigotry and communal strife? Amidst an increasingly multi-religious and culturally diverse society, can followers of Christ share the good news with neighbours of other faiths without provoking social unrest and religious conflict? For Christians who live under a prophetic mandate to be "the Voice of Truth,"[3] this presents a serious missiological question but one with burning existential implications as well.

The Challenge of Religious Pluralism

The most formidable challenge to "the Voice of Truth" today is the growing influence of the ideology of religious pluralism. This ideology constitutes an unofficial orthodoxy in much of academia, is firmly entrenched within the entertainment and media elite, and finds wide acceptance in popular culture—even among some sections of professing Christians.

Several years ago, the gauntlet was thrown in an article entitled "The Real War," published in the immediate wake of 9/11, in which columnist, Thomas Friedman, blames all faiths coming out of the Mosiac tradition (Judaism, Christianity, and Islam) for all the religious conflict in our world. He accuses these faiths of what he provocatively terms "religious totalitarianism" – "a view of the world that my faith must reign supreme and can be affirmed and held passionately only if all others are negated".[4] Portraying this caricature as the real enemy of global peace and harmony, Friedman strongly advocates pluralism as an alternative that embraces religious diversity and fosters tolerance. Citing Rabbi David Hartman in support of his view, Friedman asks:

> Can Islam, Christianity and Judaism know that God speaks Arabic on Fridays, Hebrew on Saturdays and Latin on Sundays, and that he welcomes different human beings approaching him through their own history, out of their language and cultural heritage? Is single-minded fanaticism a necessity for passion and religious survival, or can we have a multilingual view of God – a notion that God is not exhausted by just one religious path?[5]

Pluralism thus holds that no one religion can claim to be somehow normative and superior to others: all religions are complex historically and culturally

---

[3] A phrase based on the title to represent the gospel as expressed within the biblical-historic Christocentric trinitarian faith tradition.
[4] Thomas L. Friedman, "Foreign Affairs; The Real War," *The New York Times*, 27th November 2001 [Available at: https://www.nytimes.com/2001/11/27/opinion/foreign-affairs-the-real-war.html] [Last accessed: 18th March 2024].
[5] Friedman, "Foreign Affairs."

conditioned human responses to the one divine reality. People must celebrate diversity of religious experience and expression as something good and healthy and acknowledge salvation (enlightenment or liberation) as present and effective in its own way in each religion.

Friedman's case is strengthened by the observation that fundamentalism in any religion appears to generate hatred, suspicion, fear, and violent rejection of the "other" expressed in religious terrorism.[6] Pluralism thus offers an attractive irenic alternative at a time when there are increasing curbs on religious freedom in many regions of the world in which Christ followers in erstwhile colonies struggle under the burden of the cultural imperialist legacy of the colonial era, and where many also live in fear of violent opposition from extremist and militant religious organisations.[7] Pluralism, however, poses a serious threat to Christian mission and to the Christian faith itself: it strikes at the nerve centre of Christian faith at three crucial points.

First, pluralism insists that tolerance towards other religions requires that the holy scriptures of people of other faiths be accepted as possessing the same authority as the Bible. Furthermore, it undermines the central constitutive claim of the Christian faith – that Jesus of Nazareth was not simply one of many, or even the greatest of all human religious figures, but the decisive self-disclosure of the eternal God himself. Pluralists regard this claim as imperialistic, an unnecessary hindrance to interreligious harmony: Jesus may be the Saviour for Christians, but he is not the only Saviour for all peoples. A third problem in pluralism is its belief that different religions represent many different paths leading to the same goal. Pluralism holds that different religious traditions are responses from different contexts within which humans experience essentially the same salvation/enlightenment. This perspective clearly undermines the grounds and motivation for Christian mission.

Pluralism has been thoroughly weighed in the scales and found to be biblically ungrounded, theologically flawed, philosophically vacuous, and logically untenable.[8] Nonetheless, it continues to present a serious challenge to Christian

---

[6] Some studies have documented a close connection between religious fundamentalism and terrorist violence in most of the world's major religious traditions, including Christianity, Islam, Hinduism, Judaism, Buddhism, and Sikhism. See Mark Juergensmeyer, *Terror in the Mind of God* (Berkeley, CA: University of California Press, 2003).

[7] In this context, Asian voices such as Peter Phan call for abandoning Christian claims of Christ's decisiveness: "[T]he heightened consciousness, ever more widespread since modernity, of the necessarily relational and historically embedded character of all exclusive and absolute claims, including religious ones [is] a feature that seems to render [...] exclusive and absolute claims problematic if not impossible." Peter Phan, "Cultural Diversity and Religious Pluralism: The Church's Mission in Asia", *Asia Pacific Mission Studies* 1(2) (2019), 90; [Available at: https://core.ac.uk/reader/286139530] [Last accessed: 18th March 2024].

[8] A detailed critique of pluralism is beyond the scope of this presentation. In brief,

witness in the twenty-first century due to its emotional appeal and the Church's response, a crucial test of its future survival.[9]

Beyond Exclusion and Eclecticism to Embrace

The gospel does not exist as something Christians have invented but is rather a "pearl of great price" (Mt. 13:45)[10] entrusted to our stewardship. This gospel affirms that all humans are sinners in need of redemption; that God desires the salvation of peoples of every race, culture, and religion; that God's salvation comes to us through a particular person, Jesus Christ, the decisive self-disclosure of God, who made atonement for the sins of the world by his death and resurrection; and that only by faith in him can human beings experience restoration to a right relationship with God.

God has called his people to share this gospel with courage and conviction and to do so with gentleness and respect (Eph. 4:15; 1 Pet. 3:15).[11] The critical question remains: can we trust the Holy Spirit to show a way to share Christ that remains faithful to Christ and biblical truth and yet reflects a posture of sensitivity and respect towards our neighbours of other faiths?

The good news is that an approach to other faiths exists that has an impressive vintage, firmly rooted in the New Testament and which we can trace all through the history of the Church. Derived from Jesus's attitude to Judaism in Matthew 5:17, "Think not that I have come to abolish the law and the prophets; I have come not to abolish them but to fulfil them," this response is commonly referred to as the fulfilment approach. The theme in its original New Testament context

---

pluralists have two major problems: (a) they have to contend with the problem of conflicting truth claims, given the incredible diversity and mutual incompatibility of beliefs in the various religions; and (b) the pluralist vision rests on a logical inconsistency that there is no privileged religious tradition, even though pluralist philosophical presuppositions and truth claims are also inevitably tradition specific. See Ivan Satyavrata, "Jesus and Other Faiths," in Timoteo D. Gener and Stephen T. Pardue (eds), *Asian Christian Theology: Evangelical Perspectives* (Carlisle: Langham Global Library, 2019), 225-29.

[9] "This [Christian witness to people of other faiths] appears to be the most crucial missiological question facing Christians at the end of the twentieth century." See Lalsangkima Pachuau et al., "Theme Two: Christian Mission among Other Faiths", in Daryl Balia and Kirsteen Kim (eds), *Edinburgh 2010-II: Witnessing to Christ Today* (Oxford: Regnum, 2010), 34, https://www.ocms.ac.uk/wp-content/uploads/2021/01/Witnessing-to-Christ-Today-final-WM.pdf.

[10] All Scripture quotations, unless otherwise noted, are from the New International Version.

[11] For illustrations of such approaches, see: Benno van den Toren and Kang-San Tan, *Humble Confidence: A Model for Interfaith Apologetics* (Downers Grove, IL: IVP Academic, 2022); Terry Muck and Frances S. Adeney, *Christianity Encountering World Religions: The Practice of Mission in the Twenty-First Century* (Grand Rapids, MI: Baker, 2009).

applied primarily to the fulfilment of Jewish messianic expectations in the incarnation of Christ, but resources for a secondary application to other non-Christian cultures may be found in certain New Testament evangelistic texts: the concept of *Logos* in the prologue of John's Gospel, the addresses of Paul to Gentile audiences in Acts 14 and 17, and Paul's creation theology in Romans 1 and 2.[12]

Paul's address to the Greeks at Athens (Acts 17:22-31) is a unique New Testament illustration of the fulfilment model applied to the gospel culture engagement outside the Jewish context, which we now consider briefly.

Paul's Areopagus address[13] serves as a sample of Paul's proclamation to cultured pagan audiences, a *praeparatio evangelica*. He avoids any direct reference to the Old Testament and uses several concepts clearly of pagan origin.[14]

1. The inscription on *the altar to the "unknown god"* – This was one of several such altars at Athens and an integral aspect of the religious consciousness of the Athenians.[15] It served as a point of contact, a text Paul used to launch his speech. Although the ignorance rather than the worship is underlined, Paul clearly was making known to them this "unknown god" who they worshipped in ignorance.[16]

2. Paul employs *two consecutive quotations from Greek poets* to illustrate his argument: "in him we live and move and have our being" traces back to the sixth century B.C. poet, Epimenides the Cretan, and "for we are indeed his offspring" is a citation from a third century B.C. poet, Aratus of Cilicia.[17] Not only are quotations from non-biblical religious texts extremely rare in the New Testament, but this combination represents a unique occurrence.[18]

---

[12] Richard N. Longenecker, *The Christology of Early Jewish Christianity* (Grand Rapids, MI: Baker, 1970), 65-66, 79-81; Leon Morris, *The Gospel According to John* (Grand Rapids, MI: Eerdmans,1995), 102-108; F.F. Bruce, *The Acts of the Apostles* (Grand Rapids, MI: Eerdmans, 1990), 379-80, 354-56, 381-85; J.D.G. Dunn, *Romans 1-8*, Word Biblical Commentary 38A (Dallas, TX: Word Books, 1988), 57-58, 71, 105.

[13] The literature on this speech is vast; for a fairly detailed bibliography of the more important works on the subject, see Bruce, *Acts of the Apostles*, 379-80.

[14] Paul Hacker, *Theological Foundations for Evangelization* (St. Augustin: Steyler Verlag, 1980), 28-30; for historical and cultural background of Acts 17, see Colin J. Hemer, *The Book of Acts in the Setting of Hellenistic History* (Tubigen: Mohr, 1989).

[15] Ample evidence exists in ancient Greek literature attesting to the existence of such altars in Athens and the surrounding region, Bruce, *Acts*, 380-81.

[16] F.F. Bruce, *Commentary on the Book of the Acts* (Grand Rapids, MI: Eerdmans, 1987), 356; cf. Lucien Legrand, "The Missionary Significance of the Areopagus Speech", in G. Gispert-Sauch (ed), *God's Word Among Men* (Delhi: Vidyajyoti, 1973), 67-69.

[17] Hemer, *Book of Acts*, 116-118; Bruce, *Acts of the Apostles*, 384-85.

[18] Lucien Legrand, "The Unknown God of Athens: Acts 17 and the Religion of the Gentiles", *The Indian Journal of Theology* 30(3-4) (1981), 158, n.1.

3. Paul also alludes to *Stoic philosophy* in the expression, "men should seek God, in the hope that they might feel after him". In accepting the merit of the truth inherent in the Stoic conviction that God is "not far from each one of us", however, Paul does not thereby approve the pantheistic framework of Stoicism within which this truth was embedded.

In summary, we see Paul's clear intent to affirm some measure of *continuity* in his acknowledgement of *elements of truth* within the Athenian god-consciousness.[19] The inculturation/contextualisation[20] impulse guides him in his selection and employment of specific concepts familiar to his Gentile audience. In their original context, none of these expresses an exclusively "Christian" truth, but Paul recognises elements of truth within them which he then uses to relate the Christian gospel to their worldview.[21]

On the other hand, Paul's strategy does not make him overlook points of *discontinuity*: in his view, the religion of the Gentiles represents a mixture of truth and aberration.[22] While he affirms the legitimacy of the Athenians' quest for God, he goes on to explicitly indicate his disapproval of their mode of worship (Acts 17:24).[23] Likewise, Paul's acceptance of truth in the allusions to Stoicism does not imply his acceptance of the Stoic pantheistic framework.[24]

Paul's fulfilment strategy identifies elements of truth on the basis of Christological criteria, frees them from their original context, and reorients them towards his message of the good news in Christ. He then goes on to share specific new and transcendent elements of the gospel message.

Based on their reading of the New Testament, the early fathers also adopted the fulfilment approach in their apologetic engagement with the culture and religion of the Greek world.[25] Various expressions of this approach later came into prominence in the crucial period of modern missionary engagement with the religions of the East in the nineteenth and twentieth centuries. We observe these emerging simultaneously in various majority world non-Christian contexts across the globe as well. A detailed discussion of the fulfilment view is obviously beyond the scope of this treatment;[26] nevertheless, we need to highlight four key aspects that relate to this article's thesis.

---

[19] Hemer, *Book of Acts*, 118.
[20] The terms *inculturation* and *contextualisation* are used interchangeably in their broadest sense to denote the means by which the Christian faith takes on indigenous expression in any given culture.
[21] Hacker, *Theological Foundations*, 29-30.
[22] Legrand, "Unknown God," 166; cf. Hacker, *Theological Foundations*, 30.
[23] J.R.W. Stott, *The Message of Acts* (Leicester: InterVarsity Press, 1990), 278-79.
[24] Hacker, *Theological Foundations*, 29.
[25] Chrys Saldanha, *Divine Pedagogy: A Patristic View of Non-Christian Religions* (Rome: Las, 1984), 158-86; Hacker, *Theological Foundations*, 35-50.
[26] For a more detailed description and evaluation of this approach with a focus on its expression in the experience of Hindu converts in nineteenth and twentieth century

1. ***Inculturation/Contextualisation Impulse*** – The fulfilment approach is the solution that consistently emerges in response to the contextualisation strategies in the gospel-culture encounter. This impulse assumes and works on the premise/principle of the *cultural translatability* of the gospel, essential to any mission engagement with non-Christian cultures.
2. ***Continuity-Discontinuity*** – The fulfilment approach is dialectical in that it recognises *continuity* within *discontinuity* in seeking to bridge the gap with people of other faiths. Accordingly, it employs Christological criteria to identify points of contact in the truth, goodness, and beauty but also judges aspects of falsehood and evil at variance with Christian faith.
3. ***Bridges, Not Walls*** – The fulfilment approach uses points of contact as bridges to present Christ as the fulfilment of the deep-seated hopes and aspirations of people of other faiths (or no faith).
4. ***Christocentricity*** – The fulfilment approach is unapologetically Christocentric. It sees other religions as having some value in preparing pre-believers for the gospel, but only as expressing human anticipations of something fuller only found in Christ.

We now turn to this crucial question: how does dependence on the Holy Spirit's empowerment enable Pentecostals to fulfil their prophetic calling to be "the Voice of Truth" and to share the gospel with neighbours of other faiths respectfully and sensitively?

Spirit-Empowered Engagement with World Religions

Pentecostals have been at the forefront of global mission and consequently at the frontiers of engagement with non-Christian religious cultures over the last century. Some of the strange religious beliefs and cultic practices Pentecostal missionaries first encountered in the regions beyond led them to believe that the non-Christian world was totally dark and evil, devoid of any truth or goodness. Most early Pentecostals thus followed their fundamentalist theological predecessors in approaching people of other faiths with a confrontational posture. Despite that posture, Pentecostals experienced phenomenal results, with vast numbers of people turning to Christ all across the globe.[27]

In the following analysis, I suggest that, at a deeper level, effectiveness of Pentecostal engagement with the non-Christian world is due to some features of fulfilment that they were led intuitively to use in their approach to neighbours of other faiths. The Holy Spirit's empowerment has always been at the heart of Pentecostal belief and spirituality as its hallmark. This aspect of the Pentecostal

---

India, see Ivan Satyavrata, *God Has Not Left Himself Without Witness* (Oxford: Regnum, 2011).
[27] Philip Jenkins, *The Next Christendom: The Coming of Global Christianity* (New York: Oxford University Press, 2002), 8.

ethos connects naturally with the dominant religious traditions, most of which are steeped in spirituality.

Two Pentecostal theologians who have given the most attention to the development of a Pentecostal theology of religions are Veli-Matti Kärkkäinen and Amos Yong. I restrict my response to these scholars' views on this topic to just a couple of brief observations. While the views of both have provoked much discussion, Yong's pneumatological approach to religions has perhaps triggered more reactions due to his advocating a clearly inclusivist view, most explicitly illustrated in the following quote:

> [R]eligions are neither accidents of history nor encroachments on divine providence but are [...] instruments of the Holy Spirit working out the divine purposes in the world [...] the unevangelised, if saved at all, are saved through the work of Christ by the Spirit (even if mediated through the religious beliefs and practices available to them).[28]

Although Kärkkäinen is clearly sympathetic to Yong's view, his trinitarian approach is more cautious, as seen in assertions like: "[T]he Spirit is everywhere, but the Spirit is also the Spirit of the Son and the Spirit of the Father. Not every spirit hovering above in the skies is the Spirit of whom Christians speak. So, there is also particularity to the Spirit."[29] Both Yong and Kärkkäinen, however, seem to tread a fine line between their deep-seated Pentecostal commitment to the finality of Christ and conceding some measure of salvific legitimacy to the Spirit's work in other faith traditions.[30]

My response to this issue will emerge in the course of this article, but I turn now to consider four features of Pentecostal spirituality key to understanding the deep connection Pentecostals evince with respect to the lived experience of people of other faiths.

A Spirituality That Connects Deeply with the Culture

The Western missionary enterprise in the post-Enlightenment period was clearly tainted by cultural imperialism, by which Western nations assumed the intrinsic superiority of their cultures over all other cultures and viewed their calling to be the Christianisation of colonised territories.[31] The challenge of contextualisation

---

[28] Amos Yong, *The Spirit Poured Out on All Flesh: Pentecostalism and the Possibility of Global Theology* (Grand Rapids, MI: Baker Academic, 2005), 235-36.
[29] Veli-Matti Kärkkäinen, "Theology of Religions: Divine Hospitality and Spiritual Discernment", in Wolfgang Vondey (ed), *The Routledge Handbook of Pentecostal Theology* (London: Routledge, 2020), 449.
[30] For a nuanced evaluation and critique of Yong's and Kärkkäinen's approaches from a conservative Pentecostal perspective, see Robert P. Menzies, "The Nature of Pentecostal Theology: A Response to Kärkkäinen and Yong", *The Journal of Pentecostal Theology* 26(2) (September 2017), 196-213.
[31] David Bosch, *Transforming Mission: Paradigm Shifts in Theology of Mission* (Maryknoll, NY: Orbis, 1997), 374-79.

has thus never been greater than in the post-colonial period, in which Christian mission is seen as a continuation of the Western imperialist project.

Mission scholars Andrew Walls and Lamin Sanneh have made convincing cases for the essential translatability of the Christian faith. Both agree that Christianity is the most local of global faiths, and that no individual culture or language has absolute normative status in Christianity. Rather, diverse cultural forms are upheld in their plural diversity without being absolutised in their unique particularity.[32] Sociologist Paul Freston sees in the Acts 2 narrative a basis for what he describes as "polycentric globalisation" in Pentecostalism, in which God reverses Babel by employing many languages rather than restoring a common language, signifying that Pentecostalism is a universalism that affirms the particular.[33]

The essential autochthonous character of Pentecostalism is plainly asserted in the brilliantly simple subtitle *A Religion Made to Travel* of the influential text, *Globalization of Pentecostalism*. One of the editors, Byron Klaus, makes this telling observation: "Pentecostalism has been the quintessential indigenous religion, adapting readily to a variety of cultures. As a religious movement, it has taken on the likeness of a particular culture of people."[34] This cultural translatability is what makes contextualisation – a key impulse of the fulfilment approach – an organic feature of Pentecostalism and explains its extraordinary success in its encounter with non-Christian cultures.

A Spirituality That Challenges the Powers of Evil

The world of most non-Christian religions is dominated by belief in an invisible supernatural world of spirits and by fear of evil powers of darkness that exercise control over human affairs and the natural world. People perceive these forces to

---

[32] Andrew F. Walls, *The Missionary Movement in Christian History: Studies in the Transmission and Appropriation of Faith* (Maryknoll, NY: Orbis, 1996), 32; Lamin Sanneh, *Translating the Message: The Missionary Impact on Culture* (New York: Orbis, 1989), 117-51.

[33] Paul Freston, "Evangelicalism and Globalisation: General Observations and Some Latin American Dimensions", in Mark Hutchinson and Ogbu Kalu (eds), *A Global Faith: Essays on Evangelicalism and Globalization* (Sydney: Centre for the Study of Australian Christianity, 1998), 72. Support for this observation can also be found in anthropological studies, such as Joel Robbins' description of Pentecostalism as a homogenising cultural force that is at the same time most susceptible to indigenous appropriation and localisation, although his assumption that the homogenising impulse is Western is a moot point. Joel Robbins, "The Globalization of Pentecostal and Charismatic Christianity", *Annual Review of Anthropology* 33 (October 2004), 127-30 [Available at: https://doi.org/10.1146/annurev.anthro.32.061002.093421] [Last accessed: 17th March 2024].

[34] Byron Klaus, "Pentecostalism as a Global Culture: An Introductory Overview", in Murray Dempster, Byron Klaus, and Douglas Petersen (eds), *The Globalization of Pentecostalism: A Religion Made to Travel* (Oxford: Regnum, 1999), 127.

have influence in every area of life: they can cause or prevent conception, engineer sickness or health, ensure peace or turmoil in the family, success or failure in business, and so on. Witch doctors, shamans, and priests who know how to manipulate these forces through rituals and magical rites are the power brokers in these contexts. Although earlier missionary movements largely tended to bypass this "excluded middle"[35] in engaging non-Christian religions, Pentecostals live and move in this world of the supernatural.

When Pentecostals began to engage the non-Christian world, they introduced a new evangelistic approach involving "power encounters"[36] in which gospel proclamation was accompanied by power demonstrations, including miracles of healing, deliverance, glossolalia, and various signs and wonders. These signs and wonders demonstrate that the God revealed in the person and work of Jesus Christ is the ultimate Lord greater than all other all other powers in the universe.[37] Followers of other faiths are attracted to Christ when they see that the salvation that he offers includes liberation from the powers of evil and death.

This Pentecostal approach proves effective because a gospel that promises not only eternal life beyond this life but that tangibly demonstrates signs of Kingdom love and power in the present through miraculous healings and deliverance from the powers of evil resonates deeply with the immediate felt needs and aspirations of people of other faiths.

We see fulfilment principles operating here in the demonic elements identified and negated in the encounter with non-Christian cultures, as well as in the fulfilment of the aspirations of people within those cultures as they experience freedom from fear and control of the powers of evil.

A Spirituality That Meets the Real Needs of the Powerless

The economic impact of globalisation has caused growing numbers of people to slip into extreme poverty due to rising social inequality and uneven distribution

---

[35] Paul Hiebert, "The Flaw of the Excluded Middle", in Ralph D. Winter and Steven C. Hawthorne (eds), *Perspectives on the World Christian Movement: A Reader* (Pasadena, CA: William Carey Library, 1999), 414-21.

[36] The term *power encounter*, first coined by Fuller missiologist, Alan Tippett, is today widely used and accepted in missiology to describe this approach. While this is no longer exclusively a Pentecostal phenomenon, without question it remains a distinctive feature of the Pentecostal approach employed in penetrating non-Christian communities with the gospel; see Charles H. Kraft, "Three Encounters in Christian Witness", in Ralph D. Winter and Steven C. Hawthorne (eds), *Perspectives on the World Christian Movement: A Reader* (Pasadena, CA: William Carey Library, 1999), 408.

[37] Conversions as the result of "power encounters" are "a conscious and rational movement" in the direction of power as well as truth; when two religious movements with partially overlapping criteria make claims to truth and power, people tend to accept the truth claims of the faith which is able to confirm its power claims more convincingly, van den Toren and Tan, *Humble Confidence*, 147.

of wealth.[38] The COVID-19 pandemic has severely exacerbated extreme poverty, causing the number of people in extreme poverty to rise from 70 million to more than 700 million people.[39] The vast majority of those who live in extreme poverty are people with some form of religious affiliation.[40]

Social engagement is today an essential component of the Pentecostal Movement in most regions of the world,[41] and much of its extraordinary success

---

[38] For insight into some painful globalisation realities, see Ruth Valerio, "Globalisation and Economics: A World Gone Bananas", in Richard Tiplady (ed), *One World or Many? The Impact of Globalisation on Mission* (Pasadena, CA: William Carey Library, 2003), 21; Douglas McConnell, "Changing Demographics: The Impact of Migration, HIV/AIDS, and Children at Risk," in Michael Pocock, Gailyn V. Rheenen, and Douglas McConnell (eds), *The Changing Face of World Missions: Engaging Contemporary Issues and Trends* (Grand Rapids, MI: Baker Academic, 2005), 48.

[39] World Bank, "Poverty", *World Bank Website* [Available at: https://www.worldbank.org/en/topic/poverty/overview] [Last accessed: 17th March 2024]. The pandemic has pushed debt in poor countries to record levels, widening the gap between rich and poor nations; price increases at the same time as income collapse have put healthy food out of reach for billions, "Impact of COVID-19 on People's Livelihoods, Their Health and Our Food Systems", Joint Statement by ILO, FAO, IFAD and WHO, *World Health Organization*, 13th October 2020 [Available at: https://www.who.int/news/item/13-10-2020-impact-of-covid-19-on-people's-livelihoods-their-health-and-our-food-systems] [Last accessed: 17th March 2024]; Saskia Osendarp et al., "The COVID-19 Crisis Will Exacerbate Maternal and Child Undernutrition and Child Mortality in Low- and Middle-Income Countries", *Nature Food*, 19th July 2021 [Available at: https://www.nature.com/articles/s43016-021-00319-4] [Last accessed: 17th March 2024].

[40] "In the world's poorest countries – those with average per-capita incomes of $2,000 or lower – the median proportion who say religion is important in their daily lives is 95%. In contrast, the median for the richest countries – those with average per-capita incomes higher than $25,000 – is 47%." Steve Crabtree, "Religiosity Highest in World's Poorest Nations", *Gallup* 31st August 2010 [Available at: https://news.gallup.com/poll/142727/religiosity-highest-world-poorest-nations.aspx] [Last accessed: 17th March 2024].

[41] Donald Miller and Tetsunao Yamamori's four-year field study of growing churches in the developing world engaged in significant social ministries has established this beyond any reasonable doubt. They document a wide range of types of social engagement by Pentecostals, from humanitarian responses to crises such as floods, drought, and earthquakes, to education, economic development, medical work, and community development. Donald Miller and Tetsunao Yamamori, *Global Pentecostalism: The New Face of Christian Social* Engagement (Berkeley, CA: University of California Press, 2007), 42-43, 213. "[E]ngagement in social ministry by Pentecostals has practically exploded in the last few decades", Kent Duncan, "Emerging Engagement: The Growing Social Conscience of Pentecostalism", *Encounter: Journal for Pentecostal Ministry* 7 (Summer 2010), 2 [Available at: https://www.evangel.edu/wp-content/uploads/2023/08/Emerging-Engagement-The-Growing-Social-Conscience-of-Pentecostalism-by-Kent-Duncan.pdf] [Last accessed: 17th March 2024].

is due to the spiritual, social, and economic empowerment experienced by those who have been uplifted from poverty. The Pentecostal witness earns credibility and breaks through barriers of religious tradition while fulfilling the aspirations of the religious poor in two ways.

First, the appeal of the spiritual power factor is liberating to those on the periphery of society, whose experience of poverty leaves them feeling helpless and disempowered and for whom religious faith provides their only hope of survival. Second, even as Pentecostals proclaim a gospel of Christ's saving power and the promise of eternal life beyond this life, Pentecostal social engagement extends God's love and seeks to make a difference to those living on the underbelly of society in the present. As Donald Miller and Tetsunao Yamamori observe: "Instead of seeing the world as a place from which to escape, they [Pentecostals] want to make it better."[42] Pentecostals are thus optimistic about their efforts towards social transformation, viewing them as evidence that the kingdom of God has pressed into the present.

The genius of Pentecostalism has thus been its relevance to the powerless and its ability to transform the lives of the socially and economically marginalised. Pentecostals feed the hungry, pray for God to heal the sick, fight against diseases, uplift the powerless, rescue victims of sex and human trafficking, and do their best to serve the needs of the poorest of the poor. In line with the fulfilment approach, Pentecostals meet people of other faiths at the point of their need and build bridges they can then use to communicate the gospel. The powerless receive a new sense of spiritual empowerment, the gift of salvation, and hope of eternal life in the future.

A Spirituality That Is Firmly Christocentric

The Holy Spirit in the New Testament is closely associated with the life and ministry of Jesus. Jesus promised that the Spirit of truth would guide us into all truth and testify about and bring glory to him (Jn 15:26; 16:13-14). The Holy Spirit is thus pre-eminently the Spirit of Christ, the "floodlight" to Jesus,[43] who comes to indwell and empower the Church as a consequence of the finished work of Christ. The Christian notion of "Spirit" must thus not be confused either with the human spirit or with notions of "spirit" in other religions.

The fact is, the Holy Spirit is not the only spirit at work in the world; other spirits are also active. John writes of the essential criterion to identify the legitimate activity of the Spirit: "This is how you can recognise the Spirit of God: Every spirit that acknowledges that Jesus Christ has come in the flesh is from God, but every spirit that does not acknowledge Jesus is not from God" (1 Jn

---

[42] Miller and Yamamori, *Global Pentecostalism*, 30.
[43] J.I. Packer's expression in *Keep in Step With the Spirit* (Grand Rapids, MI: Baker, 2005), 57.

4:2-3).[44] Kärkkäinen's appeal for a "robustly trinitarian view of the Spirit's work in the world" must thus be taken seriously,[45] apart from which Pentecostals can easily drift into a pneumato-monism and into the embrace of Eastern religions, New Age cults, or relativistic liberal pluralism.

The Christian doctrine of the Trinity is, however, derived from the early Christian experience of and testimony to the deity of Christ as recorded in the New Testament. One must regard any trinitarian formulation not grounded in the historical fact of the Incarnation as theologically inadequate, despite its use of trinitarian vocabulary.[46] A Christocentric starting point is thus the only theologically coherent way of employing a Christian trinitarian framework to evaluate other religions. This procedure does not *a priori* dismiss truth claims in other religious traditions; instead, it provides a credible theological basis for affirming what may be of value within them.

A biblical doctrine of general revelation does not preclude the possibility of truth, goodness, and beauty in the world outside the Church – a world that includes non-Christian cultures and religions. Rather, it allows for a posture of critical openness towards all religions and cultures and permits pursuit of truth, goodness, and beauty wherever it may be found. For instance, Hindu converts winnowing Vedic texts on the basis of Christological criteria find copious references to sacrifice as a means of redemption from sin, in which they see helpful pointers to Christ's atoning death; they then can use these pointers to share the gospel with their neighbours in the Hindu community.[47]

An *a priori* Christocentricity thus provides a clear theological basis for the ongoing inculturation project of the Church and enables believers to express the gospel in contextually relevant forms. It also provides a robust apologetic framework for "the Voice of Truth" to be heard clearly as we proclaim God's love in Christ and his atoning death and resurrection and as we invite people of all faiths to put their trust in him and be restored to right relationship with God. In this respect, Pentecostalism concurs with a crucial commitment of the fulfilment approach.

---

[44] Kärkkäinen quotes two scholars of repute, one Roman Catholic and the other Protestant in underlining this truth: "Jesus Christ is 'the face of the Spirit'; looking at the Spirit is to look at Jesus Christ," Stephen B. Bevans, "God Inside Out: Toward a Missionary Theology of the Holy Spirit", *International Bulletin of Missionary Research* 22(3) (1998), 104; "[T]he Holy Spirit does not lead past, or beyond, or away from Jesus," Lesslie Newbigin, *The Light Has Come: An Exposition of the Fourth Gospel* (Edinburgh: Handsel Press, 1982), 216-17 as quoted in Veli-Matti Kärkkäinen, "The Challenge of Discerning between the Genuine and Counterfeit 'Signs of the Spirit': Toward a Pentecostal Theology of the Discernment of the Spirit(s)", *Journal of the European Pentecostal Theological Association* 39(2) (July 2019), 180 [Available at: https://doi.org/10.1080/18124461.2019.1627510] [Last accessed: 18th March 2024].
[45] Kärkkäinen, "Theology of Religions," 448.
[46] Vinoth Ramachandra, *The Recovery of Mission* (Carlisle: Paternoster, 1996), 93-94.
[47] See, for instance, Satyavrata, *God Has Not Left Himself Without Witness*, 114-70.

Pentecostals in general tend to be passionately Christ-centred in their worship, service, and witness. They regularly pray for the Holy Spirit to work in the hearts of neighbours of other faiths and even to reveal Christ supernaturally to them. They hence have no difficulty accepting that pre-Christian ancestral traditions and religious experiences could be used by God to prepare those outside the Church to eventually respond positively to the good news of Christ.

Conclusion: "The Voice of Truth" in Wonders, Works, and Word

The third millennium might well be the most culturally diverse in history, presenting both formidable challenges and enormous opportunities for the Christian Witness in Asia and across the global. The rise of religious pluralism poses a serious threat to the Church's mission and to the future survival of the Church in Asia. In a world increasingly intolerant of "otherness" and in which tolerance and harmony appear to be the only virtues worth defending, a real danger exists that "the Voice of Truth" could be muted or silenced. Asia, however, has been home to some of the earliest and most resilient Christian communities for two thousand years, and as home to most of the world's unreached religious people groups, it offers the world's greatest evangelistic opportunity in this millennium.

The diverse cultures and religions of Asia make it an exciting living laboratory for followers of Christ to explore new ways to connect the good news of Jesus with the lived experience of religious peoples across the globe. Pentecostals have demonstrated the effectiveness of the fulfilment impulse by engaging cultures critically, seeking points of contact carefully, and building bridges courageously, all while keeping Christ at the centre unapologetically. Such a Spirit-empowered approach integrates wonders, works, and word in a presentation of the gospel that connects deeply with the hopes and aspirations of neighbours of other faiths. The challenge not just to Pentecostals, but to the people of God as a whole, is to listen to the voice of the Holy Spirit as he shows us how we can amplify the voice of God's truth in Christ creatively, enabling us to share the story of Jesus with our neighbours of other faiths with humble confidence and without compromise – but with sensitivity and respect.

Bibliography

Bevans, Stephen B. "God Inside Out: Toward a Missionary Theology of the Holy Spirit", *International Bulletin of Missionary Research* 22(3), (July 1998), 102-105.

Bosch, David. *Transforming Mission: Paradigm Shifts in Theology of Mission*. Maryknoll, NY: Orbis, 1997.

Bruce, F.F. *The Acts of the Apostles*. Grand Rapids, MI: Eerdmans, 1990.

——. *Commentary on the Book of the Acts*. Grand Rapids, MI: Eerdmans, 1987.

Crabtree, Steve. "Religiosity Highest in World's Poorest Nations", *Gallup*. 31st August 2010. [Available at: https://news.gallup.com/poll/142727/religiosity-highest-world-poorest-nations.aspx] [Last accessed: 17th March 2024].

Duncan, Kent. "Emerging Engagement: The Growing Social Conscience of Pentecostalism." *Encounter: Journal for Pentecostal Ministry* 7 (Summer 2010), 1-9. [Available at: https://www.evangel.edu/wp-content/uploads/2023/08/Emerging-Engagement-The-Growing-Social-Conscience-of-Pentecostalism-by-Kent-Duncan.pdf] [Last accessed: 17th March 2024].

Dunn, J.D.G. *Romans 1-8*. Word Biblical Commentary 38A. Dallas: Word Books, 1988.

Freston, Paul. "Evangelicalism and Globalization: General Observations and Some Latin American Dimensions", In Mark Hutchinson and Ogbu Kalu, Eds. *A Global Faith: Essays on Evangelicalism and Globalization*. Sydney: Centre for the Study of Australian Christianity, 1998: 69-88.

Friedman, Thomas L. "Foreign Affairs; The Real War", *The New York Times*. 27th November 2001. [Available at: https://www.nytimes.com/2001/11/27/opinion/foreign-affairs-the-real-war.html] [Last accessed: 18th March 2024].

Hacker, Paul. *Theological Foundations for Evangelization*. St. Augustin: Steyler Verlag, 1980.

Hanciles, Jehu J. "Migration and Mission: Some Implications for the Twenty-First Century Church", *International Bulletin of Missionary Research* 27(4), (October 2003), 146-153. [Available at: https://doi.org/10.1177/239693930302700401] [Last accessed: 18th March 2024].

Hemer, Colin J. *The Book of Acts in the Setting of Hellenistic History*. Tubigen: Mohr, 1989.

Hiebert, Paul. "The Flaw of the Excluded Middle", In Ralph D. Winter and Steven C. Hawthorne, Eds. *Perspectives on the World Christian Movement: A Reader*. Pasadena, CA: William Carey Library, 1999: 412-21.

Joint Statement by ILO, FAO, IFAD and WHO. "Impact of COVID-19 on People's Livelihoods, Their Health and Our Food Systems", *World Health Organization*. 13th October 2020 [Available at: https://www.who.int/news/item/13-10-2020-impact-of-covid-19-on-people's-livelihoods-their-health-and-our-food-systems] [Last accessed: 17th March 2024].

Jenkins, Philip. *The Next Christendom: The Coming of Global Christianity*. New York: Oxford University Press, 2002.

Juergensmeyer, Mark. *Terror in the Mind of God*. Berkeley, CA: University of California Press, 2003.

Kärkkäinen, Veli-Matti. "The Challenge of Discerning between the Genuine and Counterfeit 'Signs of the Spirit': Toward a Pentecostal Theology of the Discernment of the Spirit(s)", *Journal of the European Pentecostal Theological Association* 39(2), (July 2019), 165-83. [Available at:

https://doi.org/10.1080/18124461.2019.1627510] [Last accessed: 18th March 2024].

——. "Theology of Religions: Divine Hospitality and Spiritual Discernment", In Wolfgang Vondey, Ed. *The Routledge Handbook of Pentecostal Theology*. London: Routledge, 2020: 443-53.

Klaus, Byron. "Pentecostalism as a Global Culture: An Introductory Overview", In Murray Dempster, Byron Klaus, and Douglas Petersen, Eds. *The Globalization of Pentecostalism: A Religion Made to Travel*. Oxford: Regnum, 1999: 127-30.

Kraft, Charles H. "Three Encounters in Christian Witness", In Ralph D. Winter and Steven C. Hawthorne, Eds. *Perspectives on the World Christian Movement: A Reader*. Pasadena, CA: William Carey Library, 1999: 445-50.

Legrand, Lucien. "The Missionary Significance of the Areopagus Speech", In G. Gispert-Sauch, Eds. *God's Word among Men*. Delhi: Vidyajyoti, 1973: 59-63.

——. "The Unknown God of Athens: Acts 17 and the Religion of the Gentiles", *The Indian Journal of Theology* 30(3-4), (1981), 158-67.

Longenecker, Richard N. *The Christology of Early Jewish Christianity*. Grand Rapids, MI: Baker, 1970.

McConnell, Douglas. "Changing Demographics: The Impact of Migration, HIV/AIDS, and Children at Risk", In Michael Pocock, Gailyn V. Rheenen, and Douglas McConnell, Eds. *The Changing Face of World Missions: Engaging Contemporary Issues and Trends*. Grand Rapids, MI: Baker Academic, 2005: 45-78.

Menzies, Robert P. "The Nature of Pentecostal Theology: A Response to Kärkkäinen and Yong", *The Journal of Pentecostal Theology* 26(2), (September 2017), 196-213.

Miller, Donald, and Tetsunao Yamamori. *Global Pentecostalism: The New Face of Christian Social Engagement*. Berkeley, CA: University of California Press, 2007.

Morris, Leon. *The Gospel According to John*. Grand Rapids, MI: Eerdmans, 1995.

Muck, Terry, and Frances S. Adeney. *Christianity Encountering World Religions: The Practice of Mission in the Twenty-First Century*. Grand Rapids, MI: Baker, 2009.

Netland, Harold. *Encountering Religious Pluralism*. Downers Grove, IL: InterVarsity Press, 2001.

Newbigin, Lesslie. *The Light Has Come: An Exposition of the Fourth Gospel*. Edinburgh: Handsel Press, 1982.

Osendarp, Saskia, Jonathan Kweku Akuoku, Robert E. Black, Derek Headey, Marie Ruel, Nick Scott, Meera Shekar, Neff Walker, Augustin Flory, Lawrence Haddad, David Laborde, Angela Stegmuller, Milan Thomas, and Rebecca Heidkamp. "The COVID-19 Crisis Will Exacerbate Maternal and Child Undernutrition and Child Mortality in Low- and Middle-Income Countries", *Nature Food*. 19th July 2021 [Available at:

https://www.nature.com/articles/s43016-021-00319-4] [Last accessed: 17th March 2024].

Pachuau, Lalsangkima, Niki Papageorgiou, Eunice Irwin, John Azumah, Michael Biehl, Knud Jørgensen, Gwen Bryde, Michael Jagessar. "Theme Two: Christian Mission among Other Faiths", In Daryl Balia and Kirsteen Kim, Eds. *Edinburgh 2010-II: Witnessing to Christ Today*. Oxford: Regnum, 2010: 34-60. [Available at: https://www.ocms.ac.uk/wp-content/uploads/2021/01/Witnessing-to-Christ-Today-final-WM.pdf] [Last accessed: 18th March 2024].

Packer, J.I. *Keep in Step With the Spirit*. Grand Rapids, MI: Baker, 2005.

Phan, Peter. "Cultural Diversity and Religious Pluralism: The Church's Mission in Asia", *Asia Pacific Mission Studies* 1(2), (2019), 89-108. [Available at: https://core.ac.uk/reader/286139530] [Last accessed: 18th March 2024].

Ramachandra, Vinoth. *The Recovery of Mission*. Carlisle: Paternoster, 1996.

Robbins, Joel. "The Globalization of Pentecostal and Charismatic Christianity", *Annual Review of Anthropology* 33 (October 2004), 127-30. [Available at: https://doi.org/10.1146/annurev.anthro.32.061002.093421] [Last accessed; 17th March 2024].

Saldanha, Chrys. *Divine Pedagogy: A Patristic View of Non-Christian Religions*. Rome: Las, 1984.

Sanneh, Lamin. *Translating the Message: The Missionary Impact on Culture*. New York: Orbis, 1989.

Satyavrata, Ivan. *God Has Not Left Himself Without Witness*. Oxford: Regnum, 2011.

——. "Jesus and Other Faiths", In Timoteo D. Gener and Stephen T. Pardue, Eds. *Asian Christian Theology: Evangelical Perspectives*. Carlisle: Langham Global Library, 2019: 225-29.

Stott, J.R.W. *The Message of Acts*. Leicester: InterVarsity Press, 1990.

Valerio, Ruth. "Globalisation and Economics: A World Gone Bananas", In Richard Tiplady, Ed. *One World or Many? The Impact of Globalisation on Mission*. Pasadena, CA: William Carey Library, 2003: 13-32.

Van den Toren, Benno, and Kang-San Tan. *Humble Confidence: A Model for Interfaith Apologetics*. Downers Grove, IL: IVP Academic, 2022.

Van Rheenen, Gailyn. "Religionquake: From World Religions to Multiple Spiritualities", In Michael Pocock, Gailyn Van Rheenen, and Douglas McConnell, Eds. *The Changing Face of World Missions: Engaging Contemporary Issues and Trends*. Grand Rapids, MI: Baker Academic, 2005: 79-89.

Walls, Andrew F. *The Missionary Movement in Christian History: Studies in the Transmission and Appropriation of Faith*. New York: Orbis, 1996.

World Bank, "Poverty", *World Bank Website*. [Available at: https://www.worldbank.org/en/topic/poverty/overview] [Last accessed: 17th March 2024].

Yong, Amos. *The Spirit Poured Out on All Flesh: Pentecostalism and the Possibility of Global Theology.* Grand Rapids, MI: Baker Academic, 2005.

7. The Role of Prayer and its Centrality in Sustaining the Effectiveness of Global Christianity

Young-Hoon Lee

Abbreviations

ALS	Asia Leaders Summit
CGI	Church Growth International
DMZ	Demilitarised Zone
OCCK	Overseas Chinese Conference in Korea
PWC	Pentecostal World Conference
YFGC	Yoido Full Gospel Church

Introduction

As the COVID-19 pandemic has passed, global Christianity's attention has focused on the restoration of faith by the affection of local churches, as well as the continuous growth of the kingdom of God through the gospel. The threat of infectious diseases limited worship and fellowship. Not only has the worship style changed, but Christians grew accustomed to the changed environment. As a result, diverse opinions exist on whether the church should return to life as it was before COVID-19 or experience the dynamic work of the Holy Spirit once again.

Amidst varying opinions, a new revival has drawn our attention. Since February 2023, thousands of people from all over the world have come to Asbury University in Kentucky to participate in the wave of revival that began with the voluntary participation of students and spread to nearby schools. At the core of that revival was prayer.

In the history of global Christianity, there has been a recovery of prayer in relation to revival. The recovery and revival of individual and communal spirituality after the COVID-19 pandemic depends on prayer. YFGC (Yoido Full Gospel Church) has been carrying out an active prayer movement based on the 26th World Pentecostal Conference with a DMZ prayer meeting held in October 2022. Additionally, a special prayer meeting for the 120th anniversary of the Wonsan Revival[1] was held in May 2023. Throughout the history of global Christianity, such revivals of individual and communal spirituality as those that

---

[1] This refers to the revival brought about by the Methodist missionary Robert Alexander Hardie in 1903.

have occurred since the COVID-19 pandemic have always depended on prayer. This chapter illuminates the pivotal role of prayer in sustaining the effectiveness of global Christianity. It first explores the biblical and historical meanings of prayer and then observes a relationship between the Pentecostal Movement and prayer. This study then goes on to demonstrate how prayer has played a role in the revival of the world's largest church, YFGC, and then suggests a direction for how the prayer movement should move forward to facilitate future Christian revival.

Biblical and Historical Study Concerning Prayer

While the range of historical study regarding prayer is vast, this study focuses on the centuries from the biblical age to the revival of modern churches, addressing how prayer influences revival and growth in the global Church beyond region and time.

Prayer in the Old Testament

The Old Testament depicts prayer as an act of communication between God and His people.[2] Prayer toward God is both a direct and indirect response to His work and Word. Prayer consists of poetic form performed by representatives of prayer, such as the king or a prophet in the congregation. The purpose of prayer includes praise, sadness, petition, intercession, and thanksgiving. Its weight as seen in the Old Testament is absolute, and it was the privilege and duty of the Jews as a chosen people.

In the Old Testament, those who prayed truly cried out to the living God who created the world and revealed himself in the history of Israel, not idols. Even in situations where the Israelites felt that God was not with them, they still had hope that God would respond to their earnest prayers and resolve their sorrow and pain. Furthermore, the Israelites prayed not only as individuals but also with the community. They prayed together whenever they were concerned about suffering.

In 1 Kings 8, Solomon prays to dedicate the temple. His prayer consists of five specific petitions: (1) When a person would pray to God with an oath to make an offense against his neighbour right, Solomon asked God to hear from heaven to condemn the guilty and vindicate the righteous (1 Kgs. 8:31-32); (2) When the people of Israel were defeated by an enemy because they had sinned against God, Solomon asked God to forgive and recover them from their sin (vv. 33-34); (3) When the heavens were shut up with no rain and the Israelites would repent of their sin, Solomon asked God to send rain on the land (vv. 35-36); (4) When Israel suffered from disaster or disease due to their sin, Solomon asked

---

[2] Dong-Hyun Park, "An Introductory Consideration Concerning the Prayer of the Old Testament", *JangShinNonDan* 10(11) (December 1994), 304-306. See Sang-Gi Kim, "The Prayer of the Old Testament," *SungSeoMaDang* 114(6) (Summer 2015), 10-12.

God, who knows the hearts of all men, to forgive them (vv. 37-40); and (5) When the foreigner who did not belong to the people of God comes from a distant land and prays in His name, Solomon asked God to hear from heaven and do whatever the foreigner asks of him (vv. 41-43). Among these five specific prayers, the final one shows that the prayer connected strongly with the Israelite community is extended to Gentiles. It is connected to a proclamation of the future: "For my house will be called a house of prayer for all nations" was declared by the prophet Isaiah (Is. 57:7). This implies that prayer in the temple plays an essential role in preaching the gospel in the world.[3]

Prayer in the New Testament

In the New Testament, Jesus demonstrates a life of prayer (Mk 1:34; 14:22, 26, 32-39). At that time, prayer originated from Jewish tradition. However, compared to those of the Jews, Christ's prayers have two significant characteristics. First, Jesus called God the Father (Abba) (14:36). This shows not only the intimate relationship between God and Jesus but also an attitude of obedience toward God. Through Christ's prayers, the disciples and the first church members could participate in that relationship (Lk. 11:2; Rom. 8:15; Gal. 4:6). Second, Jesus prayed to God as a petition (Mk 7:7; Lk. 11:9-13). Jesus was convinced that earnest prayer for God's Kingdom and the individual was surely answered in God's reign.

Understanding regarding Jesus's prayer life came down to his disciples, both directly and indirectly. For the disciples, prayer was considered the individual and communal petition in one's intimate relationship with God (Mt. 6:5-13; 7:7-11; 18:19-20). Furthermore, Christ's prayer became a way to participate in God's ministry. For the disciples, prayer in the name of Jesus and as the high priest was always the prayer God answered (Jn 15:7; 17:1). Prayer is the only way to establish firm faith (Lk. 18:7; 21:36) and a way to lead God's people in the power of the Holy Spirit and guidance (1 Cor. 1:7; Phil. 1:9-11).[4]

Prayer Throughout Church History

The prayer of the Early Church was connected to Jewish practices. The prayer that pious Jews prayed three times a day (Dan. 6:11), the Lord's Prayer (*Didache* 8:2), became a good example that influenced many. These prayers were quickly documented and used in worship after the second century.[5] Clement of

---

[3] Simon J. De Vries, *1 Kings*, Word Biblical Commentary 12, trans. Byung-Ha Kim (Seoul: Solomon, 2006), 326.

[4] Gordon D. Fee, "Toward a Pauline Theology of Glossolalia", in Wonsuk Ma and Robert P. Menzies (eds), *Pentecostalism in Context: Essays in Honor of William W. Menzies* (Sheffield: Sheffield Academic Press, 1997), 24-37.

[5] Justin Martyr, *First Apology*, LXV-LXVII, Christian Classics Ethereal Library [Available at: https://ccel.org/ccel/justin_martyr/first_apology/anf01.viii.ii.lxvii.html] [Last accessed: 18th March 2024].

Alexandria defined prayer as a conversation with God.[6] He stressed extemporaneous prayer, including sincerity of heart regardless of script. For Clement, this understanding concerning prayer came from the teaching of Origen. Clement also felt that the best prayer was meditative prayer in union with Christ; this type of prayer continued to influence the spirituality of the Eastern monastic tradition.[7]

In medieval churches, prayers were written by text with psalms, praise, Bible verses, or writings by Early Church authors. This form of prayer prevailed until the twelfth century.[8] In the meantime, many scholars were affiliated with mendicant orders such as Dominican orders and Franciscan orders, and their form of prayer was influenced by these orders and by scholasticism. They devised a new form of prayer combined with sermons and prayers to use during mendicancy. Unrestricted by the text, they prayed sincerely and appealed to God for those who asked for prayers.

In the late Middle Ages, the biggest problem with prayer was that it was formal – offered through priests or by way of community prayer – memorised without understanding regarding the certain passage of prayer. Martin Luther argued that individual prayer was a fundamental form of prayer.[9] He saw prayer as a response to God's Word by thanksgiving and petition and felt it should come freely from the depths of one's heart, not restricted or forced. Luther thought prayer should be filled with passion toward God with all earnestness of heart.[10] Huldrych Zwingli and John Calvin agreed with Luther that individuals' prayers before God should come before the prayer through a priest or the prayer memorised by a community.[11]

For Reformers, the understanding of prayer continued to the age of piety. Prayer was no longer bound by the Lord's Prayer and the Psalms. In particular, Pietists such as Philipp Jakob Spener considered prayer as a petition offered to

---

[6] Clement of Alexandria, *The Stromata, or Miscellanies*, Book VII, Early Christian Writings [Available at: https://www.earlychristianwritings.com/text/clement-stromata-book7.html] [Last accessed: 18th March 2024].

[7] Evagrius of Pontus, "Chapters on Prayer", in *Evagrius of Pontus: The Greek Ascetic Corpus*, trans. Robert E. Sinkewicz (New York: Oxford University Press, 2003), 197, Oxford Academic [Available at: https://doi.org/10.1093/acprof:oso/9780199259939.003.0008] [Last accessed: 18th March 2024].

[8] Young-Won Kim, "Dialectic of Doctrinal Discourse and Prayer Discourse on Proslogion of Anselm of Canterbury", *Seoul National University Religion and Culture* 29 (December 2015), 126-38.

[9] Byoung-Sik Jeoung, "Luther and Prayer", *Korean Church Historical Journal* 9(56) (2020), 246.

[10] Martin Luther, *Martin Luthers Werke: Kritische Gesamtausgabe,* vol. 17 (Weimar: Hermann Böhlau, 1883-1999), 49.18-20.

[11] Jeoung, "Luther and Prayer", 246.

God and as a sincere conversation.[12] In the same age, critical voices arose that considered personal prayer a superstitious delusion due to the influence of the Enlightenment. However, the spiritualisation of prayer centred on theologians like Immanuel Kant, from faith in their hearts.[13]

Due to the influence of Pietism, the revival movement that has taken place in England and the US since the nineteenth century has caused a recovery of the prayer movement. John Wesley, founder of the Methodist movement, pursued piety through regular prayer. After Wesley experienced the presence of the Holy Spirit, the revival movement (1739-1791) he led was also a prayer movement. At the same time, Jonathan Edwards, who led the American Great Awakening Movement, was influenced by the prayer movement. The revival movement that George Whitefield, Charles G. Finney, and Dwight L. Moody led was influenced by the prayer movement, too. Various prayer meetings created by them became increasingly popular. From 1857 to 1859, these meetings saw more than a million people converted. The Wednesday prayer meeting also became common among evangelical Protestants around 1900. In the early twentieth century, the prayer movement evolved into the Pentecostal Movement.

The Holy Spirit Movement and Prayer

From the Early Church to medieval and modern churches, prayer has had a significant influence on the Pentecostal Movement. In the early twentieth century, the Pentecostal Movement, which began in Topeka, Kansas, spread rapidly around the world. This movement influenced a remarkable revival as never seen before. This study explores a brief history of the Pentecostal Movement in the global Church – specifically in the Korean Church – analysing the role of prayer.

Prayer in the History of the Pentecostal Movement

1. Classical Pentecostal Movement[14]

The Pentecostal Movement began in Topeka, Kansas in 1901 when Bethel Bible School dean, Charles Parham, and students prayed earnestly to receive the baptism of the Holy Spirit, received it, and spoke in tongues. In 1905, Parham

---

[12] Philipp Jakob Spener, *Einfältige Erklärung der Christilichen Lehr, Nach der Ordnung des kleinen Catechismi des theuren Manns Gottes Luther* (Nachdruck: Spener, Schriften, Bd. II. 1, Hildesheim u. a. 1982), 798.

[13] Kant thought that prayer should not be through written text but through Spirit. That is why the Spirit of prayer leads the people of God to come before God. In this respect, Kant agreed that when congregations pray, they cry out in congregational worship. The important thing is the spirit of prayer. See Immanuel Kant, *Lecture on Ethics* (London: Methuen, 1930), 102.

[14] Klaude Kendrick, *The Promise Fulfilled: A History of the Modern Pentecostal Movement* (Springfield, MO: Gospel, 1961), 19.

started Faith Bible School in Houston, Texas. He taught that all Christians must receive the baptism with the Holy Spirit. He stressed that a sign of the baptism with the Holy Spirit is the gift of tongues. William J. Seymour, one of Parham's students, travelled to Los Angeles where he started a prayer meeting at the home of a church member, Edward Lee, where his preaching sparked the audience. The revival first broke out through the baptism with the Holy Spirit and tongues on Monday 9th April 1906 at 214 Bonnie Brae Street then moved to 312 Azusa Street on Friday 14th April 1906.[15] The crowd participated in prayer meetings, received the baptism with the Holy Spirit and tongues, and experienced healing. The three-year-long Azusa Street revival had been changed by the Azusa Street Mission. As a result, the Pentecostal Movement spread throughout the world. In 1914, the Assemblies of God, which has the greatest influence among Pentecostal denominations, was organised.

2. Modern Pentecostal Movement/Charismatic Movement[16]

The Classical Pentecostal Movement extended to include healing ministry by William Branham, Oral Roberts, and others from 1940 to 1960. Many people joined tent crusades, experiencing Holy Spirit manifestations including tongues and healing. In 1960, the revival extended to other denominations like the Episcopal and Catholic churches. As a result, the age of the new Pentecostal Movement began. Many denominations believed that the charismatic doctrine written in the Bible could appear as the baptism with the Holy Spirit, tongues, and healing when one prayed to God in faith. After this, the Pentecostal Movement extended throughout the world in a third wave in 1990.

Prayer in Korea the Holy Spirit Movement

The 1903 Wonsan Revival Movement and 1907 Great Pyongyang Revival Movement both resulted from the prayer movement and extended throughout Korea as a flame of revival. Afterward, the Korean Revival Movement was led by Sun-Soo Gil, Ik-Doo Kim, and Yong-Do Lee.

The Wonsan Revival Movement and the Great Pyongyang Revival Movement

In August 1903, M.C. White, a Methodist missionary, visited Wonsan from China. Missionaries with White assembled for a weeklong conference, including a prayer meeting. They had asked a medical missionary from Canada, Dr Robert Hardie, to serve as the main speaker. During the conference, Hardie experienced

---

[15] Gary B. McGee, "William J. Seymour and the Azusa Street Revival", *AG News*, 4th April 1999 [Available at: https://news.ag.org/en/article-repository/news/1999/04/william-j-seymour-and-the-azusa-street-revival] [Last accessed: 18th March 2024].

[16] Vinson Synan, *The Holiness-Pentecostal Tradition: Charismatic Movements in the Twentieth Century*, trans. Young-Hoon Lee and Myung-Soo Park (Seoul: Seoul Logos, 2000), 271-309.

the power of the Holy Spirit while leading the conference.[17] Hardie realised that his ministry had failed because he had a strong racial prejudice and was overly proud and so confessed his sin before the missionaries and the Korean people. This sincere confession greatly influenced the people who had joined the conference. Korean believers, greatly impacted by Hardie's honest confession, mutually confessed their hatred toward Hardie.[18] After that, the local church, located in a rural area nearby Wonsan, began to hold Bible conferences and prayer meetings.

After Wonsan, revival continued in a meeting at Pyongyang JangDaeHyun church in January 1907. After a sabbatical year, Dr Hardie had led a joint prayer meeting of Presbyterian and Methodist missionaries for a week in August 1906. One of the participants – Graham Lee, a missionary who eventually led the revival at Pyongyang JangDaeHyun church in January 1907 – had experienced the fullness of the Holy Spirit in the joint meeting.[19] After Lee led and preached a conference at JangDaeHyun church, he began praying to God and crying out.[20] While the church was filled with the sound of crying and prayer, participants experienced the grace of the Holy Spirit and began to confess their sin. William Blair, a North Presbyterian missionary, recorded this situation: "Like the day of Pentecost, people were gathered in one place and praying with one heart. Then, suddenly a sound like the blowing of a violent wind from the heaven came and filled the whole house where they were sitting."[21] People who were gathered in the joint meeting had experienced the fullness of the Holy Spirit. Through Wonsan and the Pyoungyang, the Korean Church grew explosively, establishing Christian foundations for their Korean traditions like early morning prayer, Tong Sung prayer, Bible study, offering life, and evangelism.[22] The experience of the baptism of the Holy Spirit enabled a steady prayer life, and obedience to the Word of God had positive results not only for quantitative revival but also for qualitative spiritual growth.[23]

---

[17] Young-Kyu Park, *The Great Pyoungyang Revival Movement* (Seoul: The Word of Life, 2000), 45.
[18] Korean Christianity History Compilation Committee, *The History of Korean Christianity 1* (Seoul: Christian Literature Press, 2011), 221-22.
[19] Korean Christianity History Compilation Committee, *The History of Korean Christianity 1*, 226-27.
[20] William Blair and Bruce Hunt, *The Korean Pentecost and the Suffering Which Followed* (Carlisle: Banner of Truth, 1977), 73-74.
[21] Blair and Hunt, *Korean Pentecost*, 71.
[22] Kyung-Bae Min, *The Korean Christian History: Forming Korean Ethnic Church* (Seoul: Yonsei University Publish Center, 1995), 286-94.
[23] Joseph B. Hingeley (ed), *Journal of the Twenty-Fifth Delegated General Conference of the Methodist Episcopal Church, Held in Baltimore, Maryland, May 6 - June 1, 1908* (New York: Eaton & Mains, 1908), 861-62 [Available at: https://www.familysearch.org/library/books/records/item/37401-journal-of-the-twenty-fifth-delegated-general-conference-of-the-methodist-episcopal-church-held-in-

People Who Led the Holy Spirit Movement

The Korean Revival Movement was led by Sun-Joo Gil, Ik-Doo Kim, and Yong-Do Lee. Gil led various seminars, Bible conferences, and revival meetings across the country, emphasising the fundamental faith based on the absolute authority of the Bible, inspired by the Holy Spirit. In particular, he emphasised the importance of reading the Bible and praying – practicing early morning prayer, fasting prayer, and all-night prayer. Among these, the early morning prayer was established as a religious heritage of Korean Christianity and considered pivotal in the its rapid growth and development.[24]

Ik-Doo Kim, with Gil, also led a revival in the Korean Church. While Kim was leading a revival meeting in October 1919, he experienced the grace of God through a sermon called, "These signs will accompany those who believe" (Mk 16:17). Kim began to pray in his heart to seek God and then received a gift of divine healing. Many people sick and in pain for a long time attended the revival meetings Kim led and received healing. In October 1920, the Seoul Presbyterian Joint Revival Meeting gathered 10,000 people daily. It was the first time that many people had gathered since the joint revival meeting was held in Korea.[25] Kim even held revival meetings on Jeju Island at the southern end of Korea and the Gando area at its northern end. Some estimated that the revival venue held 776, but the number of people healed came to more than 10,000.[26]

Yong-Do Lee, active in the 1930s, started a revival movement by emphasising Christ-centred faith and prayer. After graduating from seminary in 1928, he began his ministry at Dongcheon Church in Gangwon-do but found it difficult to minister because he had no experience with the Holy Spirit. He realised that he had a problem and went to Kumgang Mountain to pray and fast for ten days. After experiencing the power of the Holy Spirit, he was transformed into a completely different person. When he preached, people repented of their sins and experienced the power of the Holy Spirit. He travelled the country until he died on 2nd October 1933, at the age of thirty-three; Lee had done his best to evangelise through the repentance movement and Holy Spirit Movement.[27] This movement challenged the hopeless Korean Church, which was filled with nihilism and defeat in the wake of Japanese rule.

---

baltimore-maryland-may-6-june-1-1908?offset=466383] [Last accessed: 18th March 2024].

[24] Bong-Rin Ro, "The Korean Church: Growing or Declining?" *Evangelical Review of Theology* 19(4) (1995), 15-29.

[25] Young-Kyu Park, *Pastor Ik-Doo Kim Biography* (Seoul: Life Book, 1991), 120.

[26] Young-Kyu Park, *Korean Church Revival Pastor Ik-Doo Kim, Biography* (Seoul: Christian Newspaper, 1968), 104-105; Kyung-Bae Min, *History of the Korean Christian Faith Movement under Japanese Colonial Rule* (Seoul: The Christian Literature of Korea, 1991), 303.

[27] Min, *The Korean Christian History: Forming Korean Ethnic Church*, 390.

Yoido Full Gospel Church and Prayer

The revival movement in Wonsan and Pyoungyang and the Holy Spirit Movement in Korea led by Sun-Joo Gil, Ik-Doo Kim, and Yong-Do Lee, all influenced Pastor David (Paul) Yonggi Cho and the church which he founded. In the early days – between the Holy Spirit Movement in Korea and the Holy Spirit Movement of Pastor Cho – it was common to include earnest prayer (early morning prayer, fasting prayer, all-night prayer, and divine-healing prayer) to overcome desperate situations. However, unlike the Holy Spirit Movement in Korea, Pastor Cho was greatly influenced by the Classical Pentecostal Movement while studying theology at Full Gospel Bible College established in 1953 by US Assemblies of God missionaries. In this respect, YFGC could freely carry out a powerful Holy Spirit Movement unlike other denominations.

Ministry Life of Pastor Yonggi Cho and Prayer

Age of Daejo-dong in Seoul, Korea

On 18th May 1958, Pastor Cho started a tent church in the suburban area of Daejo-dong, Eunpyounggu-Seoul. In the early days of his ministry, Pastor Cho preached a gospel emphasising that people repent of their sin, encouraging them to nurture their desire for heaven. However, those living in poverty and with disease did not accept his sermon.[28] Pastor Cho thus re-examined his ministry and theology with doubts about how the gospel, which did not satisfy people's current needs, could bring hope for salvation in the future.[29]

"God is Good" and Prayer

The philosophy and faith of Pastor Cho is "God is Good," which is based on the Bible. Not only does God save our souls, but He also solves problems like poverty, diseases, and death. Cho's "God is Good" philosophy and faith greatly influenced the prayer movement. He believed that God blesses us because He is good. If sinful people know how to give good gifts to their children, how much more will our heavenly Father give good gifts to those who ask Him (Mt. 7:9-11)? Therefore, Pastor Cho argued that it is reasonable that the children of God pray and seek God's blessings. Pastor Cho delivered good faith in God; prayer based on faith gave comfort and hope to those suffering from poverty and disease. People began to flock to the tent church to hear his powerful message.

---

[28] Young-Hoon Lee, *The Critical Biography of Rev. Youngsan Yonggi Cho: The Pastor of Hope* (Seoul: Seoul Logos, 2008), 358.
[29] International Theological Institute, *The Pastor of Yoido* (Seoul: Seoul Logos, 2008), 277.

Divine Healing and Casting the Devil out through a Powerful Prayer Movement

Pastor Cho read a sermon book by Pastor Oral Roberts and developed the meaning of 3 John 1:2 as a theology of three blessings[30] and began to preach a message that people may enjoy good health, and that all may go well with them, even as their soul is getting along well. At that time, many people were suffering from diseases due to poor surroundings and economic difficulties. Pastor Cho realised the necessity of divine healing for them; so, for over five hours day after day, he prayed at the church or on mountains seeking the power of the Holy Spirit. As a result, participants experienced miracles like healing and casting out the devil. One miracle occurred as a disabled boy[31] and a woman with hearing and language disabilities from birth were both healed through the earnest prayer of Pastor Cho.[32] After the son of a shaman who was addicted to gambling and alcohol changed, the shaman repented and accepted the gospel.[33] Countless miracles occurred at the tent church in Daejo-dong. People who heard the rumours flocked, and the church grew to 500 in the first three years since the tent church was founded.

Age of Seodaemun in Seoul, Korea

In 1961, Pastor Cho moved the church to a central area of Seoul, Seodaemun. He started Full Gospel Revival Center and carried out systematic prayer campaigns. He held conferences and prayer meetings for the revival movement every day at what then came to be called Full Gospel Central Church.[34] All-night prayer meeting was held on Fridays, and a dynamic work of the Holy Spirit was filled with the church. As a result, the working of the Holy Spirit was connected to the revival and growth of the church.

Prayer in Personal Relationship with the Holy Spirit

The church that moved to Seodaemun was attended by 3,000 people in three years. However, after that, the growth of the church stopped. Pastor Cho went before God with the problem of the church's stalled growth in an early morning prayer time. He listened to the Spirit's voice: "Please, consider the Holy Spirit as a personality who wants to have a deep and intimate relationship with you, not merely a god who just brings out the best."[35] Since that encounter, Pastor Cho strove to establish a deep personal relationship with the Holy Spirit. The

---

[30] Yonggi Cho, *The Story of Five Gospels for the Modern People* (Seoul: Seoul Logos, 1988), 19.
[31] Yoido Full Gospel Church 50 Years History Compilation Committee, *Yoido Full Gospel Church 50 Years History* (Seoul: Yoido Full Gospel Church, 2008), 83.
[32] International Theological Institute, *Pastor of Yoido*, 295-99.
[33] Yoido Full Gospel Church 30 Years History Compilation Committee, *Yoido Full Gospel Church 30 Years History* (Seoul: Yoido Full Gospel Church, 1989), 25.
[34] The name changed from Full Gospel Revival Center to Full Gospel Central Church.
[35] International Theological Institute, *Pastor of Yoido*, 396-7.

expression, "Holy Spirit, I acknowledge you. I welcome you. And I embrace you," a trademark of Full Gospel Central Church, came from this realisation of a personal relationship with the Holy Spirit. The result of the campaign that Pastor Cho pursued was surprising: from 3,000 people in 1968, the church grew to 8,000 people.

Tong Sung Prayer

Worship and prayer were special at Full Gospel Central Church. Unlike other denominations which pursued piety and a calm atmosphere, the worship and prayer that Pastor Cho led were quite noisy, and other denominations denounced him. However, Pastor Cho believed that a church filled with the Holy Spirit should be noisy. He considered the noise in worship and prayer as "the Holy disorder."[36] One of the reasons why worship in Full Gospel Church was noisy was the practice of Tong Sung prayer. Pastor Cho argued that when people of God expect and desire God, he answers their prayers accordingly. Tong Sung prayer is the most representative form to express the earnestness of one's heart, as Pastor Cho wrote:

> I have heard many times as follows, "Is God deaf? Why do you scream when you pray?" Whenever we gathered, when we did Tong Sung prayer, people said, "Are you Crazy? Is God deaf? Even if you pray quietly, God will listen to your voice. Why do you pray crying out? However, it means that to cry out to God is to find Him earnestly.[37]

Prayer to Call His Name Three Times, "Lord, Lord, Lord"

While praying Tong Sung, the unique prayer style of YFGC includes a prayer to calling God's name three times: "Lord, Lord, Lord." We call it Chu-Yoi Sam Chang. Most members of YFGC were poor people. Whenever they cried out to God and prayed about their difficult realities, they would put all of their pain into their cries to demonstrate their distress. Chu-Yoi Sam Chang was a sigh about their life of hardship. The origin of Chu-Yoi Sam Chang remains unclear. Tae-Young So guessed that "the prayer of people who couldn't go to the hospital due to economic difficulties, and struggled with labour in the industrial era of the 1970s and 1980s was developed as a format of Chu-Yoi Sam Chang to cry out by calling the name of Jesus three time."[38] He also provides an answer, uploaded to the webpage of Pastor Yonggi Cho:

> Full Gospel [d]enomination[s] started to pray crying out Chu-Yoi Sam Chang naturally when church members started to pray. It seems that when pastor led prayer

---

[36] Yonggi Cho, "Calvary Cross", Yoido Full Gospel Church Sunday Sermon, 8th December 2013.
[37] Yonggi Cho, "The Faith to Bring Change and [a] Miracle", Yoido Full Gospel Church Sunday Sermon, 12th July 2009.
[38] Tae-Young So, "Chu-Yoi Sam Chang That Includes Spirituality of Lamentation and Education in the Format of Prayer", *YoungSan Theological Journal* 40 (2017), 115.

in the conference, he urged participants to start praying with Chu-Yoi Sam Chang. A long [time] ago, I remember when Pastor Ja-Sil Choi was praying, she prayed with Chu-Yoi Sam Chang. However, I do not believe that Chu-Yoi Sam Chang prayer only belongs to the tradition of the Full Gospel denomination. I think that Chu-Yoi Sam Chang prayer is an autonomy movement that originated from the saints in the Korean church who had no place to hope but God in their lives of absolute despair.[39]

It cannot be asserted that the origin of Chu-Yoi Sam Chang originated from YFGC. However, clearly YFGC played a pivotal role in actively utilising it and proving its efficiency to spread it domestically and abroad.

Yoido Era

In 1973, YFGC, continuing to experience revival, surprised the world again by moving to Yoido. More than 10,000 new members were registered every year and, by October 1979, the number exceeded 100,000. By the end of November 1981, the number exceeded 200,000. YFGC has grown into the world's largest church, recording 400,000 in 1984; 500,000 in 1985; 700,000 in 1992; and up to 750,000 in 2008.[40] With the revival of the church, Pastor Cho's prayer movement and his influence began to spread beyond Korea to around the world.[41]

The Parish System and Prayer Community

In light of the rapid growth, on 1st January 1971, YFGC began practising the parish system for effective management of church members and improvement of teaching. After moving the church to Yoido, many people began to gather from all over Seoul so that YFGC had to provide a hub for people living in each area to gather. Pastor Cho first oversaw a small parish but then extended to a large parish. Those in this large parish worshipped, gathering people who lived in the same city and county every week. Once a month, YFGC practised a mission to preach the gospel by promoting faith through the Holy Spirit Movement conference. Furthermore, the parish system had the effect of incorporating people into a small prayer community. It became a prayer community where saints belonging to one parish shared prayer requests and prayed for one another.

Domestic and International Prayer Conferences

With the church's explosive growth, Pastor Cho's influence also spread, both domestically and internationally. He toured various places throughout the country, including Seoul, Busan, Daegu, Daejeon, GwangJu, and Ulan, holding

---

[39] So, "Chu-Yoi Sam Chang", 116.
[40] Yoido Full Gospel Church 60 Years History Compilation Committee, *Yoido Full Gospel Church 60 Years History* (Seoul: Seoul Logos, 2018), 72.
[41] Young-Hoon Lee, "The Holy Spirit Movement in Korea: Its Historical and Doctrinal Development" (Ph.D. diss., Temple University, 1996), 190-91.

large rallies and conferences on an unprecedented scale.[42] In addition, YFGC's overseas mission, started in the US in 1964, expanded even further since the Yoido era, with conferences led by Pastor Cho in Europe, Asia, South America, and Africa, attracting millions of people. More than 1.2 million people attended the African Great conference in 1993, two million people attended the Indian Great conference in 1994, and 1.5 million people attended the Brazilian great conference in 1997. Numerous new believers came to faith at each conference, and many signs and wonders occurred.

Church Growth International (CGI) Foundation and Period of Prayer

Pastor Cho established CGI in November 1976 based on a mission for revival of the world church and expansion of the kingdom of God. CGI is an international organisation composed of senior pastors in megachurches in each country leading the growth of churches around the world. Since starting with the first international church growth seminar, the church growth conferences and seminars have been held every year in major cities around the world, including Seoul. CGI has practical significance as a place where all member churches gather to pray.

Conference for Asian Christians Who Visit Korea

Pastor Cho held an Asian Christian conference every year to lay the foundation for Asian missions. In August 1986, the first Asian conference was hosted by the Full Gospel Business Association at the Full Gospel International Fasting Prayer Center, and more than 450 people from Japan, Taiwan, Singapore, and Malaysia attended.[43] The 32nd Conference for Asian Christians was held in 2023 with a special seminar, the Great Holy Spirit Conference. Those who participated in the Asian Christian Conference experienced a remarkable revival by applying to their church what they had learned.

Ministry and Prayer of Pastor Young-Hoon Lee

Through Pastor Cho's prayer-centred, dynamic Holy Spirit Movement, Yoido Full Gospel Church grew into the world's largest church and came to stand as a centre of revival. For Pastor Cho, prayer was always the top priority.[44]

This chapter emphasises the continuance of the efficiency of the prayer movement for the future to continue the growth of the church by inheriting and developing Pastor Cho's philosophy as the church's spiritual teacher. This inherited philosophy also stands as my philosophy of prayer.

---

[42] Yoido Full Gospel Church 30 Years History Compilation Committee, *Yoido Full Gospel Church 30 Years History*, 149-50.
[43] "The 5th Conference for Japan Saints Who Visit in Korea", *The Full Gospel Family Newspaper*, 24th August 1986.
[44] "For Christians, the first priority is prayer, the second priority is prayer and the third is prayer, too." David Cho, *How to Pray* (Seoul: Seoul Logos, 1997), 103.

Significance of Prayer

Reality of Faith

Prayer is based on faith. No one walks with God without faith in the Trinity. As Luther states, "Prayer is a space of faith."[45] Sincere prayer is based on faith and answered by faith. In sum, prayer provides a time to stand on faith, and faith based on absolute positive thanksgiving is revealed to those who pray standing firmly only by that faith. True prayer involves believing and seeking God's faithfulness and goodness, not only prosperity and blessings.

A Path to Attain the Fullness of Jesus Christ

The purpose for which the church exists is the grace of salvation, which is both momentary and constant. In Christ, even though children of God are justified by faith, they are still on the journey of faith to attain the fullness of Jesus Christ (Eph. 4:13).[46] Christ's meekness and humility are characteristics formed in the believer by prayer to follow the will of God (Mt. 11:29). God's children need to live in prayer to dwell in the fullness of Christ. Prayer includes the life of seeking God's will every moment rather than one's own will. Therefore, prayer leads God's children to the character of Christ.

Contribution of the Fulfilment of the Holy Spirit

The fulfilment of the Holy Spirit, which includes the power to overcome temptation by the world, is the grace of God for those who are saved. Such fullness comes from God's sovereignty, not the will and effort of human beings. The power of the Holy Spirit comes only from prayer and, as Luther mentions, "Prayer is chained to the Word of God."[47] Not only does prayer help people hear the voice of God, but it also relies on God.[48] Just as Jesus, who defeated the devil with the Word of God in the wilderness, returned to Galilee (Lk. 4:14), the people of God need to hold the Word of God through prayer in order to meet God. When the people of God dwell in His Word, they experience the fullness of the Holy Spirit.

It is time for us to go before God in sincere prayer. Jesus wants people to pray to seek first His Kingdom and His righteousness. Christ also prayed that God's will would be done on earth as in heaven. So, how can the people of God concentrate on prayer?

---

[45] Martin Luther, *Martin Luthers Werke: Kritische Gesamtausgabe*, vol. 4 (Weimar: Hermann Böhlau, 1883-1999), 624.8-32.
[46] Sinclair B. Ferguson, *What Is Sanctification?* (Seoul: Revival & Reformation, 2010), 54.
[47] Luther, *D. Martin Luthers Werke: Kritische Gesamtausgabe*, vol. 5 (Weimar: Hermann Böhlau, 1883-1999), 420.
[48] Jin-Ho Kwan, *Pray with Luther* (Seoul: DaeJangGan, 2019), 67.

Chapter 7

Strengthening the Prayer Movement in the Church

Special Early Morning Prayer Meeting

In May 2008, I succeeded to serve as the second senior pastor in YFGC's history. As the year of 2009 came, I held a "twelve basketfuls" special early morning prayer for twelve days to continue the revival of the church. Even though the weather was severe in the winter, traffic was heavy around the church from 3 a.m. The main sanctuary had already filled with people an hour before beginning the prayer meeting.[49] At the request of the congregation, we held this special early morning prayer meeting once again in the second half of that year. The people who joined the meeting experienced the remarkable power of the Holy Spirit – being filled with the Holy Spirit, speaking in tongues, being cured of diseases, and seeing solutions to life problems.[50] Since then, YFGC has held the twelve baskets full special early morning prayer meeting every new year.

In addition, since 2019, we have held special early morning prayer every month for deacons, elders, exhorters, and volunteers toward the goal of making 10,000 disciples. Through this special early morning prayer, YFGC has established a vision to make one million disciples in the Korean Church.

We expect these prayer initiatives to provide momentum for the revival and growth of the Korean Church. Both early morning prayers are provided on YouTube streaming for branch churches, local churches, and mission areas abroad.

The Word of God and Prayer

YFGC stresses a return to the truth of the Bible and to the Church's first faith. In Acts, the first Church was thoroughly based on the Bible and prayer. Since May 2013, I have taught an expository sermon for balancing the Word of God and prayer by renaming "Wednesday 1st Service" to "Wednesday Bible Expository".[51] After Acts, I preached on John, Genesis, Galatians, Exodus, 1st and 2nd Samuel, Mark, and Romans. YFGC provides a Bible study for group cell meetings in the parish ministry by providing a summary of sermons. For example, the education department provides Bible school programmes, Bible college programmes, Bible graduate programmes, and a theological academy. The spiritual training department provides intercessory prayer school programmes, mothers' and fathers' dream programmes, and a Pentecostal love training school programme.

---

[49] "A Passion for Twelve Basketfuls Early Morning Prayer", *The Full Gospel Family Newspaper*, 11th January 2009.
[50] "The 2nd Twelve Basketfuls Early Morning Prayer Was Successful", *The Full Gospel Family Newspaper*, 14th June 2009.
[51] "Wednesday Service and Friday All Night Service Renamed", *The Full Gospel Family Newspaper*, 28th April 2013.

Prayer Movement for Union and the Revival of Churches

Ecumenical Movement

The Holy Spirit Movement is related to the ecumenical movement. The Holy Spirit causes all churches to be united (Eph. 4:3). I have striven for a long time to unite churches around the world according to the leading of the Holy Spirit – through a prayer meeting for the sixtieth anniversary diplomatic relationship between Korea and Israel, a breakfast prayer meeting for Korean and American Christian Leaders, the great awakening revival prayer conference, and the day of prayer in Korea.[52]

Pentecostal World Conference (PWC) and DMZ Prayer Meeting

In October 2022, the 26th Pentecostal World Conference, a festival of the Pentecostal Movement, was held at YFGC. With the title, "Pentecostal Revival for the Next Generation," more than 1,500 pastors from forty-five countries around the world, in addition to 3,500 Korean leaders, participated in the PWC. All services were broadcast live on the church's website and YouTube, and 689 million members of the global Pentecostal Church experienced this scene of grace. A DMZ prayer meeting was held the last day of PWC, in which participants prayed for North Korea.[53] Participants declared that a remarkable revival will take place around the word, mainly in South Korea, for ten years from now.[54] Pentecostal leaders believe that the PWC has become a motivation for revival in the future following the pandemic.

120th Anniversary of the Wonsan Revival

In May 2023, YFGC held prayer meetings, academic seminars, and praise celebrations titled, "Crying Out Hope in the World of Despair" to memorialise the sixtieth anniversary of its foundation. Among them, at the first celebration, the 120th anniversary of the Wonsan revival meeting, I preached a sermon titled, "If the Holy Spirit Comes to You (Acts 1:4-5, 8)," emphasising that it is God's will to revive churches as he did the first Church. I stressed that the church should strive to pray to receive the fullness of the Holy Spirit for this revival. The prayer meeting was broadcast live on YouTube. It was a big festival for the Korean Church, joined by Wesleyan association churches with four million members.[55]

---

[52] "Efforts of Yoido Full Gospel Church for Alliance and Consensus", *The Full Gospel Family Newspaper*, 21st May 2023.

[53] "The 26th World Pentecostal Conference Was Held Successfully", *The Full Gospel Family Newspaper*, 16th October 2022.

[54] "Pastor Young-Hoon Lee, Let's Join the New Wave of Revival with the Fullness of the Holy Spirit", *The Full Gospel Family Newspaper*, 23rd October 2022.

[55] "The 65th Anniversary of Challenge and Glorification, the History of Revival Being with the Holy Spirit", *The Full Gospel Family Newspaper*, 21st May 2023. There are six denominations participating in Wesleyan Association: Methodist, Assemblies of God, Holiness (Kisung), Holiness (Yesung), Nazareth, and Salvation Army.

Kenya's Great Hope Conference 2023

In July 2023, Kenya's Great Hope Conference 2023 was held in Nairobi, under the title, "One Sprit, One Hope (Eph. 4:4)." As the main lecturer of this conference, I stressed that "Christians cannot do anything without prayer. The Bible emphasises the importance of prayer to all Christians."[56] I stressed to participants the need to grow in prayer. In a seminar for more than 3,000 pastors who do ministry in twelve other East African countries including Kenya, I stressed prayer as the most important factor in church growth.

Sharing Experience with World Churches

YFGC and I personally have already experienced the presence of the Holy Spirit and revival through Tong Sung prayer, like Chu-Yoi Sam Chang (Korean Prayer). I have tried to spread Korean prayer culture by sharing my ministry experience with church leaders around the world such as in the following contexts.

Asia Leaders Summit (ALS) Foundation

ALS is a group of pastors who have achieved explosive church growth through the Holy Spirit Movement in Asian countries like Japan, Malaysia, Indonesia, Hong Kong, Singapore, and Korea. I realised the necessity of sharing a vision and uniting with others to preach the gospel in Asia and so established the ALS. At the first meeting in Hong Kong in 2013, I insisted, "Pastoring is God's work, not the work of human beings. We must pray for God's wisdom and help."[57] Since then, I have been sharing my pastoral experiences with pastors who campaign for the Holy Spirit Movement by holding an ALS conference once a year.

Church Growth International (CGI) and Inauguration of the Second President

CGI was established by Pastor Cho in 1976. At a board meeting in October 2022 in Korea, I was unanimously appointed as second president.[58] Members of CGI visit Korea every two years to attend conferences and seminars, at which pastors who lead church growth around the world lecture and explain the situation of global churches. They also share about revival, mission plans, and direction for the future. I also expect to grow churches around the world by sharing my own experiences with CGI members.

---

[56] "Pastor Young-Hoon Lee, Led the History of the Holy Spirit in Africa", *The Full Gospel Family Newspaper*, 16th July 2023.

[57] "Asia Leaders, Who Led the Holy Spirit Movement, Gathered in Hong Kong", *The Full Gospel Family Newspaper*, 3rd March 2013.

[58] "Pastor Young-Hoon Lee, Was Unanimously Appointed as CGI's New President", *The Full Gospel Family Newspaper*, 9th October 2022.

Overseas Chinese Conference in Korea (OCCK)

The thirty-second OCCK, a Holy Spirit festival of Chinese saints around the world, was held in July 2023 at YFGC and O-San-Ri Choi Ja-Sil Memorial Fasting Prayer Center under the theme, "New Era, New Oil, New Bowl." More than 1,200 pastors and saints in nine countries including Taiwan, Hong Kong, Singapore, Malaysia, and Indonesia, participated in the conference.[59] As president of the OCCK Chinese affairs headquarters in Korea, I shared with these Chinese pastors and other saints who visited in Korea secrets of church growth as well as some of my pastoral experiences.

Establishment of a Cooperative System for Evangelisation in Asia and the World

Churches in China, Japan, and Taiwan asked me for support to learn about YFGC's unprecedented growth through the Holy Spirit Movement. As a result, I have been sharing my pastoral ministry by establishing a bilateral mission network between YFGC and these churches through meetings such as the Korea-China Christian Exchange Conference, Korea-Japan Mission Cooperation Conference, and the Korea-Taiwan Pastors Meeting.[60]

Prayer for Christian Revival in the Future

As seen above, the revival of YFGC has come and continues to come as a result of prayer. However, one cannot assert that prayer is the main feature of YFGC. Prayer must be a feature of the true revival that takes place in all churches in all ages. That is how revival begins, lasts, and expands: through prayer. In the future, Christian revival will be the same as praying churches grow and revive. Prayer provides the momentum of the Holy Spirit Movement impacting the joint prayer movement of churches around the world.

Momentum of the Holy Spirit for New Revival

The Holy Spirit is the founder and manager of the Church. The subject of church growth is also the Holy Spirit. The largest Christian communities around the world are Pentecostal churches that pursue the Holy Spirit Movement. The fastest-growing, largest churches of the Majority World are also churches leading the Holy Spirit Movement. Throughout history, the move of the Holy Spirit, the driving force of church growth, has always been prompted by prayer.

The Bible testifies that the Holy Spirit is the Spirit of prayer. In the Old Testament, it was written, "I will pour out on the house of David and the inhabitants of Jerusalem a spirit of grace and supplication" (Zech. 12:10). In the

---

[59] "The 32nd OCCK Conference for Evangelization in China Has Been Successful", *The Full Gospel Family Newspaper*, 6th August 2023.

[60] "2019 Korea-China Christianity Exchange Conference Was Held", *The Full Gospel Family Newspaper*, 17th November 2019.

New Testament, Paul writes, "Pray in the Spirit on all occasions with all kinds of prayers and requests" (Eph. 6:18). The birth and revival of the first Church resulted from a move of the Holy Spirit and prayer (Acts 1:14; 2:41; 4:4; 11:21). Therefore, if the church desires Christian revival and growth, she must constantly pray for the power of the Holy Spirit.

One cannot assert that the work of the Holy Spirit Movement will be same in the future as in the past and present. So Kang-Seok argues that in the future, the Spirit's work will change – customised by the Spirit considering the individual specificity of the moment, not based on a uniform working of the Spirit through large conferences.[61] Although the Holy Spirit Movement in the future may change, the church should remember that earnest and passionate prayer serves as a spiritual channel to remember the history of the Spirit's work among us.

The Social Role of the Church

The twenty-first century calls for the Church to play a social role by paying attention to the underprivileged in society and practising lovingness and generosity. Such a role means that God's work extends beyond the church to the world he created. In walking out its social role, the Church participates in the history of God, acknowledging his providence under the order of creation. The first step to participating in that history involves prayer. The Holy Spirit leads and guides the church to embody the kingdom of God and to preach the gospel. Therefore, as Terry Teyke states, "Prayer is a means of connecting Christ with the world."[62] Prayer is a means of communication between God and people.

Intercessory prayer shows the character of prayer for neighbours. Ruth A. Meyers, Dean of Berkeley School of Theology in California and professor of worship, points out that the Church lives in a state of poverty concerning prayer.[63] Although the Church emphasises praise music, preaching, and worship, it does not stress intercessory prayer in order to participate in the history of redemption and restoration by the Holy Spirit. Intercessory prayer integrates worship and life with prayer for each other and the world.[64] The Church has a mission to pray for problems facing the current society such as low birth rates, war, famine, and the destruction of ecosystems. I had a vision from God when praying for the direction of YFGC's ministry in the future – to love neighbours through sharing and practising kindness. According to the vision, YFGC has

---

[61] Kang-Seok So, "The Influence of the Holy Spirit Movement in Korean Church", Korea Christianity the Holy Spirit 100th Anniversary 5th Theology Symposium, 5th November 2009: 55.
[62] Terry Teykl, *Pray and Grow: Evangelism Prayer* (Nashville, TN: Discipleship Resources, 1988), 43; Gi-Sung An, "Research on Overcoming Church Growth Slump by Focusing on Prayer", *Reformed Church Growth* 6 (2011), 173.
[63] Ruth A. Meyers, *Missional Worship, Worshipful Mission: Gathering as God's People, Going Out in God's Name* (Grand Rapids, MI: Eerdmans, 2014), 109.
[64] John Calvin, *The Institutes of the Christian Religion*, edited by John T. McNeill (Philadelphia, PA: Westminster Press, 1960), 3.20.19.

been taking care of the underprivileged in society, practising relief activities, and carrying out an intercessory prayer movement.

Christian Revival and the Globalisation of Prayer
(Prayer Movement United with the Churches in the World)

One of the characteristics of modern society is globalisation. This phenomenon occurs in the life of humankind not only in politics and economics but also in culture, religion, and thought. Although globalisation seems to be partially slowing down due to COVID-19 and the war in Ukraine, it is a growing trend that will not fully stop.[65]

Christianity is not excluded from the trend of globalisation. When churches around the world become one body in Christ through prayer, Christianity will exert greater power beyond any religious, racial, language, and national barriers. A flame of revival from Los Angeles' Azusa Street to Korea in the past has continued in the present. Also, the Holy Spirit Movement of YFGC spread to the United States, Europe, Asia, South America, and Africa. Revival does not stay in one place; in the future, its flame will spread to the world. Therefore, churches around the world will have to pray with one mind for the future by forming close relationships both in person and virtually. World churches will have to walk the path of revival by praying together.

Conclusion

This study explored the meaning and role of prayer from the Old Testament period to now. Prayer marks the existence of faith. Recovery of prayer means the revival of the church. Revival and the growth of Christianity come from a life of faith, believing and experiencing God. The more the Church grows in faith, the more powerful its prayer life will be. In faith, prayer makes God's people strong and makes the way for him to give them a dream to walk out through his power.

Pastor Cho stated that the Church must stand on the dream and the faith that the Holy Spirit gives. There is no way to do this but through prayer. As John Maxwell, who served at Skyline Church in California, explained in his lecture, "Six Keys to Church Growth," one key for church growth is prayer. Waymon Rodgers, who established the Evangel Christian Life Center in Louisville, KY, also stressed that out of many ministries prayer is one of the best.

There is no way to form a relationship with God or to experience revival without prayer. Although the environment of ministry changes according to globalisation, truly the Church is bound to experience revival through prayer. When the people of God pray to him with faith, the church can experience

---

[65] Yong-Hun Jo, "A Study on the Moral Characteristics of Global Ethics for the Era of Global Disasters from the Perspective of Christian Ethics", *The Korean Journal of Christian Social Ethics* 56 (2023), 407.

revival. Therefore, the church may move forward with anticipation while dreaming of revival through prayer.

Bibliography

"The 2nd Twelve Basketfuls Early Morning Prayer Was Successful", *The Full Gospel Family Newspaper*, 14th June 2009.

"The 5th Conference for Japan Saints Who Visit in Korea", *The Full Gospel Family Newspaper*, 24th August 1986.

"The 26th World Pentecostal Conference Was Held Successfully", *The Full Gospel Family Newspaper*, 16th October 2022.

"The 32nd OCCK Conference for Evangelization in China Has Been Successful", *The Full Gospel Family Newspaper,* 6th August 2023.

"The 65th Anniversary of Challenge and Glorification, the History of Revival Being with the Holy Spirit", *The Full Gospel Family Newspaper*, 21st May 2023.

"2019 Korea-China Christianity Exchange Conference Was Held", *The Full Gospel Family Newspaper,* 17th November 2019.

An, Gi-Sung. "Research on Overcoming Church Growth Slump by Focusing on Prayer", *Reformed Church Growth* 6 (2011), 151-96.

"Asia Leaders, Who Led the Holy Spirit Movement, Gathered in Hong Kong", *The Full Gospel Family Newspaper*, 3rd March 2013.

Blair, William, and Bruce Hunt. *The Korean Pentecost and the Suffering Which Followed.* Carlisle: Banner of Truth, 1977.

Calvin, John. *The Institutes of the Christian Religion.* Edited by John T. McNeill. Philadelphia, PA: Westminster Press, 1960.

Cho, David. *How to Pray.* Seoul: Seoul Logos, 1997.

Cho, Yonggi. "Calvary Cross", Yoido Full Gospel Church Sunday Sermon. 8th December 2013.

——. "The Faith to Bring Change and [a] Miracle", Yoido Full Gospel Church Sunday Sermon. 12th July 2009.

——. *The Story of Five Gospels for the Modern People.* Seoul: Seoul Logos, 1988.

Clement of Alexandria. *The Stromata, or Miscellanies.* Book VII. Early Christian Writings. [Available at: https://www.earlychristianwritings.com/text/clement-stromata-book7.html] [Last accessed: 18th March 2024].

De Vries, Simon J. *1 Kings.* Word Biblical Commentary 12. Translated by Byung-Ha Kim. Seoul: Solomon, 2006.

"Efforts of Yoido Full Gospel Church for Alliance and Consensus". *The Full Gospel Family Newspaper*, 21st May 2023.

Evagrius of Pontus. "Chapters on Prayer", In *Evagrius of Pontus: The Greek Ascetic Corpus.* Translated by Robert E. Sinkewicz, New York: Oxford University Press, 2003: 183-209. [Available at:

https://doi.org/10.1093/acprof:oso/9780199259939.003.0008] [Last accessed: 18th March 2024].
Fee, Gordon D. "Toward a Pauline Theology of Glossolalia", In Wonsuk Ma and Robert P. Menzies, Eds. *Pentecostalism in Context: Essays in Honor of William W. Menzies*. Sheffield: Sheffield Academic Press, 1997: 24-37.
Ferguson, Sinclair B. *What Is Sanctification?* Seoul: Revival & Reformation, 2010.
Hingeley, Joseph B., Ed. *Journal of the Twenty-Fifth Delegated General Conference of the Methodist Episcopal Church, Held in Baltimore, Maryland, May 6 - June 1, 1908*. New York: Eaton & Mains, 1908. [Available at: https://www.familysearch.org/library/books/records/item/37401-journal-of-the-twenty-fifth-delegated-general-conference-of-the-methodist-episcopal-church-held-in-baltimore-maryland-may-6-june-1-1908?offset=466383] [Last accessed 18th March 2024].
International Theological Institute. *The Pastor of Yoido*. Seoul: Seoul Logos, 2008.
Jeoung, Byoung-Sik. "Luther and Prayer", *Korean Church Historical Journal* 9(56), (2020), 227-56.
Jo, Yong-Hun. "A Study on the Moral Characteristics of Global Ethics for the Era of Global Disasters from the Perspective of Christian Ethics", *The Korean Journal of Christian Social Ethics* 56 (2023), 407.
Kant, Immanuel. *Lecture on Ethics*. London: Methuen, 1930.
Kendrick, Klaude. *The Promise Fulfilled: A History of the Modern Pentecostal Movement*. Springfield, MO: Gospel, 1961.
Kim, Sang-Gi. "The Prayer of the Old Testament", *SungSeoMaDang* 114(6), (Summer 2015), 9-26.
Kim, Young-Won. "Dialectic of Doctrinal Discourse and Prayer Discourse on Proslogion of Anselm of Canterbury", *Seoul National University Religion and Culture* 29 (December 2015), 126-38.
Korean Christianity History Compilation Committee. *The History of Korean Christianity 1*. Seoul: Christian Literature Press, 2011.
Kwan, Jin-Ho. *Pray with Luther*. Seoul: DaeJangGan, 2019.
Lee, Young-Hoon. *The Critical Biography of Rev. Youngsan Yonggi Cho: The Pastor of Hope*. Seoul: Seoul Logos, 2008.
——. "The Holy Spirit Movement in Korea: Its Historical and Doctrinal Development", Ph.D. diss., Temple University, 1996.
Luther, Martin. D. *Martin Luther Werke: Kritische Gesamtausgabe*, Vol. 4. Weimar: Hermann Böhlau, 1883-1999.
——. *Martin Luther Werke: Kritische Gesamtausgabe*, Vol. 5. Weimar: Hermann Böhlau, 1883-1999.
——. *Martin Luther Werke: Kritische Gesamtausgabe*, Vol. 17. Weimar: Hermann Böhlau, 1883-1999.
Martyr, Justin. *First Apology*. LXV-LXVII, Christian Classics Ethereal Library. [Available at:

https://ccel.org/ccel/justin_martyr/first_apology/anf01.viii.ii.lxvii.html] [Last accessed: 18th March 2024].

McGee, Gary B. "William J. Seymour and the Azusa Street Revival", *AG News*, 4th April 1999. [Available at: https://news.ag.org/en/article-repository/news/1999/04/william-j-seymour-and-the-azusa-street-revival] [Last accessed: 18th March 2024].

Meyers, Ruth A. *Missional Worship, Worshipful Mission: Gathering as God's People, Going Out in God's Name*. Grand Rapids, MI: Eerdmans, 2014.

Min, Kyung-Bae. *History of the Korean Christian Faith Movement under Japanese Colonial Rule*. Seoul: The Christian Literature of Korea, 1991.

——. *The Korean Christian History: Forming Korean Ethnic Church*. Seoul: Yonsei University, 1995.

Park, Dong-Hyun. "An Introductory Consideration Concerning the Prayer of the Old Testament", *JangShinNonDan* 10(11 (December 1994), 301-40.

Park, Young-Kyu. *The Great Pyoungyang Revival Movement*. Seoul: The Word of Life, 2000.

——. *Korean Church Revival Pastor Ik-Doo Kim, Biography*. Seoul: Christian Newspaper, 1968.

——. *Pastor Ik-Doo Kim Biography*. Seoul: Life Book, 1991.

"A Passion for Twelve Basketfuls Early Morning Prayer", *The Full Gospel Family Newspaper*, 11th January 2009.

"Pastor Young-Hoon Lee, Led the History of the Holy Spirit in Africa", *The Full Gospel Family Newspaper*, 16th July 2023.

"Pastor Young-Hoon Lee, Let's Join the New Wave of Revival with the Fullness of the Holy Spirit", *The Full Gospel Family Newspaper*, 23rd October 2022.

"Pastor Young-Hoon Lee, Was Unanimously Appointed as CGI's New President", *The Full Gospel Family Newspaper*, 9th October 2022.

Ro, Bong-Rin. "The Korean Church: Growing or Declining?" *Evangelical Review of Theology* 19(4), (1995), 15-29.

So, Kang-Seok. "The Influence of the Holy Spirit Movement in Korean Church", *Korea Christianity the Holy Spirit 100th Anniversary 5th Theology Symposium*, 5th November 2009.

So, Tae-Young. "Chu-Yoi Sam Chang That Includes Spirituality of Lamentation and Education in the Format of Prayer", *YoungSan Theological Journal* 40 (2017), 107-40.

Spener, Philipp Jakob. *Einfältige Erklärung der Christlichen Lehr, Nach der Ordnung des kleinen Catechismi des theuren Manns Gottes Lutheri*. Nachdruck: Spener, Schriften, Bd. II. 1, Hildesheim u. a. 1982.

Synan, Vinson. *The Holiness-Pentecostal Tradition: Charismatic Movements in the Twentieth Century*. Translated by Young-Hoon Lee and Myung-Soo Park. Seoul: Seoul Logos, 2000.

Teykl, Terry. *Pray and Grow: Evangelism Prayer*. Nashville, TN: Discipleship Resources, 1988.

"Wednesday Service and Friday All Night Service Renamed", *The Full Gospel Family Newspaper*, 28th April 2013.

Yoido Full Gospel Church 30 Years History Compilation Committee. *Yoido Full Gospel Church 30 Years History*. Seoul: Yoido Full Gospel Church, 1989.

Yoido Full Gospel Church 50 Years History Compilation Committee. *Yoido Full Gospel Church 50 Years History*. Seoul: Yoido Full Gospel Church, 2008.

Yoido Full Gospel Church 60 Years History Compilation Committee. *Yoido Full Gospel Church 60 Years History*. Seoul: Seoul Logos, 2018.

Affirmations for Global Pentecostals

Kong Hee, Byron D. Klaus, and Douglas Petersen

There was a season in the recent past when Pentecostal writers would focus on describing what were termed Pentecostal "distinctives." As a relatively new Christian tradition, it would be reasonable that these writers would make efforts to describe those biblical and theological themes that might best describe Pentecostal life. This section intentionally uses a different lens. Affirmations focus on themes or issues that Pentecostals join other Christian traditions in considering important. Using the concept of affirmation highlights collective agreement without minimising the unique perspective Pentecostals may have on these issues. Each of the themes in this section highlights an affirmation on a theme about which Christians, regardless of faith tradition, must think seriously.

Juan Angel Castro pastors in San Salvador, El Salvador. His ministry takes place in the context of extreme violence, which has been the reality in this region since the mid-twentieth century. Violence is experienced by members of most Christian traditions; Pentecostals are not unique in experiencing violence. However, Castro's narrative provides a theological reflection and narrative of ministry action indicative of Pentecostal life in El Salvador.

Castro provides a short historical account of the violence of the later part of the twentieth century. With a revolving door of one dictator after another, El Salvador erupted into a violent civil war with insurgent guerilla forces and government soldiers fighting one another with the result being thousands of civilian deaths and mass migration to *El Norte*, i.e., the USA. Children displaced by the war and who escaped to the US were provided security and community in the gangs of large urban areas like Los Angeles.

Castro notes that the peace accord of 1992 in El Salvador was an official agreement that might have yielded a lull in the fighting but little else. Violence wrought by young people who returned to El Salvador and brought with them their new *mara* (gang) identity soon filled that vacuum. Gangs like MS-13 and Mara 18 brought new levels of violence even more lethal than the previous civil strife.

Castro's theological reflection and narratives of ministry in the face of violence provide a window into Pentecostal life. His accounts of the conversion of guerrilla leaders and imprisoned gang members seem akin to the spectacular conversion of a violent Saul of Tarsus whose life was radically overhauled. Current national leadership in El Salvador has cracked down on gangs and has built huge prisons to incarcerate them. The accounts of revivals among these imprisoned gang members read like the Book of Acts.

Castro uses an analogy from auto racing where drivers follow the dictum to "never lift." Once the race starts, you don't take your foot off the gas. Using his own ministry experience of years in the context of violence, Castro posits that the commitment of Pentecostals in El Salvador is to "never lift" in the face of violence. The Spirit has empowered them to proclaim the gospel to everyone regardless of their own lack of security and safety. They will "never lift" from the task for which the Sprit has empowered them, and that includes entering the prisons with thousands of gang members and preaching the good news that Jesus saves.

J. Kwabena Asamoah-Gyadu begins his chapter with a succinct observation that Spirit-empowered Christianity is now the representative face of faith on the African continent. He clearly articulates that Christianity's presence on the African continent is not a recent intruding initiative but clearly recorded in the Book of Acts. He further states that the gift of African Christianity to the West is how to function in the power of the Holy Spirit. He notes that the visible markers of such a movement is new birth, healing of the sick, conquering of the effects of the past, casting out evil spirits, receiving answers to prayer, God speaking through dreams, and a new life of promise.

Asamoah-Gyadu notes that the Edinburgh Mission Conference of 1910 spoke of the very real possibility of Africa becoming Muslim in the twentieth century. Yet the one-hundred-year celebration of that historic conference had a majority of attendees from the Majority World with Africa well represented. He observes that while the growth of Christianity in the Majority World remains a well-documented fact, the role of Spirit-empowered Christianity in this shifting centre of Christian influence is a reality still all too often overlooked. In explaining how the new shape of global Christianity might have occurred, he refers to the late Ogbu Kalu, who posits that, in Africa, the presence of the Holy Spirit became both the evidence and the guarantee that the reign of God was being experienced in full power. By referring to the "presence of the Holy Spirit," Kalu meant miracles, healing, and transforming power that yielded ecclesiological priorities among African Pentecostals focused on divine empowerment.

The explosion of African Pentecostal Christianity, Asamoah-Gyadu observes, has not only influenced the African continent, but serves as a significant factor in the reshaping of spirituality beyond the African context. For example, Spirit-empowered Christians have been clearly central to the migratory patterns impacting the world. Although those patterns certainly have roots in geopolitical conflict, there is also a significant impact, by those migrants, on the regions they enter, becoming a de facto church planting initiative bringing spiritual vitality globally.

Asamoah-Gyadu continues by noting that Pentecostals are transforming the way Christianity will be experienced for years to come by challenging the medium in which the essence of Christianity will be articulated. In other words, Christianity will be thoroughly experiential, and that experiential quality will be spiritually democratising.

Jacqueline Grey asks why the participation of women in the global Church is a preferable reality for the Church's flourishing. She builds her answer around several key propositions in making her case for full participation of women in ministry and leadership.

She first looks to creation. Although sin has broken God's creational design and alienated the human community, God has purposed for men and women to live in unity and minister together. Additionally, she looks to the model of full participation in ministry and leadership, with reflection upon Joel's prophetic promise actualised in the Pentecost event. With the coming of the Spirit to indwell "all flesh," she observes a blessed alliance of men and women working together in the unity realised at the birth of the Church.

Grey asks how women can be released to full participation in Spirit-empowered ministry. She focuses on two primary pathways, both embodied in the advocacy of the Apostle Paul for Phoebe and Priscilla in Romans 16. The first pathway is that men should be champions of women by advocating for their inclusion in ministry and leadership opportunities. She notes that men are doorkeepers to most ministry organisations and thus hold the key to the participation of women. They can use their influence to advocate for women's entrance into roles of greater influence. They should do so simply because they can, resulting in the release of women's capacity to fully steward their spiritual gifts and human skills with the fullest impact being greater fruitfulness for the entire faith community.

Grey observes that the biblical requirement for a leader (of any gender) to have a good reputation can be another pathway to full participation in ministry. She notes that the honour-shame cultures of many Majority World contexts do place a heavy burden on women. She nonetheless views a good reputation as a key to the full participation of women in ministry. Gender bias is clearly present, and often even men with the best intentions remain blind to such bias. Pointing to the Romans 16 model again, Grey notes that Phoebe and Priscilla navigated no less daunting cultural realities in the Graeco-Roman world. Paul recognised their good character and subsequently championed their ministries. She notes that biblical and even extra-biblical examples in the Early Church can inspire God's vision for full participation of Spirit-empowered women. These women will strengthen the flourishing of Global Christianity.

Karl Hargestam and Jennifer Hargestam have spent considerable time working among unreached people groups (UPGs). This chapter not only offers missiological reflection but case studies of their work in Ethiopia with a supporting mission agency from Sweden focused on UPGs. The Hargestams address a missiological theme that is not new, but which has been understood in its current form as championed by the late Ralph Winter. His development of the concept of UPG was his descriptive effort to identify and more strategically focus the efforts of those committed to global evangelisation. His work was a more contemporary iteration of the efforts of various eras of the modern missions movements personified in leaders like William Carey or J. Hudson Taylor – or initiatives like the Student Volunteer Movement catalysed by D.L. Moody.

The Hargestams add to the current understanding of UPGs by shifting the focus of discussion from the efforts of mission agencies to the possibilities for local churches, especially those in the Majority World. Where zeal and passionate commitment are often the factors associated with efforts to evangelise UPGs, the Hargestams suggest a framework with social science roots in their investigation of the role Cultural Intelligence might play in preparing workers for ministry with UPGs.

The case studies in this chapter focus on efforts in Ethiopia. These studies demonstrate the viability of the Hargestams' proposed model and highlight its necessity in the efforts to reach those currently outside the reach of a viable local church. The efforts to reach UPGs have arguably been an effort initiated by Western mission agencies. The Hargestams' contribution to the discussion is based on the fact that Majority World Christians are more geographically and culturally close to the majority of UPGs globally. The future of vital progress on the "unfinished task" will be most fruitful as Majority World Christians lean into this potential. While Western agencies have had the financial resources to conduct this effort, those kinds of resources are not as readily available in the Majority World. The Hargestams' advocacy for ministry to UPGs, rooted in local churches, can find contemporary resonance as it highlights what Roland Allen wrote a century ago about the work of the Holy Spirit and the local church in his classic works like *Pentecost and the World* (1917), *The Spontaneous Expansion of the Church* (1927), and *Missionary Methods: St Paul's or Ours?* (1912).

Writing from his context in Indonesia, **Gani Wiyono** chronicles the ecological realities in which he lives. While chronicling the varying contributors to the ecological crisis he sees all around him, he pivots to a position that the fundamental causes of global ecological challenges may actually be more spiritual than material. He observes that what people do to their environment may in fact be related to how they view their relationships with their Creator and other living beings around them. Citing both Christian and Islamic sources, he suggests that the ecological crisis is essentially a spiritual crisis of modern humanity. He begins his foray into ecotheology from a Pentecostal perspective.

Wiyono chooses to follow the Pentecostal understanding of healing as the theme on which he will focus his theological reflection. Noting that Luther's view of salvation denied the impact of salvation being experienced in the material realm of the world, Wiyono juxtaposes that Pentecostals (unlike Luther) see direct correlation between salvation and healing for the body. It is on this point that he notes that, while Pentecostals have been quick to affirm the material dimension of salvation, they generally limit that impact to individual, physical, or economic realms. Pentecostals have been slow to broaden their understanding of salvation's impact on the material world to the larger cosmic realm. Wiyono clearly posits that Pentecostals must extend their understanding of healing to both personal and cosmic realms. He makes his case around two key themes: deep incarnation and a vision of the sacred cosmos.

The concept of deep incarnation has its roots in Eastern Christianity with such sources as St Gregory of Nazianzus. That soteriological treatise by Gregory provides the basis for more contemporary discussion on the issue of whether non-human beings can be saved. Wiyono cites current work on the concept of deep incarnation, which affirms that, in the Incarnation, Jesus not only joined to humanity but to all creation – living creatures and the cosmic dust from which all creation springs. Citing ancient sources like St Bonaventure, Wiyono makes his case that our understanding of the Incarnation could be enriched by expanding beyond the human realm to a more cosmic realm.

He continues his essay by looking at a vision of the sacred earth. He argues that a Western influenced paradigm has shaped our understanding of the cosmos. Citing the impact of Descartes and Newton, he observes that the result has been a secularisation of the cosmos now seen as merely an object of instrumental value. Citing Pentecostal scholars like Harold Hunter, who has been at the forefront of ecotheology from a Pentecostal perspective, Wiyono wonders how we can reverse the pattern of the desacralisation of nature without descending into paganism. To answer that question, he delves into the work on panentheism as described by Jürgen Moltmann. Moltmann distinguishes pantheism from panentheism by saying that pantheism identifies God with creation while panentheism sees the Divine as inseparable, always present, and involved in the world of His creation, without the need to be qualitatively identical with His creation.

The excursus into some sturdy theological inquiries leads Wiyono to offer a focused question. He is a Pentecostal who lives with the fullest impact of ecological crisis every day. He wonders whether the historic Pentecostal theology of healing, which resacralised the impact of salvation (contra Luther's view), might be extended to the macro level and include the cosmos. Might this be a way that Pentecostals can offer an alternative ecotheology to the global body of Christ?

Kong Hee, along with his wife, Sun Ho, were the co-hosts for the Global Pentecostal Summit which has resulted in this volume. It is fitting that he offers this chapter focused on his nation and the possibilities of it serving as a locus of fervent effort to extend to the gospel. While making the analogy between Antioch and Singapore might seem on the surface a bit presumptuous, this is also the comparative framework used by no less than Billy Graham and Yonggi Cho. This chapter is not a triumphalist proclamation so much as it is a thorough investigation into why the likes of Christian statesmen like Graham and Cho might have made this observation decades ago.

Hee identifies six biblical elements in Antioch shared by Singapore. He cites those similarities as the importance of urban ministry, the empowerment of laity, dependence on the Holy Spirit, focus on instruction and discipleship, compassion for the poor, and global outreach. He notes that extensive correlations exist between the effective ministry of the Antioch church and the current church in Singapore. Noting that each of those items of correlation could be their own chapter, he focuses rather on two items that present formidable challenges facing the church in Singapore; these challenges will require the Singapore Church's successful navigation in order to live up to the observations made so long ago by Graham and Cho.

While Singapore may be the most religiously diverse country in the world, it is officially a secular state. Equilibrium between its religious communities is rigorously legislated. While this yields a modicum of peace and security, the question remains as to how Christianity has fared in this religiously pluralistic context. Hee cites Singaporean scholars who observe that the Christian community at large in Singapore is somewhat apathetic to relationships with other faith traditions, let alone interfaith dialogues. Hee posits that the brilliance of Pentecostalism is its historic contribution to promoting and maintaining racial and religious harmony. A further question exists as to whether multiracial, multireligious fellowship and dialogue between Christians and religious others can take place, even if the latter remains closed to conversion. For Pentecostals, Hee posits that the answer is *yes*! He argues that because of Pentecostalism's innate belief in the Spirit – who reflects love, respect, and forbearance for all – this movement can play a vital role in fostering tolerance and understanding in religious communities.

The second challenge Hee addresses is Christian activism. Some Singaporean Christians have interpreted Graham's reference to Singapore as the Antioch of Asia to imply it should become a Christian state. The path Hee suggests is certainly counter to that of American Pentecostalism, which is increasingly aligning itself in political activism. Given the context of Singapore and its unique context of rigorous governmental regulation, Hee lives in a situation where his theological reflection must acknowledge his reality; in that space, he defers to the historical position of nascent Pentecostalism. Following the lead of Steven Land, he posits that meeting the challenge of political activism as a Pentecostal includes not engaging in direct social or political activism but rather creating communities of care, respect, and empowerment to "affective conscientisation" toward liberation. The fruit of the Spirit, coupled with gifts, unifies and builds up the community and qualifies it for effectiveness.

If the challenges presented by religious pluralism and Christian activism in Singapore can be faced effectively by living into the essence of Pentecostalism, why has the record not shown greater success in doing so? Hee expresses the opinion that the dearth of rigorous theological education for Pentecostals has been a key contributor. Acknowledging the rocky relationship Pentecostals have with rigorous theological education, he makes a further caution. Noting that the "embourgeoisement of Pentecostalism" should not veer towards toward mainline evangelicalism (and in doing so neutralise their own identity), he further advocates for a recovery of the heart of Pentecostalism, which he describes as using Walter Hollenweger's matrix of Black orality, Wesleyan, Catholic, Protestant, and ecumenical teachings.

This chapter reflects an example of a "voice loud and clear" coming from a Majority World Pentecostal who offers some deep reflection on the nature of the tradition that deserves the attention of Western Pentecostal leaders. In conclusion, Hee asks rhetorically whether Singapore is the Antioch of Asia. The response is maybe… but maybe not yet. Any hope of leaning into that descriptor of Singapore would need to include the Pentecostal Spirit.

8. The Role of the Church in the Context of Violence

Juan Angel Castro

Introduction

Violence has impacted the Church throughout its existence. The history of the Church is replete with stories of both tragedy and resilience. From Saul's efforts to thwart the growth of early Christianity to current challenges globally, contexts of violence for Christians have been a constant reality. The personal experience and theological reflection I wish to offer for your consideration comes from a recent case study from El Salvador. I offer this testimony to you as an affirmation that the Holy Spirit makes his power most evident in places of deepest tragedy and darkness.

Once the Violence Started, It Never Stopped: The Civil War and the *Maras*

The history of El Salvador in the first part of the twentieth century provides the seedbed for the violence. From the 1930s to the 1970s, one dictator followed another. Regardless of the various political ideologies of each new leader, not much changed. What remained constant was that one hundred families controlled the wealth of the nation while the popular masses lived in abject poverty.

In the 1960s and 1970s, the glaring social and economic chasm between rich and poor spawned the breeding ground for conflict and violence.[1] No one should have felt surprised when an armed insurgency emerged in opposition to the powers that controlled the nation's social and economic structures. Peasants, urban poor, young people, university students, and key Catholic religious leaders allied with an insurgency that would soon develop into a powerful guerrilla movement known as the *Farabundo Marti Nationalist Liberation Front* (FMLN). The insurgents hit like a hammer with one act of terror after another. They dynamited bridges, knocked out power towers and attacked the communication centres. Soon the violence escalated by kidnapping or murdering prominent businesspeople. In retaliation, the government mobilised the armed forces and struck back with an even more extreme lethal vengeance. Many Salvadorans allied with one side or the other with the majority repulsed by both.

---

[1] Allan Everett Wilson. *La Crisis de Integración Nacional en El Salvador 1919-1935*, vol. 17 *Biblioteca de Historia Salvadoreña*, 1st ed. (San Salvador: Consejo Nacional para la Cultura y el Arte, 2004), 101.

The war raged on for twelve long years. The atrocities, including massacres committed by both sides, were horrific.[2] Seventy-five thousand people were killed,[3] mostly civilians, and eight thousand more "disappeared".[4] Hundreds of thousands were left homeless. The nation was in shambles.[5] Finally, on 16th January 1992, "peace agreements" were signed between the government and the FMLN. The war had no winners.

The violence of the civil war forced a major exodus of the population. Parents left children behind to be raised by a relative.[6] Families, by the thousands, simply disintegrated. A generation of children grew up without parents, without a sense of values, or a set of basic principles. This generation has been called: *"The Children of War"* [Hijos de la Guerra].[7]

In the years that followed the war, the nation was marked by resentments, grudges, and bitterness. There was no period of reconciliation, no retributive justice, and no pardons granted for the innocents. The consequences were not unlike those suffered by other nations after genocide.[8] And all too soon, a new wave of violence grasped the nation by the neck: The Maras.

---

[2] Jose Victor Villavicencio, "Pentecostal Churches and Human Rights in the Framework of the Armed Conflict in El Salvador (1987-1991)", *Journal of the Department of Theology*, Universidad Evangélica de El Salvador (January-April 2017), 39-42.

[3] BBC World Newsroom, "Inocente Montano: The Massacre of Eight People for Which the Former Colonel of the Army of El Salvador Was Sentenced to More Than 130 Years in Prison in Spain [Inocente Montano: la masacre de 8 personas por la que el excoronel del ejército de El Salvador fue sentenciado a más de 130 años de cárcel en España]", *BBC*, 29th January 2020 [Available at: https://www.bbc.com/mundo/noticias-america-latina-51305046] [Last accessed: 20th March 2024].

[4] BBC World Newsroom, "Inocente Montano."

[5] Andrea Rincón, "El Salvador: From the Civil War to Decisive Elections [El Salvador: de la Guerra civil a unas elecciones determinantes]," *France24*, 2nd January 2019 [Available at: https://www.france24.com/es/20190201-el-salvador-elecciones-presidenciales-candidato] [Last accessed: 20th March 2024]. See also: "El Salvador Civil War [Guerra civil de El Salvador]", *Wikipedia* [Available at: https://es.wikipedia.org/wiki/Guerra_civil_de_El_Salvador#cite_note-53] [Last accessed: 20th March 2024].

[6] Ibid Rincon.

[7] Carlos Medrano, "Children of War [Hijos de la Guerra]", *Computer Science and Communications Unit Salvadoran Lutheran University*, 29th July 2016 [Available at: https://uls.edu.sv/sitioweb/component/k2/item/457-hijos-de-la-guerra] [Last accessed: 20th March 2024].

[8] Marcel Uwineza, "Rwanda: Conversion Continues [Ruanda: Continúa La Conversión]", *The Society of Jesus* (Jesuits Global), 12th April 2022 [Available at: https://www.jesuits.global/es/2022/04/12/ruanda-continua-la-conversion/] [Last accessed: 20th March 2024].

Chapter 8

The Rise of the Maras (Gangs), MS-13 and Mara 18

The seeds of violence sown during the civil war sprouted into a siege of unspeakable terror that, in one way or another, lurked in the doorways of every family. No one was exempt from the horrors about to transpire. The *maras* (gangs), exploding to include seventy-five thousand of El Salvador's youth, wreaked terror wherever they wished. People's lives spun out of control, and they could not do a thing about it. After the civil war, Salvadoran society – fragmented and wounded – collapsed upon itself. Soldiers in the military and soldiers from the guerrilla movement felt frustrated and angry. The war had accomplished little. It was the *status quo* all over again.[9]

Thousands of Salvadorans who fled the nation came to Los Angeles, California in the USA. Many of their young people got involved in the criminal activities of local city gangs. They would be arrested, convicted, and deported back to El Salvador. The national nightmare of violence started all over again. The ground was fertile to recruit, reproduce, and multiply. Young Salvadorans were unemployed, living in poverty, and merely surviving in the fog of utter hopelessness. Abandoned by parents who had fled after the civil war, the appeal of the gangs gave young Salvadorans a sense of family, identity, power, and money.[10] Two rival gangs, MS-13 and Mara 18, battled for power. Isaac, a former gang member said, "The gang was a brotherhood; we knew we were doing bad things, selling drugs, stealing, fighting with other gangs, but [...] we took care of ourselves, protected ourselves, and we helped each other."[11] Another former member, Nestor S., told me, "We were told we were a family, but every day was a fight between kill or die."[12] Isaac's hope for a brotherhood never materialised; "Of all my companions," he said, "only I am alive."[13]

Gang members ranged between the ages of thirteen to twenty-nine. Being young in El Salvador was synonymous with violence and crime.[14] They

---

[9] Oscar Martinez, *El Salvador el soldado y la guerrillera* [The Soldier and the Guerrilla], (San Salvador, El Salvador: UFG-Editores, 2008).

[10] Walter Murcia, "Gangs in El Salvador: Proposals and Challenges for Youth Social Inclusion in Contexts of Urban Violence [Las pandillas en El Salvador: Propuestas y desafíos para la inclusión social juvenil en contextos de violencia urbana]", *United Nations Project Document* [Naciones Unidas Documento de Proyecto], September 2015 [Available at: https://www.cepal.org/sites/default/files/publication/files/39362/S1501050_es.pdf/] [Last accessed: 20th March 2024].

[11] Personal testimony of Isaac, ex-gang member, in interview conducted with the author 1st September 2023. The name has been changed for personal safety reasons.

[12] Personal testimony of former MS13 gang member in interview conducted with author 12th September 2023. The name has been changed for personal safety reasons.

[13] Personal testimony of Isaac.

[14] Norbert Ross, "When Being Young is Synonymous with Danger, the Country is at Risk [Cuando ser joven es sinónimo de peligro, el país está en riesgo]", *Elfaro*, 16th November 2023 [Available at: https://elfaro.net/es/202207/columnas/26251/Cuando-

kidnapped, raped, trafficked in drugs, extorted, and laundered money.[15] By 2014, there were thirty-two thousand hardened criminals on the loose, sowing terror across the country.[16] By 2022, they numbered seventy-two thousand. Government forces were overwhelmed by the extent of the violence. The gangs were better armed than the military.[17]

Extortion was rampant. The gang extorted everyone: merchants, street vendors, truckers, even pedestrians. They killed anyone who refused to pay.[18] People left work early enough to arrive home before dark. No one ventured out on the streets after dark. San Salvador, the capital city, was held hostage by a youth mafia – he new gangsters of Salvadoran society.[19] Gang members' body and face tattoos identifying them with their gang, MS-13 or Mara 18 were enough to intimidate the public.

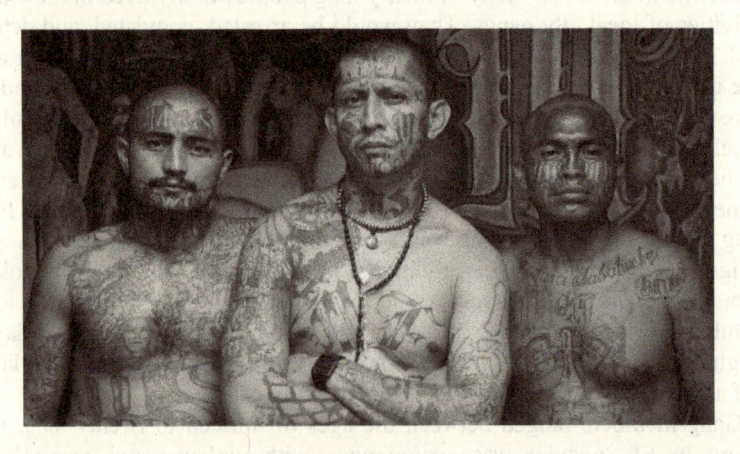

The acts of violence and barbarism were unprecedented in a nation already long accustomed to violence. Newspapers reported atrocities that had happened

---

ser-joven-es-sin%C3%B3nimo-de-peligro-el-pa%C3%ADs-est%C3%A1-en-riesgo.htm] [Last accessed: 20th March 2024].
[15] Marcos Gonzalez Diaz, "'Before We Were Under Siege': The Neighborhoods of El Salvador That Are Reunited after the 'Disappearance' of the Gangs Due to Bukele's War ['Antes estábamos sitiados': los barrios de El Salvador que se reencuentran tras la 'desaparición' de las pandillas por la guerra de Bukele]", *BBC World News*, 27th March 2023 [Available at: https://www.bbc.com/mundo/noticias-america-latina-65059584#:~:text=Ambas%20pandillas%2C%20cuyo%20origen%20se,de%20vuelta%20a%20El%20Salvador] [Last accessed: 20th March 2024].
[16] Murcia, "Gangs in El Salvador", 10-14.
[17] Murcia, "Gangs in El Salvador", 10-14.
[18] Gonzales Diaz, "Before We Were Besieged".
[19] Maria Ali-Habib, "Mass Arrests in El Salvador Raise Fears", *The New York Times*, 29th March 2022 [Available at: https://www.nytimes.com/es/2022/03/29/espanol/bukele-el-salvador-pandillas.html] [Last accessed: 20th March 2024].

the day before. For example, "A clique of Mara 18-*Revolucionarios* hijacked a minibus full of passengers. They sealed the entrance, doused the vehicle with gasoline, and set fire. They shot passengers who tried to escape through the windows. There were 17 dead, most charred."[20] One of the survivors was a young man who attended the church.

El Salvador became one of the most violent countries in the world with a homicide rate in 2015-16 of more than one hundred per 100,000 inhabitants, or a total of 6,650 murders. The government classified the gangs as terrorists.

Then it got worse. In one single day in March 2022, there were sixty-two random murders. This spike in violence was the last straw. The Legislative Assembly approved a "state of exception," expanding the powers of police and military forces to arrest any potential suspect without due process. By August 2023, they had arrested seventy-seven thousand suspected gang members.

A Critique of the Church Amidst the Violence

The Roman Catholic Church

In 1968, the Latin American Bishops held their General Council in Medellin, Colombia and issued a document critiquing the social and economic structures embedded in society as unjust and oppressive, systematically marginalising the poor while protecting the best interests of the elites. The bishops argued that existing political and economic structures and the elites who controlled them had systematically marginalised the poor. The statement by the bishops provided an affirmation that unwittingly yielded a launching pad for the formation of liberation theology in Latin America.

Liberation theologians contended that one could only understand the Bible through the lens of the poor. The theologians linked biblical justice to a condemning of the wealthy for their exploitative actions. The liberationist's view of the gospel demanded that people of faith stand for a more just society and get involved politically, with an eye to change or even overthrow the sinful structures embedded into society.

El Salvador's Archbishop, Oscar Romero, was a reluctant but strong proponent of liberation theology. Along with other Catholic leaders, Romero opted to ally with the left-wing insurgency. By aligning with the FMLN, the Roman Catholic Church had, in effect, joined ranks with a leftist insurgency. The allegiance that the Roman Catholic leadership gave to the FMLN came with

---

[20] Roberto Valencia, "Bukele vs. the Maras: Who are El Salvador's Main Gangs and Why It Is So Dangerous to Mix Them in Prisons [Bukele contra las maras: cuáles son las principales pandillas de El Salvador y por qué es tan peligroso que las mezclen en las cárceles]", *BBC World News*, 29th April 2020 [Available at: https://www.bbc.com/mundo/noticias-america-latina-52466682] [Last accessed: 20th March 2024].

tragic costs. On 24th March 1980, Archbishop Oscar Romero, while saying mass, was fatally shot.

More than twenty years after the war ended, a traditionalist voice within the Catholic Church, *Rorate Caeli*, lamented the Church's progressive efforts for responding to culture's challenges.[21] While the Church was increasingly identifying more effective means of becoming relevant to the poor, faithful Catholics abandoned the Church in droves, searching for an authentic spirituality wherever they could find it. Consequently, they found what they were looking for in charismatic groups and Pentecostal churches.

Pentecostal Churches

It is true that whether for good or bad, Pentecostals avoided direct political involvement with either the left or the right, avoiding a political situation which they viewed as a dirty business. Their critics argued that a position of neutrality was a *de facto* vote for the *status quo*. Pentecostals contended that to take a political side would almost ensure that any opposing groups would never enter their doors again. The doors of Pentecostals had to stay open for everyone.

Critiques also arose that saw these thousands of grassroots churches as nothing more than an extension of American-made missionary colonialism. Still, others complained that Pentecostals holed themselves up in the safety of their churches, avoiding the realities of life that surrounded them. These churches had more to do with "hallelujahs" focused on spiritual matters, rejecting involvement in any social efforts that ministered to the physical needs of the poor. For the most part, over the last four decades, these critiques have been debunked in a multitude of academic publications, including books, peer-reviewed journal articles and research projects.[22]

A Missional Theology: Never Lift

Race car drivers have a saying: "never lift". Simply put, when the race starts, the driver accelerates to full speed and for the rest of the race will "never lift" their foot off the accelerator, no matter what! "Never Lift" is an appropriate label to describe the role of a local Pentecostal church in El Salvador. No matter the violence of war, during times of peace or the subsequent waves of violence that

---

[21] Roberto de Mattei, "Crisis in the Church: A Historical Perspective" *Rorarte Caeli*, November 2018. Available at https://rorate-caeli.blogspot.com/2018/11/de-mattei-crisis-in-church-historical.html#more [last accessed August 18, 2024].

[22] Examples would include Edward L Cleary and Hannah W. Stewart-Gambino editors. *Power, Politics and Pentecostals in Latin America* (Boulder: Westview Press. 1997) See also David Martin, *Pentecostalism: The World Their Parish* (Oxford: Blackwell Publishers, 2002) pp 71-131. See also Miguel Alvarez, *Integral Mission: A new Paradigm for Latin America Pentecostals.* (Oxford UK: Regnum Books, 2016).

never seem to recede, the Pentecostal Church in El Salvador has remained vigilant, serving as agents of the good news of the gospel for every person. They will "never lift" from the task for which the Spirit has empowered them.

The cycle of spiritual restoration begins when a believer, often brand new, shares his or her faith with family, friends, co-workers, and passengers on the city bus – with anyone who will listen. A typical testimony: "A month ago, my life was a mess. I gave my life to Jesus. Now, I am a brand-new person. Would you like to come with me to church?" Usually, two defining experiences take place – salvation and Holy Spirit baptism – often followed by supernatural events like tongues, prophesy, divine healing, miracles, and divine answers to prayer. Congregants come together in worship, participate with a family that cares for others, and receive spiritual formation and training to serve as workers or even pastors. A small church called a *campo blanco* inevitably gives birth to another small church because, once outside the church walls, every one of these new converts now tells someone about Jesus. The cycle begins all over again. The missional priority that the Spirit-empowered church in El Salvador offers is simple: in violence or in peace, our strategy for growth is that we will "never lift".

They Overcame Him by the Blood of the Lamb and the Word of Their Testimony

Such testimonies of transformed lives through the power of the Spirit best illustrate the transforming power of the Holy Spirit in the context of extreme violence. Every story differs with a unique set of circumstances or context. In so many ways, however, each story is the same. The stories that follow are representative of hundreds, even thousands, of testimonies that have resulted from a Spirit-empowered commitment to "never lift".

Juan Angel Castro (My Story)

I was a university student when the armed insurgency took shape in the country's mountains. Some of my university friends enrolled in the Military Academy, while others decided to head for the mountains to join the guerrillas. I knew that I too would soon need to decide.

Like many young Latinos, I loved soccer. A friend told me about a soccer team I could join on the condition that I attended the youth group sponsoring the team. When I first attended, I was surprised to find students my age who were sincerely interested in others. I loved their enthusiasm when they sang or read the Bible together, but I just wanted to play soccer.

One evening, a few months later, instead of holding a practice, the leader announced that we were "evangelising". I was not a believer, but I headed out to evangelise with the others. I found three men in a grocery parking lot asking people if they could carry their groceries in return for a few pesos. I asked if they wanted to talk about God. They agreed, so I read the "four spiritual laws" I found in the tract. If someone wanted to accept the Lord, the tract instructed, ask them to kneel and repeat the prayer in the tract (I found out later that it was the sinner's prayer). As we repeated the prayer, I decided to accept the Lord for myself. That decision in a parking lot would forever change my life. Instead of heading for the mountains, I entered the ministry.

My Friend Roberto

When Roberto and I graduated from high school, we went to university. Roberto decided to head for the mountains to join the guerrilla insurgency and told me his story:

> One day, while on patrol, we were ambushed by the army. My entire squadron was annihilated. I was the only one still alive. Alone and facing certain death, I remembered a tract someone had given me that asked: "If you were to die, where would you go?" I wasn't religious, but I started to pray. I told the Lord, "I don't even believe in you, but if you exist and can deliver me from this mess, I'll serve you for the rest of my life." I took courage and carefully worked my way down the mountainside. I practically passed through the middle of the soldiers. It was as though God made me invisible. God delivered me, and I kept my word. I am a pastor.

Salvador Molina (Former Guerrilla Leader in the FMLN)

> A well-known evangelist was holding a crusade at San Salvador's national stadium. Our [...] group was ordered to kill the preacher. Five of us, our weapons hidden under our coats, entered the stadium and pushed through the crowd to get close to the platform. With our machine guns ready, we were about to take the shot; the evangelist raised his hand and said, "There are five men who have come to kill me. I tell you to repent. Give yourself to the Lord." At that moment, the five of us fell to the ground. When we got up, no one had seen us. We escaped from the stadium. We knew we had experienced the power of God. I gave my life to Jesus.

Nestor S. (Former Gang MS Who Told Me about His Conversion)

Nestor S. was the leader of a gang cell. Within the gang structure, he was prestigious and respected. His involvement in drug trafficking resulted in lots of money.

One afternoon, a pastor approached him and said, "I came to tell you that God has something better for you. He can get you out of this gang. You won't have to live in fear, constantly on the run, looking over your shoulder. You are going to serve God. God wants to make you a pastor and a preacher of the gospel." Nestor told the pastor, "I'll think about it."

Nestor was confident that because of his status near the top of the gang structure, he was almost untouchable, but Nestor was wrong. Rival drug traffickers began to view Nestor as a threat to business. They decided to find a way to eliminate him. The Narcos paid one of Nestor's own gang members to betray him. The person Nestor believed to be a loyal friend shot him five times. One of the bullets pierced his lung, and another punctured the intestine. By the time that Nestor was hospitalised, infection had set in, and he slipped into a coma. The attending doctor later reported, "I came into the room and whispered into Nestor's ear, 'If you believe God can lift you up and bring you out of this coma, squeeze my hand.'" As Nestor recounted to me, "The doctor said I squeezed her hand." Then, the doctor began to pray and prophesy. Within an hour, Nestor came out of the coma. His body began to heal rapidly. Just when he was ready to be discharged from the hospital, the police arrested him. He told me:

> While in prison, when I gave my life to Jesus, I broke down and cried like a child. I asked the Lord to transform my life, and he did. I got baptised and began to prepare to be a pastor. Other gang members heard my testimony and watched how I conducted my life. One after another, they experienced the power of the gospel through the power of the Spirit, accepted Christ, and experienced the same. For almost a year, I pastored a prison church of gang members who could not attend church.

Then, another miracle happened. Nestor was unexpectedly released from prison, a free man. He began serving in the church of the pastor who had first told me about Jesus. Now, he is the pastor of his own Pentecostal church. Nestor is right when he testifies, "Only God can change a person like me."

"Never Lift": A Strategy of the Holy Spirit

No human plan or strategy can explain the explosive growth of Pentecostals[23] except for the supernatural intervention of the power of the Holy Spirit. In 1980, at the beginning of the civil war, Catholics accounted for 91 percent of the population. evangelicals comprised less than 7 percent (of which 70 percent were Pentecostals). By the war's end in 1992, evangelical Pentecostals had more than doubled. In the most recent polls, Pentecostals and Catholics each represent 40 percent, evangelicals are in the majority in the urban centres and, perhaps most importantly, among young adults, a statistic unthinkable in 1980. Encouragingly, the Church is actively Pentecostal – with tongues, prophecy, healing, miracles, and exorcism commonly practiced by believers.

Concluding Story

A new prison in El Salvador opened in January 2023 designed to house gang members. At the time of this writing, 1,200 are members of the church in prison – the *prison*. God has transformed their lives, and most are already filled with the Spirit.

Revelation 12:11 reminds us that following Jesus is never an easy path. The nation in which I serve is a pervasive context of violence that requires my deepest

---

[23] The Spanish word *evangelico* is a literal translation of the English word evangelical. *Evangelico* is often used interchangeably in Central America with the word Pentecostal. In El Salvador the terms *evangelico* and *Pentecostal* may be used interchangeably. More precise definitions are certainly appropriate in academic research. See Douglas Petersen, *Not by Might Nor by Power* (Oxford: Regnum Books, 1996) pp 59-79.

reliance on the Holy Spirit's power just to survive. Moments where "life and death" hang in the balance are regular experiences in El Salvador. Nevertheless, I have learned that because of the power of the Spirit, I need "never lift." The same power that raised Jesus from the dead empowers my life and followers of Jesus in El Salvador. We will "never, *ever* lift!"

Bibliography

Primary Sources

Personal testimony of Isaac, ex-gang member, in interview conducted with the author 1st September 2023. The name has been changed for personal safety reasons.

Personal testimony of former MS13 gang member in interview conducted with the author 12th September 2023. The name has been changed for personal safety reasons

Secondary Sources

Ali-Habib, Maria. "Mass Arrests in El Salvador Raise Fears". *The New York Times*. 29th March 2022. [Available at: https://www.nytimes.com/es/2022/03/29/espanol/bukele-el-salvador-pandillas.html] [Last accessed: 20th March 2024].

BBC World Newsroom. "Inocente Montano: The Massacre of Eight People for Which the Former Colonel of the Army of El Salvador Was Sentenced to More Than 130 Years in Prison in Spain [Inocente Montano: la masacre de 8 personas por la que el excoronel del ejército de El Salvador fue sentenciado a más de 130 años de cárcel en España]", *BBC*. 29th January 2020. [Available at: https://www.bbc.com/mundo/noticias-america-latina-51305046] [Last accessed: 20th March 2024].

de Mattei, Roberto. "Crisis in the Church; A Historical Perspective". *Rorate Caeli*. November 2018 {Available at https://rorate-caeli.blogspot.com/2018/11/de-mattei-crisis-in-church-historical.html#more } {Last accessed August 18, 2024}

"El Salvador Civil War [Guerra civil de El Salvador]", *Wikipedia*. https://es.wikipedia.org/wiki/Guerra_civil_de_El_Salvador#cite_note-53.

Gonzalez Diaz, Marcos. "'Before We Were Under Siege': The Neighborhoods of El Salvador That Are Reunited after the 'Disappearance' of the Gangs Due to Bukele's War ["Antes estábamos sitiados": los barrios de El Salvador que se reencuentran tras la "desaparición" de las pandillas por la guerra de Bukele]", *BBC World News*. 23rd March 2023. [Available at: https://www.bbc.com/mundo/noticias-america-latina-65059584#:~:text=Ambas%20pandillas%2C%20cuyo%20origen%20se,de%20vuelta%20a%20El%20Salvador] [Last accessed: 20th March 2024].

Martinez, Oscar. *El Salvador el soldado y la guerrillera* [The Soldier and the Guerrilla]. San Salvador, El Salvador: UFG-Editores, 2008.

Medrano, Carlos. "Children of War [Hijos de la Guerra]", *Computer Science and Communications Unit Salvadoran Lutheran University*. 29th July 2016. [Available at: https://uls.edu.sv/sitioweb/component/k2/item/457-hijos-de-la-guerra] [Last accessed: 20th March 2024].

Murcia, Walter. "Gangs in El Salvador: Proposals and Challenges for Youth Social Inclusion in Contexts of Urban Violence [Las pandillas en El Salvador: Propuestas y desafíos para la inclusión social juvenil en contextos de violencia urbana]", *United Nations Project Document* [Naciones Unidas Documento de Proyecto]. September 2015. [Available at: https://www.cepal.org/sites/default/files/publication/files/39362/S1501050_es.pdf] [Last accessed: 20th March 2024].

Rincón, Andrea. "El Salvador: From the Civil War to Decisive Elections [El Salvador: de la Guerra civil a unas elecciones determinantes]", *France24*. 2nd January 2019. [Available at: https://www.france24.com/es/20190201-el-salvador-elecciones-presidenciales-candidato] [Last accessed: 20th March 2024].

Ross, Norbert. "When Being Young is Synonymous with Danger, the Country is at Risk" [Cuando ser joven es sinónimo de peligro, el país está en riesgo]", *Elfaro*, 16th November 2023. [Available at: https://elfaro.net/es/202207/columnas/26251/Cuando-ser-joven-es-sin%C3%B3nimo-de-peligro-el-pa%C3%ADs-est%C3%A1-en-riesgo.htm] [Last accessed: 20th March 2024].

Uwineza, Marcel. "Rwanda: Conversion Continues [Ruanda: Continúa La Conversión]", *The Society of Jesus* (Jesuits Global). 12th April 2022. [Available at: https://www.jesuits.global/es/2022/04/12/ruanda-continua-la-conversion/] [Last accessed: 20th March 2024].

Valencia, Roberto. "Bukele vs. the Maras: Who are El Salvador's Main Gangs and Why It Is So Dangerous to Mix Them in Prisons [Bukele contra las maras: cuáles son las principales pandillas de El Salvador y por qué es tan peligroso que las mezclen en las cárceles]", *BBC World News*. 29th April 2020. [Available at: https://www.bbc.com/mundo/noticias-america-latina-52466682] [Last accessed: 20th March 2024].

Villavicencio, Jose Victor. "Pentecostal Churches and Human Rights in the Framework of the Armed Conflict in El Salvador (1987-1991)", *Journal of the Department of Theology*. Universidad Evangélica de El Salvador (January-April 2017), 39-42.

Wilson, Allan Everett. *La Crisis de Integración Nacional en El Salvador 1919-1935*. Vol. 17 *Biblioteca de Historia Salvadoreña*. 1st ed. San Salvador: Consejo Nacional para La Cultura y el Arte, 2004.

9. In the Power of the Holy Ghost: Africa and Spirit-Empowered Christianity in the Twenty-First Century

J. Kwabena Asamoah-Gyadu

Abbreviations
CWME Conference on World Mission and Evangelism
MDCC The Mussama Disco Christo Church
PCCs Pentecostal-Charismatic Christians
WCC World Council of Churches

Introduction

This chapter deals with Spirit empowerment and the transformation of Christianity in Africa. Talk of Spirit-empowered Christianity in any context immediately brings to attention the many Pentecostal-Charismatic ministries, churches, and movements that have emerged in the history of the faith. The history of Christianity in Africa dates to the early biblical Pentecost period in which people of African descent were not only listed as present at the outpouring of the Holy Spirit, but an Ethiopian eunuch became one of the first beneficiaries of people baptised in the name of the resurrected and ascended Jesus. This highly placed Ethiopian believer presumably became an evangelist of the message of Jesus, the fulfilment of God's Suffering Servant in Isaiah.

One could use the expression, "Spirit-empowered" to refer any stream of Christianity that values, affirms, and consciously promotes the experiential dimension of life in the Spirit, i.e., the power in the name of Jesus and of the Holy Spirit, as part of normal Christian life.[1] The expression "power" in this context does not mean the arbitrary use of force, but divine interventions by which the salvation of souls, confessions of Jesus Christ as Lord, moral transformations, miracles, signs and wonders, and destruction of the powers of evil occur in human life, as part of the ministry of the Spirit of God in the age. The Spirit who was poured out at Pentecost has been working among African Christians ever since.

In the modern era, the early twentieth century saw the rise of many charismatic personalities who founded and led Holy Spirit movements and

---

[1] Kwabena J. Asamoah-Gyadu, *African Charismatics: A Study of Independent Indigenous Pentecostalism in Ghana* (Leiden: Brill, 2005a), 12.

churches across Christian Africa. Spirit-empowered Christianity is now the representative face of the faith on the continent, and this development has implications for Christianity worldwide. A primary gift of African Christianity to the West and to the world, according to Mark Gornick, is how to function in the power of the Holy Spirit; Spirit-empowered Christianity in Africa is one in which the Holy Spirit brings forth new birth, heals the sick, conquers the past, casts out evil spirits, answers prayers, speaks in dreams, and raises to new life.[2]

The Spirit-Empowerment and African Christianity

At the Edinburgh 1910 World Missions Conference, the expressed fear was that Africa would turn Islamic. However, a century later when the conference reconvened at Edinburgh in 2010, representation was overwhelmingly non-Western, with Africa clearly a leading player in terms of representation. Much has been said about the emergence of Christianity as a non-Western religion, but the fact often left out of this observation is the role of Spirit-empowered movements in the development. At the beginning of the twentieth century, many ordinary Africans experienced their own Pentecost. This occurred through such religious developments as the breakout of the East African Revival that spawned many local churches defining themselves in ecclesiological terms as "churches of the Spirit". The influence of itinerant prophets like William Wadé Harris of Liberia and Ghana, Garrick Sokari Braide of the Niger Delta, Simon Kimbangu of the Belgian Congo, and Isaiah Shembe of South Africa completely transformed the face of African Christianity.

The late African church historian, Ogbu U. Kalu, refers to the work of these itinerant prophets as sowing the seeds for the rise of the Pentecostal movements in Africa.[3] The spiritual churches – often pejoratively called African independent/initiated/instituted churches – shared critical characteristics with global churches, ministries, and movements designated using the ecclesial category, "Pentecostal." Many of these placed at the centre of the spirituality an interventionist theology that emphasised prayer, healing, and the prophetic, as hallmarks of the workings of the Spirit. Kalu describes the chief theological contributions of these early African Holy Spirits to the life of the church as follows:

> The presence of the Spirit became the evidence, as well as the guarantee that the reign of God was being experienced in its full power [...] It is the presence of the Spirit that explains the possibilities of miracles, healing, and power. These

---

[2] Mark R. Gornik, *Word Made Global: Stories of African Christianity in New York City* (Grand Rapids, MI: William B. Eerdmans, 2011), 269.
[3] Ogbu U. Kalu, *African Pentecostalism: An Introduction* (Oxford: Oxford University Press, 2008), Preface pp xiii-x.

pneumatic resources of the gospel were available in the contemporary life of believers and were not mere creedal assent.[4]

As in the title of this chapter, the enchanted African Pentecostal/charismatic formular "in the power of the Holy Ghost" is commonly used in situations needing divine intervention. At the heart of the ecclesiology of the African Pentecostal imagination is divine empowerment, which occurs by the presence and power of the Holy Spirit in human life and in Christian communities. The early independent church movements of Africa emerged precisely because of their disenchantment with the staid, ordered, and non-interventionist sort of Christianity associated with the Western mission enterprise with its emphasis on evangelisation through education and social developmental programmes. These were received as needed for the lofty purposes they served, but with the vernacular translations of the Scriptures, African also discerned that God was present in the biblical era in the power of the Holy Spirit. They opted for these charismatic dimensions of Christianity, many aspects of which resonated deeply with African religious worldviews and sensibilities.[5]

This chapter explores the explosion of African Pentecostal Christianity and how it is reshaping spirituality beyond the continent today. In the Spirit-empowered ministries and movements we encounter in Africa, soteriology focuses on existential issues and a dynamic pneumatology in which the presence of God manifests within the context of worship. This dual emphasis of Spirit-empowered Christianity in Africa is not misplaced because not only is the growth and dynamism of contemporary global Pentecostalism explained in terms of workings of "the power of the Holy Ghost", but also it is in that power that Pentecostalism could be said to have spread around and impacted the world. An observation by Harvey Cox some two decades ago on the reasons for the worldwide resurgence of religion, especially Pentecostalism, is disproportionately applicable to the case of Christian Africa: "[Pentecostalism] is about the experience of God, not about abstract religious ideas, and it depicts a God who does not remain aloof but reaches down through the power of the Spirit to touch human hearts in the midst of life's turmoil."[6] The growth of Pentecostalism, I argue, fulfils the prophetic appearance of African peoples at the global Spirit-empowered fellowship constituted following the outpouring of the Holy Spirit on the Day of Pentecost (*Shavuot*). It brought together, as we read from Acts 2:5, "devout people from every nation under heaven,"[7] including

---

[4] Kalu, *African Pentecostalism*, 9.
[5] See J. Kwabena Asamoah-Gyadu, *Sighs and Signs of the Spirit: Ghanaian Perspectives on Pentecostalism and Renewal in Africa*, Regnum Studies in Mission (Minneapolis, MN: Fortress Press, 2015).
[6] Harvey Cox, *Fire from Heaven: The Rise of Pentecostal Spirituality and the Reshaping of Religion in the Twenty-First Century* (Reading, PA: Addison-Wesley, 1995), 5.
[7] All Scripture quotations, unless otherwise noted, are from the Christian Standard Bible (CSB).

African Jews, to fellowship together under the influence or intoxication of the Holy Spirit.

The Pentecostal theological emphasis on the experience of the Spirit, Pentecostalism's lack of formal and neatly defined liturgical structures, and its versatile ecclesiology, mean that wherever Pentecostalism is found, Spirit-empowered communities can bring people together from across denominations and dissolve ethnic and religious identities.

This chapter describes the contribution of African Pentecostalism to world Christianity, based on its history, mission, and theological focus. Africa is a large continent with a significant part of it Islamic, so at all material times, the expression *African Pentecostalism* would be used to refer to the sub-Saharan non-Islamic, predominantly Christian parts of the continent. At the present time, some of the largest Pentecostal churches in the world are in the most populous African country: Nigeria.

Pentecostal Spirituality and its Popularity

Cox observes that the story of the first Pentecost has always served as an inspiration for people discontented with the way religion or the world in general is going.[8] Studies on religion in Africa have consistently concluded that people often accumulate in their personal worlds as many religious resources as can respond to their physical and spiritual needs. The result is that, in various African cultural contexts, people disenchanted with the older denominations crave a Spirit-empowered communion, attracted by an experiential spirituality that responds to their deepest needs. The non-Pentecostals may frame the haemorrhage of their members in terms of "sheep-stealing" against Spirit-empowered churches. However, the truth is that the sheep wander into places where they can find good pasture.

Spirit-empowered Christianity, we have noted, appeals strongly to African religious sensibilities, and that explains why Spirit-empowered churches attract so many disenchanted members out of historic mission denominations. We cannot talk about Spirit-empowered Christianity anywhere in the world without Pentecostalism. Generally, Pentecostals, as Walter J. Hollenweger often argued, are not given to creedal confessions because of the oral nature of their theology; they prefer to sing, dance, and pray their faith extemporaneously, rather than recite it.[9] Indeed, in many places, Pentecostalism first arose as a protest movement against human-made creeds and the coldness of worship associated with traditional churches. Cox observes that, while the beliefs of other religious

---

[8] Cox, *Fire from Heaven*, 5.
[9] Walter J. Hollenweger, *Pentecostalism: Origins and Developments Worldwide* (Peabody, MA: Hendrickson, 1997), 32-34

groups are enshrined in formal theological systems, those of the Pentecostals are embedded in testimonies, ecstatic speech, and bodily movement.[10]

This informal, expressive, and spontaneous form of spirituality resonates with African ways of being religious. African cultures tend to possess a non-literate oral character. Spirituality founded on the "power of the Holy Spirit" has therefore proven popular in African Christianity, engendering emulative action within Western, mission-related, mainline denominations, and leading to what one may describe as the "Pentecostalisation" of African Christianity.

Pentecost, according to Cheryl Bridges Johns, is an "ongoing festival" that continually calls people to participate in the work of the Holy Spirit. She observes that, contrary to traditional Christian views of Pentecost as a static historical event, "the primary mission of Pentecostalism is to renew the meaning of Pentecost for the whole church."[11] One implication of this is the recognition of an inseparable relationship between Spirit-empowered Christianity and the African primal imagination. *Spirituality* defines "the cluster of values, beliefs, and practices" that determine the distinctive religious lifestyle of a specific religious community.[12]

For indigenous Spirit-empowered Africans in particular, this proves evident first and foremost in worship, usually characterised by what Ghanaian theologian Christian G. Baëta says consists among other things, of rhythmic sways of the body to repetitious music, hand-clapping poignant cries and prayers, dancing, leaping, and motor reactions expressing intense religious emotions.[13]

André Droogers also speaks of the "normalisation" of pneumatic phenomena in Pentecostal Christianity.[14] Pentecostal spirituality, encapsulating speaking in tongues; interpretation of tongues; singing in the Spirit; seeing visions and revelations; prophesying; giving words of knowledge; and the desire for signs, wonders, and miracles is not denomination specific. The fluidity and eclectic nature of Spirit-empowered forms of worship is what has led to the rise of renewal movements within the historic mission denominations, what Cephas

---

[10] Cox, *Fire from Heaven*, 15.
[11] Cheryl Bridges Johns, "What Can the Mainline Churches Learn from Pentecostals about Pentecost?" in Andre Droogers, Cornelis van der Laan, and Wout van Laar (eds), *Fruitful in the Land: Pluralism, Dialogue and Healing in Migrant Pentecostalism* (Zoetemeer, Netherlands: Boekencentrum, 2006), 93.
[12] Russell P. Spittler, "Corinthian Spirituality: How a Flawed Anthropology Imperils Authentic Christian Experience", in Edith Blumhofer, Russell P. Spittler, and Grant Wacker (eds), *Pentecostal Currents in American Protestantism* (Chicago, IL: University of Illinois Press, 1999), 19.
[13] Christian G. Baëta, *Prophetism in Ghana: A Study of Some Spiritual Churches* (London: SCM, 1962), 1.
[14] André Droogers, "The Normalization of Religious Experience: Healing, Prophecy, Dreams, and Visions", in K. Poewe (ed), *Charismatic Christianity as a Global Culture* (Columbia, SC: University of South Carolina Press, 1994), 35.

Omenyo refers to as *Pentecost outside Pentecostalism*.[15] These pneumatic phenomena have recurred throughout Church history[16] since the era of Montanism, the sect-like charismatic movement of the second century that persisted for more than two centuries. This sort of spirituality has emerged in many non-Pentecostal churches. Thus, Spirit-empowerment draws the attention of the Church to the central place of the experience of the Holy Spirit and spiritual gifts in Christian life and ministry. The popularity of this spirituality has not only led to the growth of Pentecostalism in Africa but also to the rise of charismatic renewal movements within non-Pentecostal churches.

The Spirit Moveth

Spirit-empowerment in African Christianity has been possible because of the activity of God's Spirit in mission and because of the innovation of Pentecostal churches. Contrary to popular notions that Spirit-empowered movements in Africa seek to be culturally relevant, their primary desire is to be biblical. For the Apostle Paul, the term *spiritual* is synonymous with the Holy Spirit, referring to that which belongs to, or pertains to, the Spirit of God. The Church of the New Testament was charismatic, that is, it functioned in the gifts of grace bestowed by the Holy Spirit. Thus, in passages where Paul refers to believers as being "spiritual", he clearly meant "people of the Spirit".[17] Thus, in the Christian context, Spirit-empowerment is not a denominational idea. In Spirit-empowered movements, churches, and ministries, we encounter the practical outworking of the democratisation of charisma in which God pours out his Spirit on people; this explains why many such groups recognised the calling of women into ministry long before some of the older historic mission denominations.

Some churches may refer to themselves as Pentecostal or even Charismatic depending on their historical origins and theological orientations. In essence, however, Pentecostalism is a particular form of Christian expression that may be found within Christian communities in which the experience of the Holy Spirit is considered important, including within non-Pentecostal denominations. The development of renewal groups forming within historic mission denominations stands as a testimony to this pervasive and versatile nature of Pentecostal spirituality. This means Pentecostal-Charismatic spirituality diffuses and spreads quickly, affecting and impacting people of different religious, social, and racial backgrounds. In the last three decades in particular, the distinction that used to

---

[15] Cephas N. Omenyo, *Pentecost outside Pentecostalism: A Study of the Development of Charismatic Renewal in the Mainline Churches in Ghana* (Utrecht, Netherlands: Boekencentrum, 2002).

[16] See Stanley M. Burgess (ed), *Christian Peoples of the Spirit: A Documentary History of Pentecostal Spirituality from the Early Church to the Present* (New York: NYU Press, 2011).

[17] Gordon D. Fee, *Listening to the Spirit in the Text* (Grand Rapids, MI: Eerdmans, 2000), 38-39.

exist between Pentecostal and historic mission denominations in several sub-Saharan African countries has been eroding, as the latter continue to imbibe in, and become increasingly open to, the movement of the Spirit within their own liturgical structures.

Pentecostal Spirituality and the African Imagination

Spirit-empowered Christianity, as I have argued, resonates with traditional modes of being religious, especially African orality and senses of the supernatural and power. African cultures have a strong orientation to that which connects with the supernatural realms of existence. There is, in the African understanding, an unseen/spiritual world beyond the seen/physical world from where power, strength, protection, vitality, meaning, and fulfilment emanate for the living. There is also in the African traditional religious imagination a profound emphasis on the transcendent source of true life and existential salvation. Related to this worldview is the conviction that human beings are not alone in the universe but surrounded by a cloud of witnesses that includes the Supreme Being and other spirit beings whose benevolent help they may seek in times of need. This supernaturalist worldview has many facets that fit into the biblical material, making it easy for African Christians to appreciate resonances between the two worlds.

Additionally, the African traditional religious imagination also includes a deep sense of the human being as finite, weak, limited, and imperfect. Thus, humans stand in need of powers not their own that will not only supply their needs but, more importantly, protect them against the malevolent powers in the world.[18] In this vein, one of the most important traditional symbols of the Akan of Ghana depicts the saying, "*Ewuradze biribi wo sor ma me nsa nka*," meaning "God, there is something in the skies, let me have it." This traditional African universe, as explained by the Ghanaian philosopher Kwame Gyekye, is a spiritual one, in which supernatural beings play a significant role in the thoughts and actions of people – in African philosophical thought, therefore, "what is primarily real is spiritual".[19] This worldview is evident for instance in African warfare prayers, which amount to confrontations between the Spirit-empowered Christian battalions and the unseen forces and presences – principalities and powers in Pauline thought – and their spectacular dramatisation that impresses the psyche. Abimbola Adelakun explains that warfare prayers feature "insurrectional speech, imprecations and declamations" that seek to

---

[18] Kwame Bediako, *Christianity in Africa: The Renewal of a Non-Western Religion* (Edinburgh: Edinburgh University Press, 1995), 94.
[19] Kwame Gyekye, *African Philosophical Thought: The Akan Conceptual Scheme* (Philadelphia, PA: Temple University Press, 1995), 69.

performatively overthrow the supernatural evil powers that work against human and social flourishing.[20]

This fight against the powers of evil is also evident in the structure of a typical Akan (African) libation prayer, as shown by Kwesi Yankah.[21] Here, the officiant invokes the forces of beneficence, observing the Akan religious hierarchy where God is the Supreme Being, followed by Mother Earth, the pantheon of lesser gods, and the ancestors. The message segment of libation often highlights the occasion and purpose of the prayer. This is followed by solicitation, in which the speaker solicits support for the spiritual, moral, and material well-being of the lineage or society. The concluding segment of prayer, *mpae*, is often reserved for the pronouncement of curses on the forces of evil. In similar fashion, as Gornick observes among African immigrant Christians – dominated by the Spirit-empowered – the belief in the efficacy of prayer is joined with "regular and intense fasting", because life is about prayer; "prayer is theology lived, embodied and enacted in daily life".[22] This is, like the Pentecostal-Charismatic universe, also spiritual. In the Pentecostal worldview, that which is spiritual is also very real and active, and the spiritual encroaches daily upon human affairs. Pentecostal prayers in African contexts commonly request the same things that African traditional libation prayers request from deities and ancestors, that is, beneficence from heaven and curses upon enemies. One may question the Christian legitimacy of that, but in the last few decades, a whole prophetic movement has emerged within Spirit-empowered Christianity in Africa claiming to lead a charge against the powers working against the good in human life and society. The theological worldview underlying Spirit-empowered prayer is that God is active in the world, and that the power of the Holy Spirit can render the forces of darkness and evil working against human flourishing as impotent and ineffective. The Holy Spirit anoints the Church also to deal decisively with principalities and powers that hinder holistic Christian living. In the process, certain denominational barriers and inhibitions are overcome, as even non-Pentecostal churches begin to discover and operate in the power of the Spirit.

In Africa, as is being experienced globally, Spirit-empowered Christianity is now very much a form of media religion. In Africa, the Pentecostals dominate the media through televangelism, book and magazine publications, websites, and the uses of social media generally. The outbreak of COVID-19, which was problematised in terms of an "evil virus" unleashed on the world by the devil, brought the aggressive prayer life of Spirit-empowered Christians to the fore. Charismatic personalities and churches mobilised prayer across the continent –

---

[20] Abimbola A. Adelakun, *Powerful Devices: Prayer and the Political Praxis of Spiritual Warfare* (New Brunswick, NJ: Rutgers University Press, 2023), 2.
[21] Kwesi Yankah, *Speaking for the Chief: Okyeame and the Polities of Akan Royal Oratory* (Bloomington, IN: Indiana University Press, 1995), 174.
[22] Gornik, *Word Made Global*, 127.

destroying, cursing, pulling down, and banishing the evil virus from among God's people so that the Church would be released from lockdown to meet again.

The translatability of Pentecostal spirituality, that is, the ease with which the movement settles comfortably into cultures, has served as one of its major ecumenical strengths. Cox, commenting on the global effects of early twentieth-century North American Pentecostal revivals, refers to how the movement "became Russian in Russia, Chilean in Chile [and] African in Africa. [...] [He notes further that] It was a religion made to travel and it seemed to lose nothing in the translation."[23] In the last two decades or so, the number of African charismatic churches has burgeoned in western European cities, underscoring the shift in the centre of gravity of Christianity from the northern to the southern continents. That most of the churches in the Diaspora belong to the Pentecostal-Charismatic stream of Christianity or claim a Spirit-empowered heritage is often missed by those commenting on these developments.

The African churches in question are leading the way in demonstrating true ecumenism in the former heartlands of Christianity by bridging racial gaps. These attempts at reversing Christian mission are the focus of the modem Pentecostal Movement as a religion dedicated to preaching Christ in all nations. Indeed, a strong call has gone out to European churches to abandon their attitudes and feelings of hostility towards their new immigrant compatriots and in grateful joy "perceive the work of the Holy Spirit outside the confines of their own organised pastoral activities, and recognise the genesis of new [African] churches and congregations in European soil as the grace of God".[24] Future generations will be the judge of how well European churches have heeded this challenge from African Pentecostals now living in Europe.

Pentecostals and World Christianity

In world Christianity, Spirit-empowered streams of the faith are often bastardised as aberrations of biblical faith. Early Pentecostal literature speaks of the visible unity of the Church, but this was to occur only on Pentecostal terms because, by putting a strong emphasis on the experience of the Spirit, Spirit-empowered movements draw attention to a dimension of biblical Christianity that is neglected at our peril.[25] There have been mutual suspicions for example between the Spirit-empowered and the advocates of the ecumenical movement all over the world. In Ghana, for example, the historic mission churches operate through

---

[23] Cox, *Fire from Heaven*, 102.
[24] Claudia Wahrisch-Oblau, "We Shall Be Fruitful in This Land: Pentecostal and Charismatic New Mission Churches in Europe", in Andre Droogers, Cornelis van der Laan, and Wout van Laar (eds), *Fruitful in this Land: Pluralism, Dialogue and Healing in Migrant Pentecostalism* (Zoetermeer, Netherlands: Boekencentrum, 2006), 46.
[25] Cecil M. Robeck, "Pentecostals and Ecumenism in a Pluralistic World", in Murray W. Dempster, Byron D. Klaus, and Douglas Petersen (eds), *The Globalization of Pentecostalism: A Religion Made to Travel* (Oxford: Regnum, 1999), 243.

the Christian Council of Ghana, while the Pentecostals operate through two bodies: the Ghana Pentecostal and Charismatic Council and the National Association of Charismatic and Christian Churches. Pentecostals have had suspicions of ecumenism for two reasons: first, the older denominations regarded the Spirit-empowered as unqualified for recognition; and second, people in Pentecostal-Charismatic communities entertained serious objections to the various ecumenical councils as then constituted.[26] The dissociation of classical Pentecostals from bridge-building efforts of Pentecostal ecumenists, such as David du Plessis in the 1960s, serves as a classic example of this suspicion.

The 2005 World Council of Churches (WCC) Conference on World Mission and Evangelism (CWME) in Athens highlighted some of these concerns, as it sought to create space for ecumenical dialogue with Pentecostal-Charismatic Christians (PCCs). The Christians at the CWME sent a letter to the organisers protesting aspects of the programme that did not adequately address their concerns. This letter, signed by at least three Africans, started with a word of appreciation to the WCC for allowing PCCs consideration in the programme: "We have sensed the genuine openness in the leadership of the conference to the potential of Pentecostal contributions to the future of global Christianity." The letter went on to note that: "Pentecostals are often misunderstood, misrepresented, and even unfairly caricaturised."[27]

Pentecost and Gentile Inclusion

Spirit-empowerment, as developments in Africa indicate, is not a denominational agenda. The current spread of Pentecostal-Charismatic Christianity in Africa is reminiscent of the expansion of Christianity from Jewish into Gentile territory, following the missionary enterprise of the Early Church. God's exercise in ecumenism did not only arise from the Day of Pentecost but was also demonstrated in many other ways, including the events that took place at the house of Cornelius (Acts 10). One implication of these developments has to do with the fact that Pentecost is about experiencing the Spirit of God; this experience is not the prerogative of any Christian denomination, ethnic groups, or nationalities. It is noteworthy that, in the house of Cornelius, after being struck by the reality of the ccumenical nature of Pentecost, Peter confesses: "In truth I perceive that God shows no partiality but, in every nation, whoever fears Him and works righteousness is accepted by him" (Acts 10:34-5). Similarly, this truth appears in the words of the Apostle Paul, who went to great lengths to bring this message to the Gentiles: "Christ has redeemed us from the curse of the law [...]

---

[26] Klaude Kendrick, *The Promise Fulfilled: A History of the Modern Pentecostal Movement* (Springfield, MO: Gospel Publishing, 1961), 203-04.
[27] Allan H. Anderson, *An Introduction to Pentecostalism.* Global Charismatic Christianity (Introduction to Religion) (Cambridge: Cambridge University Press, 2004), 335-36.

that the blessing of Abraham might come upon the Gentiles in Christ Jesus, that we might receive the promise of the Spirit through faith" (Gal. 3:13-14). Abraham was the father of nations, and therefore, to inherit the blessing of Abraham means to be adopted as outsiders into the family of God. Given that Christian mission has traditionally been viewed as the West bringing the gospel to Africa, it is instructive to note that at present Africa has overtaken the West in the terms of Christian presence. The rise of Spirit-empowered movements is the single most important evidence of the importance of African Christianity in world Christianity. African immigrants are planting churches in Western Europe. In a sense, this is the fulfilment of prophecy of the outsiders now being incorporated into God's family as beneficiaries of the blessings of Abraham. In the house of the Gentile Centurion, Cornelius, the Pentecost that the disciples of Jesus experienced previously occurred outside Pentecostalism.

The Holy Spirit defied the religious protocols of the time, literally invading Gentile territory, to affirm a global Christian vision of ecumenical proportions. In Acts 11:1-18, the Apostle Peter narrates to his fellow disciples the sequence of events that led him to experience Pentecost with the Gentile Cornelius in Caesarea, and that narrative concludes: "When they heard these things, they became silent; and they glorified God saying, then God has also granted to the Gentiles repentance to life" (Acts 11:18).

This trend has continued, and today some churches are designated Pentecostal because they function in a certain experiential pneumatology. However, the events surrounding Peter's encounter with Cornelius underscores the simple fact that, in God's scheme of things, Pentecost can occur outside Pentecostalism. This is one way to understand the rise of Spirit-empowered movements within Presbyterian, Methodist, Roman Catholic, and Anglican churches in African countries, such as Ghana.

In the early 1920s, the Spirit-empowered experiences of an African Methodist catechist, William Egyanka Appiah, was described as belonging to the occult. He was "firmly ordered [...] to stop all his 'occult practices' completely and at once, as the Methodists were not like that".[28] By this statement, the superintendent minister meant that his catechist was being un-Methodist through his new spirituality. Catechist Appiah felt unable to obey the instructions, and the result was that he and his Faith Society left the Methodist Church of the Gold Coast (Ghana). They decided to meet every Thursday, "to seek the Holy Spirit as the Apostles did".[29] In about 1924, the Fellowship metamorphosed into an independent indigenous "Pentecostal" church, the Mussama Disco Christo Church (MDCC).[30] What the Methodists rejected as "occult practices" at the time were the religious phenomena that give Spirit-empowered ministries their identity, and which in fact are not alien to the Wesleyan Methodist heritage.

---

[28] Baëta, *Prophetism in Ghana*, 35.
[29] Baëta, *Prophetism in Ghana*, 36.
[30] Baëta, *Prophetism in Ghana*, 31-32.

This early twentieth-century account from Ghana serves as an example of many that occurred all over the continent at the time. The account recalls the words of Walter Hollenweger that Pentecostal movements usually begin as "ecumenical movements" within existing historic mission church traditions.[31] Similarly, towards the end of the twentieth century, many young people whose Holy Spirit experiences were considered an aberration to Christian spirituality were thrown out of historic mission denominations. Many started independent charismatic churches, which have grown to become mega-sized churches in urban Africa. They left their previous denominations because their baptism in the Holy Spirit and related experiences were rejected as unbiblical.

A useful example of this situation is the Charismatic Evangelistic Ministry located in Accra. It began as a renewal movement within the Roman Catholic Church on the campus of the University of Ghana. The inability of the hierarchical and liturgically ordered Catholic structure to accommodate the experiential, spiritual, and ecumenical outlook of the new movement led to a break in relations in 1993, culminating in the formation of the Charismatic Evangelistic Ministry. Through such indigenous initiatives in Christian expression, African Christians took their spiritual destinies into their own hands in the formation of independent indigenous churches.

According to Hollenweger, what unites Spirit-empowered churches is not doctrine but religious experience.[32] The phenomenal success of Spirit, particularly in African countries such as Ghana, is largely due to its emphasis on the experience of the Spirit.[33] Pentecostalism has succeeded in Africa because it provides ritual contexts within which people may experience God's presence and power in forceful and demonstrable ways. In Africa, such acts of power for healing, protection of wealth, success and prosperity, and deliverance from activities of witches were traditionally sought from local shrine deities. Spirit-empowered Christianity, with its emphasis on the experience of God's power, now represents, for the same people, Christian alternatives to traditional spiritual resources of supernatural succour.

Spirit-empowerment is now the hallmark of Christianity in Africa. We see its impact in the emergence of mega-sized congregations, the numbers of people subscribing to Pentecostal forms of religious manifestations and impartations in media, the growing public influence of Spirit-empowered leaders, and the sheer transformation of Christianity as a public faith. Our discussion in this chapter is not a novel attempt at pointing to the importance of the nonrational in religion, which is the stock-in-trade of Spirit-empowerment on charismatic Christianity.

---

[31] Walter J. Hollenweger, "From Azusa Street to the Toronto Phenomenon", in Jürgen Moltmann and K. Kuschel (eds), *Pentecostal Movements as an Ecumenical Challenge* (London: SCM, 1996), 6.

[32] Hollenweger, "From Azusa Street to the Toronto Phenomenon", 7.

[33] Kwabena J. Asamoah-Gyadu, "Pentecostalism and the Missiological Significance of Religious Experience", *Trinity Journal of Church and Theology* 12(1 and 2) (2002), 30-57.

In his classic work, *The Idea of the Holy*, Rudolf Otto lamented that the marginalisation of the non-rational aspect of religion by orthodoxy had resulted in the idea of the holy being given a one-sidedly intellectualistic approach: "So far from keeping the non-rational element in religion alive in the heart of the religious experience," Otto writes, "orthodox Christianity manifestly failed to recognise its value, and by this failure gave to the idea of God a one-sidedly intellectualistic and rationalistic interpretation."[34] In a sense, Spirit-empowered Christianity serves as a corrective, an inversion, to the logic of the intellectualistic approach to faith.

Russell Spittler states that whatever else can be said about them, the Pentecostal and Charismatic movements have democratised individual religious experience.[35] Donald Miller picks up the same theme of the centrality of religious experience in Spirit-empowered Christianity, in noting that these new paradigm churches, as he terms them, are changing the way Christianity looks and is experienced.[36] Miller further describes the new paradigm churches as groups which have discarded many of the attributes of establishment religion. Appropriating contemporary cultural forms, these churches have created new genres "of worship music; they are restructuring the organisational character of institutional religion; they are democratising access to the sacred by radicalising the Protestant principle of the priesthood of all believers."[37] In short, they offer people hope and meaning grounded in a transcendent experience of the people.[38]

Pentecost in New Tongues

One way to appreciate the global influence of Pentecostalism is to consider its cardinal theological emphasis of speaking in tongues (glossolalia). Glossolalia is the Spirit-inspired utterance that Pentecostals believe must accompany baptism in the Holy Spirit following conversion. Speaking in tongues plays a very democratising role in worship. The gift of tongues allows people to pray in non-rational meditative language that is not mediated. Certain things remain clear about the experience of glossolalia that have a direct bearing on the democratising nature of Pentecostal spirituality. Tongues is unintelligible speech directed toward God (1 Cor. 14:2, 14-15, 28). The Apostle Paul held in the highest esteem speaking in tongues, as a means of communicating with God. To

---

[34] Rudolf Otto, *The Idea of the Holy* (Oxford: Oxford University Press, 1923), 3.
[35] Spittler, "Corinthian Spirituality", 5-6.
[36] Donald E. Miller, *Reinventing American Protestantism: Christianity in the New Millennium* (Oakland, CA: University of California Press, 1997), 13-16.
[37] Miller, *Reinventing American Protestantism*, 1-2.
[38] Miller, *Reinventing American Protestantism*, 3.

this end, Paul's reference to "inarticulate groaning too deep for words" (Rom. 8:26) must be understood as referring primarily to glossolalia.[39]

One clearly senses that we are in profound moments in Pentecostal worship when people sing in tongues. Singing in the Spirit during worship, which invariably means "singing in tongues" can lift both the singer and the listeners to another level of spiritual experience.[40] It is at once a subduing, uplifting, overwhelming, and edifying experience that makes the presence of God palpable when it occurs during worship. The phenomenon changes the atmosphere of worship to the extent that the very presence of the living God becomes real.

Tom Smail describes the phenomenon of singing in the Spirit in the context of worship as a form of collective religious experience that by-passes the rational faculties.[41] Singing in the Spirit reminds us that alongside the praise of the renewed mind comes the praise of the renewed heart that when, evoked by the Spirit, expresses not simply our superficial feelings, but engages the deep primal emotions at the hidden centre of our being in our self-offering to the living God.[42] The experience escapes from a complicated conceptuality and a second dependence on such liturgical resources as prayer books and hymn books and responds in immediacy and freedom to the contact with the living Lord that the Spirit makes possible and, in joyous serenity, rejoices and mediates upon his poured-out grace and his revealed glory.[43]

Smail's description of speaking in tongues echoes the view of the Apostle Paul: "For if I pray in a tongue, my spirit prays, but my understanding is unfruitful" (1 Cor. 14:14). The expression "unfruitful" implies that the human intellect in this kind of ecstatic praying lies dormant contributing nothing to the process of articulating thoughts into words. Martin suggests that in enraptured fellowship with God, when the human spirit is in such deep, hidden communion with the divine Spirit, that words, arising from broken utterances sourced from within our secret selves, are actually formed by spiritual upsurge without mental effort.[44]

Because glossolalia bypasses the rational faculties and makes possible free access to the living God, it cannot be colonised within any Christian tradition;

---

[39] Frank D. Macchia, "Sighs Too Deep for Words: Toward a Theology of Glossolalia", *Journal of Pentecostal Theology* 1(1) (1992), 47-73 [Available at: https://doi.org/10.1177/096673699200100105] [Last accessed: 21st March 2024].
[40] Kwabena J. Asamoah-Gyadu, "Signs of the Spirit: Worship as Experience in African Pentecostalism", *Journal of African Christian Thought* 8(2) (December 2005b), 17-24.
[41] Tom Smail, "In Spirit and in Truth: Reflections on Charismatic Worship", in Tom Smail, A. Walker, and N. Wright (eds), *Charismatic Renewal* (London: SPCK, 1995), 109-10.
[42] Smail, "In Spirit and in Truth", 109-10.
[43] Smail, "In Spirit and in Truth", 109-10.
[44] Ralph M. Martin, "Aspects of Worship in I Corinthians 14:1-25", in Cecil M. Robeck (ed), *Charismatic Experiences in Christian History* (Peabody, MA: Hendrickson, 1985), 74.

precisely for this reason, glossolalia can have a strong and profound democratising significance for Spirit-empowered Christians worldwide. The worshipful acts of speaking, praying, and speaking in tongues amount to an inclusive experience in the Spirit which makes the marginalised and despised feel a sense of belonging when it comes Spirit empowerment. Historically, Western mission Christianity became paradigmatic of biblical faith; the reversal of the Tower of Babel experience means that what has happened within African Christianity with the experience of the Spirit cannot be dismissed as an aberration of what happens elsewhere in the world.

Pentecost: God's Empowering Presence

The experience of the Holy Spirit, as Gordon Fee would have it, amounts to encountering God empowering presence.[45] The Holy Spirit is God's empowering presence. The empowering effect of God the Holy Spirit is evident, through glossolalic experiences because, as Paul says, "We do not know how to pray so the Spirit helps us in our weakness" (Rom. 8:26). This is so that, against the backdrop of limited human speech and comprehension, the Spirit-empowered are enabled to speak mysteries to God in prayer. John V. Taylor's *The Go Between God: The Holy Spirit and the Christian Mission* appeared at a time when it was clear that the "death of God" prophets of the 1960s had been proven false. The book drew attention to the Holy Spirit as a neglected factor in Christian mission.[46] Taylor referred to the Holy Spirit as "the chief actor in the historic mission of the Christian church," noting that "the marching orders" for Christian mission and "the gift of the Holy Spirit come in the same package."[47]

There is a non-negotiable connection between the reception of power through the presence of the Holy Spirit and the ability to witness. According to the Latin American Pentecostal theologian, Juan Sepúlveda,[48] the constitutive act of the Pentecostal Movement is the offer of a direct and particularly intense encounter with God that makes possible a profound change in the life of the person who experiences it. The reference to the Holy Spirit relates fundamentally to the direct character of the encounter. Through the Holy Spirit, God makes himself directly accessible to the believer who seeks him, thus destroying the necessity of every kind of external priestly mediation.

In the contemporary Western Church, this supernatural dimension in the mission of the Church has been gravely downplayed in Christian ministry, and

---

[45] Gordon D. Fee, *God's Empowering Presence: The Holy Spirit in the Letters of Paul* (Peabody, MA: Hendrickson, 1994).
[46] John V. Taylor, *The Go Between God: The Holy Spirit and the Christian Mission* (London: SCM, 1972).
[47] Taylor, *Go Between God*, 34.
[48] Juan Sepúlveda, "Reflections on the Pentecostal Contribution to the Mission of the Church in Latin America", *Journal of Pentecostal Theology* 1(1) (1992), 100 [Available at: https://doi.org/10.1177/096673699200100107] [Last accessed: 21st March 2024].

the results have been an anaemic Christianity and empty chapel buildings. Wherever Christianity is succeeding, such as in Africa, it is doing so because the Holy Spirit, God's empowering presence, remains active. In emphasising the experience of the Holy Spirit as essential to Christian identity and mission, the various streams of Spirit-empowered movements identify the critical element in the mission of the Church. By the common experience of the Holy Spirit, Africans now come to belong because it is the single most important proof that God's visitation does not defer to or privilege any single geographical source or people.

Earlier on in this chapter, I referred to the use of media in the globalisation of Pentecostalism. One of the ways in which Spirit empowerment is mediated is through a shared genre of music. A close relationship exists between music and religious experience. The informal, affective, and expressive nature of Pentecostal meetings, facilitated by music, demonstrates that worship requires more than cognitive assent.[49] Praise and worship of God, Poloma asserts, is believed to be the medium through which the presence of God is made manifest.[50] God does indeed inhabit the praises of his people (Ps. 22:3).

Cox cites music as one of the reasons for the quick diffusion of Pentecostal Christianity globally. Music is not used by Pentecostals merely as an embellishment to worship but as the wavelength on which the message is carried.[51] There is no doubting Cox's claim that music is integral rather than peripheral to Pentecostal worship.[52] Indeed, music is the heartbeat of Pentecostal religiosity and, through this medium, it has most affected non-Pentecostal liturgies. Music plays a critical role in the therapeutic and edifying process of Spirit-empowered worship, observable in African settings. In many of the local Pentecostal-Charismatic choruses, the Holy Spirit, *Sunsum Kronkron,* comes to work among God's people when they gather for worship. In one song, He brings *ayaresa* [healing] *ogyee* [deliverance], and *emuonyam* [glory], to those who wait upon Him.

Another local Pentecostal chorus depicts the Holy Spirit in keeping with biblical images of Him as *ogya* [fire], *mframa* [wind], and *adom nsu* [water of life]. As fire he purifies, as wind he fills, and as living water he restores life to dry deserts and lands, resulting from drought. African Pentecostals worship in expectation that during the singing and prayer, the Holy Spirit will visit, and people can encounter His presence. This mode of religious expression appeals greatly to African religious sensibilities because of its experiential and therapeutic nature.

---

[49] Margaret Poloma, *Mainstream Mystics: The Toronto Blessing and Reviving Pentecostalism* (New York: Altamira, 2003), 41.
[50] Poloma, *Mainstream Mystics*, 41.
[51] Cox, *Fire from Heaven*, 121.
[52] Cox, *Fire from Heaven*, 122.

Conclusion

We cannot talk about Christianity in Africa today without acknowledging its Spirit-empowered streams. In Pentecostalism, says Miller, we are witnessing a second reformation, transforming people who will experience Christianity in this millennium. The Pentecostal reformation challenges the medium through which the message of Christianity is articulated.[53] In Africa, where Pentecostalism has become the representative face of Christianity, Allan H. Anderson also speaks of the situation as an *African Reformation*.[54]

This reformation is thoroughly experiential in character and experientially democratising in orientation because it is not bound by denominational bureaucracy and the restraint of religious tradition. Spirit-empowered Christianity represented by Pentecostalism is not only a faith of the present but also the Christianity of the future. Its greatest strength is its emphasis on Christianity as an *experience* or *encounter* with a living God who revealed himself in Jesus Christ and, at Pentecost, poured himself out on the Church.[55]

Right from its biblical origins in the prophecy of Joel through to the promise of the Spirit after the resurrection of Christ and its fulfilment on the Day of Pentecost, Spirit-empowered Christianity has been thoroughly infectious in its effects. Spirit empowerment offers a form of religion not defined by denominational boundaries. In other words, this spirituality is not denomination-specific but an experience that people can encounter inside and outside of denominational, ethnic, social, geographical, economic, and political boundaries.

Pentecost, unlike Babel, was a divine action in which God reached out to all flesh by the outpouring of His Spirit. While the Tower of Babel created confusion and dispersion of nations, Pentecost announces the possibility of a new unity among people. This unity, which transcends linguistic and ethnic differences and gives communal value to the individual emotional experience, transforms Spirit-empowered Christianity into the greatest expression of religious communication. Wherever it is found today, Pentecostalism breaks down rigid traditional ecclesiastic structures and joins the secular, modem world, reaching out in all languages to all peoples and nations.[56]

To celebrate Pentecost is not to recall an event locked in time and space but rather to participate in a continuing festival ever more mysterious, frightening,

---

[53] Miller, *Reinventing American Protestantism*, 11.
[54] Allan H. Anderson, *African Reformation: African Initiated Christianity in the 20th Century* (Trenton, NJ: Africa World Press, 2001).
[55] Amos Yong, *The Spirit Poured Out on All Flesh: Pentecostalism and the Possibility of Global Theology* (Grand Rapids, MI: Baker Academic, 2005).
[56] Waldo Cesar, *From Babel to Pentecost: A Social-Historical-Theological Study of the Growth of Pentecostalism* (Bloomington, IN: Indiana University Press, 2001), 31-32.

and wonderful than we could ever imagine.[57] Rather than allowing denominational inclinations to divide us, each one of us should remain open to the empowerment of the Spirit, sincerely desiring his gifts, so that when God reaches out to us, we can recognise His presence wherever we meet. For in Christ, as the Apostle Paul tells the Church at Ephesus, we "also are being built together for a dwelling place or God in the Spirit" (Eph. 2:22).

Bibliography

Adelakun, Abimbola A. *Powerful Devices: Prayer and the Political Praxis of Spiritual Warfare*. New Brunswick, NJ: Rutgers University Press, 2023.

Anderson, Allan H. *African Reformation: African Initiated Christianity in the 20th Century*. Trenton, NJ: Africa World Press, 2001.

———. *An Introduction to Pentecostalism*. Global Charismatic Christianity (Introduction to Religion). Cambridge: Cambridge University Press, 2004.

Asamoah-Gyadu, Kwabena J. *African Charismatics: A Study of Independent Indigenous Pentecostalism in Ghana*. Leiden: Brill, 2005a.

———. "Pentecostalism and the Missiological Significance of Religious Experience", *Trinity Journal of Church and Theology* 12(1 and 2), (2002), 30-57.

———. *Sighs and Signs of the Spirit: Ghanaian Perspectives on Pentecostalism and Renewal in Africa*. Regnum Studies in Mission. Minneapolis, MN: Fortress Press, 2015.

———. "Signs of the Spirit: Worship as Experience in African Pentecostalism", *Journal of African Christian Thought* 8(2), (December 2005b), 17-24.

Baëta, Christian G. *Prophetism in Ghana: A Study of Some Spiritual Churches*. London: SCM, 1962.

Bediako, Kwame. *Christianity in Africa: The Renewal of a Non-Western Religion*. Edinburgh: Edinburgh University Press, 1995.

Burgess, Stanley M., Ed. *Christian Peoples of the Spirit: A Documentary History of Pentecostal Spirituality from the Early Church to the Present*. New York: NYU Press, 2011.

Cesar, Waldo. *From Babel to Pentecost: A Social-Historical-Theological Study of the Growth of Pentecostalism*. Bloomington, IN: Indiana University Press, 2001.

Cox, Harvey. *Fire from Heaven: The Rise of Pentecostal Spirituality and the Reshaping of Religion in the Twenty-first Century*. Reading, PA: Addison-Wesley, 1995.

---

[57] Wout van Laar, "Introduction: It's Time to Get to Know Each Other", in Andre Droogers, Cornelis van der Laan, and Wout van Laar (eds), *Fruitful in this Land: Pluralism, Dialogue and Healing in Migrant Pentecostalism* (Zoetermeer, Netherlands: Boekencentrum, 2006), 14.

Dempster, Murray W., Byron D. Klaus, and Douglas Petersen, Eds. *The Globalization of Pentecostalism: A Religion Made to Travel.* Carlisle, UK: Paternoster, 1999.

Droogers, André. "The Normalization of Religious Experience: Healing, Prophecy, Dreams, and Visions", In K. Poewe, Eds. *Charismatic Christianity as a Global Culture.* Columbia, SC: University of South Carolina Press, 1994: 33-49.

Fee, Gordon D. *God's Empowering Presence: The Holy Spirit in the Letters of Paul.* Peabody, MA: Hendrickson, 1994.

——. *Listening to the Spirit in the Text.* Grand Rapids, MI: Eerdmans, 2000.

Gifford, Paul. *African Christianity: Its Public Role.* London: Hurst, 1998.

Gornik, Mark R. *Word Made Global: Stories of African Christianity in New York City.* Grand Rapids, MI: William B. Eerdmans, 2011.

Gyekye, Kwame. *An Essay on African Philosophical Thought: The Akan Conceptual Scheme.* Philadelphia, PA: Temple University Press, 1995.

Hollenweger, Walter J. *The Pentecostals: The Charismatic Movement in the Churches.* London: SCM, 1972.

——. "From Azusa Street to the Toronto Phenomenon", In Jürgen Moltmann and K. Kuschel, Eds. *Pentecostal Movements as an Ecumenical Challenge.* London: SCM, 1996: 3-14.

——. *Pentecostalism: Origins and Developments Worldwide.* Peabody, MA: Hendrickson, 1997.

Johns, Cheryl Bridges. "What Can the Mainline Churches Learn from Pentecostals about Pentecost?" In Andre Droogers, Cornelis van der Laan, and Wout van Laar, Eds. *Fruitful in the Land: Pluralism, Dialogue and Healing in Migrant Pentecostalism.* Zoetemeer, Netherlands: Boekencentrum, 2006: 93-99.

Kalu, Ogbu U. *African Pentecostalism: An Introduction.* Oxford: Oxford University Press, 2008.

Kendrick, Klaude. *The Promise Fulfilled: A History of the Modern Pentecostal Movement.* Springfield, MO: Gospel Publishing, 1961.

Macchia, Frank D. "Sighs Too Deep for Words: Toward a Theology of Glossolalia", *Journal of Pentecostal Theology* 1(1), (1992), 47-73. [Available at: https://doi.org/10.1177/096673699200100105] [Last accessed: 21st March 2024].

Martin, Ralph M. "Aspects of Worship in I Corinthians 14:1-25", In Cecil M. Robeck, Eds. *Charismatic Experiences in Christian History.* Peabody, MA: Hendrickson, 1985: pp 66-73

Miller, Donald E. *Reinventing American Protestantism: Christianity in the New Millennium.* Oakland, CA: University of California Press, 1997.

Omenyo, Cephas N. *Pentecost outside Pentecostalism: A Study of the Development of Charismatic Renewal in the Mainline Churches in Ghana.* Utrecht, Netherlands: Boekencentrum, 2002.

Otto, Rudolf. *The Idea of the Holy.* Oxford: Oxford University Press, 1923.

Phiri, Isabel. "President Frederick J.T. Chiluba of Zambia: The Christian Nation and Democracy", *Journal of Religion in Africa* 33(4), (2003), 401-28.

Poloma, Margaret. *Mainstream Mystics: The Toronto Blessing and Reviving Pentecostalism*. New York: Altamira, 2003.

Robeck, Cecil M. "Pentecostals and Ecumenism in a Pluralistic World", In Murray W. Dempster, Byron D. Klaus, and Douglas Petersen, Eds. *The Globalization of Pentecostalism: A Religion Made to Travel*. Oxford: Regnum, 1999: 338-62.

Sepúlveda, Juan. "Reflections on the Pentecostal Contribution to the Mission of the Church in Latin America", *Journal of Pentecostal Theology* 1(1), (1992), 93-108. [Available at: https://doi.org/10.1177/096673699200100107] [Last accessed: 21st March 2024].

Smail, Tom. "In Spirit and in Truth: Reflections on Charismatic Worship", In Tom Smail, A. Walker, and N. Wright, Eds. *Charismatic Renewal*. London: SPCK, 1995: 109-10.

Spittler, Russell P. "Corinthian Spirituality: How a Flawed Anthropology Imperils Authentic Christian Experience", In Edith Blumhofer, Russell P. Spittler, and Grant Wacker, Eds. *Pentecostal Currents in American Protestantism*. Chicago, IL: University of Illinois Press, 1999: 3-19.

Taylor, John V. *The Go Between God: The Holy Spirit and the Christian Mission*. London: SCM, 1972.

van Laar, Wout. "Introduction: It's Time to Get to Know Each Other", In Andre Droogers, Cornelis van der Laan, and Wout van Laar, Eds. *Fruitful in this Land: Pluralism, Dialogue and Healing in Migrant Pentecostalism*. Zoetermeer, Netherlands: Boekencentrum, 2006: 133-45.

Wahrisch-Oblau, Claudia. "We Shall Be Fruitful in This Land: Pentecostal and Charismatic New Mission Churches in Europe", In Andre Droogers, Cornelis van der Laan, and Wout van Laar, Eds. *Fruitful in this Land: Pluralism, Dialogue and Healing in Migrant Pentecostalism*. Zoetermeer, Netherlands: Boekencentrum, 2006: 32-46.

Yankah, Kwesi. *Speaking for the Chief: Okyeame and the Polities of Akan Royal Oratory*. Bloomington, IN: Indiana University Press, 1995.

Yong, Amos. *The Spirit Poured Out on All Flesh: Pentecostalism and the Possibility of Global Theology*. Grand Rapids, MI: Baker Academic, 2005.

10. Spirit Empowered Women: Why and How the Full Participation of Women in Spirit Empowered Ministry Strengthens Global Christianity

Jacqueline Grey

Introduction

This chapter explores why and how the full participation of women in ministry remains crucial for the flourishing of the global Church. First, I address why a biblical vision for the contribution of women proves essential, and what that vision might look like. In many contexts of global Christianity today, women experience exclusion from key leadership roles and thereby from full participation in church ministry. Yet, imagine the positive impact on the global Church if women were fully released into Spirit-empowered ministry. Second, to envision what this could look like necessitates a return to the Early Church. Using the example of Romans 16, I retrieve biblical models for women's leadership. In this passage, Paul promotes the public ministry of Phoebe and commends Priscilla, among various other women. He emphasises these women as gifted, honourable, and hard-working. Paul's emphasis on their good reputation acts as a mechanism by which they could exercise influence and pursue leadership opportunities in a culture that often restricted women from the public sphere. The women in Romans 16 turned this cultural challenge into an opportunity to pursue the ministries for which God had called and gifted them. With these examples in mind, I conclude by considering some practical suggestions to assist contemporary women, particularly in the Majority World.

Why Is Participation of Women Needed?

Considering mechanisms for releasing women in ministry requires first being convinced that women are necessary for the flourishing of the church. *Why* is the full participation of women in ministry crucial for the global Church? Of course, women are necessary. Who else will clean the toilets and provide hospitality? No doubt the church needs women's ministries for the many tasks that keep Christian communities operational. But is the *full* participation of women in all activities and levels of ministry – including leadership – truly needed and wanted? Why is the full participation of women in ministry crucial? I offer here three key arguments why women remain central for the flourishing of the global Church: first, because women and men were created to work together; second, the Bible models women's ministry and leadership; and third, Spirit-empowerment is for daughters as well as sons.

God Created Women and Men to Work Together

In Genesis 1, God created men and women in his image and gave them the task of stewarding the earth together (Gen. 1:26-28). Carolyn Custis James refers to this creational design of men and women ministering together as a "Blessed Alliance".[1] God blessed them to be fruitful and gave them both the shared responsibility to act as God's caretakers of creation. This role of stewardship rested on the foundation of their shared nature as God's image bearers. In ministering together in loving relationship to serve the needs of the world, men and women together best reflect the image of the triune God. God designed for women and men to work together in unity towards the flourishing of the earth and human communities.

Similarly, the narrative of Genesis 2 begins with the man (*ish*) placed in the Garden as its caretaker. However, God recognised that it was not good for the man to be alone; no individual is intended to stay independent of community. We need one another. As a solution, God made the woman (*ishah*). The woman was not created to function as the man's assistant. God presented her to the man as *ezer kennedo*, which refers to someone comparable or equal to the man, to serve with him.[2] The text describes the man and woman as uniting together to become one (Gen. 2:23-24). Genesis 2 reinforces God's original design of women and men working together. Of course, sin has broken this creational design and alienated human community. Humanity chose (and so often continues to choose) autonomy and independence. Too often we think we don't need God or each other. Yet, in turning to God, we acknowledge our total dependence on him. As part of the family of God, we also recognise our bond with, and reliance on, one another as brothers and sisters in Christ. Although we live in a world broken by sin, including social structures that have distorted this blessed alliance, God has purposed for men and women to live in unity and minister together. Only human sin and brokenness subjugates one person over another based on gender or ethnicity, such as the development of the patriarchal culture described but not prescribed in the Bible.[3] Instead, for Christians, "There is neither Jew nor Gentile, neither slave nor free, nor is there male and female, for you are all one in Christ Jesus" (Gal. 3:28).[4]

---

[1] Carolyn Custis James, *Half the Church: Recapturing God's Global Vision for Women* (Grand Rapids, MI: Zondervan, 2010), 137.
[2] Alice Mathews, *Gender Roles and the People of God: Rethinking What We Were Taught about Men and Women in the Church* (Grand Rapids, MI: Zondervan, 2017), 39.
[3] Mathews, *Gender Roles*, 93.
[4] All Scripture quotations, unless otherwise noted, come from the New International Version.

The Bible Models Women's Ministry and Leadership

Throughout the Bible, we see examples of women empowered by the Holy Spirit for their God-given task. So often God unexpectedly used people of low social status, such as women, to do his remarkable and Spirit-empowered work. We see God speak through female prophets, such as Miriam and Huldah. We see women courageously speak truth to power, including Hannah and Abigail. These women ministered as agents of change. We see a female judge, Deborah. We see Queen Esther making and implementing decisions at national level. These types of roles and activities were not normally open to women in the cultural context of the ancient world, yet God empowered these women by his Holy Spirit to act in counter-cultural ways to do his work of ministry and leadership. These female ministers and leaders were known for their integrity, strength, and good character. Yet these few examples in the Old Testament serve only as a signpost of what God would do at Pentecost when he would pour out his Spirit on his sons and daughters together.

Spirit Empowerment is for Daughters and Sons

God's vision for his daughters and sons in each community across the globe is for the Holy Spirit to empower them for the flourishing of the Church and God's work in the world. In fact, this was the purpose of Pentecost. The Book of Acts records how Jesus promised the gift of the Holy Spirit to empower believers for mission (Acts 1:4-5; 8). Luke highlights the presence of female disciples alongside the apostles expectantly awaiting the promise of the Spirit (v. 14). When the Holy Spirit was poured out on the Day of Pentecost, these disciples were all together in one place (2:1). Both women and men received the Holy Spirit equally and were initiated for ministry. Peter adopted the words of the prophet Joel to articulate this new thing God was doing:

> In the last days, God says,
> I will pour out my Spirit on all people.
> Your sons and daughters will prophesy,
> your young men will see visions,
> your old men will dream dreams.
> Even on my servants, both men and women,
> I will pour out my Spirit in those days,
> and they will prophesy (Acts 2:17-18).

At Pentecost, the Spirit empowered both daughters and sons for ministry. Joel's promise of the blessed alliance of men and women working together in unity was realised at the birth of the Church. This empowerment of the Holy Spirit did not end at Pentecost or with the apostles but continued through the Early Church period and up to the church today. Therefore, Pentecost provides a paradigm and model for ministry in which the old walls of division that alienated human community – walls of gender, ethnicity, and social class – are torn down.[5] What follows in the Book of Acts and the letters of the New Testament are countless examples of women empowered by the Holy spirit ministering in all different activities and levels of leadership in the Early Church.

What Spirit-Filled Women Did in the New Testament

This next section explores some examples of women in the New Testament that model for us the blessed alliance of men and women working together in ministry. I focus on the roles and activities of two women commended by Paul in Romans 16: Phoebe and Priscilla. However, in addition to exploring the Spirit-empowered gifting of these women to minister and lead, I also observe how Paul promoted their excellence of character and diligence. This focus remains important when considering the implications of these biblical models for the promotion of female ministers in the Majority World.

As a backdrop, we need to understand the culture of the Graeco-Roman world in which the New Testament Church was birthed. It is identified as an honour-shame culture. In such cultures, including many today, clear boundaries exist between the public and private spheres, as well as expectations regarding gendered roles in those spaces. Mostly, women cannot participate in the public sphere, with some exceptions for wealthy and socially elite women.[6] Generally, however, women must adhere to a strict code of moral behaviour and maintain their reputation as virtuous to ensure the family's honour.[7] So what does Romans 16 tells us about how the New Testament women navigated this honour-shame culture to engage in public ministry?

It was standard practice in the Graeco-Roman world to conclude a letter with a list of greetings and commendations. As Nijay Gupta observes, this list is "the kind of thing we might just skip over when reading this weighty letter, like the closing credits of a movie."[8] Yet, Paul's list of commendations in Romans 16 reveals much data to us about men and women working together in the Early Church.[9] In this list, we see that Paul refers to a total of twenty-six people, including ten women, with the names of the women and men all mixed in together. He also often refers to the men and women in the same way. Gupta

---

[5] Melissa L. Archer, "Women in Ministry: A Pentecostal Reading of New Testament Texts", in Margaret English de Alminana and Lois E. Olena, Eds. *Women in Pentecostal and Charismatic Ministry: Informing Dialogue on Gender, Church, and Ministry*, vol. 21 of Global Pentecostal and Charismatic Studies, series editors William K. Kay and Mark Cartledge (Leiden: Brill, 2016), 37-38.
[6] See Susan E. Hylen, *Women in the New Testament World* (Oxford: Oxford University Press, 2019).
[7] Julia Pizzuto-Pomaco, *From Shame to Honor: Mediterranean Women in Romans 16* (Lexington, KY: Emeth Press, 2017), 99.
[8] Nijay K. Gupta, *Tell Her Story: How Women Led, Taught, and Ministered in the Early Church* (Downers Grove, IL: InterVarsity Press, 2023), 4.
[9] Gupta, *Tell Her Story*, 4.

suggests then that "Paul did not treat women differently than men when it came to church ministry and leadership."[10] Paul publicly honoured both his female and male co-workers as model leaders.

Phoebe tops the head of this list of commendations in Romans 16. Paul begins with commending Phoebe because she functions as the courier of this letter to the Roman Church on behalf of Paul. Yet, this role involved more than just a personalised postal service. Phoebe served as Paul's ambassador. The role as letter-bearer required Phoebe to read Paul's letter to the Church in Rome, answer any questions local church leaders and members had about the contents of the letter, and respond on behalf of Paul. This required Phoebe to stay in Rome and receive their hospitality. Her credentials, cited by Paul, emphasise her competency to act as his representative. Paul entrusted the transportation and explanation of the Book of Romans – often considered his masterpiece – to a woman. Her role as letter-bearer also points to her strength of character. That she would travel to Rome, using her own resources and going at her own personal risk, points to her courage and self-sacrificial nature.

In terms of Phoebe's credentials, Paul commends her for her relational, ministry, and leadership roles. She is a sister, deacon, and benefactor. As a sister in the Lord, Phoebe had a close, trusted, relational connection to Paul. Interestingly, no reference occurs regarding her marital status or her natural family, but the emphasis remains on her status as part of God's family. Paul also recognises Phoebe for her key leadership role in her hometown of Cenchreae (located next to Corinth). Paul honours her as a "deacon," which means "servant"; a title Paul also uses of himself (see 1 Cor. 3:5; 2 Cor. 6:4). Since Paul emphasises the importance of Spirit-gifting for ministers in the church, notably in 1 Corinthians 12, we can assume that Phoebe also evidenced the gifting of the Holy Spirit in her ministry as a deacon. This term *deacon* seems to develop later in the Early Church as an actual title for leaders in the Christian community. In fact, 1 Timothy 3:8-13 outlines the qualifications for and expectations of a deacon, including "being worth of respect" (v. 8). While the passage in 1 Timothy assumes most deacons were male, clearly women like Phoebe also functioned in this type of leadership role.

The final qualification of Phoebe that Paul mentions in Romans 16 is that she served as a benefactor to many, including him. To function as a patron suggests that Phoebe had wealth and status in the community. Yet, she used this wealth and status to benefit others. Overall, Romans 16 demonstrates that Paul promotes Phoebe to the Church in Rome and endorses her ministry. The text upholds her as a Spirit-gifted minister of the gospel of Jesus Christ and describes her – like many of the women of the Old Testament – as a woman of strength and noble character.

The second person Paul names in Romans 16 is Priscilla, along with her husband Aquila. Unusually, Paul here lists Priscilla's name before her husbands

---

[10] Gupta, *Tell Her Story*, 98-99.

in his greeting. In fact, in four out of the six references to this couple (Acts 18:2, 18, 19, 26; Rom. 16:3; 1 Cor. 16:19; 2 Tim. 4:19), Priscilla's name is deliberately mentioned first. Scholars generally agree that Paul lists Priscilla first because she had a more prominent ministry role than Aquila through her well-known gift of teaching. Paul did not reinforce hierarchy based on gender or social status, but highlighted Priscilla as a model for ministry. He describes this wife-husband team as "my co-workers" (Rom. 16:3), a term he uses for close colleagues in ministry.[11] Paul then describes his gratitude for this couple because they had risked their lives for him. We don't know the circumstances of the event to which Paul refers, but it points to their courage, self-sacrifice, and humility. This couple, known for their Spirit-gifting and character, also led a house-church in Rome. Priscilla and Aquila were clearly held in high esteem by Paul, the Church in Rome, and believers elsewhere.

While Paul commends many more women and men in Romans 16, space does not allow for a full exploration of their merits. We can note, however, that Paul endorses the ministries of women, men, couples, families, and singles. Andronicus and Junia, most likely a married couple (like Priscilla and Aquila), had been imprisoned with Paul. This couple were at the vanguard of ministry and persecuted for their faith. Paul endorsed both husband and wife as "outstanding among the apostles" (16:7). Others in the list are commended for their hard work, resilience, and motherly care of Paul. In fact, Paul repeats the praise of many of the Romans 16 women as being "women who work hard in the Lord" (v. 12). Yet, what stands out in this list is that the men and women worked together for the gospel and flourishing of the church in the blessed alliance. Women in the Early Church functioned in all roles according to their gifts and calling, together with the men.

While other sections in NT letters seem to limit the roles of women, these must be read in the light of Paul's actions and attitudes towards women highlighted here. For Paul, the gospel and health of the church remained the priority. Therefore, to advance the gospel may have required some women in particular contexts to limit their freedom and activities. This meant that the behaviour of Christian women (and men) would need to stay consistent with the culture in which they lived while maintaining Christian values. As Cynthia Long Westfall notes, Paul's intentions were for "believers to fit into the culture while remaining ethically pure."[12] Therefore, Paul encouraged the Corinthians to think of themselves as slaves to everyone to win as many as possible to the gospel (1 Cor. 9:19). Therefore, as described in 1 Corinthians 11:2-16, if some women had to limit their freedom by wearing headscarves to ensure that the gospel would not be held in disrepute, then Paul thought they should wear the headscarf. Similarly, if some unlearned women had questions that disrupted the church

---

[11] Other examples include Romans 16:9, 16, 21; 2 Corinthians 8:23.

[12] Cynthia Long Westfall, *Paul and Gender: Reclaiming the Apostle's Vision for Men and Women in Christ* (Grand Rapids, MI: Baker Academic, 2016), 13.

service, as described in 1 Corinthians 14:6-40, then Paul instructed them to wait and ask their husbands at home to ensure order in the church but still allowing the women to learn. Or, if some uneducated women who had accepted wrong teaching had to be silent and learn, as was the situation with the woman in 1 Timothy 2:12, then they should get educated and learn as students.

However, the seeming restrictions of women's activities noted above had to do with particular situations in local churches at that time. They were not universal commands. Instead, all believers, women and men, must live worthy of the gospel to which God has called us (Eph. 4:1). Paul – counter-cultural in many ways as demonstrated in his commendations of Phoebe and Priscilla – would not have promoted these two women unless they were known as honourable women. However, when it came to his mission, Paul wanted women and men to ensure that their behaviour did not hinder the advancement of the gospel. While Paul promoted the full participation of women, the promotion of the gospel came first. Yet, he did not want the full resources of the church and the gifting of women to go untapped.

So, what can we learn from Phoebe to help release women for ministry in the global church today? We can learn that both character and gifting remain essential for women operating in the cultural context of an honour-shame culture. Many women in the Majority World also live in this type of context. For many years, I lived and worked in Izmir, Turkey. I experienced that honour-shame culture, albeit as an outsider, and the difficulties navigating it. Therefore, learning from these models of women in Romans 16 can also help women navigate leadership and ministry in their own contexts today.

How We Can Release the Full Participation of Women in Spirit-Empowered Ministry?

What would the global Church look like if gifted and called women were released into the fullness of their ministry potential? What would the global Church look like if space was made for godly women to lead, speak, and minister like Phoebe? What would the global Church look like today if men in our world acted like Paul – commending godly women in their communities and promoting their ministry? To do so would require that courageous men share space at the table, trusting that room enough exists for everyone. God's vision for his daughters and sons in each community across this globe is for the Holy Spirit to empower them for the flourishing of the Church and for his work in the world. Yet, while God's vision is universal, it is not universal in application but must find its outworking in the specifics of geography, culture, and context. Two simple mechanisms can help release Spirit-gifted women into their full potential and full participation in the global Church – male champions and a good reputation.

Male Champions Are Necessary

As evidenced in Romans 16, Paul championed many women in his sphere of influence. He identified women such as Phoebe and Priscilla as both gifted and of good reputation. Paul publicly named women as his co-workers and leaders in the Early Church. He promoted these women and commended them to others. Paul, despite many misconceptions about him, championed women. While few formal titles existed in the Early Church and no official ordination, we could ask: if Paul was around today, would he have ordained Phoebe? We speculate, but based on his comments in Romans 16, I think Paul would. This is one significant way that male leaders can champion women. They can look for the call and gifts of ministry on a woman's life and encourage those giftings. Giftings evidenced in one person's life may look different to those evidenced in another person. For example, a leadership gift in a woman might look and be expressed differently to a leadership gift in a man, yet both have the same outcome of influencing others. Phoebe was very different to Paul. Paul was a male Jew. Phoebe was a female Gentile. Yet, Paul could look beyond these differences to see her gifts and strength of character and promote her ministry to others.

Having an official position and formal title in the church or Christian organisation gives women agency to lead and influence others in cultural contexts that do not normally accept women as leaders. The same proves true for official endorsement of women by male pastors. This is also another way men (or powerholders) can champion women: give public recognition of their gifts and ministries in congregational and denominational meetings.[13] This sponsorship and promotion of women gives confidence to other ministers that this person is trustworthy and has a valuable ministry. Similarly, men can bring women into their networks for ministry. Brothers in Christ, like Paul, can help women identify their calling and Spirit-empowered giftings. Men should seek to mentor women and nurture the development of their sisters with the goal of seeing male and female leaders carry out God's mission together. To do this requires that men open doors of ministry to women, as they often function as the gate keepers. It is not enough to say, "Women just need to rise up." How can women step into the room if the doors are locked, with men holding the key?

The Importance of a Good Reputation

Women do have agency. The question remains how to identify their opportunities. In many contexts of an honour-shame culture, a key mechanism for women to be released into ministry is having a good reputation in the community. This is true for men as well but vital for female leaders in many cultures that have strong expectations about female behaviour and requirements of female purity. In fact, 1 Timothy 3:7 requires that church leaders "have a good

---

[13] Kimberly Ervin Alexander and James P. Bowers, *What Women Want: Pentecostal Women Ministers Speak for Themselves* (Eugene, OR: Wipf & Stock, 2018).

reputation with outsiders". While these expectations may seem to present an obstacle, they can provide an opportunity for women to engage in public ministry. In a recent study of women in Khyber Pakhtunkhwa (KP), a province in northwest Pakistan, Susan Smith found that women identified a key mechanism by which they obtained influence in the public sphere – being known as honourable and hard-working women.[14] These women found that, as they could demonstrate compliance to social norms through their personal integrity and hard work, this in fact gave them a voice and opportunity to work in public roles, despite the social restrictions of their culture. This mechanism of good reputation and hard work proved effective even when women worked in public roles alongside men who were not family members.

This strategy of women promoting their good reputation has to do with turning a cultural obstacle into an opportunity. In essence, it serves as a pragmatic approach to empower women in cultural contexts which may restrict their participation. In fact, while the Early Church did not seek to destabilise their culture, the impact of the gospel resulted in cultural reform. May such reform continue today through contemporary examples of the blessed alliance of men and women working together and bring positive changes to cultures that diminish the contribution of women. While this emphasis on a woman's honourable character may not be required in all contexts of the global Church, many women, particularly in the Majority World, operate in such situations. Therefore, a key method for Spirit-gifted women to be released into public ministry involves their demonstrating – and others promoting (as Paul did for Phoebe) – their honour and hard work. This requires support from their male family members as well as their Christian brothers.

Conclusion

Upholding reputational purity and hard work may seem heavy requirements for women. We must ask: do these requirements put an additional burden on women? Yes and no. They unfortunately present an additional weight our sisters in the Majority World must carry, and they reflect the reality of gender bias embedded in our cultural systems that women must navigate, but of which many men remain unaware. However, as noted above, the Bible requires that all leaders in the church have a good reputation in their communities regardless of gender. Yet, as we have seen with Phoebe and Priscilla, they navigated the limitations women encountered in the Graeco-Roman culture through the mechanism of promoting their good character and hard work. Paul aided their navigating these limitations by championing their ministries. As Genesis reminds us, gender hierarchies were not God's intention for human communities. Yet, despite the

---

[14] Susan Smith, "Sitting with Melons: A Critical Evaluation of the Mechanisms by Which Women Exercise Public Sphere Influence in Khyber Pakhtunkwa", PhD diss., Alphacrucis University College, Australia, 2023.

cultural obstacles resulting from our broken world, the New Testament shows women working alongside men in the public sphere. Women's leadership in the Early Church was real and is well evidenced in the biblical and extra-biblical data.[15] Such rich data provides models to emulate, especially for young men and women in the Majority World who will benefit from seeing women upheld as examples. These examples can also inspire us today to see God's vision for the full participation of Spirit-empowered women that will strengthen and benefit global Christianity.

Bibliography

Alexander, Kimberly Ervin, and James P. Bowers. *What Women Want: Pentecostal Women Ministers Speak for Themselves*. Eugene, OR: Wipf & Stock, 2018.

Archer, Melissa L. "Women in Ministry: A Pentecostal Reading of New Testament Texts", In Margaret English de Alminana and Lois E. Olena, Eds. *Women in Pentecostal and Charismatic Ministry: Informing Dialogue on Gender, Church, and Ministry*. Vol. 21 of Global Pentecostal and Charismatic Studies, series edited by William K. Kay and Mark Cartledge. Leiden: Brill, 2016: 35-56.

Custis James, Carolyn. *Half the Church: Recapturing God's Global Vision for Women*. Grand Rapids, MI: Zondervan, 2010.

Gupta, Nijay K. *Tell Her Story: How Women Led, Taught, and Ministered in the Early Church*. Downers Grove, IL: InterVarsity Press, 2023.

Hylen, Susan E. *Women in the New Testament World*. Oxford: Oxford University Press, 2019.

Long Westfall, Cynthia. *Paul and Gender: Reclaiming the Apostle's Vision for Men and Women in Christ*. Grand Rapids, MI: Baker Academic, 2016.

Mathews, Alice. *Gender Roles and the People of God: Rethinking What We Were Taught about Men and Women in the Church*. Grand Rapids, MI: Zondervan, 2017.

Pizzuto-Pomaco, Julia. *From Shame to Honor: Mediterranean Women in Romans 16*. Lexington, KY: Emeth Press, 2017.

Smith, Susan. "Sitting with Melons: A Critical Evaluation of the Mechanisms by Which Women Exercise Public Sphere Influence in Khyber Pakhtunkwa", PhD diss., Alphacrucis University College, Australia, 2023.

Taylor, Joan E., and Ilaria L.E. Ramelli. "Introduction", In Joan E. Taylor and Ilaria L.E. Ramelli, Eds. *Patterns of Women's Leadership in Early Christianity*. Oxford: Oxford University Press, 2021: 1-10.

---

[15] Joan E. Taylor and Ilaria L.E. Ramelli, "Introduction", In Joan E. Taylor and Ilaria L.E. Ramelli (eds), *Patterns of Women's Leadership in Early Christianity* (Oxford: OUP, 2021), 5.

11. Unreached People Groups and the Cultural Intelligence Model

Karl Hargestam and Jennifer Hargestam

Abbreviations

CQ	Cultural Intelligence
UPGs	Unreached People Groups
UUPGs	Unengaged Unreached People Groups

Introduction

Since the time of the Cross, places exist throughout the world where the people have received no gospel presentation. These people are classified as being a part of an Unreached People Group (UPG) or "least-reached people", defined as follows:

> [...] a people group among which there is no indigenous community of believing Christians with adequate numbers and resources to evangelise this people group without outside assistance. A number of years ago Joshua Project introduced the term "least-reached" to communicate that the status of people groups is found on a spectrum, rather than an on/off toggle as implied by the "reached"/"unreached" terminology. However, the term "unreached" is so widely used in the global missions community there has not been a significant shift to "least-reached." Both terms mean the same thing and are used interchangeably on this [Joshua Project] website. The original Joshua Project editorial committee selected the criteria less than or equal to 2% Evangelical Christian and less than or equal to 5% Professing Christians.[1]

Unengaged Unreached People Groups (UUPGs) have "no known active church planting underway."[2] Ninety percent of UUPGs live between 10 and 40 degrees north latitude stretching across North Africa, the Middle East, Central and East Asia. Of all UPGs worldwide, 74 percent can be found within the Asian circle. Seventy nine percent of the world's UUPGS are also found in Asia.[3]

---

[1] Joshua Project, "Unreached/Least Reached", *Joshua Project Website* [Available at: https://joshuaproject.net/help/definitions] [Last accessed 22nd March 2024].
[2] Joshua Project, "Unengaged", *Joshua Project Website* [Available at: https://joshuaproject.net/help/definitions] [Last accessed 22nd March 2024].
[3] Joshua Project, "People Groups: Lists: All Continents: Continent: Asia", *Joshua Project Website* [Available at: https://joshuaproject.net/continents/ASI] [Last accessed: 22nd March 2024].

Islam is practiced by 24.8 percent of the world's population among 4,032 people groups; of those, 85.9 percent of the groups are considered "unreached".[4] Hinduism is practiced by 15.1 percent of the world's population among 2,399 people groups, of which 92 percent are considered "unreached".[5] Buddhism is practiced by 6.3 percent of the world's population among 666 people groups, with 76.7 percent of those considered "unreached".[6] There exists, worldwide, a great need to reach the unreached with the good news of Jesus Christ.

In 2022, the Pew Research Center published an article noting a significant change in religious practices – specific to the United States – when respondents are asked their religion.[7] Since 2007, the percentage of adults reporting to have no religion, being agnostic or even atheist, has increased thirteen percent (13 percent) from 16 percent in 2007 to 29 percent in 2022. The decline of those reporting to profess the Christian faith has declined, from 78 percent in 2007 to 63 percent in 2022. Those interested in UPG pioneer work must be culturally competent. Sadly, research is showing that such competency is lacking:

- Many Americans cannot name the Four Noble Truths of Buddhism or the Five Pillars of Islam.
- Only 38 percent know that Vishnu and Shiva are Hindu gods.
- Most do not know what Ramadan is or when the Jewish Sabbath begins.

A Gallup poll revealed that only half of American adults can name even one of the four Gospels of the New Testament.[8]

UPG/UUPGs represent the areas of the world with few or no gospel workers. It is estimated that for every thirty cross-cultural workers of Christian faith, only one goes to a UPG field.[9] For the unreached to be reached, something must change. It will require the Global Church to recognise the importance of engaging in areas where there is no gospel witness. We must explore different avenues to develop strategies to engage in each UPG/UUPG.

---

[4] Joshua Project, "Religion: Islam", *Joshua Project Website* [Available at: https://joshuaproject.net/religions/6] [Last accessed: 22nd March 2024].
[5] Joshua Project, "Religion: Hinduism", *Joshua Project Website* [Available at: https://joshuaproject.net/religions/5] [Last accessed: 22nd March 2024].
[6] Joshua Project, "Religion: Buddhism", *Joshua Project Website* [Available at: https://joshuaproject.net/religions/2] [Last accessed: 22nd March 2024].
[7] Pew Research Center, "How U.S. Religious Composition Has Changed in Recent Decades", Pew Research Center's Religion & Public Life Project, *Pew Research Center*, 13th September 2022 [Available at: https://www.pewresearch.org/religion/2022/09/13/how-u-s-religious-composition-has-changed-in-recent-decades/] [Last accessed: 22nd March 2024].
[8] Pew Research Center, "The Global Religious Landscape."
[9] Joshua Project, "People Groups: Lists: Unreached: Unreached: 100 Largest", *Joshua Project Website* [Available at: https://joshuaproject.net/unreached/1] [Last accessed: 22nd March 2024].

Communicating the Gospel across Cultures

Communicating the gospel cross-culturally to unreached people groups can prove difficult; looking at our own missionary journey, engaging in UUPG missions has presented many challenges including language, culture, safety, and geographical difficulties. Yet, in the Gospel of Matthew, Jesus commissions his followers to go make disciples of all nations (*ethnos*), meaning all ethnicities (Mt. 28:19). Regardless of the complexities, we must willingly cross barriers to fulfil the Great Commission as Jesus has asked us to do. The good news is that we do not do this in our own strength and abilities. Jesus premised the entire Great Commission by stating, "All power and authority belong to me, therefore go" (Mt. 28:18-19). What comfort and blessing to know we go in the authority of Jesus.

This chapter proposes two elements that local churches could quite easily integrate into a local church Unreached People Groups (UPG) training curriculum. The first, formation of Cultural Intelligence (CQ), is defined as the capability of an individual or group to function effectively in situations characterised by cultural diversity. CQ research conducted by Soon Ang[10] and others provides compelling insight into why some individuals and organisations thrive in culturally diverse settings while others do not. Emerging from the research evidence comes a globally accepted model where one can develop and measure the effectiveness of cultural knowledge, strategies, and actions. Many Fortune 500 companies around the world have adopted the CQ model. This should also be considered by the global church. Serving in Ethiopia among UPGs for over seventeen years, we saw tribes once considered UUPG respond to the good news of the gospel. When engaging with UPGs, it remains crucial to have a deep understanding of specific UPG culture and needs. The globally recognised concept of Cultural Intelligence has proven successful on many levels as a tool to develop competence where pioneer workers – those who do initial gospel work – can receive adequate training and equipping to engage in UUPGs. Not having cultural competence could result in good intentions without long-term sustainability. The Cultural Intelligence approach remains crucial to reaching the unreached. No other global need of greater significance exists than reaching people who have never had a chance to hear the name of Jesus.

The second element which local churches could easily adapt into their UPG training curriculum involves application of an established method for understanding religion. A church's grasp of cultural similarities and differences remains incomplete without a basic understanding of the beliefs, rituals, and practices of Unreached People Groups.

---

[10] Soon Ang and Linn Van Dyne, "Conceptualization of Cultural Intelligence: Definition, Distinctiveness, and Nomological Network", In Soon Ang and Linn Van Dyne (eds), *Handbook of Cultural Intelligence: Theory, Measurement, and Applications* (Armonk, NY: M.E. Sharpe, 2008), 3-15.

Cultural Intelligence as a Tool for UPG Training Curriculum

The Value of CQ

As a globally recognised way of assessing and improving effectiveness for culturally diverse situations, Cultural Intelligence is rooted in rigorous academic research conducted by scholars around the world. Leading organisations in business, education, government, and health care are adopting CQ as a key component of personal development and competitive advantage.

CQ includes the leaders' capability to function effectively across a variety of cultural specific contexts. As improvements in technology and communication have caused the workplace to globalise, CQ has emerged "as a specific form of intelligence focused on an individual's ability to grasp and reason correctly in situations characterised by cultural diversity."[11] David Livermore believes it is "an individual capability"[12] that some have, and others only possess in limited quantities, although all can increase their cultural intelligence.

The driving question behind CQ is, "why do some but not other individuals easily and effectively adapt their views and behaviours cross culturally?"[13] The concept of CQ, through the research of Soon Ang, P. Earley, and Mei Ling Tan,[14] builds on Robert J. Sternberg and D.K. Detterman's 1986 four-factor model for conceptualising individual intelligence: metacognitive, cognitive, motivational, and behavioural.[15] Livermore identifies the Four Capabilities of Culturally Intelligent Leaders: CQ Drive, CQ Knowledge, CQ Strategy and CQ Action.[16] In practical terms, the most effective leaders in multicultural settings are highly motivated in their work (Drive), work hard to determine what matters most about the culture they are seeking to engage (Knowledge), think strategically when determining how to best reach and connect with the people of a new culture (Strategy), and put their motivation, understanding and strategy effectively into action (Action) through well-planned work and communication in key locations with the right leaders. Reaching the unreached can be made more effective through the successful implementation of the CQ model.

---

[11] Ang and Van Dyne, "Conceptualization of Cultural Intelligence", 4.
[12] David Livermore, *Leading with Cultural Intelligence: The Real Secret to Success*, 2nd ed. (New York: AMACOM American Management Association, 2015), 26.
[13] Linn Van Dyne, Soon Ang, and David Livermore, "Cultural Intelligence: A Pathway for Leading in a Rapidly Globalizing World", In Kelly Hannum, Belinda B. Mcfeeters, Lize Booysen, and Center for Creative Leadership (eds), *Leading Across Differences: Cases and Perspectives* (San Francisco, CA: Pfeiffer, 2010), 582.
[14] Soon Ang, Linn Van Dyne, and Mei Ling Tan, "Cultural Intelligence", In Robert J. Sternberg and Scott B. Kaufman (eds), *The Cambridge Handbook of Intelligence* (New York: Cambridge University Press, 2011), 582-602.
[15] Robert J. Sternberg and D.K. Detterman, *What is Intelligence? Contemporary Viewpoints on its Nature and* Definition (Westport, CT: Praeger, 1986); see Ang, Van Dyne, and Tan, "Cultural Intelligence."
[16] Livermore, *Leading with Cultural Intelligence*, 27.

As Livermore says, "It's impossible to be an effective leader without having some insight into how culture shapes the thoughts and behaviours touched by your leadership."[17] For organisations to expand into new areas, a strong understanding of CQ remains vital, and "research consistently demonstrates a high level of failure when expansion into international markets is done without an awareness of how people from other cultures think and behave."[18] CQ has also been shown to positively impact the effects of visionary-transformational leadership within organisations that seek to be innovative.[19] CQ has emerged as a key capability of successful leaders within organisations when expanding into new, unreached cultures and people groups.

Four Factors of Culturally Intelligent Leaders

The following sections further describe Livermore's identified capabilities of CQ leaders: Drive, Knowledge, Strategy, and Action[20] – each followed by an application or illustration of this component.

CQ Drive

The first capability of a culturally intelligent leader is CQ Drive, or motivation. For Christians, this is an easy one. Our drive comes straight from Scripture. This is clearly shown in the words of the Apostle Paul: "How, then, can they call on the one they have not believed in? And how can they believe in the one of whom they have not heard? And how can they hear without someone preaching to them? And how can anyone preach unless they are sent?" (Rom. 10:14-15).[21] Paul's ambition was to preach the gospel. As Christians, we, too, must be motivated (CQ Drive) to share our faith to all nations, just as Jesus commands. Unless some people are commissioned for the task, there will be no gospel preachers; unless the gospel is preached, sinners will not hear Christ's message and voice; unless they hear him, they will not believe the truths of his death and resurrection; unless they believe these truths, they will not call on him; and unless they call on his name, they will not be saved.

As followers of Christ, our CQ drive should come through Scripture. We must be motivated to adapt to culture to be able to communicate the most important message – the gospel message. To tell people who have never heard, UPGs, requires that we have curiosity about who we are reaching. Adaptation is the key to CQ Drive. Leaders with high CQ Drive are motivated to learn and adapt to new and diverse cultural settings.

---

[17] Livermore, *Leading with Cultural Intelligence*, 67.
[18] Livermore, *Leading with Cultural Intelligence*, 67.
[19] Ang, Van Dyne, and Tan, "Cultural Intelligence".
[20] Livermore, *Leading with Cultural Intelligence*, 27.
[21] All Scripture quotations, unless otherwise noted, are from the New International Version.

CQ Drive Application: Ato Bekele's Story:

An illustration of CQ Drive can be seen in the story of a friend, Ato Bekele, an evangelist and a simple man who lives in a remote village in Ethiopia. One day, Ato Bekele experienced a supernatural encounter with God where he heard a voice telling him to walk south until he would come to a place where two rivers intersect. The voice said that when he would come to the two rivers, he would find people who had never heard the name of Jesus. Ato Bekele obeyed the voice and walked for approximately eight days: he found a people group called the Tara tribe. This tribe was so isolated that later we found out that the Ethiopian government did not even know the tribe existed. Ato Bekele had a CQ Drive initiated first by the Spirit and confirmed through Scripture: "How then, can they call on the one they have not believed in? And how can they believe in the one of whom they have not heard?" (Rom. 10:14).

CQ Knowledge (Cognition), Understanding Intercultural Norms and Differences

Livermore notes that "To lead effectively, you need to understand how communication styles, predominant religious beliefs, and role expectations for men and women differ across cultures. General knowledge about different types of economic, business, legal, and political systems that exist throughout the world is important."[22] As businesses and mission organisations have sought to expand globally, there has been an increasing desire to focus on CQ. In this quest to understand and apply CQ, much effort has been spent on applying CQ Knowledge to organisational work. Knowledge of how culture influences the thoughts and behaviours of others[23] is precisely what leading mission organisations are charged to do as they seek to reach the unreached. In pioneering among UPGs, workers need to have an intense focus on knowledge so that much of what was previously unknown about the UUPG is now a part of shared knowledge within the church to begin the process of a strategic plan.

By immersing oneself in the Tara people's regional dynamics, including their customs, traditions, and unique cultural practices, one can tailor the message of the Gospel to resonate with their distinctive worldview. This nuanced approach not only acknowledges and respects the Tara people's cultural identity, but also ensures that the message is presented in a manner that aligns with their values and beliefs.

One cannot understand this global world without some basic grasp of the religious beliefs, experiences, behaviours, and attitudes that shape the way people think and act. Furthermore, understanding those things relative to a particular people group helps the global worker understand the answers they may have to life's common questions: Who am I? Is there a God or an ultimate reality? Why is there evil in the world? How should I live?

---

[22] Livermore, *Leading with Cultural Intelligence*, 28.
[23] Ang, Van Dyne, and Tan, "Cultural Intelligence".

The study of religions involves the disciplines of history, theology, philosophy, literature, sociology, psychology, anthropology, and art. It is multidisciplinary.

Doug Petersen provides a basic framework for the study of religion:
- Origins
- Founder/Key Figures
- Sacred Texts
- Core Beliefs
- Ultimate Reality and Divine Beings
- The Purpose of Life
- Soteriology (Salvation/Liberation)
- Suffering/Good and Evil
- Afterlife
- Rituals (Context & Categories) Sacred time
- Sacred Space, Sacred Ceremonies, Sacred Symbols
- Behaviour and Community
- Challenges (Insider)
- Opportunities (Outsider)[24]

Studying a world religion when reaching out to an unreached people group remains crucial for effective and culturally sensitive communication, trust-building, and sustainable efforts. It allows for a more respectful and nuanced approach that can increase the chances of successful outreach and engagement with the unreached group.

CQ Knowledge Application: Ato Bekele

Ato Bekele's drive led him to move and live among the Tara. He became a student of their culture, language, society, and religious systems. Ato Bekele actively sought knowledge. He discovered that understanding their religion played a pivotal role in making necessary adaptions to build trust. It became evident that understanding the religion was essential for a comprehensive grasp of the people's values, traditions, and behaviours.

One critical cultural factor was that the Tara had a tribal king who ruled the people. Bekele was able to build a trusting relationship with the king, and eventually this relationship led the king to receive Jesus as Lord.

Bekele's willingness to gain knowledge demonstrates a CQ competence. The more that he discovered about the people, the more he adapted. He spent months researching in order to share his knowledge and help find ways to reach across cultural divides so he could share the gospel.

In his research, Bekele discovered that infant deaths were high among the Tara due to lack of sanitation. This type of basic understanding of the Tara people and their culture served as a basis for a clear gospel strategy to begin to unfold.

---

[24] Doug Petersen, "Great World Religions", presentation, Vanguard University, 2023.

Bekele became our CQ "agent" relative to knowledge; he helped us discover how to best reach the Tara tribe and share Jesus with them. We began by flying in soap to the Tara, while teaching them about practical sanitation. Over time, their hygiene practices improved; they became healthier and more open to the gospel.

CQ Strategy: Strategising and Making Sense of Culturally Diverse Experiences
Strategy is the third capability of CQ leaders. As Livermore observes, "Leaders with high CQ Strategy develop ways to use their cultural understanding to develop plans for new intercultural situations. These leaders are better able to monitor, analyse, and adjust their assumptions and behaviours in different cultural settings."[25] While mission organisations often thrive in CQ Drive and Knowledge, CQ Strategy remains an area requiring much growth for long-term sustainability. To accomplish the overall goal of planting a church within a UPG, mission leaders must consider carefully the needs of the specific people group. What works with one UPG may not work for another. CQ Strategy will determine the needs and the next, most effective, steps to share the gospel.

When working with a UPG, challenges will be highlighted as the culture becomes more evident. CQ Strategy is all about how to address the challenges, thoughtfully and often subtly, to guide powerful change. "CQ Strategy is the key link between our cultural understanding and behaving in ways that result in effective leadership".[26] Livermore's insights highlight the role of CQ strategy in navigating the cultural diversities within UPGs. It is not just about understanding, it is about leveraging that understanding to drive effective action. This underscores the importance of competently utilising cultural insights to steer gospel work so UPGs are introduced to salvation through Christ.

CQ Strategy Application: Ato Bekele
In Ethiopia, Ato Bekele and our team worked together to employ a high level of CQ Strategy. Our strategy followed that which Livermore recommends: (1) Plan cross-cultural interactions; (2) Become more aware; and (3) Check whether your assumptions were appropriate.[27] As the team gained knowledge, we put into practice analysing and adjusting for long-term sustainability. It became clear that this was where the hard work began. To share the gospel with the Tara tribe, an oral-only people, we put into place the orality method of chronological Bible stories translated into their language. Our hard work produced effective results as a church was planted.

---

[25] Livermore, *Leading with Cultural Intelligence*, 135.
[26] Livermore, *Leading with Cultural Intelligence*, 137.
[27] Livermore, *Leading with Cultural Intelligence*, 138.

CQ Action: What Behaviours Do I Need to Adjust?

CQ Action, the fourth and final capability of effective CQ leadership, "is primarily the outcome of our CQ Drive, Knowledge and Strategy."[28] CQ Action is the focus on the results of the internal and external actions taken as one seeks to fully implement Cultural Intelligence. When one has successfully applied CQ Drive, Knowledge, and Strategy, it will be clear what behaviours and actions are needed to appropriately adapt to reach the unreached people groups. Actions taken will vary as the people groups change. The successful employment of CQ Action will involve communication adapted to the specific cultural environment, leadership that engages the needs of the community, and appropriate implementation of actions that effectively address the needs of the affected community.[29] "CQ Action becomes the natural outgrowth of the other three CQ capabilities."[30] CQ Action requires the successful implementation of Drive, Knowledge and Strategy, which will result in a holistic and sustainable approach to sharing the gospel in an unreached setting. Without Cultural Intelligence, the focus could be placed on the outsider rather than on the people being reached. CQ Action enables the pioneer to authentically engage cross-culturally where Jesus is revealed as the Saviour who loves and accepts all cultures, people groups, and individuals.

Conclusion to the Story of Ato Bekele and the Tara People

Missional work continued with the Tara people. Support was frequent as we flew in by helicopter and continued to provide resources to the Tara people monthly. This resulted in the formation of a local team tasked to plant a local church. Support of Ato Bekele and the Tara people included training in orality, or chronological biblical storytelling. As we continued to learn language and key components of the culture, we continued to adapt the Bible stories to a more contextual approach to the Tara people. God's presence was felt among the Tara people and our team. We observed miracles as God made his power evident. An indigenous church was planted for the Tara people, and Christianity continues to grow in their area.

This story of Ato Bekele and the Tara people illustrates the success that can be achieved through missional outreach to a UPG. It also represents the success experienced through the successful implementation of the CQ model. As Christians seek to fulfil the challenge of the Great Commission, to "make disciples of all nations" (Mt. 18:19), implementation of a structured approach, the CQ model, can positively increase the effectiveness of Christian outreach to UPGs. As training programmes are developed for those seeking to minister to UPGs worldwide, CQ can serve as the structure for future training. Christian leaders can utilise the structure provided by CQ: Drive, Knowledge, Strategy and

---

[28] Livermore, *Leading with Cultural Intelligence*, 158.
[29] Livermore, *Leading with Cultural Intelligence*, 30.
[30] Livermore, *Leading with Cultural Intelligence*, 160.

Action, to develop training curriculum. A significant understanding of the UPG (CQ knowledge) and a plan to address their needs (CQ strategy) will aid in the development of training curriculum which will guide missionaries in their efforts to work with UPGs and lead the people toward salvation and a relationship with Christ.

The Story of the Shining Man

The story of the Shining Man illustrates that the Cultural Intelligence (CQ) model is paramount for individuals venturing into pioneering work in Unreached and Unengaged People Groups (UUPs). While cultural competency is undeniably crucial for such endeavours, it is essential to recognise that God supernaturally operates within and through the pioneering efforts of His people. It is not solely cultural competence that is needed; rather, it is the acknowledgment that God precedes us, working in hearts and drawing people toward Him. This perspective underscores that the success of pioneering work goes beyond human capabilities and cultural understanding; it hinges on divine intervention and the Gospel's transformative power. The following narrative of The Bodi Tribe illustrates God's profound love and concern for ensuring that the Gospel reaches those who have never heard it before.

While identifying the importance of CQ in the work of reaching UPGs, one cannot underestimate the role of the Holy Spirit when working with UPGs. The work is complex and involves the supernatural, not just the work of humans.

The Bodi Tribe is an ethno-linguistic people group, nomadic pastoralists known for their violence and feared by neighbouring tribes, along the southwest corner of the Omo River of Southern Ethiopia. This area was roadless with extremely harsh conditions. Because of the difficult terrain and the people's violent nature, we used the assistance of a helicopter to survey the Bodi territory. It took a CQ process to develop a team and plan to initiate a gospel work.

The day came for our team to fly to the Bodi area. We prayed that God would grant us favour to speak with the leaders of the tribe, knowing that was key to initiating a conversation. As we landed the helicopter, it took only a few minutes for more than sixty people to gather to see what they called "the big chicken from the sky". One of our team members, Ben, was a pioneer worker in a neighbouring tribe, fluent in the language. He started to communicate and introduce the purpose of our visitation. He conversed in a nomad style, saying, "May God bless you, and may your cattle all be healthy and give you much milk." He continued by stating how God cares about their well-being. At the time, the tribe's cattle were being harmed by a deadly animal disease carried by flies. We offered to bring medicine to treat the cattle. The word *medicine* in Bodi language is the same word for *Saviour*.

It was then that a chief elder stood up and asked about the name "Kristos," which translates to Jesus Christ. We were shocked and wondered how he knew of the name. The chief began to explain: "Five nights ago, as I was sleeping in my hut, a bright light woke me up. It was a man in shining clothes, whose face I could not see. The shiny man announced that in five days, people were going to come from the sky and tell a message of truth. They will explain who I am and what I have done for the Bodi people; it will be a message that will set you and your people free." In response, the chief asked the shining man his name, and he replied, "My name is Kristos!" The tribal chief turned and let us know that they had been waiting to hear the message. They wanted to learn more about the shiny man named "Kristos".

This story reveals a couple of key components in effective UPG pioneer work. First, even with all of our team's efforts to reach the Bodi, God showed himself faithful to reveal how much he loved the Bodi people. Even with this visitation, however, reaching the Bodi people required that people *go*. Acts 10 teaches that it took Peter to share the gospel with Cornelius and his household; God entrusted His message to Peter. The same truth applies today – someone must go.

Second, Cultural Intelligence played a significant part in approaching the Bodi tribe; the four capabilities of culturally intelligent leaders that David Livermore describes can be found in the interactions: drive, knowledge, strategy, and action.[31] Our team possessed a God-given desire to share the gospel with all people, including those in understanding of the tribal culture and to know how to reach many Ethiopian tribes initially. This knowledge included where the helicopter would land, who we would initially meet, and how we should best connect with the leader(s) of this UPG. With great assistance from the divine revelation given to the tribal chief, we were able to work with the elders of the tribe to develop a plan for sharing the gospel through chronological Bible storying that led to the establishment of a church.

Understanding people's religious beliefs gives insight into their world view and serves as a compass for building relationships without deconstructing one's individual identity. The significance of religious literacy can be the impetus for success within the ability to adapt culture.

Conclusion: Reaching the Unreached

The story of the Bodi tribe is beautifully encapsulated in Revelation 5:9, "And they sang a new song, saying: 'You are worthy to take the scroll and to open its seals, because you were slain, and with your blood you purchased for God persons from every tribe and language and people and nation" (Rev. 5:9). This passage unveils that all people from every tribe, language and nation will be represented in Heaven. This illustrates the value of all people, including UPGs, to God. To spread the Gospel effectively, we must be willing to take the necessary action to reach Unreached People Groups (UPGs) which first is engaged by going; then, it takes a willingness to become competent in crossing cultural boundaries.

---

[31] Livermore, *Leading with Cultural Intelligence*, 27.

As Christians, we must finish the most important task that God has given to us. We need local churches to begin training pioneer workers willing to cross cultures and to value other people groups as if they were our own. We need to see others as God sees them. We must plant churches and make disciples of all people groups. Working together, we must formulate an action plan to place a disciple-making church within every people group.

Missionally, no greater need has ever existed worldwide. We must respond to this need by giving at least one chance to every person to respond to the good news of the gospel. There currently exist throughout the world people groups who will live their full life, from birth to death, without ever hearing the name of Jesus. This is our challenge.

Bibliography

Ang, Soon, and Linn Van Dyne, Eds. "Conceptualization of Cultural Intelligence: Definition, Distinctiveness, and Nomological Network", In Soon Ang and Linn Van Dyne, Eds. *Handbook of Cultural Intelligence: Theory, Measurement, and Applications*. Armonk, NY: M.E. Sharpe, 2008: 3-15.

Ang, Soon, Linn Van Dyne, and Mei Ling Tan. "Cultural Intelligence", In Robert J. Sternberg and Scott B. Kaufman, Eds. *The Cambridge Handbook of Intelligence*. New York: Cambridge University Press, 2011: 582-602.

Farhadian, Charles E. *Introducing World Religions: A Christian Engagement*. Ada, MI: Baker, 2021.

Joshua Project. "People Groups: Lists: All Continents: Continent: Asia", *Joshua Project Website*. [Available at: https://joshuaproject.net/continents/ASI] [Last accessed: 23rd March 2024].

——. "People Groups: Lists: Unreached: Unreached: 100 Largest", *Joshua Project Website*. [Available at: https://joshuaproject.net/unreached/1] [Last accessed: 23rd March 2024].

——. "Religion: Buddhism", *Joshua Project Website*. [Available at: https://joshuaproject.net/religions/2] [Last accessed: 23rd March 2024].

——. "Religion: Hinduism", *Joshua Project Website*. [Available at: https://joshuaproject.net/religions/5] [Last accessed: 23rd March 2024].

——. "Religion: Islam", *Joshua Project Website*. [Available at: https://joshuaproject.net/religions/6] [Last accessed: 23rd March 2024].

——. "Unengaged", *Joshua Project Website*. [Available at: https://joshuaproject.net/help/definitions] [Last accessed: 23rd March 2024].

——. "Unreached/Least Reached", *Joshua Project Website*. [Available at: https://joshuaproject.net/help/definitions] [Last accessed: 23rd March 2024].

Keener, Craig S. *Romans: A New Covenant Commentary*. Eugene, OR: Cascade Books, 2009.

King, Winston. *Introduction to Religion*. New York: Harper & Brothers, 1954.

Livermore, David. *Leading with Cultural Intelligence: The Real Secret to Success.* 2nd ed. New York: AMACOM American Management Association, 2015.

Ng, Kok-Yee, Linn Van Dyne, and Soon Ang. "Cultural Intelligence: A Review, Reflections, and Recommendations for Future Research", In Ann Marie Ryan, Frederick T. L. Leong, and Frederick L. Oswald, Eds. *Conducting Multinational Research: Applying Organizational Psychology in the Workplace.* Washington, DC: American Psychological Association, 2012: 29-58. [Available at: https://doi.org/10.1037/13743-002] [Last accessed: 23rd March 2024].

Petersen, Doug. "Great World Religions." Presentation. Vanguard University, 2023.

Pew Research Center. "The Global Religious Landscape", *Pew Research Center Website.* 18th December 2012. [Available at: https://www.pewresearch.org/religion/2012/12/18/global-religious-landscape-exec] [Last accessed: 23rd March 2024].

Pew Research Center. "How U.S. Religious Composition Has Changed in Recent Decades", Pew Research Center's Religion & Public Life Project, *Pew Research Center Website.* 13th September 2022. [Available at: https://www.pewresearch.org/religion/2022/09/13/how-u-s-religious-composition-has-changed-in-recent-decades/] [Last accessed: 23rd March 2024].

Sternberg, Robert J., and D.K. Detterman. *What is Intelligence? Contemporary Viewpoints on its Nature and Definition.* Westport, CT: Praeger, 1986.

Van Dyne, Linn, Soon Ang, and David Livermore. "Cultural Intelligence: A Pathway for Leading in a Rapidly Globalizing World", In Kelly Hannum, Belinda B. Mcfeeters, Lize Booysen, and Center for Creative Leadership, Eds. *Leading across Differences: Cases and Perspectives.* San Francisco, CA: Pfeiffer, 2010: Chapter 7.

12. Healing God's Creation: A Contribution of Pentecostal Understanding of Divine Healing to Ecotheology in Response to the Global Ecological Crisis

Gani Wiyono

Abbreviations

C	Carbon
H	Hydrogen
O	Oxygen
N	Nitrogen
P	Phosphorus
S	Sulfur
Cl	Chlorine
Ca	Calcium
K	Kalium
Na	Natrium
DNA	Deoxyribonucleic Acid

Introduction

As I began writing the draft of this paper, the air quality in Jakarta, where I live, was recorded as the worst in the world.[1] Undoubtedly, the leading causes are the industrial activities and the use of fossil-fuelled transportation by the residents of Jakarta and its surrounding cities which continue to produce pollutants almost twenty-four hours a day.

In another part of Indonesia, in a region known as Puncak, Central Papua, extreme weather has caused severe drought and cold. As a result, the local population has suffered crop failure and is in danger of starving to death. The latest news I received reported that six people have died of starvation so far.[2]

---

[1] Tim | CNN Indonesia, "Foreign Media Highlights Jakarta's Worst Air Pollution in the World [Media Asing Soroti Polusi Udara Jakarta Terburuk di Dunia]", *CNN Indonesia*, 16th August 2023 [Available at: https://www.cnnindonesia.com/internasional/20230816092108-113-986655/media-asing-soroti-polusi-udara-jakarta-terburuk-di-dunia] [Last accessed: 23rd March 2024].

[2] Anugrah Andriansyah, "Jokowi: Famine in Central Papua Triggered by Extreme Weather [Jokowi: Kelaparan di Papua Tengah Dipicu Cuaca Ekstrem]", *VOA Indonesia*,

A few weeks ago, at the end of July 2023, Hurricane Doksuri hit the Philippines, Taiwan, China, and Vietnam, causing extensive damage in the affected areas. Even in Beijing and the surrounding provinces where it passed through, they received the heaviest rainfall in 140 years, resulting in millions of people evacuated, dozens of people reported missing, and twenty-one deaths. According to climate experts, rising sea temperatures caused by the climate crisis are to blame for the extreme weather in China.[3]

July 2023, according to *Scientific American*, was the hottest month on record; based on evidence in sediments, ancient ice sheets, and other palaeoclimate data, it was the hottest month in the last 120,000 years.[4] Analysis of available data also suggests that such a significant temperature rise links to the abundance of greenhouse gases produced by fossil fuel use.

Unchecked global emissions of greenhouse gases have the potential to bring the planet to the brink of global collapse. If, by 2030, the threshold of 1.5 degrees Celsius above pre-industrial average temperatures is exceeded; experts predict climate disasters so extreme that humans will find it challenging to adapt. Heat waves, violent storms, melting glaciers, rising sea levels, extreme floods, and droughts will trigger food shortages and infectious diseases, potentially taking millions of human lives by the end of the twenty-first century.[5]

Climate change is not the only environmental problem humans face. Plastic pollution also poses a serious threat to freshwater and marine ecosystems across the globe. A study in the journal, *Science*, states that twenty-four to thirty-four million metric tons of plastic are dumped into the ocean every year. This figure is predicted to rise sharply to fifty-three to ninety million metric tons annually by 2030.[6] The scale of ecosystem damage due to plastic pollution remains unknown. Nevertheless, clearly, apart from causing the death of marine animals such as sharks, rays, and whales, plastic decomposition – microplastics – has

---

[1] 1st August 2023 [Available at: https://www.voaindonesia.com/a/jokowi-kelaparan-di-papua-tengah-dipicu-cuaca-ekstrem/7205348.html] [Last accessed: 23rd March 2024].
[3] Damien Gayle, "Aftermath of Typhoon Doksuri Brought Beijing Floods, Meteorologists Explains", *The Guardian*, 2nd August 2023 [Available at: https://www.theguardian.com/environment/2023/aug/02/aftermath-of-typhoon-doksuri-brought-beijing-floods-meteorologists-explain] [Last accessed: 23rd March 2024].
[4] Andrea Thompson, "July 2023 is Hottest Month Ever Recorded on Earth", *Scientific American*, 27th July 2023, 2023 [Available at: https://www.scientificamerican.com/article/july-2023-is-hottest-month-ever-recorded-on-earth/] [Last accessed: 23rd March 2024].
[5] Sarah Kaplan, "World is on Brink Catastrophic Warming, U.N. Climate Change Report Says", *Washington Post*, 20th March 2023 [Available at: https://www.washingtonpost.com/climate-environment/2023/03/20/climate-change-ipcc-report-15/] [Last accessed: 23rd March 2024].
[6] Stephanie B. Borrelle et al., "Plastic Pollution: Predicted Growth in Plastic Waste Exceeds Efforts to Mitigate Plastic Pollution", *Science* 369(6510) (18th September 2020), 1515 [Available at: https://www.science.org/doi/10.1126/science.aba3656] [Last accessed: 24th March 2024].

appeared in almost every ecosystem on Earth, from the Equator to the Antarctic.[7] Humans, as plastic users, are no exception. Studies show that microplastic particles are found in human bodies and faeces.

The Earth is not doing well. The Earth is sick. The ecological crisis that began with the advent of the Industrial Revolution and worsened in recent decades now threatens the survival of all species on the planet.

Many humans have attempted to find the roots of this ecological crisis to prevent a global ecological disaster. The once dominant approach involved looking for the causes of this ecological crisis in technology, population density, and other material elements. While such a material approach is valid, the fundamental causes of the global ecological crisis are more spiritual than material. What people do with their environment is strongly influenced by what they believe about themselves in relation to their Creator and other living beings and objects around them. Lynn White raised this kind of understanding in her controversial work in 1967,[8] claiming that an anthropocentric understanding of Christian theology had caused ecological degradation.[9] A similar conclusion emerged from the observations and reflections of the great Iranian Islamic thinker, Seyyed Hossein Nasr, who states that the ecological crisis is essentially a spiritual crisis of modern humans.[10] If White and Nasr's observations are correct, theology plays a significant role in helping humans prevent further ecological damage.

From the Christian side, ever since White launched a sharp critique of the significant role of Christianity in ecosystem degradation, a wide range of ecotheology works have emerged, encouraging active involvement of Christians to prevent the continuation of the ecological crisis on our planet. As the youngest tradition of Christian thought, Pentecostals have been included. Since the beginning of the twenty-first century, Pentecostal thinkers have begun to explore and produce ecotheology-oriented works.[11] Admittedly, there have not been too

---

[7] Gita Laras Widyaningrum, "Latest Study: The Earth's Plastic Waste Problem Is out of Control [Studi Terbaru: Masalah Sampah Plastik di Bumi Sudah di Luar Kendali]", *National Geographic*, 21st September 2020 [Available at: https://nationalgeographic.grid.id/read/132346281/studi-terbaru-masalah-sampah-plastik-di-bumi-sudah-di-luar-kendali] [Last accessed: 24th March 2024].

[8] Lynn White Jr, "The Historical Roots of Our Ecologic Crisis", *Science* 155(3767) (10th March 1967), 1203-07 [Available at: https://www.science.org/doi/10.1126/science.155.3767.1203] [Last accessed: 24th March 2024].

[9] White, "Historical Roots", 1205-06.

[10] Seyyed Hossein Nasr, "The Spiritual and Religious Dimensions of the Environmental Crisis", *The Ecologist* 30(1) (Jan/Feb 2000), 18-20 [Available at: https://traditionalhikma.com/wp-content/uploads/2015/03/The-spiritual-and-religious-dimensions-of-the-environmental-crisis-Seyyed-Hossein-Nasr.pdf] [Last accessed: 24th March 2024].

[11] See Anita Davis, "Pentecostal Approaches to Ecotheology: Reviewing the Literature", *Australasian Pentecostal Studies* 22(1) (2021), 1-33 [Available at: https://aps-

many, and ample room remains to explore ecotheology from a distinct Pentecostal perspective.

In light of the above consideration, in this paper, I explore divine healing, one of the facets in the full gospel theology of the Pentecostals (whether four-fold or five-fold), as a source for building a typical Pentecostal ecotheology. Why choose healing? First, because healing serves as one of the dominant characteristics in the message and praxis of Pentecostals. Second, healing connects Pentecostals with the larger Christian tradition. As Amanda Porterfield points out, "Healing is a persistent theme in the long history of Christianity, threading its way over time through ritual practice and theological belief, and across space through the sprawling, heterogeneous terrains of Christian community life and missionary activity."[12] Thus, by using healing as a source to build an ecotheology, I speak about the need for ecological awareness for Pentecostals and people from other Christian traditions.

Divine Healing within Pentecostalism

Divine healing and the doctrine of the baptism in the Holy Spirit are undoubtedly the most prominent features of modern Pentecostalism. From the beginning, Pentecostal preachers proclaimed the availability of God's power to touch and heal the weak and sick in their evangelistic campaigns. Even today, healing is one of the most influential spiritual advertisements to attract people to revival services on both small and large scales. Not surprisingly, some researchers see healing as critical to Pentecostalism's growth and global expansion.

How do Pentecostals view healing in their tradition? According to Kimberly Alexander, the answer to this question varies. Some see healing as a sign of God's coming Kingdom,[13] while others see healing as part of Jesus' finished

---

journal.com/index.php/APS/article/view/9572] [Last accessed: 24th March 2024], for a brief but useful description of the development of Pentecostal ecotheology. Some important works on ecotheology from Pentecostal Perspective include, A.J. Swoboda, "Tongues and Trees: Towards a Green Pentecostal Pneumatology" (PhD diss., University of Birmingham (United Kingdom), 2011) [Available at: https://etheses.bham.ac.uk//id/eprint/3003/1/Swoboda11PhD.pdf] [Last accessed: 24th March 2024]; Amos Yong (ed), *The Spirit Renews the Face of the Earth: Pentecostal Forays in Science and Theology of Creation* (Eugene, OR: Pickwick, 2009); A.J. Swoboda (ed), *Blood Cries Out: Pentecostals, Ecology, and the Groans of Creation* (Eugene, OR: Pickwick, 2014).

[12] Amanda Porterfield, *Healing in the History of Christianity* (Oxford: Oxford University Press, 2005), 3.

[13] See Candy Gunther Brown, *Global Pentecostal and Charismatic Healing* (Oxford: Oxford University Press, 2011) and Joseph W. Williams, *Spirit Cure* (Oxford: Oxford University Press, 2013).

work on Calvary.[14] Although the theories of soteriology underlying their healing beliefs and practices may differ, they agree on one thing: they emphasise the materiality of salvation.

This emphasis on the materiality of salvation distinguishes Pentecostal theology from the classical (and to a large extent modern) Protestant theology, which, "since Luther[,] has retained its radical distinction between salvation and well-being and denied that salvation can be partly experienced in the realm of bodily existence in the world."[15] However, for Pentecostals, salvation is not identical to the betterment of earthly conditions. In other words, the materiality of salvation as manifested in physical healing exists as one aspect but not a gospel in and of itself. However, if the materiality of the salvation is omitted or neglected, the gospel they preach will not be a full gospel. Guy Duffield and Nathaniel Van Cleave, two Pentecostal theologians from the Foursquare Church, say, "Salvation for the soul and healing for the body are inseparable benefits of Christ's Atoning Work."[16] Like two sides of a coin, both are essential; one cannot exist without the other. Thus, both should be preached together.

Even though Pentecostals seem right to recover the material dimension of salvation – often omitted or neglected by the classical Protestant tradition – they generally limit the concrete application of this understanding only to the individual-physical-economic realms: supernatural healing for the sick person and economic miracles for those in need. They seem slow in applying this understanding in cosmic realms in the present age of ecological crises. This shortage may be partly due to the apocalyptic eschatology of Pentecostals. Having been influenced by dispensationalism, some Pentecostals see the current world as destroyed in a cataclysmic event and replaced by a new world – thus discontinuity between the present world and the world to come. Thus, for some Pentecostals, it seems pointless to talk about or fight for preservation of the world we live in today. What Todd Strandberg, a dispensationalist, says may represent a typical Pentecostal attitude toward environmental crisis:

> The main job of a Christian leader is to guide lost souls to redemption. I can only ask where the Bible even hints that saving the whales and fighting global warming are part of the Great Commission. Dealing with environmental problems needs to be left to the politicians. In my view, any preacher who decides to get involved in

---

[14] Wesleyan Pentecostals believe that healing is a foretaste of the coming Kingdom, while non-Wesleyan Pentecostals believe that as justification and sanctification, healing is provided for all in the Atonement. Just as justification and sanctification should be received by faith, so too with healing. For a fuller explanation of these two models of Pentecostal healing, see Kimberly Ervin Alexander, *Pentecostal Healing: Models in Theology and Practice* (Dorset, UK: Deo, 2006), 195-225.

[15] Miroslav Volf, "Materiality of Salvation: An Investigation in the Soteriologies of Liberation and Pentecostal Theologies", *Journal of Ecumenical Studies* 26(3) (Summer 1989), 453.

[16] Guy P. Duffield and Nathaniel M. Van Cleave, *Foundations of Pentecostal Theology* (San Dimas, CA: L.I.F.E. Bible College, 1987), 412.

environmental issues is like a heart surgeon who suddenly leaves an operation to fix a clogged toilet.[17]

To cure the deficit, Pentecostals must extend their theology of healing – to understand it at both personal and cosmic levels. In this regard, two concepts described below, deep incarnation and a vision of the sacred cosmos, can help Pentecostals construct a cosmic healing theology.

Deep Incarnation

St Gregory of Nazianzus' dictum:[18] "For [w]hat is not assumed is not healed,"[19] was born amid a polemic with Apollinarianism that rejected the perfect humanity of Jesus (i.e., that the Logos substitutes the human spirit/mind in the human nature of Jesus Christ).[20] St Gregory's dictum emphasises the importance of the Logos being perfectly human to save humanity ideally because if only the body and soul are embraced, then only the body and soul are saved, excluding the human spirit/mind. How then? In his following sentence, St Gregory writes: "what is united to God, will be saved."[21] In other words, St Gregory states that only by uniting humanity with Christ, who is truly God and truly human, can humanity experience salvation.

The next question that arises is, are only humans saved? What about non-humans? Are they also saved? Answering this question, John Zizioulas, the late orthodox theologian, holds that non-human beings will be saved through human intercession; in other words, human beings become the mediators (priests) who will elevate or bring creation before God so that, in the end, they gain sacredness and salvation in God.[22] Zizioulas' understanding is seen as too anthropocentric, placing humans above nature.[23]

---

[17] Todd Strandberg, "Bible Prophecy and Environmentalism", *Rapture Ready*, 8th August 2016 [Available at: https://www.raptureready.com/2016/08/08/bible-prophecy-vs-the-environment/] [Last accessed: 24th March 2024].

[18] St Gregory Nazianzus (330-390), along with Basil of Caesarea and Gregory of Nyssa, was one of the famous Cappadocian Fathers. His *Letter 101* to the presbyter Cledonius was probably written in the spring of 382 or the spring of 383. See Bradley K. Storin, "Gregory of Nazianzus, Letter 101 to Cledonius", in Mark DelCogliano (ed), *Christ Through Nestorian Controversy*, vol. 3 of *The Cambridge Edition of Early Christian Writings* (Cambridge: Cambridge University Press, 2022), 483.

[19] Storin, "Gregory", 392.

[20] Apollinarianism believes that the Logos substitutes the human mind in the human nature of Jesus Christ.

[21] Storin, "Gregory", 392.

[22] John Zizioulas, "Orthodoxy and the Ecological Crisis", in John Chryssavgis and Nikolaos Asproulis (eds), *Priest of Creation: John Zizioulas on Discerning an Ecological Ethos* (London: T&T Clark, 2021), 58.

[23] See Emannuel G. Singgih, *Introduction to Ecological Theology [Pengantar Teologi Ekologi]* (Yogyakarta: Penerbit Kanisius, 2021), 136.

An alternative view worth considering is called deep incarnation. Danish theologian, Neils Gregersen first introduced the term *deep incarnation*,[24] which means that the Incarnation not only joins Jesus to humanity but also extends beyond humanity to all living creatures and the cosmic dust of which all earthly life is constituted. Elizabeth Johnson, a feminist theologian who developed Gregerson's initial ideas, explains further:

> In the incarnation, Jesus, the self-expressing Wisdom of God, conjoined the material conditions of all biological life forms (grasses and trees) and experienced the pain common to all sensitive creatures (sparrows and seals). The flesh assumed in Jesus connects with all humanity, all biological life, all soil, the whole matrix of the material universe down to its very roots.[25]

So, the Incarnation, in this kind of understanding, is not merely a historical event that occurred in a particular time and space (Bethlehem, 2000 years ago); the deep incarnation is a cosmic event in which matter becomes part of God himself.

Biblical support for deep incarnation can be found in several texts. One of these is the Gospel of John 1, which presents a Christology from above. The Logos, described as being one with God and through whom all things were made, is said by John to have been incarnated into flesh (*sarx*), "The Word became flesh and made his dwelling among us. We have seen his glory, the glory of the one and only Son, who came from the Father, full of grace and truth" (John 1:14, NIV).[26] It is interesting how John uses words in the prologue of his Gospel. He uses the word *sarx* (flesh). Indeed, this word has been used negatively in the Pauline corpus as an antithesis of the Spirit (for example, in Gal. 5:19-23). However, in this passage, *sarx* is not negative! The rise of docetism, which introduced an anti-material Christology, seems one of the reasons why John wrote his Gospel.[27] John refutes this understanding of Christology. For John, materiality itself is not inherently evil! That is why the Logos became *sarx* (flesh). The emphasis on materiality (as an antidote to gnostic docetism) rather than on the human person may be the reason why John ignores the word *anthropos* or *aner* (which exclusively refer to the human being) and chooses *sarx*, with a broader scope. The *sarx* of John 1:14 "which the Word became not only weds Jesus to other human being in species; it also reaches beyond us to the

---

[24] "Deep Incarnation" first appeared in Neils H. Gregersen's "The Cross of Christ in an Evolutionary World", *Dialog: A Journal of Theology* 40(3) (2001), 192-207.
[25] Elizabeth A. Johnson, *Ask the Beast: Darwin and the God of Love* (New York: Bloomsbury, 2014), 196.
[26] All Scripture quotations, unless otherwise noted, are from the New International Version.
[27] See the work of Udo Schnelle, *Antidocetic Christology in the Gospel of John: An Investigation of the Place of the Fourth Gospel in the Johannine School*, trans. Linda Maloney (Minneapolis, MN: Fortress, 1992).

whole biological world of living creatures and the cosmic dust of which we are composed."[28] The Incarnation, then, for John has a cosmic significance.

The understanding that *sarx* has a broader meaning than just man appears further in St. Bonaventure's (1221–1274) understanding of the Incarnation. In one of his sermons, he says:

> As a human being, Christ has something in common with all creatures. With the stone, he shares existence; with plants, he shares life; with animals, he shares sensation; and with the angels, he shares intelligence. Therefore, all things are said to be transformed in Christ since – in his human nature – he embraces something of every creature in himself when he is transfigured.[29]

Thus, Bonaventure believes that the Incarnation has a cosmic scope, encompassing living beings with consciousness and cognitive abilities and inanimate objects such as sands and stones.

Unfortunately, the dominant theological reflection has generally limited the Incarnation in the flesh to the human realm. The understanding that the Logos became human could explain why a dominance of anthropocentric soteriology exists until today. That indeed cannot be wrong. However, the scientific era in which we live today understands humans as an inseparable part of the existence of the rest of creation synchronically and diachronically. Synchronically, humans are not only *homo sapiens*, *homo faber*, or *homo economicus*; they are also *homo ecologicus*, which means that humans cannot exist and survive without existential connection with other existences outside themselves (whether non-human living things or inanimate objects, for example, water, air, sunlight, etc.) that serve as their living space and source of life. Diachronically, based on the dominant understanding of science today, materially, humans exist as the result of a long process of evolution of the universe that began with the big bang that produced stardust 13.7 billion years ago. Stardust produced the universe and the Earth, and from the Earth came life, ranging from the simplest to the most complex, including *homo sapiens*.

In the Incarnation, Jesus became part of this material universe. His body, like ours, is composed of the elements C, H, O, N, P, S, Cl, Ca, K, and Na, also part of the elements found in stardust.[30] Like us, the DNA in his cellular structure makes Jesus part of a community of common ancestors. When he lived for about thirty-three years on Earth, like us, he also became *homo ecologicus*, adrift and

---

[28] Johnson, *Ask the Beast*, 197.
[29] Bonaventure, *Sermo I, Dom. II, in Quad.* (IX, 218). This translation is quoted from Dahan Lee, "The Ecological Meaning of St Bonaventure's Theology of the Created World", Ph.D. diss. (Australian Catholic University, 2020), 108.
[30] Kerry Lotzof, "Are We Made of Stardust?" *Natural History Museum* [Available at: https://www.nhm.ac.uk/discover/are-we-really-made-of-stardust.html] [Last accessed: 24th March 2024].

inseparable from the existence of other living things and other objects that existed outside himself.[31]

If all elements of the cosmos come within reach of Jesus's Incarnation and, if the Incarnation involves a radical embodiment that reaches down to the roots of human biological and material existence, then in using the dictum of St Gregory of Nazianzen, "for that which is not assumed, is not healed" as a kind of formula, we can say all creation (not only human) will be healed.

This kind of soteriological expansion will bring consequences to one of the facets of Pentecostal's full gospel theology, Jesus as the divine healer. Humanity now can understand Jesus as the one able to cure not only the sick body but also the sick creation – thus creating an ecotheology from a Pentecostal perspective.

A Vision of Sacred Earth

Like the Christian traditions that developed in the post-Enlightenment West, Pentecostalism was heavily influenced by the Cartesian-Newtonian paradigm that shaped modern worldviews. Briefly, the Cartesian-Newtonian paradigm[32] can be described as follows:

- Subjectivism-anthropocentric: Rene Descartes' creed: *Cogito Ergo Sum* (I Think Therefore I Exist) clearly describes the form of consciousness of the subject that leads to himself (human), which is the basis for the formation of anthropocentrism and the hierarchical order of the universe. (Humans are superior to the universe.)
- Dualism: Subject-Object, Mind-Body. The sharp separation between mind and body, subject consciousness, and external reality (object) has had a tremendous impact on the mind of modern man. Nature that was once considered as "You" (to borrow a term used by Martin Buber) has now become "It" to exploit in such a way as to benefit the subject (human).
- Mechanistic: This means that nature is seen as a lifeless machine with no symbolic meaning, value, or sense of ethics and aesthetics. Alfred North Whitehead writes, "Nature is a dull affair, soundless, scentless, colourless, merely the hurrying of material, endlessly, meaninglessly."[33] The consequence of this mechanistic understanding is that humans can do anything to this lifeless nature for their benefit.

---

[31] It is important to clarify that the concept of deep Incarnation does not suggest that the divine nature shown in the incarnation of Jesus was simultaneously infused into all aspects of the created world. (I thank Dr Frank Macchia for raising this issue during the Q&A session.)

[32] Rene Descartes and Isaac Newton are the figures shaping modernism. Descartes was the pioneer of rationalism, while Newton was the scientist who built modern science with classical Newtonian physics dominant in the scientific world before the birth of quantum mechanics in the twentieth century.

[33] Alfred North Whitehead, *Science, and Modern World* (New York: The Free Press, 1967), 54.

This Cartesian-Newtonian paradigm has led to the secularisation of the cosmos. Once considered sacred and with intrinsic value, the universe is now considered nothing more than an object with only instrumental value.

One can see the influence of the Cartesian-Newtonian paradigm in Pentecostalism in the practice of Pentecostal congregational life, which is very focused on humans and their life problems with only a minimal concern for ecological issues. Even if such concern exists, it more accurately appears as charity rather than as engagement or advocacy on ecological issues. Seeing this kind of condition, Harold Hunter, a Pentecostal theologian who cares about ecological issues, offers a sobering reflection that summarizes well the dilemma facing Pentecostals:

> Thus, even those Pentecostals who prohibit cigarette smoking and drinking alcohol find themselves passively taking in many of the same chemicals and seem little concerned about keeping enough air for future generations to breathe. […] One of the gifts of the Pentecostal Movement to the Twentieth Century was its commitment to the possibility of physical healing. Yet, how does the movement now respond to caring for God's creation when the sickness of creation makes us ill?[34]

How can Pentecostals reverse the desacralisation of nature without going back to a paganism that often identifies nature with God, the Creator (pantheism)? The answer may lie in the willingness to embrace panentheism! Unlike pantheism, which identifies God with His creation, panentheism sees the Divine as inseparable, always present and involved in the world of His creation, without the need to be qualitatively identical with His creation. Various versions and explanations of panentheism exist; however, the most relevant one to present here is Jürgen Moltmann's panentheism, since he gives ample space to the Holy Spirit, often closely associated with Pentecostalism.

Jürgen Moltmann's Panentheism

Moltmann argues that too strict a separation between God and His creation is the cause of ecological degradation. In *God in Creation*, he writes: "The ruthless conquest and exploitation of nature which fascinated Europe during this period [modernity] found its appropriate religious legitimation in that ancient distinction between God and the World."[35] To overcome the problems of overemphasising God's transcendence, we need a model that gives space to God's immanence without sacrificing or discarding His transcendence. According to Moltmann, God is never distant and separate from His creation but present and involved in it. However, one should not equate or identify God with

---

[34] Harold D. Hunter, "Pentecostal Healing for God's Sick Creation?" *The Spirit and The Church*, 2(2) (November 2000), 153-54.
[35] Jürgen Moltmann, *God in Creation: An Ecological Doctrine of Creation*, trans. Margaret Kohl (London: SCM, 1985), 13-14.

His creation because, at one time, creation did not exist. This idea of *creatio ex nihillo* "indicates God's self-distinction from the world and entails that the world is neither in itself divine nor an emanation from God's eternal being".[36]

Moltmann then borrows the idea of *Shekinah* from ancient Jewish religious literature (for example, the Mishnah and the Talmud)[37] and Kabbalistic traditions to describe God's transcendence and immanence. *Shekinah* is the embodiment of God's promise to His people that he will dwell within the midst of his people. At the time of the Exodus, God's *Shekinah* was a pillar of cloud by day and a pillar of fire by night, leading the Israelites out of Egypt to the Promised Land. The *Shekinah* was also present in the Ark of the Covenant, the Tabernacle of Moses, and the Temple of Israel in Jerusalem. In the time of the Exile, the *Shekinah* of God became a partner in suffering as the people of Israel lived in misery in a foreign country. So, the *Shekinah* is none other than God himself, present in a particular time and space.[38] However, God's local and temporal presence must be distinguished from himself, which the universe cannot contain. Moltmann writes:

> The Shekinah is not a divine attribute. It is the presence of God himself. However, it is not God in his essential omnipresence. It is his special, willed, and promised presence in the world. The Shekinah is God himself, present at a particular place and time. "When two sit down together to study the Torah, the Shekinah is in their midst." The descent and habitation of God at a particular place and time among particular people must, therefore, be distinguished from the very God himself, whom even the heavens are unable to contain. The Shekinah is certainly the present God, but this presence is distinguished from his eternity. If the Shekinah is the earthly, temporal, and spatial presence of God, then it is at once identical to God and distinct from him.[39]

Furthermore, Moltmann understands this *Shekinah* to be the Holy Spirit himself.[40]

The Holy Spirit, the *Shekinah* of God, dwells in the universe. He is in us, others, and the rest of creation.[41] However, interestingly, by dwelling in the universe, God does not dissolve in the universe, as classical pantheism does. Thus, we can metaphorically summarise Moltmann's panentheism with the words, God who is at once "above" and "within the world".

---

[36] Steven Bouma-Prediger, *The Greening of Theology: The Ecological Models of Rosemary Radford Ruether, Joseph Sittler, and Jürgen Moltmann* (Atlanta, GA: Scholar Press, 1995), 116.
[37] *Shekinah* shows up for example in *Pirkei Avot 3:2* (the Mishnah), *Berakhot 6* and *Menachot 43b* (the Talmud).
[38] Jürgen Moltmann, *The Coming of God*, trans. Margaret Kohl (London: SCM, 1996), 266.
[39] Jürgen Moltmann, *The Spirit of Life: A Universal Affirmation*, trans. Margaret Kohl (Minneapolis, MN: Fortress, 1994), 48.
[40] Moltmann, *Spirit of Life*, 51.
[41] Moltmann, *Spirit of Life*, 51.

If God is present in creation, and creation serves as his dwelling place through the inhabitation of the Holy Spirit (cosmic pneumatology), then the universe remains sacred and has intrinsic value in itself. The next question arises: how does Pentecostal divine healing relate to the vision of a sacred universe? At first glance, there seems no connection between the two, but as shown in the following paragraphs, they can be linked through resacralisation.

Body Resacralisation in Divine Healing

Jonathan Baer states that incipient or early Pentecostals "resacralised the body and rejected secular authority on it".[42] Their views stood diametrically opposed to the typical Reformation Protestants' view, which tended to desacralise the body. Philip Mellor and Chris Shilling explain that the Protestant Reformation brought about not only a transformation of beliefs that led to the separation of Church and State, the promotion of individualism and rationalism, but also what they call a re-formation of embodiment.[43] In general, medieval Catholicism, the background for the birth of the Reformation, saw the body as sacred. This sacredness of the body is obtained through "a collective effervescence of social relationships that can be typified as sacred eating communities".[44] In the Eucharist, for example, when individuals gather together as a sacred eating community, God incorporates himself into the body of the individual as bread and wine, thereby incorporating the individual into the body of Christ.[45]

In contrast, Reformation Protestantism views the here-and-now world (including the body) as entirely profane, utterly detached from the sacred. Even the association of embodied people sacralised through the Eucharist is seen as nothing more than a profane association. When the world is entirely profane, with God far away as the radical transcendence, the world, on the one hand, becomes closed to what Max Weber calls "magic"[46] and utterly open to the intervention of human ratios. Thus, there was a strict separation between the supernatural and the natural, which led the Protestant reformers to reject all forms of present-day miracles (cessationism). According to this view, all miracles, including divine healing, had been limited to the apostolic times, whose function was to aid the establishment of Christianity. Divine healing and other miracles emphasised in Catholicism as signs of God's presence in the universe

---

[42] Jonathan R. Baer, "Redeemed Bodies: The Functions of Divine Healing in Incipient Pentecostalism", *Church History* 70(4) (December 2001), 765.
[43] Philip A. Mellor and Chris Shilling, *Re-Forming the Body: Religion, Community, and Modernity* (London: Sage, 1997), 98.
[44] Mellor and Shilling, *Re-Forming the Body*, 16.
[45] Mellor and Shilling, *Re-Forming the Body*, 16
[46] See Jack Baberlet, "Magic and Reformation Calvinism in Max Weber's Sociology", *European Journal of Social Theory* 21(4) (29th October 2017), 1-18 [Available at: https://doi.org/10.1177/1368431017736996] [Last accessed: 25th March 2024], for a detailed interpretation of Weber's magic.

were seen as the work of Satan to deceive humanity. Consider what John Calvin says:

> We may also fitly remember that Satan has his miracles, which, though they are deceitful tricks rather than true powers, are of such a sort as to mislead the simple-minded and untutored (1 Thess. 2:9-10). Magicians and enchanters have always been noted for miracles. Idolatry has been nourished by wonderful miracles, yet these are not sufficient to sanction the superstition either of magicians or of idolaters.[47]

For John Calvin, all-present-day miracles are counterfeit miracles, not genuine miracles performed by the power of God. Such understanding (cessationism) had dominated traditional Protestantism at least until the rise of Charismatic Protestantism in the second half of the twentieth century.

Early Pentecostals challenged this traditional Protestant belief to desacralise the body and its intended consequence, namely the denial of post-apostolic miracles. For them, the body was a site of divine grace and power. The sacred was not experienced in abstract terms but in tangible and physical ways. The experience of the Holy Spirit's infilling power was authenticated through trances, body shaking, and speaking in tongues. The apex of experience of the sacralisation of the body is undoubtedly divine healing since it represents "not only bodily expressions but also concrete physical change".[48]

Just as resacralisation of the body paved the way for healing the sick body among early Pentecostals, resacralisation of Earth should also pave the way for healing the sick creation. As the human body, Earth is the temple of God because the Holy Spirit is present and permeates all elements of the Earth. God desires to heal not only the sick body but also the sick Earth. Thus, the expansion of divine healing theology from the micro level (human body) to the macro level (cosmos) might be an alternative ecotheology that can be offered by Pentecostals to the body of Christ.

Epilogue

I close this chapter with an idea from one of Jesus' most famous stories, the Good Samaritan (Lk. 10:25-37), highlighting two points. First, this story explicitly deconstructs the traditional understanding of whom we should love. In Jesus' time, those to be loved were people of the same nation and religion. However, Jesus deconstructs this understanding! We are to love everyone, including those seen as enemies! At the beginning of the twenty-first century, amidst the ecological crisis that has hit the world, we must deconstruct the traditional understanding we have inherited, which sees our neighbours as only fellow

---

[47] John Calvin, *Institute of the Christian Religion Vol. 1*, trans. by Ford L. Battles, edited by John T. McNeill (Louisville, KY: John Knox Press, 2006), 17.
[48] Baer, "Redeemed Bodies", 765.

human beings. Our neighbours should now be not only human beings but also the (non-human) elements of creation on this Earth.

Second, in the story of the Good Samaritan, we find the healing process experienced by an injured person. The person cannot heal himself; he needs help to experience recovery. The Good Samaritan helps in the healing process. Right now, "our neighbour" – the Earth – is sick like the wounded man in the story. It looks like she cannot help herself! In such conditions, we Pentecostals can act as the Good Samaritan for the Earth. One of the things that we can do to help heal the Earth is to change the theological perspective of our people: we should extend healing not only to the sick in body but to the sick earth as well.

Bibliography

Alexander, Kimberly Ervin. *Pentecostal Healing: Models in Theology and Practice*. Dorset, UK: Deo, 2006.

Andriansyah, Anugrah. "Jokowi: Famine in Central Papua Triggered by Extreme Weather [Jokowi: Kelaparan di Papua Tengah Dipicu Cuaca Ekstrem]", *VOA Indonesia*. 1st August 2023 [Available at: https://www.voaindonesia.com/a/jokowi-kelaparan-di-papua-tengah-dipicu-cuaca-ekstrem/7205348.html] [Last accessed: 23rd March 2024].

Baberlet, Jack. "Magic and Reformation Calvinism in Max Weber's Sociology." *European Journal of Social Theory* 21(4), (29th October 2017), 1-18 [Available at:https://doi.org/10.1177/1368431017736996] [Last accessed: 25th March 2024].

Baer, Jonathan R. "Redeemed Bodies: The Functions of Divine Healing in Incipient Pentecostalism", *Church History* 70(4), (December 2001), 735-71.

Borrelle, Stephanie B. *et al.* "Plastic Pollution: Predicted Growth in Plastic Waste Exceeds Efforts to Mitigate Plastic Pollution", *Science* 369(6510), (18th September 2020), 1515-18 [Available at: https://www.science.org/doi/10.1126/science.aba3656] [Last accessed: 23rd March 2024].

Bouma-Prediger, Steven. *The Greening of Theology: The Ecological Models of Rosemary Radford Ruether, Joseph Sittler, and Jürgen Moltmann*. Atlanta, GA: Scholar, 1995.

Calvin, John. *Institute of the Christian Religion Vol. 1*. Translated by Ford L. Battles. Edited by John T. McNeill. Louisville, KY: John Knox, 2006.

Davis, Anita. "Pentecostal Approaches to Ecotheology: Reviewing the Literature", *Australasian Pentecostal Studies* 22(1), (2021), 1-33 [Available at: https://aps-journal.com/index.php/APS/article/view/9572] [Last accessed: 24th March 2024].

Duffield, Guy P., and Nathaniel M. Van Cleave. *Foundations of Pentecostal Theology*. San Dimas, CA: L.I.F.E. Bible College, 1987.

Gayle, Damien. "Aftermath of Typhoon Doksuri Brought Beijing Floods, Meteorologists Explain", *The Guardian*. 2nd August 2023 [Available at: https://www.theguardian.com/environment/2023/aug/02/aftermath-of-typhoon-doksuri-brought-beijing-floods-meteorologists-explain] [Last accessed: 23rd March 2024].

Gregersen, Neils H. "The Cross of Christ in an Evolutionary World", *Dialog: A Journal of Theology* 40(3), (2001), 192-207.

Gunther Brown, Candy. *Global Pentecostal and Charismatic Healing*. Oxford: Oxford University Press, 2011.

Hossein Nasr, Seyyed. "The Spiritual and Religious Dimensions of the Environmental Crisis", *The Ecologist* 30(1), (Jan/Feb 2000), 18-20 [Available at: https://traditionalhikma.com/wp-content/uploads/2015/03/The-spiritual-and-religious-dimensions-of-the-environmental-crisis-Seyyed-Hossein-Nasr.pdf] [Last accessed: 24th March 2024].

Hunter, Harold D. "Pentecostal Healing for God's Sick Creation?" *The Spirit and The Church* 2(2), (November 2000), 153-54.

Johnson, Elizabeth A. *Ask the Beast: Darwin and the God of Love*. New York: Bloomsbury, 2014.

Lee, Dahan. "The Ecological Meaning of St Bonaventure's Theology of the Created World", Ph.D. diss., Australian Catholic University, 2020.

Lotzof, Kerry. "Are We Made of Stardust?" *Natural History Museum*. [Available at: https://www.nhm.ac.uk/discover/are-we-really-made-of-stardust.html] [Last accessed: 24th March 2024].

Kaplan, Sarah. "World is on Brink Catastrophic Warming, U.N. Climate Change Report Says", *Washington Post*, 20th March 2023. [Available at: https://www.washingtonpost.com/climate-environment/2023/03/20/climate-change-ipcc-report-15/] [Last accessed: 24th March 2024].

Mellor, Philip A., and Chris Shilling. *Re-Forming the Body: Religion, Community, and Modernity*. London: Sage, 1997.

Moltmann, Jürgen. *The Coming of God*. Translated by Margaret Kohl. London: SCM, 1996.

——. *God in Creation: An Ecological Doctrine of Creation*. Translated by Margaret Kohl. London: SCM, 1985.

——. *The Spirit of Life: A Universal Affirmation*. Translated by Margaret Kohl. Minneapolis, MN: Fortress, 1994.

Porterfield, Amanda. *Healing in the History of Christianity*. Oxford: Oxford University Press, 2005.

Schnelle, Udo. *Antidocetic Christology in the Gospel of John: An Investigation of the Place of the Fourth Gospel in the Johannine School*. Translated by Linda Maloney. Minneapolis, MN: Fortress, 1992.

Singgih, Emmanuel G. *Introduction to Ecological Theology [Pengantar Teologi Ekologi]* Yogyakarta: Penerbit Kanisius, 2021.

Storin, Bradley K. "Gregory of Nazianzus, Letter 101 to Cledonius", In Mark DelCogliano, Ed. *Christ through Nestorian Controversy*. Vol. 3 of *The Cambridge Edition of Early Christian Writings*. Cambridge: Cambridge University Press, 2022: 388-98.

Strandberg, Todd. "Bible Prophecy and Environmentalism", *Rapture Ready*. 8th August 2016. [Available at: https://www.raptureready.com/2016/08/08/bible-prophecy-vs-the-environment/] [Last accessed: 24th March 2024].

Swoboda, A.J. *Blood Cries Out: Pentecostals, Ecology, and the Groans of Creation*. Eugene, OR: Pickwick, 2014.

——. "Tongues and Trees: Towards a Green Pentecostal Pneumatology", PhD diss., University of Birmingham (United Kingdom), 2011. [Available at: https://etheses.bham.ac.uk//id/eprint/3003/1/Swoboda11PhD.pdf] [Last accessed: 24th March 2024].

Thompson, Andrea. "July 2023 is Hottest Month Ever Recorded on Earth", *Scientific American*. 27th July 2023 [Available at: https://www.scientificamerican.com/article/july-2023-is-hottest-month-ever-recorded-on-earth/] [Last accessed: 23rd March 2024].

Tim | CNN Indonesia. "Foreign Media Highlights Jakarta's Worst Air Pollution in the World [Media Asing Soroti Polusi Udara Jakarta Terburuk di Dunia]", *CNN Indonesia*. 16th August 2023 [Available at: https://www.cnnindonesia.com/internasional/20230816092108-113-986655/media-asing-soroti-polusi-udara-jakarta-terburuk-di-dunia] [Last accessed: 23rd March 2024].

Volf, Miroslav. "Materiality of Salvation: An Investigation in the Soteriologies of Liberation and Pentecostal Theologies", *Journal of Ecumenical Studies* 26(3), (Summer 1989), 447-67.

White, Lynn Jr. "The Historical Roots of Our Edological Crisis", *Science* 155(3767) (10th March 1967), 1203-07. [Available at: https://www.science.org/doi/10.1126/science.155.3767.1203] [Last accessed: 24th March 2024].

Whitehead, Alfred North. *Science, and Modern World*. New York: The Free Press, 1967.

Widyaningrum, Gita Laras. "Latest Study: The Earth's Plastic Waste Problem Is out of Control [Studi Terbaru: Masalah Sampah Plastik di Bumi Sudah di Luar Kendali]", National Geographic. 21st September 2020 [Available at: https://nationalgeographic.grid.id/read/132346281/studi-terbaru-masalah-sampah-plastik-di-bumi-sudah-di-luar-kendali] [Last accessed: 24th March 2024].

Williams, Joseph W. *Spirit Cure*. Oxford: Oxford University Press, 2013.

Yong, Amos, Ed. *The Spirit Renews the Face of the Earth: Pentecostal Forays in Science and Theology of Creation*. Eugene, OR: Pickwick, 2009.

Zizioulas, John. "Orthodoxy and the Ecological Crisis", In John Chryssavgis and Nikolaos Asproulis, Eds. *Priest of Creation: John Zizioulas on Discerning an Ecological Ethos*. London: T&T Clark, 2021: 55-60.

13. Singapore: The Antioch of Asia?

Kong Hee

Abbreviations

AG	Assemblies of God
AG USA	Assemblies of God USA
AWARE	Association of Women for Action and Research
CMIO	Chinese-Malay-Indian-Others
LGBTQ	Lesbian, Gay, Bisexual, Transgender, and Queer

Introduction

Singapore first received the designation as the "Antioch of Asia", from Billy Graham in 1978 and then from Yonggi Cho in 1982.[1] There are good reasons why these prominent leaders made this claim. Antioch, the ancient capital of Syria, was well-known for its strategic location as an important centre of commerce, culture, art, and philosophy.[2] As a cosmopolitan city of 500,000 inhabitants, Antioch had a multiracial population, attracting Syrian, Greek, Cretan, Cypriot, Jewish, Persian, Indian, and Chinese settlers.[3] Some of the languages Antiochenes spoke or read included Greek, Latin, Hebrew, Syriac, and Persian. They were also multireligious, worshipping a myriad of Greco-Roman deities like Zeus, Tyche, Aphrodite, Artemis, Athena, Dionysus, Hermes, and

---

[1] May Ling Tan-Chow, *Pentecostal Theology for the Twenty-First Century: Engaging with Multi-Faith Singapore* (Abingdon-on-Thames: Routledge, 2016), 15.
[2] John R.W. Stott, *The Message of Acts*, The Bible Speaks Today (Downers Grove, IL: InterVarsity Press, 2014), Acts 11. Antioch is a crossroads of trade routes south to and from Egypt, Asia Minor, Greece, Italy, Mesopotamia, and later Armenia and India. See Worcester Art Museum, "Antioch: The Lost Ancient City – City of Antioch," *Worcester Art Museum*, Webpage about October 2000 exhibition. [Available at: https://archive.worcesterart.org/exhibitions/antioch.html] [Last accessed: 27th March 2024]. See also Eric P. Costanzo, "Antioch of Syria", John D. Barry *et al.* (eds), *The Lexham Bible Dictionary* (Bellingham, WA: Lexham, 2016) [Available at: https://biblia.com/books/lbd/word/Antioch_of_Syria] [Last accessed: 27th March 2024].
[3] By AD 165, Antioch was the third largest city in the Roman Empire. See Trent C. Butler (ed),"Antioch", in *Holman Bible Dictionary* (Nashville, TN: Holman Bible, 1991) [Available at: https://www.studylight.org/dictionaries/eng/hbd/a/antioch.html] [Last accessed: 27th March 2024]; David Noel Freedman, "Antioch (Place)", in *A-C*, vol. 1 of *The Anchor Yale Bible Dictionary*, 1st ed. (New York: Doubleday, 1992), 264-69.

Jupiter, and their deified Roman emperors were well-represented in the city.[4] The Antiochenes were upwardly mobile, since commerce thrived, luring aspiring entrepreneurs from all over the Mediterranean into the city.[5]

When reflecting on the question whether Singapore today stands as the "Antioch of Asia", one can see the similarities of these two cities. Like Antioch, Singapore is one of the world's most strategically located countries, situated along the world's major trade, shipping, and aviation routes.[6] Although a small tropical island in Southeast Asia with a land area of merely 728 square kilometres, Singapore is highly urbanised, and culturally, socially, and economically diverse and complex.[7] The 5.92 million population has a multiracial makeup consisting of four main communities: Chinese, Malay, Indian, and Eurasian,[8] although more than 120 nationalities live and work in the city.[9] Singaporeans are multilingual with most being bilingual in English – the lingua franca and working language for government and business, and one of the other three official languages.[10] The Pew Research Center considers Singapore the most religiously diverse country in the world with its population practising at least eight religions, including Christianity, Islam, Buddhism, Taoism (including several Chinese "folk religions"), Hinduism, Sikhism,[11] and Judaism.[12] Singaporeans epitomise upward mobility, and like Antioch, the city-

---

[4] Freedman, "Antioch (Place)", 264-69.
[5] Worcester Art Museum, "City of Antioch".
[6] EDB Singapore, "Global Connectivity", *EDB Singapore* [Available at: https://www.edb.gov.sg/en/why-singapore/global-connectivity.html] [Last accessed: 27th March 2024].
[7] J. Clammer, *Singapore: Ideology, Society and Culture* (Singapore: Chopmen, 1985), 5.
[8] Singapore Ministry of Foreign Affairs, "About Singapore", *Singapore Ministry of Foreign Affairs*, updated 12th October 2023 [Available at: https://www.mfa.gov.sg/Overseas-Mission/Washington/About-Singapore] [Last accessed: 27th March 2024]; *Population in Brief 2023: Key Trends*, National Population and Talent Division (Singapore: Prime Minister's Office, 2023), 19-20.
[9] Lemuel Teo, "The Church Going Urban", *Singapore Centre for Global Missions*, updated 14th June 2018 [Available at: https://www.scgm.org.sg/the-church-going-urban] [Last accessed: 27th March 2024].
[10] Wai Yin Pryke, "Singapore's Journey: Bilingualism and Role of English Language in Our Development", Transcript of presentation to British Council, Chile, 2013 [Available at: https://www.britishcouncil.cl/sites/default/files/escrito-way-yin-pryke.pdf] [Last accessed: 27th March 2024].
[11] Joseph Chinyong Liow, "Managing Religious Diversity and Multiculturalism in Singapore", in Terence Chong (ed), *Navigating Differences: Integration in Singapore* (Singapore: ISEAS, 2020), 20; Pew Research Center, "Global Religious Diversity", *Pew Research Center*, 4th April 2014 [Available at: https://www.pewresearch.org/religion/2014/04/04/global-religious-diversity/] [Last accessed: 27th March 2024].
[12] Singapore Infopedia, "Jewish Community", *National Library Board Singapore*, updated April 2018 [Available at: https://www.nlb.gov.sg/main/article-detail?cmsuuid=b176a5a8-100e-49f7-9dbc-

state's thriving economy, exceptional educational system, and diverse cultural tapestry magnetise individuals from across the globe.

Although separated by time, culture, and space, one can observe six insightful biblical elements shared between Antioch and Singapore: (a) the importance of urban ministry: Antioch marked the first time the Church crossed the fundamental divide between rural people and city dwellers;[13] (b) the empowerment of the laity: unnamed lay disciples from Cyprus and Cyrene brought about the Antiochene conversion (Acts 11:20-21);[14] (c) dependence on the Holy Spirit: Barnabas and Paul were clearly men of the Spirit, and Antiochene believers respected the *charismata* (11:24, 28; 13:2); (d) instruction and discipleship: for an entire year, the members received thorough instruction (11:26); (e) compassion for the poor: when Agabus prophesied about an impending famine, the Antiochene Christians "as each one was able" helped "the brothers and sisters living in Judea" (11:27-29);[15] and (f) global outreach: Antioch became the mother church of all the Gentile churches, from which Paul and Barnabas were sent on missionary journeys throughout the Mediterranean and Europe. From Antioch, Christianity became a world religion.

In many ways, Christianity[16] in Singapore exemplifies these six biblical Antiochene characteristics. Many churches are adept at urban ministry. Lay volunteerism remains high. Many identify as Pentecostal or have Pentecostal leanings[17] and thus are open to the *charismata* of the Spirit. Singapore has emerged as a major centre of theological education in Asia. Many churches have vibrant ministries to the poor, and a recent national missions report rightly observes that the Singapore church has done "extensive work" in global missions.[18] Each of these shared characteristics merits its own treatment. This

---

41b0b31779d7#:~:text=The%20history%20of%20the%20Jewish,their%20exile%20from%20ancient%20Israel] [Last accessed: 27th March 2024].

[13] Wayne A. Meeks, *The First Urban Christians: The Social World of the Apostle Paul* (New Haven, CT: Yale University Press, 1983), 11; Gerhard A. Krodel, *Acts*, Augsburg Commentary on the New Testament (Minneapolis, MN: Augsburg, 1986), 207. In 1970, Donald McGavran said, "Discipling urban populations is perhaps the most urgent task confronting the Church." See *Understanding Church Growth* (Grand Rapids, MI: Eerdmans, 1970), 295.

[14] Lay ministry brings diverse perspectives, expertise, and energy, extending the reach of the church into the marketplace.

[15] All Scripture quotations, unless otherwise noted, are from the New International Version.

[16] A Christian believes in Christ and seeks to live according to his teachings. See Millard J. Erickson, "Christian," in *The Concise Dictionary of Christian Theology*, rev. ed. (Wheaton, IL: Crossway, 2001), e-book.

[17] Mathew Mathews, "Pentecostalism in Singapore: History, Adaptation and Future", in Denise A. Austin, Jacqueline Grey, and Paul W. Lewis (eds), *Asia Pacific Pentecostalism* (Leiden: Brill, 2019), 271-94.

[18] Singapore Centre for Global Missions, *An Antioch of Asia: The National Missions Study 2019 Report* (Singapore: Singapore Centre for Global Missions, 2019), 11

chapter, however, focuses on two formidable challenges that the Singapore Church must confront on its journey to emulate the Antioch model.

Multiracial and Multireligious Harmony

The first challenge has to do with fostering racial and religious harmony. One interesting feature often overlooked is that Antiochene Christianity thrived in a multiracial, multireligious context in which social harmony was maintained. From its founding, the church was a mixed congregation of Jews and Gentiles, rich and poor, enjoying table fellowship with one another.[19] The Antiochene leadership reflected that diversity (Acts 13:1).[20] Breaking down the prejudices of their day, the church echoed Galatians 3:28: "There is neither Jew nor Gentile, neither slave nor free, nor is there male and female, for you are all one in Christ Jesus." More than that, it flourished without causing tension with other faiths. Can the same be said of Christianity in Singapore?

Considering that Singapore is the most religiously diverse country in the world and ranks as the world's third richest and sixth safest country,[21] sociologist Joseph Liow argues that these factors suggest that Singapore has successfully maintained multiracial and multireligious harmony whilst achieving an enviable level of development.[22] Many Asian countries politicise race and religion because it is an attractive and powerful rallying point in the face of dislocation, oppression, poverty, and powerlessness. Singapore's vulnerable position – in relation to its neighbours and its own complex and fragile ethnic structure –

[Available at: https://www.scgm.org.sg/wp-content/uploads/2020/04/NMS2019-Report.pdf] [Last accessed: 27th March 2024].

[19] Stott, *Message of Acts*, Acts 11.

[20] Barnabas was a Jew from Cyprus (4:36). Simeon was likely a black West African man, whose alias was "Niger", Latin for "black". Lucius of Cyrene was from North Africa; his Latin praenomen suggests important Roman connections. Manaen was the suntrophos (foster brother) of Herod the Tetrarch and a man of position in the royal court. Paul came from Tarsus in Cilicia. Despite their racial, cultural, and socioeconomic backgrounds, these five men by the Spirit loved one another and served together. See Freedman, "Antioch (Place)", 264-69; Stott, *Message of Acts*, Acts 13.

[21] Luca Ventura, "Richest Countries in the World 2023", *Global Finance*, 30th January 2023 [Available at: https://www.gfmag.com/global-data/economic-data/richest-countries-in-the-world] [Last accessed: 27th March 2024]; "Overview of Safety and Security Situation in 2022", *Ministry of Home Affairs*, Press Release, 8th February 2023 [Available at: https://www.mha.gov.sg/mediaroom/press-releases/overview-of-safety-and-security-situation-in-2022] [Last accessed: 27th March 2024].

[22] Liow, "Managing Religious Diversity", 20; Reuters, "Religious Conflict in Global Rise", *The Telegraph*, 14th January 2014 [Available at: https://www.telegraph.co.uk/news/worldnews/middleeast/10572342/Religious-conflict-in-global-rise-report.html#:~:text=Violence%20and%20discrimination%20against%20religious,by%20the%20Pew%20Research%20Centre] [Last accessed: 27th March 2024].

compels the government to adopt the ideology of a secular state. Religion in Singapore, although widespread, is not a public function but only a private conscience upholding Asian values, such as filial piety, thriftiness, diligence, and group interest above all else.[23]

Historical events, such as the 1950 Maria Hertogh riots, underscore the fragility of this equilibrium. Maria was a Dutch Catholic girl raised by Malay-Muslim foster parents during World War II. After the war, her biological parents were awarded custody. The Muslim community strongly opposed this decision, leading to massive violence that left many dead or injured.[24] Since then, Singapore has encountered several incidences where communal tensions threatened to spill over into conflict and violence.[25] The government enacts "tough laws to prevent race and religion [from] being used to create divisions", to "protect our racial, religious harmony", and to ensure all Singaporeans have "the freedom to practise his or her religion"[26] while fostering the greatest likelihood of avoiding unnecessary cultural disequilibrium.

The Societies Act allows the government to ban religious groups that are "prejudicial to public peace, welfare or good order".[27] The Penal Code makes it a criminal offence to defile or disturb a place of worship, utter words to insult any religion, or to arouse animosity between religious groups or "promote enmity [...] on grounds of race".[28] The Internal Security Act allows the detention of individuals without trial for the purposes of national security or public order.[29] Finally, and most specifically, the Maintenance of Religious Harmony Act, passed in 1990, allows the government to issue a restraining order on any religious leader causing hostility between different religious groups, promoting

---

[23] Tan-Chow, *Pentecostal Theology*, 9.
[24] Singapore Infopedia, "Maria Hertogh Riots", *National Library Board Singapore*, updated 28th September 2014 [Available at: https://www.nlb.gov.sg/main/article-detail?cmsuuid=fbc266c5-4f6f-49d8-b77e-d37e20742087] [Last accessed: 30th March 2024].
[25] Liow, "Managing Religious Diversity", 26.
[26] K. Shanmugam, "The 2nd SRP Distinguished Lecture and Symposium 2016 – Opening Address by Mr K. Shanmugam, Minister for Home Affairs and Minister for Law", *Ministry of Home Affairs*, 19th January 2016 [Available at: https://www.mha.gov.sg/mediaroom/speeches/the-2nd-srp-distinguished-lecture-and-symposium-2016---opening-address-by-mr-k-shanmugam-minister-for-home-affairs-and-minister-for-law/] [Last accessed: 30th March 2024].
[27] "Societies Act (2020 rev. ed.), section 24 (1) (a) (Singapore)", *Singapore Statutes Online*, updated 1st December 2021 [Available at: https://sso.agc.gov.sg//Act/SA1966] [Last accessed: 30th March 2024].
[28] "Penal Code 1871 (2020 rev. ed.), sections 298, 436 (Singapore)", *Singapore Statutes Online*, updated 1st December 2021 [Available at: https://sso.agc.gov.sg/Act/PC1871] [Last accessed: 30th March 2024].
[29] "Internal Security Act 1960 (2020 rev. ed.), section 8 (Singapore)", *Singapore Statutes Online*, updated 1st December 2021 [Available at: https://sso.agc.gov.sg/Act/ISA1960] [Last accessed: 30th March 2024].

a political cause or political party, or carrying out subversive activities under the guise of religious programmes.[30] Apart from strict laws, the government has set up many "racial and religious harmony circles" to promote greater social cohesion and more interfaith dialogues among Singaporeans.[31] Singapore's Chinese-Malay-Indian-Others (CMIO) system of ethnic classification enforces ethnic quotas in public housing to prevent the creation of enclaves. Every town also has land equally allocated for churches or temples.[32]

Pentecostalism, Harbinger of Plurality

How does Christianity fare in Singapore with respect to fostering religious harmony? May Ling Tan-Chow, a theologian from Singapore who earned her PhD from Cambridge University, observes that most Singaporean churches have an apathetic attitude towards ecumenism among different Christian traditions, let alone interfaith dialogues with religious others.[33] This is because of one of the possible outgrowths of fundamentalism in Singapore, in which conservative piety, eschatological understanding, and a largely exclusive view of religious others militate against a positive engagement with them.[34] I refer to a dispensational view of the Spirit that is "unreservedly opposed to Modern Pentecostalism, including the speaking in unknown tongues, and [...] healing in the atonement".[35] Dispensational premillennialism can result in a focus on building separatist churches and schools that would allow them to shun the corrupting influence of society and competing forms of Christianity.[36] Tan-Chow notes that, while evangelicalism distances itself from the anti-intellectual and parochial characteristics of fundamentalism,[37] their core beliefs can end up being similar. Fear of getting labelled *liberal* and *unorthodox* can result in a refusal to participate in multireligious events, despite the government's push for greater interfaith dialogues. At the same time, the tendency here is the church's

---

[30] Terence Chong, "Christian Activism in Singapore", in Terence Chong (ed), *Navigating Differences: Integration in Singapore* (Singapore: ISEAS, 2020), 47–48.
[31] Harmony Circle, "About Harmony Circle", *Racial & Religious Harmony Circle* [Available at: https://www.harmonycircle.sg/about-harmonycircle/] [Last accessed: 30th March 2024].
[32] Liow, "Managing Religious Diversity", 30.
[33] Tan-Chow, *Pentecostal Theology*, 21.
[34] Tan-Chow, *Pentecostal Theology*, xvii; 21; 26–27; 90.
[35] Walter J. Hollenweger, *Pentecostalism: Origins and Developments Worldwide* (Peabody, MA: Hendrickson, 1997), 191.
[36] The Pluralism Project, "Fundamentalism, Evangelicalism, and Pentecostalism", Harvard University: The Pluralism Project, updated 25th October 2023 [Available at: https://pluralism.org/files/pluralism/files/evangelicalism_fundamentalism_and_pentecostalism.pdf?m=1648211809] [Last accessed: 28th March 2024].
[37] "Fundamentalism, Evangelicalism, and Pentecostalism".

demonisation of the ecumenical movement as a liberal project, while triumphalistically absolutising itself over others.[38]

Tan-Chow argues that Christianity has thrived in Singapore precisely in a context of complex ethnic, social, and religious plurality.[39] The Christian population has surged from 10.1 percent in 1980 to 18.9 percent in 2020, while other religious affiliations have registered a decline in the same period. Its growth trumps even secularisation, as those professing "no religion" increased only from 14.1 to 20.0 percent in the same period.[40] The brilliance of Pentecostalism lies in its contribution in promoting and maintaining racial and religious harmony, when Pentecostals tap into its ecumenical roots of openness and dialogue, as practised by William J. Seymour and David du Plessis.[41]

Analysing Pentecostal spirituality requires understanding its Azusa Street origin. Steven Land agrees with Walter Hollenweger that Pentecostalism's first decade represents its "heart" and not its infancy.[42] From its inception, Azusa Street was multiracial, multicultural, and manifestly ecumenical.[43] Journalist Frank Bartleman, who witnessed the revival, writes that as whites and blacks intermingled, "The 'color line' was washed away in the blood."[44] Led by Seymour, a black ecumenist, the experience of the Spirit gave these "voiceless" people a new freedom and language to praise God, and a new status and relationship not defined by race, colour, class, or gender – but by their relationship together in Christ.[45] The Azusa miracle was a solution to people marginalised by societal segregation and racism. Assemblies of God (AG) Superintendent Doug Clay quotes Seymour as writing, "The Pentecostal power, when you sum it all up, is just more of God's love. If it does not bring more love,

---

[38] Tan-Chow, *Pentecostal Theology*, 21; 26-27; 90.
[39] Tan-Chow, *Pentecostal Theology*, 16.
[40] Daniel P.S. Goh, "Grace, Megachurches, and the Christian Prince in Singapore", in Terence Chong (ed), *Pentecostal Megachurches in Southeast Asia: Negotiating Class, Consumption and the Nation* (Singapore: ISEAS-Yusof Ishak Institute, 2018), 181; See also "Share of Population in Singapore in 2020, By Religion", *Statista*, updated 22nd May 2023 [Available at (behind a paywall): https://www.statista.com/statistics/1113870/singapore-share-of-population-by-religion/] [Last accessed: 28th March 2024]. Christians come from all ethnolinguistic groups, and Christianity is popular among the middle class – those socially mobile, English-speaking, and well-educated. See Tan-Chow, *Pentecostal Theology*, 16.
[41] Hollenweger, *Pentecostalism*, 1; See also Tan-Chow, *Pentecostal Theology*, xvii.
[42] Walter J. Hollenweger, "Pentecostals and the Charismatic Movement", in Cheslyn Jones, Geoffrey Wainwright, and Edward Yarnold (eds), *The Study of Spirituality* (London: SPCK, 1986), 551.
[43] Tan-Chow, *Pentecostal Theology*, 29.
[44] Frank Bartleman, *What Really Happened at Azusa Street?* (Northridge, CA: Voice Christian), 29.
[45] Tan-Chow, *Pentecostal Theology*, 44.

it is simply a counterfeit."[46] Bartleman writes further of Azusa, "Divine love was wonderfully manifest in the meetings. They would not even allow an unkind word said against their opposers or the churches. The message was 'the love of God.'"[47] As such, Pentecostal belief, affection, and practice are amicable, encouraging an unconditional love and respect for all people regardless of race, language, or religion.

Can multiracial, multireligious fellowship and dialogue between Christians and religious others take place, even if the latter remains closed to conversion? For Pentecostals, the answer is yes. Robert Menzies argues that Pentecostals staunchly view the Book of Acts as the model for the contemporary Church.[48] In Acts 17, when Paul came to Athens, a city filled with adherents of other religions, he engaged them with humility, respect, and kindness. He did not insult or condemn their religious beliefs but critically sought to find commonalities without surrendering his own conviction in the centrality of Christ (17:22-34). Liow posits that a central principle of interreligious dialogue is to "agree to disagree",[49] something Paul obviously could do. In Acts 10:28, Peter says, "God has shown me that I should not call anyone impure or unclean". The Spirit opened Peter to God's inclusive love and hospitality. Peter gladly had fellowship with Cornelius, even before Cornelius' conversion (v. 23).[50]

The Spirit's outpouring in the Book of Acts remains central to the Pentecostal *Weltanschauung* (worldview). Frank Macchia rightly observes that, at Pentecost, Christ fulfilled the promise of the Father when he imparted the Spirit on all flesh, overflowing all social boundaries and privileges regardless of age, gender, race, or socio-economic class (Acts 2:17-18).[51] In Acts, the Spirit came upon the Jews of Jerusalem and the Jews of the Diaspora (2:9-11) and then upon the Samaritans (8:14-17), the Caesarean Gentiles (10:44), and the Ephesians (19:1-7).[52] The Spirit's outpouring not only effected territorial expansion, but it also enlarged the apostles' mental landscapes of God's nature and generosity, reaching out to and seeking reconciliation with all flesh (1 Cor. 12:13; Eph. 3:6). Antioch's

---

[46] Doug Clay, "Five Leadership Lessons of William J. Seymour", *Influence Magazine*, 22nd February 2021 [Available at: https://influencemagazine.com/en/Practice/Five-Leadership-Lessons-of-William-J-Seymour] [Last accessed: 30th March 2024].

[47] Bartleman, *What Really Happened at Azusa Street?*; See also Frank Bartleman, "The Great Earthquake", *Revival Library* [Available at: https://revival-library.org/revival-histories/pentecostal-revivals/american-pentecostal-revival/azusa-street-revival/] [Last accessed: 30th March 2024].

[48] Robert P. Menzies, "Pentecost: This Story is Our Story", *Enrichment Journal* (Fall 2013), 40 [Available at: https://enrichmentjournal.ag.org/Issues/2013/Fall-2013] [Last accessed: 30th March 2024].

[49] Liow, "Managing Religious Diversity", 31.

[50] Tan-Chow, *Pentecostal Theology*, 159.

[51] Frank D. Macchia, *Jesus the Spirit Baptizer: Christology in Light of Pentecost* (Grand Rapids, MI: Eerdmans, 2021), 204.

[52] Tan-Chow, *Pentecostal Theology*, 31.

multiracial congregation celebrated and embraced diversity, not fearing or suppressing it, thus exemplifying this Pentecostal ethos.[53]

Amos Yong rightly cautions against uncritically joining fundamentalists and evangelicals in their antagonistic disposition towards religious others. The Spirit's outpouring on all flesh requires a respectful orientation towards religious others because the Spirit can redeem traditions and communicate the gospel in new ways.[54] Recognising that the Spirit can speak through even religious others demands a listening ear, a willingness to be self-critical, and an openness to learn from and even be corrected by them. The Wesleyan theological tradition provides a proto-pneumatological theology of religions to discern the Spirit's presence and activity in others. Without affirming universalism, it argues the possibility for the unevangelised to be saved if they respond to the light that they have received (Rom. 2:12-16).

For example, a Pentecostal pneumatology can provide a way forward in Christian-Muslim interactions since a commonality is the Spirit in both the Bible and Quran.[55] In the Quran, *ruh* (the Arabic counterpart to *ruach*) is the source of Allah's word and human breath. *Ruh* was given to Mary to bear Jesus and declared him the perfect man. *Ruh* was the Spirit of holiness imparted to him. *Ruh* is the comforter and strengthener of all Allah's believers.[56] Volf argues that Muslims' denial of the Incarnation and Trinity is not dissimilar to the Jews, yet Christians nonetheless accept that the God of Christianity and the God of Judaism is one and the same. Since these three monotheistic religions all claim to believe in the God of Abraham, should Christians not accord Muslims the same courtesy and respect as they do the Jews?[57]

Liow has observed that post-9/11, the resilience of interreligious harmony has grown more acute against the backdrop of terrorism and religious extremism.[58] To truly foster understanding towards religious others, one must emphasise the importance of everyday interaction. Knowing others' religious beliefs,

---

[53] This required intentional effort by the leaders and church members to overcome divisive barriers to shape Christian theology and missions. Diversity and inclusivity in Christ reflect the gospel truth that humankind are created in God's image, equal in value and dignity. A diverse community is vibrant, resilient, adaptable, and creative, making the local church better and stronger, a powerful witness of God's love and grace to a fallen world (Jn 13:34).

[54] Amos Yong, *The Spirit Poured Out on All Flesh: Pentecostalism and the Possibility of Global Theology* (Ada, MI: Baker Academic, 2005), 237–47.

[55] The word translated "spirit" in the Qur'an, *ruh*, has etymological roots similar to those of the Hebrew *ruah*, "wind".

[56] Yong, *Spirit Poured Out*, 260–61.

[57] Miroslav Volf, "Wheaton Professor's Suspension is about Anti-Muslim Bigotry, Not Theology", *The Washington Post*, 17th December 2015 [Available at: https://www.washingtonpost.com/news/acts-of-faith/wp/2015/12/17/wheaton-professors-suspension-is-about-anti-muslim-bigotry-not-theology] [Last accessed: 30th March 2024].

[58] Liow, "Managing Religious Diversity", 31.

traditions, and customs humanises them by identifying similarities instead of differences.[59] Tan-Chow rightly argues that Pentecostalism can be "a peaceful harbinger of plurality".[60] Paul, too, exhorts us to pray for those in authority to create social stability and a conducive environment wherein everyone can practise their faith without fear or anxiety (1 Tim. 2:1-4). We are to heed God's command and take the responsibility to seek the *shalom* and flourishing of our city (Jer. 29:7). Because of Pentecostalism's innate belief in the Spirit who instantiates love, respect, and forbearance for all, this movement can play a vital role in fostering tolerance and understanding among different religious communities. Tolerance does not mean being soft or weak but kind and respectful – treating religious others with courtesy and consideration, without compromising one's own values and beliefs.

Pentecostalism Eschews Christian Activism

The second challenge to the Singapore church functioning as the "Antioch of Asia" concerns Christian activism, a potential problem of both fundamentalism and evangelicalism,[61] but something Pentecostals tend to avoid. Sociologist Terence Chong defines Christian activism as the mobilisation of the Christian community to resist or publicly express objections to events or public policy based on Christian morality and values. Since its independence, Singapore's conservative government was perceived as guarding the populace against decadence and vice, protecting cultural conservatism, dominant heterosexual values, and traditional institutions like the nuclear family unit.[62] Christian activism began in earnest in the 1990s when the government began to liberalise not just the banking and financial sectors but also the arts and entertainment industry to make Singapore a culturally vibrant global city. To attract global talent and dissuade Singaporeans from immigrating, the government relaxed censorship regulations.[63] In 2004, the government approved the building of two casinos and the now-defunct topless Parisian cabaret show, *Crazy Horse*.[64] Conservative Christians felt particularly troubled by the spectre of

---

[59] Liow, "Managing Religious Diversity", 32.
[60] Tan-Chow, *Pentecostal Theology*, xvi. David Martin used this phrase in his lecture "Missions and the Plurality of Faiths", presented at the Faculty of Divinity, University of Cambridge, October 2001.
[61] Fundamentalists tend to be effective political organisers for conservative moral reform. See "Fundamentalism, Evangelicalism, and Pentecostalism". Evangelicalism is marked by the four distinctives of conversionism, biblicism, crucicentrism, and activism. See David W. Bebbington, *Evangelicalism in Modern Britain: A History from the 1730s to the 1980s* (New York: Routledge, 2003), 3.
[62] Chong, "Christian Activism", 39.
[63] Chong, "Christian Activism", 9. Movie ratings allowed themes like nudity, sex, homosexuality, and other taboo issues for certain age groups.
[64] Chong, "Christian Activism", 41.

homosexuality and gay lifestyles.[65] For many conservatives, the country had sacrificed its moral values on the altar of economic growth and global-city ambitions.[66]

In 2009, a group of Christian women challenged the women's rights group, Association of Women for Action and Research (AWARE), for straying from its original objective of championing workplace gender equality towards actively promoting homosexuality and lesbianism amongst the young.[67] AWARE thus became a battleground for the pro-LGBTQ and anti-LGBTQ activists.[68] Chong observes that this marked the coming of age of Singapore's Christian activism.[69] That year, the first "Pink Dot" annual festival publicly celebrated Singapore's LGBTQ community. By 2014, Pink Dot had a turnout of 26,000.[70] One Christian alliance, together with their Muslim counterparts, publicly expressed their displeasure at such "alternative lifestyles" with their "Wear White" campaign.[71] This is the most visible example of Singapore's culture war, not a transplant of a Western or American problem (although the comparative influence is obvious), and it is happening in the social milieu of public morality grounded in Asian family values.[72]

Of particular concern is the rhetoric that Singapore should be a Christian nation with a Christian moral framework. Some have interpreted Billy Graham's call for Singapore to be the "Antioch of Asia" to mean that it should not merely serve as a centre for missions but as a Christian state.[73] In 2001, a prominent interchurch network's goal of seeing two million Singaporeans receiving Christ[74]

---

[65] The term "conservative Christian" should not necessarily denote intolerance or narrow-mindedness. After all, for most local Christians, personal adherence to conservative moral values does not inevitably lead to the desire to impose them on others. Indeed, Christian activism is confined to a minority within the community. However, this minority may be argued to be disproportionately impactful in light of its socio-economic profile. See Chong, "Christian Activism", 38; M. Nirmala, "Govt More Open to Employing Gays Now", *The Straits Times*, 4th July 2003.
[66] Chong, "Christian Activism", 42.
[67] Zakir Hussain, "Dr Thio Upset about Sexuality Programme", *The Straits Times*, 24th April 2009.
[68] LGBTQ stands for lesbian, gay, bisexual, transgender, and queer.
[69] Chong, "Christian Activism", 36.
[70] "26,000 Crowd Celebrate the Freedom to Love at Pink Dot 2014", *The Online Citizen*, 28th June 2014 [Available at: http://www.theonlinecitizen.com/2014/06/26000-crowd-celebrate-the-freedom-to-love-at-pink-dot-2014] [Last accessed: 29th March 2024].
[71] Chong, "Christian Activism", 46.
[72] Daniel P.S. Goh, "Protest and the Culture War in Singapore", in Terence Chong (ed), *Navigating Differences: Integration in Singapore* (Singapore: ISEAS, 2020), 143.
[73] Chong, "Christian Activism", 46.
[74] Tan-Chow, *Pentecostal Theology*, 77. Full disclosure: I was a committee member of that interchurch network in 2001.

was viewed by some as an attempt to "Christianise" Singapore.[75] One senior clergyman prophesied that *Singapura* (Sanskrit for "lion city") would be returned from the demonic lion of Sang Nila Utama (the Malay prince who founded the pre-colonial settlement) to Christ the Lion of Judah in its fiftieth jubilee year.[76] Observers fear that such aspirations may trigger Muslims, Buddhists, Taoists, or Hindus to similarly express their religious identities to restore some semblance of symmetry[77] if they get anxious that Christian activism is shrinking public spaces.[78]

How can concerns over public morality issues not lead to greater societal tensions? Can Pentecostals, adept at evangelism and missions, live as socially moderate Christians? If the Book of Acts provides a model for the contemporary Church, one must admit that little Christian activism appears in it, if any at all. Paul certainly has misgivings about homosexuality (Rom. 1:27; 1 Cor. 6:9) but he does not force Christian values upon the Roman society through lobbying and demonstration. In fact, all New Testament writers seek to win the ungodly to Christ by living exemplary lives in obedience to God's will.

A major social ill in the time of the Early Church was slavery. John Stott notes that while the New Testament does not condone slavery, it also does not outrightly condemn it.[79] Paul neither incites slaves to revolt against their owners and seize their freedom, nor does he command slave-owners to emancipate their slaves. Slavery was an indispensable part of the Roman world, with many cities having more slaves than free people. It would have been impossible to abolish slavery in one stroke without the complete disintegration of society. Even if Christians had liberated their slaves, those freed slaves would face unemployment and penury. The Early Church's way to eradicate this structural evil was by exemplifying the gospel in everyday living. Paul's letters talk about the transformed slave-master relationship in a countercultural way, with equality, justice, and mutual love between masters and slaves (Eph. 6:9; Col. 4:1; Philem. 1:16). All those in Christ are sons and daughters of God, and there is "neither slave nor free", for all are "one in Christ Jesus" (Gal. 3:28). Such teachings *ipso facto* issued a radical challenge to an evil institution separating them as proprietor and property. Instead of Christian activism, Paul allows

---

[75] Simon Chan, "Chan on Tan-Chow, '*Pentecostal Theology for the Twenty-first Century: Engaging with Multi-Faith Singapore*'", *H-Pentecostalism*, December 2007 [Available at: https://networks.h-net.org/node/9663/reviews/11358/chan-tan-chow-pentecostal-theology-twenty-first-century-engaging-multi] [Last accessed: 29th March 2024].

[76] Daniel P.S. Goh, "State and Social Christianity in Post-Colonial Singapore", *SOJOURN: Journal of Social Issues in Southeast Asia* 25(1) (2010), 81.

[77] Chong, "Christian Activism", 45; 47.

[78] Chong, "Christian Activism", 47–50.

[79] John R.W. Stott, *The Message of Ephesians*, The Bible Speaks Today (Downers Grove, IL: IVP Academic, 1979), Ephesians 6:9.

"slavery to be abolished from within", as William Hendriksen notes, by the Spirit through his Word.[80]

Steven Jack Land argues that most Pentecostals do not believe that worldly politics, manipulation, and coercion will bring in the Kingdom.[81] Historical, social, and theological reasons exist for this. Pentecostals in the early twentieth century were cultural and premillennial pessimists, eschewing politics, and believing Jesus alone rewards covenant faithfulness to his Word and to the neighbour, not the world.[82] This does not mean Pentecostals have no social conscience. Douglas Petersen defines the Pentecostal view of social justice as meeting essential human needs within a community and creating an environment where the poor and oppressed can flourish through "experiences of the divine".[83] As such, Pentecostals were, and are, very much involved in rescue missions, medical help, building orphanages and schools, feeding the hungry, and clothing the naked. Their focus, however, remains clear: the church must spread the gospel, relieve suffering, and prepare the faithful for the Lord's coming – not crush social injustice.[84] At times, individuals may emulate figures like Joseph and Esther from the Old Testament, speaking truth to power without resorting to overt activism or resistance. They employ the soft power of wisdom, humility, and unwavering commitment to moral convictions; they seek common ground and show respect for the human rights of all, including non-believers and established authority.

Hollenweger notes that the earliest Pentecostals were pacifists. In 1917, the Assemblies of God USA (AG USA) sent a statement to President Woodrow Wilson officially declaring itself a pacifist church.[85] The community within the church was the Spirit's strategy for transforming the world and them with it. Christian activism was considered the "works of the flesh" and destructive to love, unity, and missions. Land argues that most Pentecostal full-time workers do not engage in direct socio-political action but have created communities of care, respect, and empowerment, thus developing their own "affective

---

[80] William Hendriksen, *Exposition of Ephesians* (Ada, MI: Baker, 1967), 263. See also P.R. Coleman-Norton, "The Apostle Paul and the Roman Law of Slavery", in *Studies in Roman Economic and Social History in Honor of Allan Chester Johnson* (Princeton, NJ: Princeton University Press, 1951), 155-77; Ephesians 6:21.
[81] Pentecostals are often criticised for their lack of social consciousness and responsibility.
[82] Steven Jack Land, *Pentecostal Spirituality: A Passion for the Kingdom* (Cleveland, TN: CPT, 2010), 179.
[83] Douglas Petersen, *Pentecostals and Social Justice*, unpublished paper for The Pentecostal Movement of Sweden, Sweden, 25th March 2020: 9.
[84] Land, *Pentecostal Spirituality*, 179.
[85] Hollenweger, *Pentecostalism*, 188.

conscientisation" toward liberation.[86] The fruit of the Spirit, coupled with the gifts, unify and build up the community and qualify it for effective witness. Pentecostal liberation brings great joy because peace – not violent coercive manipulation – is the means and the goal of the fruit and gifts of the Spirit, respectively.[87] This chapter argues that this remains the best strategy for the Church today.[88]

The Urgent Need for Pentecostal Theological Education

If Pentecostalism is inherently well-suited for fostering racial and religious harmony, as well as preventing social strife caused by Christian activism, why do Pentecostals not pursue it more? It is my opinion that a dearth of rigorous Pentecostal theological education prevents such a pursuit. This was not the case at Antioch. Barnabas and Paul met with the church "for an entire year" and taught "a great many people" (Acts 11:23-26). Paul himself was a theologian par excellence. His fourteen years in Syria and Cilicia (Gal. 1:18-19, 21; 2:1), where he received revelations and spiritual experiences (Eph. 3:3-5; 2 Cor. 12:1-7), were mostly spent in Antioch.[89] There, Paul honed his understanding of christology, teaching the significance of Jesus' life, death, resurrection, exaltation, his present reign, and future coming.[90] The word "Christ" was constantly on the lips of believers to an extent that witty Antiochenes coined the moniker *Christianoi* (Acts 11:26).[91]

The necessity for rigorous theology was made abundantly clear at Antioch. For a while, Gentile believers were baptised without circumcision. When Judaisers arrived in the city, they insisted that Gentile converts must submit to circumcision and other law observance (Gal. 2:12). Paul's indignation increased when the Judaisers won Peter over to their side, stumbling many Jewish believers into joining him "in his hypocrisy"; even Barnabas was "led astray" (v. 13). Paul confronted Peter by asserting that "a person is not justified by works of the law,

---

[86] Cheryl Bridges Johns, *Pentecostal Formation: A Pedagogy among the Oppressed*, vol. 2 of *Journal of Pentecostal Theology Supplement Series* (Sheffield: Sheffield Academic Press, 1993).

[87] Certainly, individuals have the option to engage in social activism through non-violent and non-manipulative means, aligning with the perspective on addressing injustice as defined by Douglas Petersen above.

[88] Land, *Pentecostal Spirituality*, 207.

[89] Wayne Meeks believes that Paul resided in Antioch for more than a decade. Meeks, *First Urban Christians*, 10.

[90] Stott, *Message of Acts*, Acts 11.

[91] Edward Arbez, "Antioch", in *The Catholic Encyclopedia Vol. 1* (New York: Robert Appleton Company, 1907). No evidence suggests that it arose elsewhere. Among the Apostolic Fathers, it occurs only in Ignatius' letters, and again in Theophilus' apology. The verb form in Acts 11:26 does not specify whether the Antiochene Christians gave themselves that name or it was given to them by outsiders.

but through faith in Jesus Christ" (v. 16). To resolve the issue,[92] the Antioch Church appointed Paul and Barnabas to consult with the Jerusalem apostles (Acts 15:2) to clarify doctrine, end controversy, and promote peace. The outcome was a landmark decision: Gentile believers neither needed to follow Jewish customs and laws nor convert to Judaism. The message was clear: the sinner is saved by grace through faith in Christ alone. Justification is by *sola fide* (by faith alone), not a mixture of faith and works, grace and law, Christ and Moses. Gentile believers thus can have fellowship as authentic members of a multinational family.[93]

The Jerusalem Council served as a watershed of Christianity.[94] Galatians 2 and Acts 15 show the importance of theological clarity. Once the theological principle was firmly established, Paul made two conciliatory concessions. First, he accepted the four cultural abstentions (Acts 15:29) for Gentile converts, to ease Jewish conscience and facilitate Jewish-Gentile social intercourse. Second, he circumcised Timothy out of consideration for the Jews who would feel offended otherwise (16:3). With theological adeptness, Paul diffused an explosive situation. Antioch was the place where Paul formulated his theology. Many believe that the Gospel of Matthew,[95] the Gospel of Luke, the Acts of the Apostles, and the Epistle of James were all written there.[96] Antioch was home to many Christian leaders and theologians like Peter, Luke, Ignatius, and Chrysostom.[97] For the first six centuries, it was a centre of theological education.[98]

Alas, Pentecostals, in general, have not been known for theological sophistication. Many remain wary of academic theology, prioritising experience over disciplined theologising. Systematic thought is often equated with "the dry rot of orthodoxy" and the saying that "Pentecost is not a creed but an

---

[92] Scholars who hold the "South Galatian" view believe that the context of Acts 15 is Galatians 2. In addition to circumcision, Judaisers insisted that Gentile believers were "required to keep the law of Moses" (15:5). These Judaisers were teaching that faith in Jesus was insufficient for salvation, which undermined the very foundation of the Christian faith.
[93] Stott, *Message of Acts*, Acts 15.
[94] Ernst Haenchen, *Acts of the Apostles: A Commentary* (Louisville, KY: Westminster, 1971), 461.
[95] The Gospel of Matthew was used by Syrian writers such as Ignatius of Antioch.
[96] Freedman, "Antioch (Place)", 264–69.
[97] Eusebius of Caesarea, *Church History*, Book III, Documenta Catholica Omnia, 2006 [Available at: https://www.documentacatholicaomnia.eu/03d/0265-0339,_Eusebius_Caesariensis,_Church_History,_EN.pdf] [Last accessed: 29th March 2024]; See Horatio Balch Hackett, *A Commentary on the Original Text of the Acts of the Apostles* (Gould, AR: Gould and Lincoln, 1858), 12; See also Chrysostom Baur, "St John Chrysostom", in *The Catholic Encyclopedia Vol. 8* (New York: Robert Appleton, 1910).
[98] Britannica, "School of Antioch", *Encyclopaedia Britannica* [Available at: https://www.britannica.com/topic/School-of-Antioch] [Last accessed: 29th March 2024].

experience".[99] Such rhetoric makes the "traditioning" of experiences problematic because of the lack of an adequate theological foundation.

The embourgeoisement of Pentecostals should not cause them to seek evangelical respectability at the cost of their conviction on themes like political neutrality, women's equality, and the embracing of ecumenism. Pentecostals have their own identity in relation to mainstream evangelicalism, moving in directions in tension with the doctrines of Calvinism, dispensationalism, and cessationism.[100] Their eschatological understanding and piety are arguably more robustly pneumatological than conservative evangelicalism. Pentecostal theology rejects an arid, rationalistic, formalistic, unemotional, non-experiential, and non-charismatic approach,[101] as espoused by Charles Hodge and B.B. Warfield.[102] Pentecostals are evangelical only in the sense that they believe in the inspiration of Scripture. The Spirit, however, is prior to the written Word, and his purpose is not just to illumine Scripture and apply salvation's benefits to believers. Pentecostals believe that while "the Spirit does not contradict the Scriptures [...] his job is more than just repeating what we can find by reading there".[103] The Spirit remains actively involved in every part of salvation history, featuring a Spirit christology, Spirit soteriology, and Spirit ecclesiology. Hollenweger argues that Pentecostals should not be enamoured by evangelical and Protestant scholasticism but instead combine the Spirit's dynamic with cognitive academic theology.[104] More than ever, an urgent need exists for rigorous theological reflection that strengthens Pentecostal identity and witness in polycentric cultures like Singapore.[105]

Recovering the "Heart" of Pentecostalism

Pentecostalism must recover its historical roots, which are black oral, Wesleyan, Catholic, Protestant, and ecumenical.[106] The black spirituality root was mediated through Seymour, characterised by oral liturgy, narrative theology, participation

---

[99] Tan-Chow, *Pentecostal Theology*, 31–32.
[100] Hollenweger, *Pentecostalism*, 201–2.
[101] Donald R. Wheelock, *Spirit-Baptism in American Pentecostal Thought* (Atlanta, GA: Emory University, 1983), 334; See Douglas J. Nelson, "For Such a Time as This: the Story of Bishop William J. Seymour and the Azusa Street Revival; a Search for Pentecostal/Charismatic Roots" (Birmingham, UK: University of Birmingham, 1981).
[102] David R. Nichols, "The Search for a Pentecostal Structure in Systematic Theology", *Pneuma* 6(1) (1984), 73.
[103] J.W. Jones, *The Spirit and the World* (New York: Hawthorn, 1975), 98-99.
[104] Hollenweger, *Pentecostalism*, 303.
[105] Singapore is uniquely situated in a global centre of high technology, commerce, and trade. Here, we Pentecostals desire to be a people who stay attentive to the Spirit's impulse in expressing the *imago Dei* through expanding lay ministry and creativity in the church, as well as through believers flourishing in workplace spirituality.
[106] Hollenweger, *Pentecostalism*, 2.

of the whole church in prayer and worship, visions and dreams, witnessing, and the healing ministry.[107] Their media were sermons, songs, pamphlets, testimonies, and conferences, not unlike the first hundred years of Christianity.

Pentecostalism also has a Wesleyan root, with shared beliefs like Arminianism, supernaturalism, and the *ordo salutis* of a subsequent experience after conversion.[108] Wesley's creative Protestant-Catholic construction was drawn from both Eastern and Western traditions, while always seeking to remain faithful to Scripture.[109]

Pentecostal spirituality thus embodies Catholic transformation of a deep and personal union with God through contemplative prayer, mystical experiences, and ascetic practices.[110] Instead of calling it "mysticism", we term it "divine encounters" and "being touched by the Lord". At the same time, Eastern Orthodox pneumatology stresses each member of the Trinity equally in a *perichoresis* seeking to bring creation into their loving embrace.[111] Pentecostal soteriology is, therefore, more than just forensic justification by the removal of guilt, but an ever-deepening communion with the Father by the Spirit, leading to a transformative *theosis* in conformation to image of the Son (2 Cor. 3:18). The greatest evidence of the indwelling Spirit is love for God and for all others. Pentecostals also reject the Calvinistic pneumatology of *filioque*, that the Spirit has no dignity on his own but is an inferior member of the Trinity.[112]

A new intercultural, ecumenical theology is also needed. Pentecostalism from its inception was manifestly ecumenical – freely crossing denominational, social, racial, and economic boundaries. Unity and embrace within the body of Christ were intuited as the necessary correlates of the Spirit's presence and outpouring. Pentecostals should return to their ecumenical root through dialogue with other church traditions and organised ecumenism. Because Pentecostalism understands the third article ("I believe in the Holy Spirit") well, it is tolerant and open to new unknown moves of the Spirit. It can easily consult with non-Christians on religion and peace and embrace a global ethos of love.[113] No doubt this might inflame some evangelicals, but it would also make clear that

---

[107] Land, *Pentecostal Spirituality*, 52. See Walter J. Hollenweger, "After Twenty Years' Research on Pentecostalism", *Theology* 87(720) (1984), 405-6 [Available at: https://doi.org/10.1177/0040571X8408700602] [Last accessed: 30th March 2024]. See also Leonard Lovett, "Black Origins of Pentecostalism", in Vinson Synan (ed), *Aspects of Pentecostal-Charismatic Origins* (Plainfield, NJ: Logos, 1975), 145-58; See also Walter J. Hollenweger, "The Black Pentecostal Concept: Interpretations and Variations", *Concept* 30 (1970), 16-17.

[108] Hollenweger, *Pentecostalism*, 143.

[109] Land, *Pentecostal Spirituality*, 222.

[110] Sung Jin Song, "John Wesley and Mysticism", 14th Institute of The Oxford Institute of Methodist Theological Studies, Pembroke College, 12th–19th August 2018.

[111] Hollenweger, *Pentecostalism*, 218.

[112] Hollenweger, *Pentecostalism*, 218, 221.

[113] Hollenweger, *Pentecostalism*, 399.

Pentecostals are not just "evangelical plus fire" but have their own identity as pioneers in new areas of the Spirit's workings, as seen in the work of du Plessis and others.

Finally, Pentecostals must engage in humble self-reflection. Heretical theologies, outrageous visions, preposterous fundraising schemes, financial improprieties, and scandalous moral failures among its ranks expose Pentecostal hermeneutics as deficient and inadequate in translating biblical principles to everyday moral application.[114] However, the wholesale adopting of a fundamentalist and evangelical hermeneutics that ultimately rejects Pentecostalism is not the answer. After more than a century, the Pentecostal Movement today consists of classical, charismatic, neo-Pentecostals (third wavers) and neo-charismatics. We should humbly repent and honestly deal with the abuse of theologies within our ranks and not allow fringe doctrines like hyper-faith, hyper-grace, the prosperity gospel, and dominion theology to hijack Pentecostalism. Where is the place of suffering? How do we ride the tension of the already and not yet? Pentecostal theology is a serious study of immense depth and breadth.

Conclusion

I feel strongly convinced that Pentecostalism remains pivotal in maintaining and fostering racial and religious harmony, and in preventing social strife caused by Christian activism. However, the need exists for an educational renaissance within Pentecostal circles for theological clarity and robust understanding. Pentecostalism is not anti-intellectual and anti-ecumenical. Is Singapore the "Antioch of Asia"? Perhaps. Or perhaps not yet. Suffice it to say, the Pentecostal Spirit remains key to us drawing ever closer to the fulfilment of that dream.

Bibliography

Harmony Circle. "About Harmony Circle", *Racial & Religious Harmony Circles Website*. [Available at: https://www.harmonycircle.sg/about-harmonycircle/] [Last accessed: 30th March 2024].

Anderson, Gary L. "The Changing Nature of the Moral Crisis of American Christianity". Unpublished paper presented to the 38th Annual Meeting of the Society for Pentecostal Studies, 1990.

Arbez, Edward. "Antioch", In *The Catholic Encyclopedia Vol. 1* New York: Robert Appleton, 1907.

---

[114] Gary L. Anderson, "The Changing Nature of the Moral Crisis of American Christianity", Unpublished paper presented to the 38th Annual Meeting of the Society for Pentecostal Studies, 1990: 3. Cited by Hollenweger, *Pentecostalism*, 312.

Bartleman, Frank. "The Great Earthquake", *Revival Library*. [Available at: https://revival-library.org/revival-histories/pentecostal-revivals/american-pentecostal-revival/azusa-street-revival/] [Last accessed: 30th March 2024].

——. *What Really Happened at Azusa Street?* Northridge, CA: Voice Christian, 1962.

Baur, Chrysostom. "St John Chrysostom", In *The Catholic Encyclopedia Vol. 8*. New York: Robert Appleton, 1910.

Bebbington, David W. *Evangelicalism in Modern Britain: A History from the 1730s to the 1980s*. New York: Routledge, 2003.

Bridges Johns, Cheryl. *Pentecostal Formation: A Pedagogy among the Oppressed*. Vol. 2 of *Journal of Pentecostal Theology Supplement Series*. Sheffield: Sheffield Academic Press, 1993.

Britannica. "School of Antioch", *Encyclopaedia Britannica*. [Available at: https://www.britannica.com/topic/School-of-Antioch] [Last accessed: 29th March 2024].

Butler, Trent C., Ed. "Antioch", In *Holman Bible Dictionary*. Nashville, TN: Holman Bible, 1991. [Available at: https://www.studylight.org/dictionaries/eng/hbd/a/antioch.html/] [Last accessed: 27th March 2024].

Chan, Simon. "Chan on Tan-Chow, '*Pentecostal Theology for the Twenty-first Century: Engaging with Multi-Faith Singapore*'", *H-Pentecostalism*. December 2007. [Available at: https://networks.h-net.org/node/9663/reviews/11358/chan-tan-chow-pentecostal-theology-twenty-first-century-engaging-multi] [Last accessed: 29th March 2024].

Chong, Terence. "Christian Activism in Singapore", In Terence Chong, Ed. *Navigating Differences: Integration in Singapore*. Singapore: ISEAS, 2020: 36-55.

Clammer, John. *Singapore: Ideology, Society and Culture*. Singapore: Chopmen, 1985.

Clay, Doug. "Five Leadership Lessons of William J. Seymour", *Influence Magazine*. 22nd February 2021. [Available at: https://influencemagazine.com/en/Practice/Five-Leadership-Lessons-of-William-J-Seymour] [30th March 2024].

Coleman-Norton, P.R. "The Apostle Paul and the Roman Law of Slavery", In P.R. Coleman-Norton, Ed. *Studies in Roman Economic and Social History in Honor of Allan Chester Johnson*. Princeton, NJ: Princeton University Press, 1951: 155-77.

Costanzo, Eric P. "Antioch of Syria", In John D. Barry *et al.*, Eds. *The Lexham Bible Dictionary*. Bellingham, WA: Lexham, 2016. [Available at: https://biblia.com/books/lbd/word/Antioch_of_Syria] [Last accessed: 27th March 2024].

EDB Singapore. "Global Connectivity", *EDB Singapore Website*. [Available at: https://www.edb.gov.sg/en/why-singapore/global-connectivity.html] [Last accessed: 27th March 2024].

Erickson, Millard J. "Christian", In *The Concise Dictionary of Christian Theology*. Rev. ed. Wheaton, IL: Crossway, 2001. E-book.

Eusebius of Caesarea. *Church History*. Book III. Documenta Catholica Omnia. 2006. [Available at: https://www.documentacatholicaomnia.eu/03d/0265-0339,_Eusebius_Caesariensis,_Church_History,_EN.pdf] [Last accessed: 29th March 2024].

Freedman, David Noel. "Antioch (Place)", In *The Anchor Yale Bible Dictionary*, Vol. 1 A-C. 1st ed. New York: Doubleday, 1992.

Goh, Daniel P.S. "Grace, Megachurches, and the Christian Prince in Singapore", In Terence Chong, Ed. *Pentecostal Megachurches in Southeast Asia: Negotiating Class, Consumption and the Nation*. Singapore: ISEAS-Yusof Ishak Institute, 2018: 181-206.

——. "Protest and the Culture War in Singapore", In Terence Chong, Ed. *Navigating Differences: Integration in Singapore*. Singapore: ISEAS, 2020: 129-47.

——. "State and Social Christianity in Post-Colonial Singapore", *SOJOURN: Journal of Social Issues in Southeast Asia* 25(1), (2010), 54-89.

Hackett, Horatio Balch. *A Commentary on the Original Text of the Acts of the Apostles*. Gould, AR: Gould and Lincoln, 1858.

Haenchen, Ernst. *Acts of the Apostles: A Commentary*. Louisville, KY: Westminster, 1971.

Hendriksen, William. *Exposition of Ephesians*. Ada, MI: Baker, 1967.

Hollenweger, Walter J. "The Black Pentecostal Concept: Interpretations and Variations", *Concept* 30 (1970), 1-70.

——. *Pentecostalism: Origins and Developments Worldwide*. Peabody, MA: Hendrickson, 1997

——. "Pentecostals and the Charismatic Movement", In Geoffrey Cheslyn Jones and Edward Yarnold Wainwright, Eds. *The Study of Spirituality*. London: SPCK, 1986: 549-53.

——. "After Twenty Years' Research on Pentecostalism", *Theology* 87(720), (1984), 403-12 [Available at: https://doi.org/10.1177/0040571X8408700602] ,[Last accessed: 30th March 2024].

Hussain, Zakir. "Dr Thio Upset about Sexuality Programme", *The Straits Times*, 24th April 2009.

Jones, J.W. *The Spirit and the World*. New York: Hawthorn, 1975.

Krodel, Gerhard A. *Acts*. Augsburg Commentary on the New Testament. Minneapolis, MN: Augsburg, 1986.

Land, Steven Jack. *Pentecostal Spirituality: A Passion for the Kingdom*. Cleveland, TN: CPT, 2010.

Liow, Joseph Chinyong. "Managing Religious Diversity and Multiculturalism in Singapore", In Terence Chong, Ed. *Navigating Differences: Integration in Singapore*. Singapore: ISEAS, 2020: 19-35.

Lovett, Leonard. "Black Origins of Pentecostalism", In Vinson Synan, Ed. *Aspects of Pentecostal-Charismatic Origins*. Plainfield, NJ: Logos, 1975: 145-58.

Macchia, Frank D. *Jesus the Spirit Baptizer: Christology in Light of Pentecost*. Grand Rapids, MI: Wm. B. Eerdmans, 2021.

Martin, David. "Missions and the Plurality of Faiths", Lecture presented at the Faculty of Divinity, University of Cambridge, October 2001.

Mathews, Mathew. "Pentecostalism in Singapore: History, Adaptation and Future", In Denise A. Austin, Jacqueline Grey, and Paul W. Lewis, Eds. *Asia Pacific Pentecostalism*. Leiden: Brill, 2019: 271-94.

McGavran, Donald. *Understanding Church Growth*. Grand Rapids, MI: Eerdmans, 1970.

Meeks, Wayne A. *The First Urban Christians: The Social World of the Apostle Paul*. New Haven, CT: Yale University Press, 1983.

Menzies, Robert P. "Pentecost: This Story is Our Story", *Enrichment Journal* (Fall 2013), 38-45. [Available at: https://enrichmentjournal.ag.org/Issues/2013/Fall-2013] [Last accessed: 30th March 2024].

Ministry of Home Affairs. "Overview of Safety and Security Situation in 2022." *Ministry of Home Affairs*, Press Release. 8th February 2023. [Available at: https://www.mha.gov.sg/mediaroom/press-releases/overview-of-safety-and-security-situation-in-2022] [Last accessed: 27th March 2024].

National Population and Talent Division. *Population in Brief 2023: Key Trends*. Singapore: Prime Minister's Office, 2023.

Nelson, Douglas J. "For Such a Time as This: the Story of Bishop William J. Seymour and the Azusa Street Revival; a Search for Pentecostal/Charismatic Roots". Birmingham, UK: University of Birmingham, 1981.

Nichols, David R. "The Search for a Pentecostal Structure in Systematic Theology", *Pneuma* 6(1), (1984), 57-76.

Nirmala, M. "Govt More Open to Employing Gays Now", *The Straits Times*, 4th July 2003.

The Online Citizen. "26,000 Crowd Celebrate the Freedom to Love at Pink Dot 2014", *The Online Citizen*. 28th June 2014. [Available at: http://www.theonlinecitizen.com/2014/06/26000-crowd-celebrate-the-freedom-to-love-at-pink-dot-2014] [Last accessed: 29th March 2024].

Petersen, Douglas. "Pentecostals and Social Justice", Unpublished paper for The Pentecostal Movement of Sweden, Sweden, 25th March 2020.

Pew Research Center. "Global Religious Diversity", *Pew Research Center Website*. 4th April 2014. [Available at: https://www.pewresearch.org/religion/2014/04/04/global-religious-diversity/] [Last accessed: 27th March 2024].

The Pluralism Project. "Fundamentalism, Evangelicalism, and Pentecostalism", *Harvard University: The Pluralism Project*. Updated 25th October 2023. [Available at:

https://pluralism.org/files/pluralism/files/evangelicalism_fundamentalism_and_pentecostalism.pdf?m=1648211809] [Last accessed: 28th March 2024].

Pryke, Wai Yin. "Singapore's Journey: Bilingualism and Role of English Language in Our Development", Transcript of presentation to British Council, Chile, 2013. [Available at: https://www.britishcouncil.cl/sites/default/files/escrito-way-yin-pryke.pdf] [Last accessed: 27th March 2024].

Reuters. "Religious Conflict in Global Rise", *The Telegraph*. 14th January 2014. [Available at: https://www.telegraph.co.uk/news/worldnews/middleeast/10572342/Religious-conflict-in-global-rise-report.html#:~:text=Violence%20and%20discrimination%20against%20religious,by%20the%20Pew%20Research%20Centre] [Last accessed: 27th March 2024].

Shanmugam, K. "The 2nd SRP Distinguished Lecture and Symposium 2016 – Opening Address by Mr. K. Shanmugam, Minister for Home Affairs and Minister for Law", *Ministry of Home Affairs*. 19th January 2016. [Available at: https://www.mha.gov.sg/mediaroom/speeches/the-2nd-srp-distinguished-lecture-and-symposium-2016---opening-address-by-mr-k-shanmugam-minister-for-home-affairs-and-minister-for-law/] [Last accessed: 30th March 2024].

Statista. "Share of Population in Singapore in 2020, By Religion", *Statista Website*. Updated 22nd May 2023. [Available at (behind a paywall), https://www.statista.com/statistics/1113870/singapore-share-of-population-by-religion/] [Last accessed: 28th March 2024].

Singapore Centre for Global Missions. *An Antioch of Asia: The National Missions Study 2019 Report*. Singapore: Singapore Centre for Global Missions, 2019. [Available at: https://www.scgm.org.sg/wp-content/uploads/2020/04/NMS2019-Report.pdf] [Last accessed: 27th March 2024].

Singapore Infopedia. "Maria Hertogh Riots", *National Library Board Singapore*. 28th September 2014. [Available at: https://www.nlb.gov.sg/main/article-detail?cmsuuid=fbc266c5-4f6f-49d8-b77e-d37e20742087] [Last accessed: 30th March 2024].

——. "Jewish Community", *National Library Board Singapore*. April 2018. [Available at: https://www.nlb.gov.sg/main/article-detail?cmsuuid=b176a5a8-100e-49f7-9dbc-41b0b31779d7#:~:text=The%20history%20of%20the%20Jewish,their%20exile%20from%20ancient%20Israel] [Last accessed: 27th March 2024].

Singapore Ministry of Foreign Affairs. "About Singapore", *Singapore Ministry of Foreign Affairs*. Updated 12th October 2023. [Available at: https://www.mfa.gov.sg/Overseas-Mission/Washington/About-Singapore] [Last accessed: 27th March 2024].

Singapore Statutes. "Internal Security Act 1960 (2020 rev. ed.), section 8 (Singapore)", *Singapore Statutes Online*. 1st December 2021. [Available at: https://sso.agc.gov.sg/Act/ISA1960] [Last accessed: 30th March 2024].

Singapore Statutes. "Penal Code 1871 (2020 rev. ed.), sections 298, 436 (Singapore)", *Singapore Statutes Online*. 1st December 2021. [Available at: https://sso.agc.gov.sg/Act/PC1871] [Last accessed: 30th March 2024].

Singapore Statutes. "Societies Act (2020 rev. ed.), section 24 (1) (a) (Singapore)", *Singapore Statutes Online*. 1st December 2021. [Available at: https://sso.agc.gov.sg//Act/SA1966] [Last accessed: 30th March 2024].

Song, Sung Jin. "John Wesley and Mysticism", 14th Institute of The Oxford Institute of Methodist Theological Studies, Pembroke College, 12th–19th August 2018.

Stott, John R.W. *The Message of Acts*, The Bible Speaks Today. Downers Grove, IL: InterVarsity, 2014.

——. *The Message of Ephesians*. The Bible Speaks Today. Downers Grove, IL: IVP, 1979.

Tan-Chow, May Ling. *Pentecostal Theology for the Twenty-First Century: Engaging with Multi-Faith Singapore*. Abingdon: Routledge, 2016.

Teo, Lemuel. "The Church Going Urban", *Singapore Centre for Global Missions*. Updated 14th June 2018. [Available at: https://www.scgm.org.sg/the-church-going-urban] [Last accessed: 27th March 2024].

Ventura, Luca. "Richest Countries in the World 2023", *Global Finance*. 30th January 2023. [Available at: https://www.gfmag.com/global-data/economic-data/richest-countries-in-the-world] [Last accessed: 27th March 2024].

Volf, Miroslav. "Wheaton Professor's Suspension is about Anti-Muslim Bigotry, Not Theology", *The Washington Post*. 17th December 2015. [Available at: https://www.washingtonpost.com/news/acts-of-faith/wp/2015/12/17/wheaton-professors-suspension-is-about-anti-muslim-bigotry-not-theology] [Last accessed: 30th March 2024].

Wheelock, Donald R. *Spirit-Baptism in American Pentecostal Thought*. Atlanta, GA: Emory University, 1983.

Worcester Art Museum. "Antioch: The Lost Ancient City – City of Antioch", *Worcester Art Museum*. Webpage about October 2000 exhibition. [Available at: https://archive.worcesterart.org/exhibitions/antioch.html] [Last accessed: 27th March 2024].

Yong, Amos. *The Spirit Poured Out on All Flesh: Pentecostalism and the Possibility of Global Theology*. Ada, MI: Baker Academic, 2005.

Contemporary Challenges Facing Global Pentecostalism

Kong Hee, Byron D. Klaus, and Douglas Petersen

Numerous challenges face Pentecostalism in today's global society. The natural process of secularisation inevitably impacts any revivalist movement. Additionally, the geopolitical volatility of the Majority World creates an ever-changing array of challenges for the continued effectiveness of the Global Pentecostal Movement. The challenges addressed in this section are not an exhaustive list but are real and daunting, thus requiring sturdy theological reflection.

Kim-Kwong Chan is a noted scholar on the state of the Church in China. Currently living in Hong Kong, he maintains close relationships with a broad spectrum of Christians in China. He makes clear that the significant growth of Chinese Christianity over the last four decades is facing a new and formidable challenge as the leadership of Xi Jinping exhibits its full intent. Undoubtedly, the COVID-19 era further highlighted the design of Xi to restrain all challenges to governmental control, with religion clearly in the crosshairs of those efforts. This new reality requires that global Pentecostal leaders see beyond the reports of devout spirituality in the face of persecution or the potential of global mission from China connected to the pathways that China's Belt Road Initiative might have provided.

Chan highlights the fact that the historic bias against Christianity, as a Western intruder to Chinese culture, is further exploited with an intentional *Sinicisation* of Christianity. Reading this chapter is likely to elicit déjà vu to a similar process during the 1930s in Germany.

Chan does note that the meteoric growth of Christianity since the 1980s seems to have levelled off. While differing points of view about the number of Christians in China are present, clearly, a triumphalist view of Christianity's growth in China must be exchanged for serious theological reflection on what it means in China to follow Jesus today. Additionally, a sense of unity among Christian groups within China is not evident.

As with any historical example of significant growth of the Church in Christian history, the inevitable challenges related to coming of age are present. While the last forty years of Christianity's growth in China have occurred in the face of brutal persecution, the current realities would seem to indicate an unprecedented systemic effort to neutralise the Church in China.

While Asia certainly represents a region where the growth of Christianity is increasingly documented, relatively little has been told about the role of women sacrificially involved in missionary efforts in the region. **Julie Ma** not only tells some of those stories in her chapter but embodies someone herself who has effectively faced the stiff headwinds that culture places in front of women who make a faith commitment to Christ and make subsequent efforts in pioneering missionary activity.

Ma begins her chapter with two assumptions. She cites the fact the two-thirds of the world's Christians presently reside in the Global South. Additionally, she notes that the typical global Christian is a non-White woman living in the Global South. She then refers to the reality facing women in Asia (and other regions of the Majority World) whose identity is formed in reference to their relationship to a man – or in reference to lack of such a relationship. She highlights the inevitable societal exploitation that can occur and the roadblocks that face women in ecclesial settings. She uses her own experience as a biographical case study to demonstrate the long road she has had to traverse in her career as a missionary to unreached people groups and as a theological educator.

Ma's chapter does not take the usual tact of describing the obvious injustices that face women in the Global South or even opining those additional challenges facing women called to ministry in the region. Rather, she offers narratives of female Christian leaders in Asia and uses their stories to demonstrate the democratising power of Pentecost. She asks rhetorically: "What would it take for Pentecostal churches or denominations to elect or appoint women to significant ecclesial roles in their organisations?" She encourages women to counter Asian culture's expectation that women should always defer. She calls them instead to follow her personal stance of moving forward with confidence and to see themselves as qualified because of the transformative power of Christ. (As a special note, Dr Ma's original presentation at the Global Pentecostal Summit was heard by over 400 people; 90 percent of whom were young, Asian women. Dr Ma represented a living embodiment of what she presented. Her story was a "voice loud and clear" as a source of empowerment for that young, primarily female audience.)

Mary K. Mahon serves as president of a large Pentecostal ministry to children born in poverty throughout Latin America and the Caribbean. Working with over 100,000 children in twenty countries, she has experienced the debilitating aspects of poverty that rob children of their God-given human dignity. The challenges she faces working with these children is mirrored throughout the Majority World. Dr Mahon focuses her chapter on investigating how the Holy Spirit's work in children's lives can serve as the doorway to agency in their human development.

Mahon cites research from the social sciences about the development of agency in a child's growth. She provides integration of social scientific research with stories of children born into poverty and how each of their "personal Pentecosts" have emerged as narratives of empowerment. She posits that such a Holy Spirit-empowered process develops cognitive growth that the experience of poverty usually crushes. She uses the language of developmentalists like

James Fowler, Robert Coles, David Hay, and Rebecca Nye to describe what the transforming moment of a "personal Pentecost" can mean in a child's life.

Mahon's work proposes much more than simply creating a more informed ministry to children. She acknowledges the debilitating reality of children born into poverty. Women and children regularly experience the most violent aspects of the volatility that accompanies the rapidly changing political and economic landscapes of the Majority World. Integration of development literature and the narratives of children's transformative Holy Spirit encounters, however, provides an alternative picture of human agency created in the most debilitating circumstances – the kingdom of God revealed in the most unlikely places.

Joel Tejedo provides a pertinent look into megachurch life using focused research among megachurch attendees in Metro Manila. This research was made possible by grant funding from the John Templeton Foundation. The pertinence of this research applies to Global Pentecostalism in that there is no lack of Pentecostal megachurches globally. The narratives that get the most visible press (to date) tend to report the examples of exploitive leadership and shallow theological teaching that yields a stereotype of Pentecostal spirituality as shallow rooted. While those narratives are not without foundation, Tejedo provides an alternative to the usual framing of megachurch life. He moves from focusing on the megachurch and its organisational qualities and activities to a broadened picture of its impact on the social context in which it exists.

Tejedo provides the methodology and results of his research, which serves as at least one well-documented example that counters the usual negativity surrounding megachurches. Positing that megachurches have had obvious influence on Global Christianity, Tejedo offers evidence in his research of some broader social realities. He notes that megachurches have offered an urban face to Christianity that resonates well with the flourishing of life in urban contexts. In addition, megachurches can serve as therapeutic institutions with a repository of transcendent values that can heal a nation. Megachurches provide moral empowerment and can provide influential opposition to corruption.

In Tejedo's comprehensive research, he arrives at conclusions that both substantiate popularly held views about megachurches as well as counter some broadly held assumptions. In his research in Metro Manila, megachurch attendees are young – primarily Millennials and Gen Z. Congregants have had genuine conversion experiences that occur in contexts that foster a deep commitment to intentional discipleship and to the authority of Scripture and its prescriptive teaching on moral issues. Attendees were digitally savvy and ubiquitous users of technology. While some participated in political processes, they tended not to align with particular political parties.

Although Tejedo delimits his research to Metro Manila, the project of which he is a part continues to explore the megachurch phenomenon in other Majority World urban centres. His research proves quite useful in that it provides an alternative and generally positive picture that needs to be considered as the megachurch continues to function as an influential force in Global Christianity.

Guichun Jun provides a fascinating foray into the metaverse. With the pervasive influence of the Internet and the resulting world of virtual reality facing Global Christianity, this presentation goes where few have dared to tread. While the negative impact of technology can be argued, Jun's presentation offers a diligent investigation of what untapped opportunities the Holy Spirit might be providing for the Church.

Jun's chapter certainly delves into the details of the metaverse, and digital immigrant's eyes may initially glaze over and move on; what readers will encounter, however, is serious, technologically informed theological reflection. The author affirms that the presence and power of the Holy Spirit are not confined to physical space but permeate the entirety of created order. He desires a deeper and wider understanding of the Holy Spirit in the digital age.

To that end, you will see themes including virtual churches and the role of the Holy Spirit in creating community and unity in virtual spaces. You will see queries into how the Holy Spirit's power and presence operate in the metaverse. For example, he discusses this in reference to regeneration, sanctification, and impartation. To seriously venture into spaces that must not be avoided, Jun also diligently explores the interplay of the transcendent nature of the Holy Spirit and the immanence of God's presence. For those who might resist such a journey, this is not a new idea. Even in the early days of television, Oral Roberts asked people to put their hands on the television as a "point of contact" to release the healing power of God. When one considers the words of Oral Roberts more than a half century ago, Jun's investigation into the Holy Spirit in the metaverse does not seem out of line.

The German research firm *Statista* (http://www.statista.com) clearly places the population of the Majority World as overwhelmingly young. For example, the African continent has 40 percent of its population under fifteen years of age. Asia and Latin America have about one-quarter of their population under fifteen years of age. While cultural differences exist around the world, the Internet and a globalised economy have created surprising homogeneity among the younger inhabitants of our planet.

Antipas Harris provides an in-depth study of Gen Z and why they hold such a critical place in the continued growth of Global Christianity. While using Gen Z as a precise category, Harris also points out pitfalls of "tribalising" people into age groups. However, he posits that the challenges which Gen Z face are taking a different form than those faced by previous generations. Even in more traditional regions, historic religious assumptions are meeting secularised views of the world. The institution of the family is morphing and is less stable than in previous times. Undoubtedly, modern technology has impacted Gen Z in ways that older adults could never have imagined, and that technology has led to social isolation on an unprecedented scale (exacerbated by the COVID-19 pandemic).

Harris notes that the internal questions that exist as part of the development growth of people in Gen Z have taken on a different shape. "Who am I, and why am I here?" seem unchanged. However, a reshaping of one's perception of the transcendent has occurred, with the question, "Is there a power greater than me, and can life be better for me?" Also, "Does the 'ultimate being' care about what's going on in the world?" These questions represent a morphing of the developmental process reflective of a postmodern focus on self and a reframing of the place of the transcendent in our lives.

Harris makes clear that churches whose community life is negative, with infighting as a social dynamic, will *not* attract Gen Z. Rather, churches that welcome Gen Z into leadership opportunities *will* be attractive to them. Above all, Gen Z must not be seen as an object of ministry activity so much as partners in the mission of a congregation.

14. The Challenges of the Church in China in the Next Decade

Kim-Kwong Chan

Abbreviations

ACC   Autonomous Christian Communities
BRI   Belt Road Initiatives
CPC   Chinese Communist Party
PRC   People's Republic of China
TSPM/CCC   Three Self Patriotic Movement/China Christian Council

Introduction

After the end of China's Great Proletarian Cultural Revolution (1966–1976), China began to adopt an Open and Reform Policy with the marketisation of China's economy, which resulted in an economic boom. Part of the Open and Reform Policy included re-opening religious venues such as churches and allowing religious believers to practice religion hitherto banned during the Cultural Revolution. Christianity, once considered as decimated from Chinese society after three decades of suppression by the Chinese Communist regime, suddenly emerged from the shadows. Christianity rapidly expanded among the official affiliated Three Self Patriotic Movement/China Christian Council (TSPM/CCC)[1] and among the various unregistered Autonomous Christian Communities (ACC),[2] also known as house churches, underground churches, or family churches.

From the Governments' official figures which only counted those Christians who were under the Government's registered churches, there were only three million Chinese Protestants in 1982 (0.38 percent of the population). This number raised to ten million in the 1990s (1 percent of the population), twenty-three million in 2010 (2 percent of the population) and in 2018, thirty-eight million (2.7 percent of the population).[3] However the number would be much

---

[1] "Home Page," China Christian Council National Committee of Three-Self Patriotic Movement of the Protestant Churches in China (TSPM/CCC) [Available at: https://en.ccctspm.org/] [Last accessed: 1st April 2024].
[2] Alan Hunter and Kim-Kwong Chan, *Protestantism in Contemporary China* (Cambridge: Cambridge University Press, 1993), 81.
[3] Kim-Kwong Chan, *Understanding World Christianity: China*, series edited by Dyron B. Daughrity (Minneapolis, MN; Fortress, 2019), 32.

higher if one includes those churches which were not operating under the Government's control. For example, in 2011, Pew Research Center presented the figure of fifty-eight million Protestants in China (4 percent of the population) as its methodology included those not registered with the authority – hence with a higher figure than what the authority had provided.[4] The Christians population had grown ten to twenty times larger within a short span of thirty years, depending on if one included the non-registered Christians or not. In 2014, Professor Yang Fenggang of Purdue University suggested that, by 2030, the number of Chinese Protestants would outpace the number of Chinese Communist Party (CPC) Members.[5] With such rapid growth, the Protestant community in China established theological training, pastoral formation, ecumenical connection, local church planting, and even overseas missions. Such phenomenal development of the Church in China drew attention from the global Christian community, especially with respect to its impressive church growth while under political constraint, its development of spirituality while facing persecution, and its remarkable potential in global missions as China has increasingly connected with the world through its Belt Road Initiatives (BRI).[6]

Since assuming the leadership over China in 2013, Xi Jinping has not only reversed China's Reform and Open Policy (a marketed economy adopted since the 1980s) back to the pre-1980 Socialist Planned Economic Policy but he has also governed China under a strong CPC autocratic governance; this has decreased room for individual freedom and increased control over all sectors of life including religion. Furthermore, Xi positioned China as a rival with the West and shielded China from Western influences such as democracy, human rights, and even religious cultures such as Christianity.

Under Xi's reign, which has also covered the period of the COVID-19 pandemic (2020–2023), the Church in China has faced many new restrictions, challenges, transformations, and opportunities. This chapter looks at the challenges ahead of this vibrant and dynamic Christian people numbering in the tens of millions living under an autocratic regime at the juncture of entering a

---

[4] C. Hackett, B. Grim, V. Skirbekk, M. Stonawski, and A. Goujon, *Global Christianity: A Report on the Size and Distribution of the World's Christian Population* (Washington DC: Pew Research Center, 2011), 84, 97-110.
[5] Alison Lesley, "The Christian and Muslim Community in China is multiplying", *World Religion News*, 7th September 2015 [Available at: https://www.worldreligionnews.com/religion-news/christianity/the-christian-and-muslim-community-in-china-is-multiplying/] [Last accessed: 1st April 2024]. See also Jamil Anderlini, "The Rise of Christianity in China", *Financial Times*, 11th November 2014 [Available at: https://www.ft.com/content/a6d2a690-6545-11e4-91b1-00144feabdc0] [Last accessed: 1st April 2024].
[6] For a brief summary, see Jie Yu and Jon Wallace, "What is China's Belt Road Initiative?" *Chatham House Explainer*, 13th September 2021 [Available at: https://www.chathamhouse.org/2021/09/what-chinas-belt-and-road-initiative-bri] [Last accessed: 1st April 2024].

new world order. First, the chapter provides a general orientation of Xi Jinping's governance, particularly those elements with a direct bearing on the present state of the Christian Church in China. Then I highlight several issues that I perceive as major challenges facing the Church in China in the coming decade: ecclesial manifestation and internalisation of faith; Christian unity; Sinicisation (Christianity in China or Chinese Christianity), and lastly, missiology, diasporas, and nationalistic sentiment.[7] Some of these challenges may prove particular to the Church in China, and some may resonate with other Christian communities due to living in a digitalised world with inter-connectivity often transcending geographic boundaries. After all, Christian communities all embrace similar values, live in the same world, connect through the same Internet, and are affected by similar global trends.

Xi Jinping's Reign 2012-2023 and Its Implication for Chinese Christianity

Over the past decade, the world has faced many challenges – from global warming and the effects of climate change; to multiple refugee crises; to the war against Ukraine; to the devastating COVID-19 pandemic when schools, public institutions, churches, and shops were closed, and physical contact was discouraged. Virtual reality became a daily reality. This pandemic not only took nearly seven million lives[8] but also slowed the global economy by shutting down factories, interrupting supply chains, and the decrease in consumer demands affecting every country including China. The world is still recovering from the pandemic as other global crises emerge daily.

Xi Jinping became China's paramount leader during the past decade of global turbulence – a time when China has been at its strongest moment in history in terms of wealth, military capability, production, average per capita income, mobilisation capacity, political control, and geopolitical ambition. Xi has a vision for China: a China that would demand respect from the world by its newly gained national strength, a China that would become the economic engine of Eurasia via the Belt Road Initiatives, a China that would format a multipolar world order with China as one of the most important players, a China that would regain all its sovereign territories including Taiwan, and, most significantly, a China governed by an ideological construct encompassing the vision of a Socialist China under the authorship of Xi's name: "Xi Jinping Thought on Socialism with Chinese Characteristics for a New Era."[9] Xi's vision on China

---

[7] Chan, *Understanding World Christianity: China*, 198-200.
[8] This was the figure as of August 2023. See WHO, "WHO Coronavirus (COVID-19) Dashboard", *World Health Organization Website* [Available at: https://covid19.who.int/] [Last accessed: 1st April 2024].
[9] Xi's thoughts were enshrined in the Party's Constitution at the 20th CPC National Congress, in October 2022. Xi's Thought is now on par with Karl Marx, Vladimir

was the realisation of the promises made to the Chinese people by the CPC since the foundation of People's Republic of China (PRC) in 1949: an egalitarian and prosperous society, a proud nation to build upon its historical and cultural heritage, a nation on par with Western powers to shape the global geopolitical order, and a sovereign and unified China. To achieve his goals, Xi consolidated his leadership over the Party, established direct Party control over all social sectors, and promoted his form of socialist ideology along with a unified nationalistic political culture.

The last decade from 2013 to 2023 has witnessed drastic changes in China's domestic governance affecting every sphere of life, including religion and certainly Christianity in particular. Radical changes in China's foreign relations during this time have seen anti-Westernism sentiments affecting the links that Chinese Christians have with fellow Christians abroad. As well, these changes have impacted many other relationships. Religion in China, as with all other civil organisations there, has followed the political guidance of Xi during this time. In Xi's vision, China would experience rejuvenation along with her long cultural heritage coupled with xenophobia and strong nationalistic sentiment.

China has long regarded Christianity as a product of Western culture and associates it with Western imperialistic aggression that humiliated, bullied, and colonised China by robbing China of its once proud cultural heritage. Islam was regarded as a religion carrying foreign symbols, such as Arabic characters. Buddhism and Daoism were regarded as Chinese cultural heritage to promote as part of the nascent Chinese rejuvenated culture.

Under Xi, three major policies have existed on religion: de-foreignisation, Sinicisation, and loyalty to the Party. Since 2015, the Zhejiang Province ordered the forceful removal of crosses from churches, a campaign that gradually extended from Zhejiang Province to other parts of China.[10] It seems that the authorities would like to cut down visible Western or foreign influence – such as crosses on Christian churches – from the surface of the Chinese society. Not long after that initiative, the government also banned all Christmas celebrations in public and instead promoted Chinese festival days and traditions to counter Western influences. In 2016, Xi chaired the important once-every-five-years National Religious Work Conference and declared that all religion must be sinicised to support the authorities' national policy and interests through religious teachings. With respect to this, he said that religious organisations should:

Lenin, and Mao Tse Tung's thoughts, as the guiding principle of the CPC. See Xinhua (New China News Agency), "Full Text of Resolution on Party Constitution Amendment", *China SCI,* 22nd October 2022 [Available at: http://english.scio.gov.cn/20thcpccongress/2022-10/22/content_78480782.html] [Last accessed: 1st April 2024].

[10] Nanlai Cao, "Spatial Modernity, Party Building, and Local Governance: Putting the Christian Cross Removal Campaign in Context", *The China Review* 17(1) (February 2017), 29-52. Additionally, crescents from mosques were also removed since this time.

[...] merge religious doctrines with Chinese culture, abide by Chinese laws and regulations, and devote themselves to China's reform and opening up drive and socialist modernisation in order to contribute to the realisation of the Chinese dream of national rejuvenation. [...] [Religious groups should] dig deep into doctrines and canons that are in line with social harmony and progress, and favourable for the building of a healthy and civilised society, and interpret religious doctrines in a way that is conducive to modern China's progress and in line with our excellent traditional culture.[11]

Finally, the clergy of all religious organisations initiated by the Party Loyalty Campaign would have to pledge their obedience and loyalty to the Party, just as in any other social organisation in China submitting to the Party's leadership. This pledge usually centres on the following slogans or some variants of it: "Adhere to the Words of the Party, Follow the Party's Lead, and Be Thankful to the Graciousness of the Party."[12] The requirement for those who wish to observe religion in China has changed from patriotism – love the nation – to the new demand of obedience to the Party. This requirement reflects the increase of Party dominance in China under Xi's governance. The Church in China (those in TSPM/CCC), abided by these new measures to organise sinicisation seminars and to stage loyalty to Party activities – all while keeping to their usual ecclesial activities. The non-registered fractions became less visible as the authorities' surveillance and social control intensified with sporadic reports of harassments and arrests. During the three-year lockdown measures due to the COVID Zero-Tolerance policy, the whole nation came to a halt, and almost all ecclesial physical activities were suspended.

Ecclesiology Manifestation and Internalisation of Faith

One of the most well-known characteristics of the Church in China is its rapid growth during the past several decades despite the unfavourable socio-political environments such as hostile authority and lack of resources. This rapid increase of believers caught the attention of the Christian world especially during the 1980s and 1990s as the Chinese Christian community developed from merely a

---

[11] Xinhua, "Xi Calls for Improved Religious Work", *Xinhua News*, 24th April 2016 [Available at: http://www.china.org.cn/china/2016-04/24/content_38312410.htm] [Last accessed: 1st April 2024].
[12] For a Tibetan example, see Gong Cun, "Be a Good Monk and Nun, Who always Listens to the Party, Feels Grateful to the Party and Follows the Party", *Xizang Ribao* [Tibetan Daily], 13th January 2023 [Available at:
http://www.tibet.cn/cn/religion/202301/t20230113_7345261.html] [Last accessed: 1st April 2024]. For a Catholic example, see Leshan Diocese's study campaign, "Learn the History of the Party, Adhere to the Words of the Party, and Follow the Party's Lead", *Sichuan Catholic Web*, 21st June 2021 [Available at:
https://www.chinacatholic.cn/html/report/21060924-1.htm] [Last accessed: 1st April 2024].

few million into tens of millions in a couple of decades. Based on such a growth rate, one can easily project that China may soon have the largest bloc of Christian population in the world.[13] Although the diverse reasons for such astonishing growth lies beyond the scope of this chapter,[14] one thing certainly agreed upon by all is the significance of the large number of Christians there.

The answer to the question, "How many Christians are there in China?" has long been a contentious issue with wide variations depending on methodologies and political stances. Official figures tend to be on the conservative side, and the ACC fractions and their sympathisers abroad would usually suggest a higher figure. A recent report from the Pew Research Center – the same centre that gave a high figure of sixty-seven million in 2011 – now came up with a lower figure of twenty million, suggesting a decline of Christian population.[15] Many scholars, such as Yang Fenggang of Purdue University, hold strong reservations on this finding.[16] While the number of Christians in China is an important one, the strong governmental containment on Christianity in China would also contribute to the distortion on the validity of the methodologies as well as the results that further frustrate meaningful discussion on this issue. Despite the vastly different headcount of Christians in China, an implicit narrative seems to interpret these numbers on socio-political constructs – namely the greater the number, the stronger the socio-political representation and influence the Church in China has on Chinese society.

The above assumption may prove valid in sociological studies or political science since the numerical strength of a civil group or institution with clear membership – especially in a democratic society where equal socio-political rights are granted to every individual – may represent the desire or aspiration of a certain portion of the population that helps shape that society. However, two interrelated questions need attention vis-à-vis the number of Christians in China: (1) does the number of Christians have a direct correlation with Christian socio-political influence? and (2) more importantly, how does the number of believers relate to ecclesiastical manifestation such as the population of saved souls, the quality of spirituality, and even the nature of the Church's socio-religious witness?

From a theological perspective, several different understandings of Church membership exist other than headcount. In ecclesiology, a church member is one

---

[13] Chan, *Understanding World Christianity: China*, 186-8.
[14] For some of the reasons, see Chan, *Understanding World Christianity: China*, 176-81.
[15] Pew Research Staff, "Measuring Religion in China", *Pew Research Center*, 30th August 2023 [Available at: https://www.pewresearch.org/religion/2023/08/30/measuring-religion-in-china] [Last accessed: 1st April 2024].
[16] Isabel Ong, "Have China's Christians Peaked? Pew Researches the Data Debate", *Christianity Today*, 30th August 2023 [Available at: https://www.christianitytoday.com/news/2023/august/china-christian-churches-pew-measuring-religion-surveys.html] [Last accessed: 1st April 2024].

who embraces the Christian faith along with the initiation rite of communion with all the Saints. Such a commitment would usually be active but could also be in a passive or delegated mode as in the case of paedobaptism. In soteriology, as one makes a conscious decision to accept the lordship of Jesus Christ, that person would live in the realm of eternal salvation. Thus, any number of Chinese Christians would include those who made such a confession from the time of the resurrection of Jesus until the Eschaton. Pastorally speaking, ecclesial functionality would include those members actively engaging with (and hence physically connecting to) the group of believers and catechumens or seekers; this would not necessarily involve church membership. Thus, very different understandings exist between theological and sociological aspects relative to the number of believers.

In the case of the Church in China, the high number of believers would probably indicate the increasing number of people known by others to have embraced the Christian faith; this provides a soteriological indication relative to the increase of saved souls. However, the zero number on Christianity by Chinese officials during the Cultural Revolution when the authority declared that religion had been cleansed from Chinese society in 1970s – as well as the low number released by official documents since the 1980s – does not affect the functionality of the ecclesial communities in China since Christian perseverance and hope have not only preserved but also influenced many with consequences not manifested until years later. The current suggestion of a decline in the number of Christian believers in China proves sociologically significant. The primary theological narrative would be the ecclesial functionality on preservation and propagation of faith regardless of a high or low number of members.

The low number presented by current reports on the decline of the Church in China may reflect those who have since withdrawn from publicly professing their Christian faith as a sociological interpretation. The same result can also suggest Christian withdrawal from the public sphere due to political pressure; these may have instead turned inward as a spiritual journey into a typological wilderness. They may have concentrated on and consolidated into ecclesial functionality or internalised their faith – all these are signs of ecclesial maturity.

The Church in China needs to develop its ecclesial self-understanding with both sociological and theological narratives. The challenge is to go beyond the triumphalism of a high conversion number into the often-silent phase of in-depth theological reflection to focus on ecclesial-spiritual maturity – a qualitative rather than quantitative approach. Although the Church in China exists as part of the social fabric of Chinese society, it is also a spiritual community in communion with the *ekklesia* beyond time and space, distinguishing itself from any other social groups in China.

"How many Christians are there in China?" I once asked a wise old Christian in China in the evening. He said, "Look at the sky and how many stars do you see?" It was a cloudy night. He said, "If the weather is good, you see more. If it is overcast, you may not see any. Yet all the stars are there."[17] He gave a soteriological narrative in the context of the socio-political reality.

Christian Unity

Unlike Catholics, no demand exists for Protestants to organically join as one visible ecclesial entity. Protestants have ecclesial flexibility to start their own church should they have a unique emphasis on a particular doctrine or polity. Such allowances serve as a safety valve; if a group has too much tension within it, instead of fighting one another, one can always protest and form another group in the true spirit of Protestantism.

Due to political and theological differences, the Church in China has split into the TSPM/CCC and ACCs factions. Such divisions cause tremendous hurt and bitterness between these two groups. However, as with original denominational traditions relative to diverse doctrines and liturgies, the never-ending divisions of the ACCs and the internal power factions within each community – along with competition for support from ecclesial communities abroad – challenges unity in the Church in China. In fact, unity remains in short supply among Christians in China. Inter-ecclesial fights were not uncommon and at times even surprised Chinese officials. One senior Party officials who served at a Provincial Religious Affairs Bureau, perplexed by such inter-ecclesial tension, once asked me:

> Are you Christians not believing in the very same God? If so, why are you people fighting so much among yourselves, treating your co-religionists worse than your ideological enemies like us atheists, even appealing to us atheists for intervention? Why can't you people resolve your differences among yourselves through your religious teaching? Or do you people believe in different Gods? Is it only happening in China – Christianity with Chinese characteristics?[18]

I was speechless to answer this contextual challenge despite my years of training in Christian theology.

The rapid growth of Christianity in China during the past decades may have eased some of the inter-ecclesial tensions due to the overwhelming influx of new converts. This influx has focused ecclesial attention on the need to minister to new believers rather than on fighting each other and competing for new converts since there are plenty of unreached souls around. However, the competition for loyalty from new believers may at times also escalate existing tensions. Additionally, often a group will make exclusive claims over all Chinese Christians with the often-arbitrary use of the all-inclusive term, "Church in China" to denote their group. This is misleading to say that they represent all Christians in China, using terms such as the "House Church in China," to denote

---

[17] Interview by author with a brother in Christ, Miao Shuzhi, in Yantai, Shangdong, April 1980.
[18] Personal interview, Northwestern China, winter 2012, name, and location withheld for security reasons.

their comprehensive representation. Such claims are theologically invalid in the Protestant tradition as Protestantism implies diverse voices and groups where one group cannot represent or rule over other groups. Such exclusive ecclesial claims implicitly imply that other groups are either under this group's leadership or are apostates/heretics. This presents more of a theological narrative like Catholicism rather than Protestantism and denies the true ecclesial nature of the Church in China – further escalating inter-ecclesial tensions.

The Chinese Protestant community, despite the significant number of adherents, is divided into endless groups and factions that render this community weak. Such divisions cause a lack of consensus and increase the inability of believers to make collective decisions and take common actions. In contrast, Chinese Muslims, with far fewer numbers, have clearly made more of a socio-political impact in China, often successfully challenging the government to address their common needs. Protestants in China have yet to unite to champion their common interests.

As the Chinese authorities exercise increasing social control to shape a monolithic Chinese society, all Christians – regardless of their theological spectrum – are affected. However, as long as Chinese Protestant groups stress the common spiritual needs of Chinese society and the overall welfare of the Chinese Church in general above the needs of their own ecclesial factions or groups and achievements of their particular community, hope remains that Chinese Christians will move in the direction of authentic Christian unity as demonstrated by many signs of reconciliation.[19] However, increasing socio-political pressure on the Church in China may also cause different factions to strive for their own survival at the expense of other Christian groups that have fallen into the self-fulfilling prophecy of the Chinese authority on Christianity, who sees them as divided and conquered. Or, hopefully, the socio-political pressure may facilitate different Christian groups to draw closer together through their common interest in striving for survival. The current spiritual challenges for Chinese Christian leaders of both factions are indeed great, relative to their ecclesial vision beyond the self-interest of their own groups; meeting those challenges in unity will serve as a true mark of spiritual leadership.

Sinicisation: Christianity in China or Chinese Christianity

Christianity has long been regarded by both Chinese general population and authorities as a foreign – specifically Western – religion, given its mission history in China. The Chinese authorities' official historical narrative interpreted the Western world as an imperialistic force that exploited China, using

---

[19] Kim-Kwong Chan, "Tensions and Reconciliation between the Autonomous Christian Community and the China Christian Council/Three Self Patriotic Movement", in Robert Schreiter and Knud Jorgensen (eds), *Mission as Ministry of Reconciliation* Regnum Edinburgh Centenary Series, vol. 16 (Oxford: Regnum, 2013), 290-92.

Christianity as a form of cultural colonialism that damaged China's cultural heritage. Whether Western missionaries committed such cultural atrocity against China remains an important agenda item in academic discussions, currently inviting more controversy than consensus.

Despite different interpretations regarding the cultural impact of Christianity on China, one thing remains unambiguous: Chinese Christians consciously or otherwise have taken on a Western façade with respect to their manifestation of Christian faith. Church buildings in China today often look Western and are often incongruous in the surrounding landscape especially in the countryside. Church worship music is often translated Western hymnody. However beautifully written and composed, this music differs greatly from the musicological milieu of China. At present, Christianity in China is commonly perceived and even referred to as a foreign religion that happens to have inserted itself into China.

Chinese Christians in general also explicitly choose a Western appearance. Perhaps this has emerged as a subtle form of reaction to the authorities' accusation – or as a deliberate attempt to assert their identity separate from the rest of the Chinese social milieu in a dualistic worldview shaped by the Christian Fundamentalism commonly embraced by Chinese Christians. Regardless of the cause, the Western (or non-Chinese) appearance of Christianity in China became a part of Xi's xenophobic discourse against the West. Xi ordered all religions in China to sinicise as a political objective of governance on religion. Such a call for sinicisation seemed like more of a political campaign to foster a nationalistic society than a genuine indigenisation of religion. Xi clearly framed and proclaimed his content about this in political terms with respect to religious groups, saying they should "Merge religious doctrines with Chinese culture, abide by Chinese laws and regulations, and devote themselves to China's reform and opening up drive and socialist modernisation [sic] in order to contribute to the realisation of the Chinese dream of national rejuvenation".[20] Since Xi's proclamation, the TSPM/CCC has devoted a tremendous amount of resources at all ecclesial administrative levels, also involving Christian groups abroad, responding to this government-induced political campaign. They held conferences, conducted workshops, and published books on the theme of the sinicisation of Christianity. They have promoted this topic in all churches in China as the top ministerial priority. They even constructed an English term with Chinese characteristics for this supposed theological endeavour – the Chinanisation of Christianity.[21] The ACCs, however, basically kept their distance on this matter.

Despite the political nature of this sinicisation campaign, it has challenged the Church in China to *become* the Church of China. One of the major challenges

---

[20] Xinhua, "Xi Calls for Improved Religious Work".
[21] TSPM/CCC News, "Seminar on Chinanization of Christianity Commences in Hong Kong", *TSPM/CCC*, 31st May 2023 [Available at:
https://en.ccctspm.org/newsinfo/16342] [Last accessed: 1st April 2024].

facing Chinese Christianity is its need to be accepted as a genuine part of Chinese society – not as an extension of a foreign entity intruding into China. Chinese Christians have paid a high price trying to gain a foothold in China. Although now at the highest percentage of the population reached since the introduction of Christianity at least fourteen hundred years ago, a long journey remains ahead for Christianity to be accepted as part of the Chinese social fabric. Hopefully, a day will come when Chinese Christians feel confident enough to incorporate their cultural heritage into their Chinese Christianity identity without fearing the betrayal of their Christian faith which they embraced with great cost. One can hope that they will feel comfortable enough to take down any cultural barriers separating them from the general Chinese population, a form of Christianity than can be accepted as a part of Chinese socio-cultural milieu.

Missiology, the Chinese Diaspora, and Nationalistic Sentiment

Since the 1980s, more than ten million Chinese people have emigrated to other countries,[22] swelling the number of ethnic Chinese in the diaspora to more than forty-six million.[23] This number does not even include the tens of thousands of Chinese merchants, professionals, volunteers, and workers engaging in various business and construction activities in more than 140 countries under the general scheme of the Belt Road Initiatives promoted by Xi since 2013. The BRI has since that time become one of the largest infrastructure projects in the world.[24] This entity exists as a new geopolitical entity which Xi has named "a community with a shared future for [hu]mankind [*sic*]."[25]

The rapid church growth in China compounded by the increased Chinese population leaving China captured the imagination of mission-minded leaders to suggest that the Chinese Church operate as a potential major stakeholder in global mission. If there are ten million Chinese who have migrated to different countries in the last three decades, and if the Christian population among Chinese is about 3 percent (taking the mean average), then that should mean that about

---

[22] IOM, "China", *International Organization for Migration*, 2020 Figures [Available at: https://www.iom.int/countries/china] [Last accessed: 1st April 2024].
[23] Academy for Cultural Diplomacy, "Chinese Diaspora", *Academy for Cultural Diplomacy Website* [Available at: https://www.culturaldiplomacy.org/academy/index.php?chinese-diaspora] [Last accessed: 1st April 2024].
[24] For a brief summary and update, see Shannon Tiezzi, "How China's Belt and Road Took over the World", *The Diplomat*, 12th September 2023 [Available at: https://thediplomat.com/2023/09/how-chinas-belt-and-road-took-over-the-world/] [Last accessed: 1st April 2024].
[25] China Daily, "A Community with a Shared Future for Mankind", *China Daily*, 18th January 2021 [Available at: https://language.chinadaily.com.cn/a/202101/18/WS60054e10a31024ad0baa35af.html] [Last accessed: 1st April 2024].

300,000 Chinese Christians have carried the ecclesial characteristics and experiences of rapid Church growth to different countries. These potential Christian migrants would provide an important impetus for global mission to continue the legacy of Chinese mission movements since the late 1940s in the name of the *Back to Jerusalem* mission movement.[26] Furthermore, the Lausanne Movement has promoted Business as Mission (BAM),[27] which fits right into many mission-minded Chinese Christian entrepreneurs taking advantage of China's BRI to promote Chinese business engaging in BRI regions – which largely overlap with the 10/40 Window. In fact, Christians under Socialist China engaged in global mission much earlier than the initiation of BRI, so the BRI simply facilitated this mission dynamic with a few dozen mission training centres already in operation by 2017 to prepare for Chinese missionaries.[28]

Most of these Chinese Christians in the diaspora, however, tended to congregate among themselves based on their origin hometown, their dialect, and their established ecclesial communities. For example, Wenzhou Christians formed Wenzhou churches that operated their Christian services in their dialects that were almost incomprehensible to non-Wenzhouese. These dialect- and regional-based Chinese Christian Churches abroad may serve also as a club for mutual support through a religious platform. In fact, the socio-ecclesial function of ethnic churches in hosting countries is rather common, such as the Congolese Christian traders in China who have formed their own churches in China serving both as a religious and a socio-commercial supporting group extending from the Democratic Republic of Congo into China.[29]

These Chinese churches have also actively evangelised among their kinsfolk in the diaspora as shown by the fact that the Chinese Christian population has grown in the diaspora.[30] These dialect-based or ethnic Chinese Churches may also turn inward into an ecclesial ghetto holding onto their own traditions, customs, and identities, similar to Hasidic Jews in Europe during the medieval time.

---

[26] See Kim-Kwong Chan, "The Back to Jerusalem Movement: Mission Movement of the Christian Community in Mainland China", in Wonsuk Ma and Kenneth R. Ross (eds), *Mission Spirituality and Authentic Discipleship* Regnum Edinburgh Centenary Series, vol. 14 (Oxford: Regnum, 2013), 182.
[27] Lausanne, "Business as Mission", *Lausanne Movement* [Available at: https://lausanne.org/networks/issues/business-as-mission] [Last accessed: 1st April 2024].
[28] Chan, *Understanding World Christianity: China*, 194.
[29] Gerda Heck, "Religion as Infrastructure: Congolese Migration, Diaspora, and Religious Networks", 25th January 2021, Webinar Hong Kong University BRIFAITH lecture [Available at: https://asiar.hku.hk/event/religion-as-infrastructure-congolese-migration-diaspora-and-religious-networks/.] [Last accessed: 6th April 2024].
[30] For example, see Fenggang Yang, *Chinese Christians in America: Conversion, Assimilation, and Adhesive Identities* (Philadelphia, PA: The Pennsylvania State University Press, 1999) and many of his subsequent writings.

Chinese Christians could contribute to the richness of the global Christian communion by both their unique ecclesial manifestations sustainable in a hostile environment, along with the spirituality of their suffering and resilience.[31] If they launch out beyond their ethnic boundary to evangelise the local population, they may unconsciously convey a form of Christianity which carries a strong Chinese cultural-political characteristic. Such introduction of a socio-culturally shaped theology may re-enact what the missionaries from the West had presented to China a Western interpretation of Christianity, which was criticised by the Chinese authority as cultural imperialism and a Christianity hitherto tainted among the Chinese population. Chinese missionaries may easily draw similar criticisms from the hosting population as the Western missionaries drew from the Chinese population in the past.

The rise of Chinese nationalism and national prominence in various global contexts does facilitate Chinese global mission yet may accentuate the Chinese hegemonic undertone in their mission endeavours for a "Chinese" Christianity (a non-contextualised form of Christianity in other cultural milieus).

A major challenge in cross cultural mission engaged in by Chinese Christians – and in fact by all Christians – has to do with staying aware to not re-enact any sense of cultural superiority, which can result in a lack of genuine contextualisation of the gospel. Chinese Christians are new entrants to global mission, and they can benefit from many valuable experiences from other people without re-inventing the wheel or repeating the mistakes of their predecessors. Chinese Christians must do their utmost to learn from history with God's help.

Conclusion

In merely forty years (since 1980), the People's Republic of China has transformed from a humble nation into the seconding largest economic entity with global influence. Concurrently, Chinese Christianity has emerged from the ruins of the Cultural Revolution as a remnant community into a formidable force of tens of millions of followers with potential impact in global Christianity. Their visibility has increased all while existing in an environment hostile to religion. Both the PRC and Church in China are rather new in their respective self-identities as both have experienced rapid development often outpacing any previous experiences one could rely upon.

China, now flexing its muscles in different parts of the world, has increasingly made its mark in those regions. However, such outward venturing is new to China, and the Chinese authority has constantly adjusted to balance Sinophilia and Sinophobia tensions in the international community to exercise its global influence. Likewise, Christianity in China now finds its identity both in Chinese

---

[31] Daniel H. Bays, *A New History of Christianity in China* (West Sussex: Wiley-Blackwell, 2012), 225.

society and in the global Christian world. The Church in China has numerical strength, just as China has economic power.

However, the real strength of a nation lies not in its wealth or armaments but also in moral integrity and universal values such as honouring human rights, equality, and sharing. The ecclesial community must focus not only on the size of its followers but also on spiritual maturity evidenced by humility, servanthood, justice, and compassion. The Church in China must embark on a journey of consolidating its ecclesial community in terms of spiritual formation, striving for Christian unity, identifying with its cultural milieu, and balancing tensions between Chinese nationalistic aspirations and developing a vision on God's Kingdom beyond ethnicity and nationality. If it does not do these things, then it could end up falling into many fragmented groups squabbling among themselves with little more than some ethno-centric ecclesial modes to share with others, despite any relevancy they may have to others beyond the Chinese milieu.

Lastly, in the context of China, the Christian population is merely a small percentage of the general population, and more than 90 percent remain unreached – the largest single geopolitical entity of the global unreached population. China itself is already the biggest mission challenge the Church in China faces. China has the largest aging population with a rapid decrease in the youth population – due to the prolonged One-Child Policy – and this will negatively impact future civil and ecclesial society structures. Future leaders will have to face caring for an increasingly aging population as well as a highly distorted gender ratio. Many Asian countries with low birth rates, such as Korea, Singapore, Japan, and Taiwan, face similar challenges with varying degrees of magnitude. This population issue presents an impending national socio-political challenge for China far beyond the scope of this chapter, yet it carries detrimental consequences for Chinese society.

These questions remain: will the Church in China continue to develop as a vibrant ecclesial community with an increasing number of believers that outpace the rate of population growth? Or will the Church in China gradually become a religious club for the elderly with only a few youth seen among its rank and file as observed in many churches of Christianised nations in the West? We shall have a better idea in 2033, if we shall live that long, and if Christ has not yet returned.

Bibliography

Academy for Cultural Diplomacy. "Chinese Diaspora", *Cultural Diplomacy Website*. [Available at: https://www.culturaldiplomacy.org/academy/index.php?chinese-diaspora] [Last accessed: 1st April 2024].

Bays, Daniel H. *A New History of Christianity in China*. West Sussex: Wiley-Blackwell, 2012.

Cao, Nanlai. "Spatial Modernity, Party Building, and Local Governance: Putting the Christian Cross Removal Campaign in Context", *The China Review* 17(1), (February 2017), 29-52.

Chan, Kim-Kwong. "The Back to Jerusalem Movement: Mission Movement of the Christian Community in Mainland China", In Wonsuk Ma and Kenneth R. Ross, Eds. *Mission Spirituality and Authentic Discipleship.* Regnum Edinburgh Centenary Series. Vol. 14. Oxford: Regnum, 2013: 172-92.

——. "Tensions and Reconciliation between the Autonomous Christian Community and the China Christian Council/Three Self Patriotic Movement." In *Mission as Ministry of Reconciliation*, edited by Robert Schreiter and Knud Jorgensen, 287-93. Regnum Edinburgh Centenary Series. Vol. 16. Oxford: Regnum 2013.

——. *Understanding World Christianity: China.* Minneapolis, MN: Fortress, 2019.

Cun, Gong. "Be a Good Monk and Nun, Who always Listens to the Party, Feels Grateful to the Party and Follows the Party", *Xizang Ribao* [Tibetan Daily], 13th January 2023. [Available at: http://www.tibet.cn/cn/religion/202301/t20230113_7345261.html] [Last accessed: 1st April 2024].

China Daily. "A Community with a Shared Future for Mankind", *China Daily.* 18th January 2021. [Available at: https://language.chinadaily.com.cn/a/202101/18/WS60054e10a31024ad0baa35af.html] [Last accessed: 1st April 2024].

Hackett, C., B. Grim, V. Skirbekk, M. Stonawski, and A. Goujon. *Global Christianity: A Report on the Size and Distribution of the World's Christian Population.* Washington DC: Pew Research Center, 2011.

Heck, Gerda. "Religion as Infrastructure: Congolese Migration, Diaspora, and Religious Networks", 25th January 2021. *Webinar Hong Kong University BRIFAITH lecture.* [Available at: https://asiar.hku.hk/event/religion-as-infrastructure-congolese-migration-diaspora-and-religious-networks/] [Last accessed: 6th April 2024].

Hunter, Alan, and Kim-Kwong Chan. *Protestantism in Contemporary China.* Cambridge: Cambridge University Press, 1993.

International Organization for Migration. "China", *IOM Website*, 2020. [Available at: https://www.iom.int/countries/china] [Last accessed: 1st April 2024].

Lausanne Movement. "Business as Mission", *Lausanne Movement Website.* [Available at: https://lausanne.org/networks/issues/business-as-mission] [Last accessed: 1st April 2024].

Sichuan Catholic. "Learn the History of the Party, Adhere to the Words of the Party, and Follow the Party's Lead", *Sichuan Catholic Web.* 21st June 2021. [Available at: https://www.chinacatholic.cn/html/report/21060924-1.htm] [Last accessed: 13th April 2024].

Lesley, Alison. "The Christian and Muslim Community in China is Multiplying", *World Religion News.* 7th September 2015. [Available at:

https://www.worldreligionnews.com/religion-news/christianity/the-christian-and-muslim-community-in-china-is-multiplying/] [Last accessed: 1st April 2024].

Ong, Isabel. "Have China's Christians Peaked? Pew Researches the Data Debate," *Christianity Today*. 30th August 2023. [Available at: https://www.christianitytoday.com/news/2023/august/china-christian-churches-pew-measuring-religion-surveys.html] [Last accessed: 1st April 2024].

Pew Research Staff. "Measuring Religion in China", *Pew Research Center*. 30th August 2023. [Available at: https://www.pewresearch.org/religion/2023/08/30/measuring-religion-in-china/] [Last accessed: 1st April 2024].

Tiezzi, Shannon. "How China's Belt and Road Took over the World", *The Diplomat*. 12th September 2023. [Available at: https://thediplomat.com/2023/09/how-chinas-belt-and-road-took-over-the-world/] [Last accessed: 1st April 2024].

TSPM/CCC. "Home Page", *China Christian Council National Committee of Three-Self Patriotic Movement of the Protestant Churches in China* (TSPM/CCC). [Available at: https://en.ccctspm.org/] [Last accessed: 1st April 2024].

TSPM/CCC News. "Seminar on Chinanization of Christianity Commences in Hong Kong", *TSPM/CCC*. 31st May 2023. [Available at: https://en.ccctspm.org/newsinfo/16342] [Last accessed: 1st April 2024].

World Health Organization. "WHO Coronavirus (COVID-19) Dashboard", *WHO*. [Available at: https://covid19.who.int/] [Last accessed: 1st April 2024].

Xinhua (New China News Agency). "Full Text of Resolution on Party Constitution Amendment", *China SCI*. 22nd October 2022. [Available at: http://english.scio.gov.cn/20thcpccongress/2022-10/22/content_78480782.html] [Last accessed: 1st April 2024].

Xinhua. "Xi Calls for Improved Religious Work", *Xinhua News*. 26th April 2016. [Available at: http://www.china.org.cn/china/2016-04/24/content_38312410.htm] [Last accessed: 1st April 2024].

Yang, Fenggang. *Chinese Christians in America: Conversion, Assimilation, and Adhesive Identities*. Philadelphia, PA: The Pennsylvania State University Press, 1999.

Yu, Jie, and Jon Wallace. "What is China's Belt Road Initiative?" *Chatham House Explainer*. 13th September 2021. [Available at: https://www.chathamhouse.org/2021/09/what-chinas-belt-and-road-initiative-bri] [Last accessed: 1st April 2024].

15. Women's Leadership in Asia and Their Influence on Global Christianity

Julie Ma

Abbreviations

APTS	Asia Pacific Theological Seminary
ISACC	Institute for Studies in Asian Church and Culture
OCMS	Oxford Centre for Mission Studies
SAIACS	South Asia Institute of Advanced Christian Studies

Introduction

God has placed both men and women in his Kingdom to carry out God-given purposes, spanning all spheres of social life. Thus, God calls women to contribute to his Kingdom globally and locally by exercising their leadership.

Traditionally, women have suffered victimisation due to gender inequality and inequity in education, employment, and leadership opportunities in the church and wider society. The situation worsens in Asia because of its current cultural views on women. Many socio-cultural circumstances frequently impede the roles God ordained for women.[1] However, as time passes, society and churches allow women to take advantage of possibilities to pursue higher education, careers in teaching, etc.

This chapter discusses the role of women in the context of the Asian Church and how they influence Christianity worldwide. After addressing the challenges alluded to above, I discuss select Asian women who have made an impact on both their local church and the global Church. I also reflect on personal experiences throughout my academic journey in the hope that our examples serve as a valuable window through which other women may come to understand their unique and yet significant role in shaping global Christianity.

This discussion considers two assumptions: more than two-thirds (67 percent in 2020) of the world's Christians today reside in the Global South, making global Christianity a "Southern" religion.[2] Additionally, the discussion assumes that most Christians are women, since the *World Christian Encyclopedia*

---

[1] Julie Ma, "The Role of Christian Women in the Global South", *Transformation* 31(3) (2014), 194.
[2] Todd M. Johnson and Gina A. Zurlo (eds), *World Christian Encyclopedia*, 3rd ed. (Edinburgh: Edinburgh University Press, 2020), 917.

describes a typical Christian today as "a non-White woman living the Global South."[3] Based on these presumptive facts, Asian Christian women have a significant role in influencing global Christianity in various ways and helping women in the Global South overcome the many challenges they face, described in the following section.

Challenges of the Women in the Global South

Women play a unique role in every level of social life, encompassing personal, familial, and societal arenas. However, women in the Global South face many difficulties such as living with "lower-than-average levels of societal safety and proper health care."[4] Many cultures and communities restrict women's access to resources, opportunities, and leadership positions in the public sphere.

Creating Identity in the Face of Cultural Social Perceptions

The biggest obstacle women face involves overcoming restrictions they may face in creating their identity in a particular social context. How women are perceived and treated in many regions of Asia, Africa, and Latin America remains problematic due to many cultural practices needing eradication. For instance, a woman's identity often stems from her husband or children in many regions of Asia; she is frequently referred to as so-and-so's wife or mother. Her name is, therefore, less used and, thus, less well-known. When I became a Christian, I was surprised to hear women addressed by name in the church, an utterly countercultural norm in Korea.[5]

Many of these perceptions find their basis in the religious observances present in various Asian cultures. For example, the notion that men are the "sky" and women are the "earth" is another Confucianism-influenced Asian worldview. This can become the basis for injustice and discrimination instead of promoting a harmonious relationship of complementarity. For instance, even today, in some households, mothers and children do not join the table when the father and his guests are eating. They hold off until the men are finished eating. The mother and her children receive any leftovers. This gender inequality also results in favouritism toward males. Some families express disappointment that their daughters are not males by dressing them in boy's clothing or giving them a boy's name. This also creates confusion in gender roles even after they have grown up. In many societies, this practice has reinforced the idea that men are superior to women.

When practicing religions like Islam, women must publicly cover their faces and bodies. Due to the long history of these intense religious constraints, women have also rarely questioned such restrictions. Even if regarded as cultural norms,

---

[3] Johnson and Zurlo, *World Christian Encyclopedia*, 3.
[4] Johnson and Zurlo, *World Christian Encyclopedia*, 3.
[5] Ma, "Role of Christian Women", 196.

however, such restrictions placed on women's access to school, employment, and other opportunities are in truth a matter of injustice rather than culture:

> In some nations, female rape victims are imprisoned for adultery while their attackers go free. "Honour killings" of women and young girls are also on the rise. A woman doesn't have to be guilty of doing something immoral to be killed. Her father, husband, brothers, and uncles may kill her simply because she is the subject of gossip. No one knows the exact number of honour killings, but in just one region of one of these nations, 350 young women – some as young as twelve – were murdered in one year. The preferred method of killing women to restore honour to the family is to burn them alive or throw acid on them.[6]

Although cultural practices are changing in modern societies, in certain countries in Asia or Africa, the notion of women remains the same or only gradually changes.

Human Trafficking

Another serious issue for women and girls especially in the Global South is human trafficking. Approximately 800,000 persons are trafficked internationally each year: 50 percent are minors, and 80 percent are women or girls. Although the extent of human trafficking varies between nations and continents, it has clearly emerged as a serious issue on a global scale. Although sex trafficking victims might be of any age and either sex, as the above percentage clearly shows, women and adolescent girls as the majority face the greatest threat. Even though many countries have made female trafficking illegal, it remains a problem on a global scale.[7]

The most typical motives for human trafficking include exploitation for forced labour and sex. Victims of sex trafficking are forced into engaging in one or more types of sexual exploitation. It is critical to understand that prostitution is merely one type of work that sex trafficking victims are forced into, and human trafficking and prostitution are different.[8] However, commercial sex activities

---

[6] Barbara Ehrenreich and Deirdre English, *For Her Own Good: Two Centuries of the Experts' Advice to Women* (New York: Anchor Books, 1978), 31.

[7] Tiffany Dovydaitis, "Human Trafficking: The Role of the Health Care Provider", *J Midwifery Women's Health* 55(5) (Sep-Oct 2010), 462-67 [Available at: https://doi.org/10.1016/j.jmwh.2009.12.017] [Last accessed: 14th April 2024]. See also Amy Novotney, "7 in 10 Human Trafficking Victims are Women and Girls. What are the Psychological Effects?" *American Psychological Association*, 24th April 2023 [Available at: https://www.apa.org/topics/women-girls/trafficking-women-girls] [Last accessed: 14th April 2024].

[8] There is a similarity between human trafficking and prostitution but the fundamental difference is that, in human trafficking, some people are physically locked behind closed doors, threatened with their family's safety, and paying off debts by servicing men in brothels or working without pay. In prostitution, many women, particularly those living in impoverished areas, turn to sex work because few economic opportunities exist elsewhere. An uneducated woman can make fast money, she is under pressure to provide for her family, and she lives within widespread cultural acceptance of the sex

like prostitution, pornography, exotic dance, stripping, live sex shows, mail-order brides, military prostitution, and sexual tourism are closely related to sex trafficking.[9]

Most frequently, victims are presented with bogus marriage proposals that evolve into bonds of servitude or promises of a good career, education, or citizenship in a foreign nation. Parents, husbands, and other family members sell their family members, especially young girls, into the sex trade; sometimes traffickers kidnap victims against their will. Debt bondage is the coercive method utilised the most by perpetrators. In this complex criminal world, victims must provide personal services to repay their debt, such as travel or living expenses. Human traffickers frequently approach low-income families to buy girls or young women with the promise of a better life in a more affluent country.[10]

Women's Ordination

Women's ordination has been a contentious and complex issue in the Global South and even in more developed countries. For instance, although Pentecostals generally have more readily embraced women's ordination than more traditional churches, the Church of God in Christ, the biggest African American Pentecostal denomination, still does not ordain women. As Elizabeth Dabney notes, women can only serve as replacements for male pastors:

> In the absence of a pastor and with official approval, a woman can "act" in the role of pastor. Official support may come from the pastor who designates which woman will serve while he is absent from his church. In the event of a vacancy of the pastorate, a district superintendent or jurisdictional bishop may authorise a woman to act in the role of pastor until a permanent appointment can be made. But, she cannot assume the title of "pastor." She may be called by other titles, such as, "missionary," "mother," or "shepherdess." If the woman acts as pastor, she must use the "covering" of a man – a husband, father, brother, uncle, son or nephew – in order to carry out pastoral and other chief leadership roles.[11]

Female pastors shouldn't merely be a substitute or replacement to a male pastor but a full understanding of equality would allow them to pastor in their own right.

---

industry. Sex work quickly becomes a viable option – sometimes seemingly the only one. For more information, see Au'Vonnie Alexander, "Prostitution & Human Trafficking: What's the Difference?" *United Against Human Trafficking* [Available at: https://uaht.org/prostitution-and-human-trafficking/] [Last accessed: 14th April 2024].
[9] Dovydaitis, "Human Trafficking", 462-67.
[10] Neha A. Deshpande and Nawal M. Nour, "Sex Trafficking of Women and Girls", *Rev Obstet Gynecol* 6(1) (2013), e22-7, *National Library of Medicine* [Available at: https://pubmed.ncbi.nlm.nih.gov/23687554/] [Last accessed: 14th April 2024].
[11] Elizabeth Juanita Dabney, *What It Means to Pray Through: A True Mystical Journey of Spiritual Awakening to Find Divinity in the Heart of Self* (Memphis, TN: iUniverse, 2012), 45.

Even though Asian women encounter many such difficulties related to their identity and equality issues, they still can be exposed to theological education and can make an impact globally. The following sections, followed by reflections from my own experience in theological education, illustrate the various fields in which women can contribute significantly while they also demonstrate the difficulties and barriers they all too often confront in their particular social contexts.

Reflections on My Involvement in Theological Education

I first worked as a theological educator at Asia Pacific Theological Seminary (APTS), a Pentecostal graduate school in Baguio, Philippines (1996–2006), immediately following the completion of my doctorate. This school's student body consisted of more than twenty other nations, including non-Asians. Its faculty was equally diverse, representing seven different countries, both Western and Asian. The mission of the school was to prepare regional and global leaders by complementing national schools which trained local and national leaders. An urgent need had emerged for this international leadership development due to the expansion of Christianity in the Global South. Training Pentecostal leaders for the Global South served as an explicit goal of the school's establishment, since being Spirit-filled and empowered stands as a key tenet of Pentecostal-Charismatic leadership training and development in an educational setting.

I taught mission courses at the seminary. Some students were preparing for missionary work, while others had already had field experience in cross-cultural settings. Given the student body's multicultural makeup, this diversity frequently gave students a unique chance to learn from one another by exchanging their real-world experiences. A more comprehensive global image or glocal interactions began to take shape as different local perspectives were shared. The need for Spirit empowerment in theological education applied not only to training leaders but training students for mission because Spirit-filled leaders affect people and change their lives, as Amos Yong and Dale Coulter note:

> Being centred on the formation of the person, education concerns the cultivation and a *habitus* that shapes and orients the individual toward the proper ends for human flourishing. In Christian terms, education is about being Christ-shaped and Spirit-infused. Christ is the pattern, while the Spirit is the transforming presence driving the educational process.[12]

For an Asian woman, teaching was never easy. Eiko Takamizawa, a Japanese scholar who has taught missiology at Torch Trinity Graduate University, Seoul, South Korea, for fourteen years – and who also regularly visits Londrina Biblical Seminary in Londrina, Brazil to teach mission courses – has had a similar challenging experience: cultural diversity and a different education system.

---

[12] Amos Yong and Dale M. Coulter, *The Holy Spirit and Higher Education: Renewing the Christian University* (Waco, TX: Baylor University Press, 2023), 1.

After leaving the Philippines, I transitioned to the United Kingdom to teach at the Oxford Centre for Mission Studies (OCMS) from 2006-2016. The move was more than geographical: from graduate to postgraduate programmes, from relational to global, from Pentecostal to radical evangelical, and more. It felt both enriching and challenging to serve at this global institution. The school's primary focus was training high-level church and mission practitioner leaders from the Global South. Its numbers of PhD students increased from 80 to 120 during my time. Their research topics were broad with subjects ranging from HIV/AIDS to biblical studies. Regnum Books, its publishing arm, grew to more than twenty academic titles per year. The school's quarterly journal, *Transformation*, also increased in subscription and influence.

The school aligned with the realities of global Christianity since theological education must take the realities of life seriously for theological thought to impact mission practices and how mission is understood. The ideal theologian or theological educator will, therefore, be a reflective practitioner who frequently lives in and participates in a specific social and local environment. One can only contribute to the creation of global theology if one is truly local. This proves especially true if theological education in the future reflects the realities of the regions where Christianity is developing and spreading, i.e., the Global South:

> As children of the Enlightenment, we distinguished between theory and practice. An encounter with theologies from the Global South will help us to understand that theology cannot and must not be separated from the concrete world. Truth cannot be separated from practice, and orthopraxis is as crucial as orthodoxy. Theology must, therefore, be based on missional/missionary experience; that was how the theology of the Early Church came into being as a theoretical framework of conceptual thinking based on concrete mission experience. Theological reflection must be missiological thinking to hold together practice and theory.[13]

It is so true that theology and practice go hand in hand; they are not separated at all. Our theological understandings of God, our Saviour Jesus, the Holy Spirit, and mission must be applied to practical settings as Jorgensen clearly notes.

OCMS faced the realities of global theological education. Institutional resources were minimal with less than a dozen academic staff, half a dozen administrative staff, and a modest annual budget. As an independent institution, donations provided the most significant income, much of which was used to assist the students. My most striking encounter while there had to do with the creativity of the academic system. Taking full advantage of the UK higher education system, the school contracted more than 300 scholars from the United Kingdom and worldwide to serve as dissertation supervisors.

However, I was the only female resident research tutor and most external supervisors were male. Although the number of female students improved over the years, more than two-thirds of the student body was male. However, many studies were on issues related to women and children, such as health, education,

---

[13] K. Jorgensen, "Mission in the Post-Modern Society" (Unpublished Paper, 2009), 7.

human trafficking, and cultures reinforcing gender inequality. Even topics that did not appear gender-related had profound implications for women. Several dissertations on microfinance, for example, had an overwhelming influence regarding the role of women.

When I transferred to Oral Roberts University (ORU) in 2016 (where I have served until the present time), my teaching career continued. Contextual Theology Ph.D. coursework at ORU began in 2018. The worldwide Spirit-empowered movement has experienced extraordinary growth, and this degree examines the contextual theologies of world Christianity with a primary focus on that movement's development. I have experience mentoring, supervising, and instructing.

As discussed in the section on the challenges of women in the Global South, living with lower-than-average levels of societal safety and proper health care are only some of the numerous challenges women in the Global South endure. Many cultures and groups restrict women's access to resources, opportunities, and leadership roles in public life. The issues of human trafficking and women's ordination are issues churches are facing and agendas they are having to deal with. My involvement in education through teaching, mentoring, and supervising in several academic institutions was a scarce opportunity; as well, publication and paper presentation were also great privileges. These hands-on mission experiences while teaching in the classroom at APTS served as valuable ministry, making theology *living* theology.

The Impact of Asian Women on Global Christianity

Asian Christian female leaders have made an international impact on the Christian Church through their involvement in various ways, despite the challenges they have had to surmount and their having fewer opportunities to participate in local and global activities. This section discusses some of those key areas: academic leadership, influence in publishing, important contributions at academic conferences, involvement in missions, and the creation of new knowledge by their scholarly work. Even with those contributions, however, the challenge of the glass ceiling remains – serving as top-level denominational decisionmakers who can participate equitably with their male partners in making significant Kingdom impacts on Global Christianity.

Academic Leadership

Asian women have made their most notable advancements within general and Christian education, including church-based education, with many female scholars teaching at colleges, universities, and seminaries all around the world. However, Asian women's leadership in higher education still needs to catch up with that of their male counterparts. This is particularly true within Asian contexts. According to my experience, for instance, the participation of women at international gatherings is substantially less than that of men. Furthermore, men's voices are more frequently heard than women's. Therefore, I encourage female academics to participate and assert their voices more proactively. Female academic leaders sometimes organise such gatherings when the opportunity presents itself. Nevertheless, Asian women's leadership is increasing in educational settings, as the following examples demonstrate.

Jung-sook Lee in Korea has exercised significant leadership in Christian higher education. Educated at Princeton Theological Seminary with a PhD in church history, she served as the first female president of Torch Trinity Theological University, Seoul; the Korean Association of Accredited Theological Schools; and the Church History Society in Korea. She also served as a vice president of the Asia Theological Association; a member of the executive board for the Oxford Centre for Mission Studies, Oxford, United Kingdom; and a presidium for the International Congress for Calvin Research. She formerly worked as a co-moderator for the Doctoral Initiatives Steering Committee for the International Council of Evangelical Theological Education. She was actively involved in the Asia Forum for Theological Educators and the Global Forum for Theological Educators.[14]

Havilah Dharamraj is another example of an Asian woman making a significant impact in educational settings. She serves as Academic Dean and Professor of Old Testament at the South Asia Institute of Advanced Christian Studies (SAIACS) in Bangalore, India. After studying Biochemistry and Theology, she earned a Theology PhD from the University of Durham, UK. Dharamraj's research areas are Old Testament, biblical and theological studies, and innovation in theological education and ministry training. One of her publications is "We Reap What We Sow: Engaging Curriculum and Context in Theological Education."[15]

Another example among the many Asian female academics is Jayachitra Lalitha in India. In addition to serving as an ordained minister in the Church of South India, she has academic positions at the Tamilnadu Theological Seminary in Tamil Nadu, India. One of her works, *Re-Reading Household Relationships Christologically: Ephesians, Empire and Egalitarianism*,[16] is highly acclaimed and has had an important effect on other women.

Yet another example is Protestant systematic theologian Elizabeth (Lisa) Sung, a visiting theology professor at Mundelein Seminary and the University of Saint Mary of the Lake. She also previously served as an Associate Professor in Trinity Evangelical Divinity School's Department of Biblical and Systematic Theology. She belongs to the Evangelical Theological Society and the American Academy of Religion. Additionally, Sung teaches in the "Global Theologies" course by seminaries affiliated with the evangelical, mainstream, and Roman

---

[14] Dr Jung-sook Lee, email message with author, 17th July 2023.
[15] Havilah Dharamraj, "We Reap What We Sow: Engaging Curriculum and Context in Theological Education," *Evangelical Review of Theology* 38(4) (2014), 2-14.
[16] Jayachitra Lalitha, *Re-Reading Household Relationships Christologically: Ephesians, Empire and Egalitarianism* (New Delhi: Christian World Imprints, 2017).

Catholic traditions. Theological hermeneutics, theological anthropology, the relationships between theology and science and culture, and theologies of sanctification and spiritual formation are the main topics of her literature. Her publications include *"Race" and Ethnicity Discourse and the Christian Doctrine of Humanity: A Systematic Sociological and Theological Approach* (2011) and *"Race" and Ethnicity Discourse and the Christian Doctrine of Humanity: A Systematic Sociological and Theological Appraisal.*[17]

Publishing

Several ways exist to share newly created knowledge, with publication being the first and most obvious path. Both print and online publications are available for monographs and scholarly papers. It is encouraging to see a rise in the quantity and quality of doctoral dissertations written by thoughtful individuals in the Global South. This used to happen only in theological schools in the West, but now more research-based postgraduate programmes exist in Africa, Asia, and Latin America than ever before. However, since so few of these researchers are published, fresh studies from the new churches face an even greater uphill battle.

Fortunately, progress has taken place on several fronts. First, the rise of contemporary communication technology has radically expanded spaces to share knowledge. Publishing media now includes institutional and personal websites that regularly publish studies. Such publishing media have added functions such as audio and video material to augment the texts and allow conversation between authors and readers. Search capability also adds convenience to traditional books. Shareability is another revolutionary function of electronic publishing, evidenced by the increasing number of portals offering complementary material. Online libraries have also become more widely available, holding numerous studies not easily shared otherwise. Both in traditional and new publishing spaces, both established Western publishers and an ever-growing number of non-Western authors are now publishing their works. A select number of publishers even give non-Western authors priority. At the same time, more publishers in Latin America, Africa, Asia, and Eastern Europe are producing high-quality studies for global consumption.[18]

---

[17] Graham Joseph Hill, "18 Asian Female Theologians You Should Know About (Plus Others for You to Explore)", *Global Church Project,* 16th December 2023 [Available at: https://theglobalchurchproject.com/18-asian-female-theologians/] [Last accessed: 20th April 2024]. See also "10 Asian Christian Women to Start Following during #WomensHistoryMonth," 7th March 2020, *Grace Ji-Sun Kim ~ Loving Life Website* [Available at: https://gracejisunkim.wordpress.com/2020/03/14/10-asian-christian-women-to-start-following-during-womenshistorymonth/] [Last accessed: 20th April 2024].

[18] For example, "The Globethics Library is the world's largest free, open online library aimed at providing quality resources in the field of ethics, higher education, policy engagement, and ethical leadership, with a specific focus on the thematic priorities defined in the Globethics Strategy 2023-2027. The library currently holds more than 3.8

For this reason, editorial work can serve as a unique gift of empowering new minds from the Global South to stand with established Western scholars in the same co-edited book. The editor creates a new space where scholars from various parts of the world are brought together for collaboration. In the process, contributors experience empowerment from the Lord and one another, expanding their understanding and discovering new implications of their studies in new contexts, such as South-to-North and South-to-South exchanges. I am familiar with several academic journal editors promoting such exchanges by recruiting young scholarly voices from the Global South.[19]

Professional Academic Seminars and Conferences

Professional conferences provide another venue for the exchange of newly produced knowledge. Sharing many essential components with publishing, these events offer an opportunity to develop new relationships, have lively discussions, and empower younger scholars. After receiving my PhD in June 1996 at Fuller Theological Seminary, I was first invited to present a paper at the conference on "Pentecostalism in Globalization" in Costa Rica. This opportunity came my way as a greenhorn scholar from the Global South, thanks to a good friend who encouraged me to participate, along with my husband. I recognised many well-known conference speakers when I first viewed the conference flyer. Standing with them required much courage, primarily due to my lack of experience. Since that nerve-racking but warmly empowering experience, I have attended many events, frequently on invitation.[20]

Naturally, more exposure leads to better recognition, thanks to the empowering hospitality of established scholars and organisers. Over time, I have contributed to the broader process of knowledge creation regularly. This experience has also helped me handle critical responses to my study gracefully, with a learning attitude and increased clarity of my views. As people naturally tend to get fearful and demoralised by criticism, handling it takes continued exposure and experience. Later, I learned that academics should trust each other for their unique viewpoints and contexts, strengthening the greater Christian community.

---

million documents, including Globethics publications, books, reference works, research papers, dissertations, conference proceedings, case studies, reports, textbooks, and educational resources, carefully selected and curated in over 75 collections and more than 170 journals, accessible free of charge, and via a multilingual portal." "About Globethics Library," *Globethics Library* [Available at: https://repository.globethics.net/pages/about] [Last accessed: 20th April 2024].

[19] Julie Ma and Allan Anderson, "Pentecostalism", in Todd M. Johnson and Kenneth R. Ross (eds), *Atlas of Global Christianity* (Edinburgh: University of Edinburgh Press, 2010), 100-101.

[20] Jungja (Julie) Ma, "Pentecostal Challenges in East and South-East Asia", in Murray Dempster, Byron D. Klaus, and Douglas Petersen (eds), *The Globalization of Pentecostalism: A Religion Made to Travel* (Carlisle, UK: Regnum, 1999), 183-202.

I also learned to respect and accept different views and methodologies as a result of these conferences. At the same time, affirmations motivate us. Indeed, such is the environment where academic engagements and progress are made. I soon discovered that networking with thoughtful and creative colleagues proved incredibly beneficial for me and the organisations which I serve. The most helpful conference experiences for me have been those where I have gotten to know many groups with vibrant national and religious perspectives. For example, I met Eiko Takamizawa, a Japanese mission scholar who presented at the International Symposium on Asian Mission in Manila in January 2002. Another scholar was a Filipino female social anthropologist, Melba P. Maggay, who contributed a study to the same conference.[21] I have grown even more appreciative of others, as many come from different experiences and academic disciplines. Knowing that my own specialty may be unfamiliar to others, I could confidently share my understanding and findings.

Another conference I attended was the 2005 Conference for World Mission and Evangelism of the World Council of Churches in Athens, Greece, with about 800 attendees, including delegates, guests, and staff from diverse churches and mission agencies. Like many others, this conference exposed me to fresh and new experiences. Six to eight people came daily for *lexio divina* devotion and reflection. Reading a passage slowly and several times deepened my understanding and my relationship with God and others. The range of worship services offered by various church traditions proved equally valuable. For instance, Orthodox worship was ritualistic, whereas Pentecostal worship was spontaneous. I could welcome diversity rather than fear it because of such dynamic experiences.

Yet another conference I attended was the 52nd annual meeting of the Society for Pentecostal Studies (SPS) held at Oral Roberts University 16th–18th March 2023. The theme was "In Our Own Tongues", emphasising amplifying Pentecostalism's minoritised voices. Around 250 people, local and international Pentecostal scholars, church leaders, and lay leaders attended. The ethnically diverse keynote speakers presented on quite challenging subjects. The parallel sessions went well with beneficial topics and meaningful discussions among the members who attended. I found it an enriching experience academically and enjoyed seeing Pentecostal scholars who have become friends of mine and having fellowship over coffee or tea with them and new friends during the breaks.

---

[21] Melba P. Maggay, director of the Institute of Institute for Studies in Asian Church and Culture (ISACC), Manila, Philippines, presented on "Early Protestant Missionary Efforts in the Philippines: Some Intercultural Issues", International Symposium on Asian Mission, Manila, January 2002.

Missionary Reflection and Involvement

At the start of the twentieth century, women ran forty evangelical missionary organisations, with many female missionaries founding hospitals, schools, and orphanages. Ralph Winter refers to this as a "burst of female energy" into missions. One of the top medical schools in Vellore, India was founded and is managed predominantly by women. They have accomplished this in the most inhospitable locations, but as one writer observes, "The more difficult and dangerous the work, the higher the ratio of women to men."[22] Female missionaries really do shine.

God has raised up and empowered numerous Asian women. For instance, Susan Tang has founded and led churches in Sabah, Malaysia, for over twenty years. Her dedication to God's cause has produced innumerable Christ followers, pastors, and evangelists who have received training. Teo Kwee Keng has led a thriving church in Batu Pahat, Malaysia, for fourteen years while founding at least four other congregations in the area.

Many Asian women also serve as intercultural missionaries. To mention a few, Erlynda Reyes has collaborated on worldwide training projects with missionary workers from different nations. Nora Catipon, a single Filipino woman missionary, travelled to Cambodia to plant churches and teach in the Bible school which she and her fellow missionaries established. Another example is Maria Gomez, whose story Bill Snider recounts:

> In the 1960s, Maria Gomez in East Timor was called to service at a particular island where a prison stands and various criminals were confined. She and her husband spent many years planting the seeds of the gospel through the means of building churches and training young people. One night when they had an evening service, the Holy Spirit fell upon the congregation, people confessed their sins, and great healings took place. Now the whole Island is called an "Assemblies of God island." Gomez is the current General Superintendent in East Timor.[23]

Mission history contains endless examples of how women have used their gifts for God's Kingdom. Female missionaries are often more receptive to the holistic expression of God's mission because of their inherent sensitivity. They frequently demonstrate extraordinary dedication, a more profound understanding of human pain, and incredible tenacity. Additionally, they tend to have easier access to local people because they can approach and interact with other women.

Equally encouraging is the growing number of female missionaries from the Southern Church, some of whom I have already mentioned above. The areas of their missionary engagement are vast. Some started Bible schools, while others translated the Bible into hundreds of different languages worldwide.

---

[22] J. Herbert Kane, *Life and Work on the Mission Field* (Grand Rapids, MI: Baker Books, 1980), 143.
[23] Bill Snider (Assemblies of God World Mission Area Director for Southeast Asia), speaking at the Missions Emphasis Week at Asia Pacific Theological Seminary, 10th October 2001.

Along with my husband, Wonsuk Ma, I spent three decades serving as a missionary. We were intensely active in holistic ministries among the mountain tribal communities in Northern Luzon, the Philippines, in addition to our theological education ministry. Women actively led many mountain churches in those areas. Through my research on the transmission of the gospel and the impact of Christianity on Kankana-ey life and culture, I could carefully construct their Christian history, spiritual journey, and conciliate it with conventional culture and religion. Although this research may seem exotic, it has proven helpful when applied to other contexts. One local Oxford congregation proved useful for my study, which mixed church planting techniques with theological and anthropological considerations. A parish pastor who had read about my research sought my advice on improving his plan to grow churches in foreign countries.

New Christian Knowledge Being Created

"Theology in the Global South will dominate the next Christianity," predicts Knud Jorgensen, "even though it may take some strange forms. It is from this part of the world that renewal of theology and church life may come."[24] He continues, saying:

> Bediako sees African Christianity as a rediscovery of Biblical Christianity in an African context, particularly the experience of the transcendent in the midst of the immanent is one of the characteristics: God lives and acts and weeps and dances amid the world. Further, what is true about the African experience may also be witnessed by the liberated faith of Latin America – liberated in both a socio-political sense and a deep existential and religious sense. Alternatively, if we visit some of the open and house churches in the provinces of China and we will meet the same living, invigorating, shouting, praying, and infectious faith.[25]

Without writing and publication, no opportunity will exist for people to learn about the remarkable encounters and reflections happening within vibrant Christian communities in the Global South. Literature lasts much longer than us and travels much farther. As an Asian woman, I faced significant barriers with respect to writing and publication. First, my early education in Asia could have better prepared me for critical and thoughtful thought. We were simply taught to reproduce or regurgitate existing knowledge. While working in multinational institutional settings, I have received training and encouragement to create my own expertise. However, I have tried to express such storylines in an Asian manner because I appreciate my Asian thinking and writing styles as well.

The task of determining the theological future of the Global South will need to be carried out by insiders within the various global communities, i.e., Africans, Asians, Latin Americans, and Eastern and Central Europeans, even though Western theological intellectuals can provide a helping hand in the process.

---

[24] Jorgensen, "Mission in the Post-Modern Society", 8.
[25] Jorgensen, "Mission in the Post-Modern Society," 8.

Philip Jenkins makes a critical point that needs to be remembered: "I somehow doubt that the contribution of the Global South to theological inquiry will be limited to rhythmic dancing or hand-clapping."[26] Ironically, it may turn out that the old adage "Publish or perish!" is true.

Women Decisionmakers: The Challenge That Remains

Even in view of all the contributions Asian women have made to Global Christianity, the question remains regarding the extent of their serving in the national executive bodies of the Pentecostal churches. Such positions include top-level denominational officers, district-level administrators, and national mission committee members. Men typically hold most leadership positions at the national level, and women only sometimes do. Nonetheless, the lack of women in these positions shows a glass ceiling for their advancement in leadership. The majority of women only continue to be active at the level of schooling, missionary work, or local church ministry. Evangelical churches generally follow this tendency as well.

In Corinth, Paul held Priscilla and Aquila in high regard. Priscilla's function is undoubtedly that of a leader in her local congregation and in leadership development, even if the church organisation had not yet attained its current degree of sophistication. Paul received help from Priscilla and Aquila in establishing churches in Ephesus and Rome. He highly praised their leadership abilities and included them among his most reliable colleagues. Paul valued their opinions and listened to their advice (Acts 18:18-19, 24-26; Rom. 16:3-5; 1 Cor. 16:19; and 2 Tim. 4:19).

Women can contribute significantly to church and denominational decision-making through their keen attention to detail and relational sensitivity. The position and contributions of women are so important for politics; how much more critical that they have greater agency and impact in the Church.

As I close this section on the impact that Asian women have had, do have, and should have on global Christianity, I pose this challenging question: what would it take for Asian Pentecostal churches and denominations to elect or appoint women as denominational heads or heads of various departments of their denomination? Among Pentecostal churches, it is rare to see a female denominational leader. One recent surprise came from a young Pentecostal church, the Mongolian Assemblies of God, which elected a female general superintendent, but such exceptions actually demonstrate that the highest position in these ecclesial organisations is still reserved for men. Thus, the glass ceiling remains in place.

---

[26] Philip Jenkins, *The Next Christendom: The Coming of Global Christianity* (Oxford: Oxford University Press, 2002), 103.

Conclusion

In discussing the role of women in Asia and their influence on global Christianity, this chapter first discussed the challenges women face in the Global South, highlighted their involvement in theological education, depicted areas of their impact on international Christianity, and then posed the challenge of how to address the glass ceiling that still remains – female executive denominational leadership.

Certainly, the Southern Church, especially the Asian women which make up a large proportion, have played meaningful roles in the global context, yet in the face of culturally unfavourable circumstances, their unique gifts are frequently hidden. Therefore, women must remain conscious of the opportunities and gifts God has given to them. Women in the Global South must not undervalue themselves while pretending to be humble but must strengthen their conviction of God's calling and enablement so they can cultivate and use their abundant potential for Christian missions and activities worldwide and hide it no longer.

I can encourage Asian women to walk this path in confidence because, in my experience, I needed to see myself as qualified. As an Asian female theologian, my main concern now involves how to effectively manage my own opportunities and education while expanding the knowledge God has given me to advance his Kingdom. As one of the Pentecostals' favourite verses reads, "Everything is possible for him who believes" (Mark 9:23).

Women in the Global South have the chance to play a significant part in creating a new global Christianity. The Church must empower women by recognising their potential and enablement to live out the gospel. I strongly invite select women who have earned higher education degrees while actively participating in academic and missionary endeavours. As our paths have crossed, I could only sample a small portion of their potential, but I hope that all those women, especially in academic circles, will maintain their involvement in academic and mission activities to continue to serve as thoughtful practitioners and develop content that will impact the future of Christianity worldwide.

Bibliography

Primary Source

Lee, Jung-sook, email with author, 17th July 2023.

Secondary Sources

Aano, K. "Going Global: A Reflection on Being a Western Christian in a Global Church". Unpublished Paper, 2008.

Alexander, Au'Vonnie. "Prostitution & Human Trafficking: What's the Difference?" *United against Human Trafficking*. [Available at: https://uaht.org/prostitution-and-human-trafficking/] [Last accessed: 14th April 2024].

Bediako, Kwame. "The Stone Lecture", Princeton Theological Seminary, 21st October 2003.

Dabney, Elizabeth Juanita. *What It Means to Pray Through: A True Mystical Journey of Spiritual Awakening to Find Divinity in the Heart of Self.* Memphis, TN: iUniverse, 2012.

Deshpande, Neha A., and Nawal M. Nour. "Sex Trafficking of Women and Girls", *Rev Obstet Gynecol* 6(1), (2013), e22-7. [Available at: https://pubmed.ncbi.nlm.nih.gov/23687554/] [Last accessed: 14th April 2024].

Dharamraj, Havilah. "We Reap What We Sow: Engaging Curriculum and Context in Theological Education", *Evangelical Review of Theology* 38(4), (2014), 2-14.

Dovydaitis, Tiffany. "Human Trafficking: The Role of the Health Care Provider", *J Midwifery Womens Health* 55(5), (Sep-Oct 2010), 462-67. [Available at: https://doi.org/10.1016/j.jmwh.2009.12.017] [Last accessed: 14th April 2024]

Ehrenreich, Barbara, and Deirdre English. *For Her Own Good: Two Centuries of the Experts' Advice to Women.* New York: Anchor, 1978.

Globethics. "About Globethics Library", *Globethics Library Webpage*. [Available at: https://repository.globethics.net/pages/about] [Last accessed: 20th April 2024].

Hill, Graham Joseph. "18 Asian Female Theologians You Should Know About (Plus Others for You to Explore)", *Global Church Project*. 15th December 2023. [Available at: https://theglobalchurchproject.com/18-asian-female-theologians/] [Last accessed: 20th April 2024].

Hyman, Paula. "The Other Half: Women in the Jewish Tradition", In Elizabeth Koltun, Ed. *The Jewish Woman: New Perspectives.* New York: Schocken, 1976: 105-13.

Jenkins, Philip. *The Next Christendom: The Coming of Global Christianity.* Oxford: Oxford University Press, 2002.

Johnson, Todd M., and Gina A. Zurlo, Eds. *World Christian Encyclopedia.* 3rd ed. Edinburgh: Edinburgh University Press, 2020.

Jorgensen, K. "Mission in the Post-Modern Society", Unpublished Paper, 2009.

Kane, J. Herbert. *Life and Work on the Mission Field.* Grand Rapids, MI: Baker, 1980.

Lalitha, Jayachitra. *Re-Reading Household Relationships Christologically: Ephesians, Empire and Egalitarianism.* New Delhi: Christian World Imprints, 2017.

Ma, Julie. "The Role of Christian Women in the Global South", *Transformation* 31(3), (2014), 194-206.

Ma, Jungja (Julie). "Pentecostal Challenges in East and South-East Asia", In Murray Dempster, Byron D. Klaus, and Douglas Petersen, Eds. *The Globalization of Pentecostalism: A Religion Made to Travel.* Carlisle, UK: Regnum, 1999: 183-202.

Ma, Julie, and Allan Anderson. "Pentecostalism", In Todd M. Johnson and Kenneth R. Ross, Eds. *Atlas of Global Christianity*. Edinburgh: the University of Edinburgh Press, 2010: 335-47.

Maggay, Melba P. "Early Protestant Missionary Efforts in the Philippines: Some Intercultural Issues", *International Symposium on Asian Mission*, Manila, January 2002.

Novotney, Amy. "7 in 10 Human Trafficking Victims are Women and Girls. What are the Psychological Effects?" *American Psychological Association*. 24th April 2023. [Available at: https://www.apa.org/topics/women-girls/trafficking-women-girls] [Last accessed: 14th April 2024].

Reyes, Michelle. "10 Asian Christian Women to Start Following during #WomensHistoryMonth," *Grace Ji-Sun Kim ~ Loving Life Website*. 7th March 2020. [Available at: https://gracejisunkim.wordpress.com/2020/03/14/10-asian-christian-women-to-start-following-during-womenshistorymonth/] [Last accessed: 20th April 2024].

Snider, Bill. *Sermon: "God's Mission"*. Missions Emphasis Week. Asia Pacific Theological Seminary, 10th October 2001.

Yong, Amos, and Dale M. Coulter. *The Holy Spirit and Higher Education: Renewing the Christian University*. Waco, TX: Baylor University Press, 2023.

Yung, Hwa. *Mangoes or Bananas?: The Quest for an Authentic Asian Christian Theology*. Oxford: Regnum Books International, 1997.

16. Spirit-Empowered Global Christianity: The Pathway to Agency for Children at Risk

Mary Mahon

Introduction

Luis Gonzalez grew up in Linda Vista, a community in extreme poverty on the margins of the capital of Costa Rica. He experienced hardship throughout his childhood: violence, fear, anxiety, a lack of affection, and hunger leading to malnutrition. As the eldest of five children, he was often called upon to care for his younger siblings. Luis was a hard worker and a good student who attended a Christian school which was a ministry outreach for children in poverty. When Luis was eleven years old, the local church held a Bible memory verse competition. The child who could recite sixty verses would win a new bicycle. Luis was determined to win that bicycle, so he memorised the verses. Luis remembers the day of the competition:

> That day I had to recite the sixty verses, and I thought I could not, literally *could not*. Because of my condition at that moment of poverty in self-esteem and of intra-family aggression, I felt paralysed. It was there, in total dependence when I heard the voice of the Lord telling me, "Yes, you can! I am with you!" And it was precisely there that I received the baptism in the Holy Spirit with the initial evidence of speaking in tongues. What a glorious moment! I have that image in my heart. It never goes away: the pew, the church, the children, the altar, and me receiving the empowerment to be able to win.[1]

Luis was a child living at risk. *Children at risk* is a term that can be intuitively understood. Perhaps one thinks of street children in Brazil or Romania fending for themselves. Or perhaps the girls trafficked by modern-day slave runners come to mind. Children at risk could also be closer to home: a neighbourhood child who trembles in fear of abuse from a drunken stepfather. We could say that all children are at risk due to their vulnerability and dependence on adults. For that matter, it could also be argued that all humans live at risk.

Children at Risk

The Lausanne definition for children at risk highlights that children are considered at risk when they are living with risk factors that could prevent them

---

[1] Luis Gonzalez, personal communication with Mary Mahon, in-person interview, 27th May 2022.

from fulfilling their God-given potential.[2] Risk factors restrict a child from developing within the safe and healthy environment God intended. The presence of poverty is the most consistent risk factor among children at risk. Many ministries exist to reach children at risk and to help mitigate the effects of the risk factors on the lives of the developing child. However, more than external factors need to be considered to bring about sustainable transformation in the life of a child at risk. I propose that an essential protective factor, that reduces the negative outcomes due to such risk factors in the lives of children, is agency. Additionally, I propose that Pentecostal Spirit empowerment can provide a pathway to agency contributing to the resiliency needed for children living in risk to thrive and fulfil their God-given potential.

Lausanne calls on those who work in mission to children at risk to empower children as "vulnerable agents" by embracing them as active participants in ministry and the mission of God.[3] I would like to take this concept a bit further. While those who work in mission to children at risk can empower children to participate in ministry activities, I believe that the empowerment of the Spirit can prove more impactful in the development of the child. Spirit empowerment in the life of a child can spark a sense of agency within a child who otherwise may feel powerless. This Spirit-empowered agency enhances a child's ability to overcome their risk factors and to truly flourish.

Winning the bicycle was a turning point in Luis' life. He says he does not know what he learned to love more in his little Christian school – education or the Lord – but he learned to love them both. Spirit empowerment that day gave Luis hope for his future. As he says, "Empowerment in the Holy Spirit offered hope for a better tomorrow because I began to realise that people were telling me that surely God had a plan for me. That definitely gave me a hope that I did not know."[4] Today, Luis holds multiple degrees in both theology and education, including two doctorates. He serves in pastoral leadership, teaches Bible school, and works as an elementary school teacher. Luis acknowledges that it was the Spirit's empowerment the day he won the bicycle that began his path toward agency.

---

[2] Lausanne Consultation on Children at Risk, "Who are Children-at-Risk: A Missional Definition", Quito, Ecuador: Lausanne Movement, 2015 [Available at: https://lausanne.org/statement/children-at-risk-missional-definition] [Last accessed: 23rd April 2024].

[3] Desiree Segura-April et al., "Mission with Children at Risk", Lausanne Occasional Paper 66, 17th–19th November 2014, Quito, Ecuador: Lausanne Movement [Available at: https://lausanne.org/content/lop/mission-children-risk-lop-66] [Last accessed: 23rd April 2024].

[4] Luis Gonzalez, personal communication.

Chapter 16

Children at Risk and the Pentecostal Encounter

Several Pentecostal affirmations are impactful in the lives of children living in risk that can help them build the internal strength they need. Three emerge from the stories of the children: the presence of the Holy Spirit in one's day-to-day life; the guidance given to the individual by the Spirit; and the empowerment that comes from a Spirit encounter.

Pentecostalism as a "religion made to travel"[5] has adapted across national, cultural, and social barriers which accounts for its rapid growth throughout the world.[6] Expressions of Pentecostalism worldwide have been both adaptive and pragmatic, reaching a variety of groups and subcultures.[7] Children at risk exist as one of these groups. Many Pentecostal ministries direct their mission toward children living in risk. For that matter, most Pentecostal churches are located in communities of poverty and high social vulnerability within the Majority World where the greatest risk factors for children are prevalent. The question remains, however, as to the response within the child when the Holy Spirit empowers them and what enduring difference the Spirit makes in their life as a child at risk.

Edward Cleary notes that Pentecostals centre their lives on experience.[8] This is true among children as well, as the experience with the Spirit generates transformation in their lives. Although Pentecostal empowerment in the lives of adults is to gift them for service[9] or to help them bear witness,[10] in the life of a developing child, Spirit empowerment can build a pathway toward a better future by fostering agency within that child. Everett Wilson notes that rather than persuasion, crisis is what most often brings people to their "personal Pentecost".[11] This can be true for children as well. The crisis may result from a parent leaving the home, not having enough food for the family, or even the

---

[5] Murray W. Dempster, Byron D. Klaus, and Douglas Petersen (eds), *The Globalization of Pentecostalism: A Religion Made to Travel* (Oxford: Regnum, 1999). pp. xiii-xvi.

[6] Harvey Cox, *Fire from Heaven: The Rise of Pentecostal Spirituality and the Reshaping of Religion in the Twenty-First Century* (Reading, MA: Addison-Wesley, 1995), 102.

[7] Edward L. Cleary, "Latin American Pentecostalism", in Murray W. Dempster, Byron D. Klaus, and Douglas Petersen (eds), *The Globalization of Pentecostalism: A Religion Made to Travel* (Oxford: Regnum, 1999), 145.

[8] Cleary, "Latin American Pentecostalism", 143.

[9] Frank D. Macchia, "The Struggle for Global Witness: Shifting Paradigms in Pentecostal Theology", in Murray W. Dempster, Byron D. Klaus, and Douglas Petersen (eds), *The Globalization of Pentecostalism: A Religion Made to Travel* (Oxford: Regnum, 1999), 15.

[10] Macchia, "Struggle for Global Witness", 24.

[11] Everett A. Wilson, "They Crossed the Red Sea, Didn't They? Critical History and Pentecostal Beginnings", in Murray W. Dempster, Byron D. Klaus, and Douglas Petersen (eds), *The Globalization of Pentecostalism: A Religion Made to Travel* (Oxford: Regnum, 1999), 87.

stresses of school for a child with academic aspirations higher than those of their parents.

For Danny Gonzalez, that crisis happened when he was in first grade. His family was thrust into extreme poverty when their father left the home, and the loss of his father caused a personal crisis for Danny. He recalls a deep sadness because he missed his father. An intuitive teacher responded to Danny's crisis and told him about his Heavenly Father who would never leave him. As she led Danny in prayer, he arrived at his "personal Pentecost." Danny remembers that day: "I no longer felt sad about the absence of an earthly father but focused my hope on the fact that I had a Father in heaven who would always be with me and make all my dreams come true. Not only was this an experience of a new birth, but also one of having joy because of having the Holy Spirit in my heart."[12] As Danny grew, the presence of the Spirit in his life empowered and guided him to good decisions that would help him achieve his goals. Today, Danny is medical doctor and serves on the pastoral team at his local church.

The Development of the Child

The construct of self begins early in a child's life. Children are not born with social roles or self-representations to define themselves. Their identities are developed as they grow and interact with others in various social settings and cultural environments. Yet, once these identities form, they play a crucial role in the control and management of everyday life.[13] The development of a child's identity takes place within a cultural context and occurs as the developing child participates in social interactions within a particular cultural-historic situation.[14] The self helps to maintain the permanence of the culture, as well as reacts to its evaluation of the culture. Jerome Bruner compares the self to a barometer, which in essence responds to the local cultural weather.[15] The self also has the capacity to overcome the negative aspects of the culture. By using its capacity for reflection and imagining alternatives, the self can reframe what the culture is offering and envisage a better future.[16] This agentive nature of self must develop in order to help children overcome the risk factors that may prevent them from thriving.

---

[12] Danny Gonzalez, personal communication with Mary Mahon, WhatsApp audio, 23rd August 2023.
[13] Richard M. Ryan and Edward L. Deci, "On Assimilating Identities to the Self: A Self-Determination Theory Perspective on Internalization and Integrity within Cultures", in Mark R. Leary and June Price (eds), *Handbook of Self and Identity* (New York: Guilford, 2003), 253.
[14] Jerome S. Bruner, *Acts of Meaning* (Cambridge, MA: Harvard University Press, 1990), 107.
[15] Bruner, *Acts of Meaning*, 110.
[16] Bruner, *Acts of Meaning*, 110.

Agency

The quality of agency within the construct of self is particularly important in the empowerment of the developing individual. A sense of agency over the world and oneself includes a recognition of the individual's control over their own destiny.[17] Agency refers to the capacity of the individual to initiate and carry out activities and thereby implies skill and know-how.[18] A Pentecostal community of faith can play a critical role in the formation of self and the development of agency through Spirit empowerment in the life of a child at risk.

A child is in the unique stage of being and becoming. In this process of development, the child constructs a theory of self in order to make sense out of their world and experiences.[19] A child born living within vulnerable circumstances experiences the reality of the powerlessness of the world in which they live. Their agency is constrained by these realities. Jayakumar Christian explains this powerlessness as captivity in a web of lies – a "world of flawed assumptions and interpretations."[20] For a child born into poverty and living at risk, the lies influence their worldview and can negatively affect the development of self. Powerlessness is perpetuated by the worldview of the people living in a vulnerable community.[21] It is not only a current reality but a continuous disempowerment in the lives of the children.[22] This cycle of disempowerment within this context presents a risk factor that limits a child's dreams for the future, preventing them from fulfilling their God-given potential.

María Meza, a child of immigrants who lived in a community of extreme poverty, had struggled with disempowerment her whole life.[23] The influence of her community and the culture that prevailed caused her to battle insecurity in her own abilities to achieve her goals and make something out of her life. If her success had depended on her environment, she would have had little to no sense of agency. María was raised by her grandmother and her mother. From an early age, Maria's Pentecostal grandmother, who sensed her negative self-perception, prayed with her and shared Scriptures with her. The belief that she could do all things through Christ who strengthens her became a personal motto. This

---

[17] Daniel N. Stern, *The Interpersonal World of the Infant* (New York: Basic, 1985), 123.
[18] Jerome S. Bruner, *The Culture of Education* (Cambridge, MA: Harvard University Press, 1996), 34.
[19] Susan Harter, *The Construction of the Self: Developmental and Sociocultural Foundations*, 2nd ed. (New York: Guilford, 2013), 1.
[20] Jayakumar Christian, *God of the Empty Handed: Poverty, Power and the Kingdom of God* (Monrovia, CA: MARC, 1999), 161.
[21] Christian, *God of the Empty Handed*, 160.
[22] Christian, *God of the Empty Handed*, 157.
[23] María Meza, personal communication with Mary Mahon, WhatsApp Audio, 10th September 2023.

message and subsequent empowerment were echoed in her Christian school class devotional times and weekly chapels services.[24]

María has reached one of her goals: she graduated from high school and is studying at university. As she looks back on her journey, she recognises that it has been the Holy Spirit empowering her from early on. Even when she was alone, the Spirit would remind her of that verse, and she could overcome her doubts. As she recounts, "God has helped me a lot. I have achieved things I never thought I would be able to do at this moment. I have a job, I am healthy, and I am studying. All those things I never thought would happen to me, but God helped me, and I owe it all to him."[25]

Children's Spiritual Development

Children's spirituality is important to the development of a child and is an ongoing focus of research that overlaps multiple disciplines within the social sciences.[26] While earlier research focused on areas of religious education and used cognitive and moral development stage methodologies to determine a child's grasp of concepts about God, current research is based on the theory of spirituality as an innate aspect of the developing child and not culturally constructed. As David Hay, Helmut K. Reich, and Michael Utsch observe, spiritual awareness is biologically structured in human beings and expressed culturally.[27] Therefore, spirituality is a universal feature of humanity regardless of religious beliefs or lack thereof.

These concepts are key as we consider Spirit empowerment in the lives of children at risk. I review here several key religious and spiritual formation theorists to provide a basis for understanding spirituality and Spirit empowerment within the lives of children. James Fowler[28] was a pioneer in faith development and the first to study how a person's concept and understanding of God evolves. Robert Coles[29] listened to the stories of children, many of whom were facing great difficulties, as they applied their spirituality to provide meaning to what was happening around them. These two individuals lay the

---

[24] María received a scholarship to attend a Christian school that was an outreach of a local Pentecostal church in her community.
[25] Meza, personal communication.
[26] David Hay and Rebecca Nye (eds), *The Spirit of the Child*, rev. ed. (London: Fount, 2006); Donald Ratcliff (ed), *Children's Spirituality: Christian Perspectives, Research and Applications* (Eugene, OR: Cascade, 2006); Eugene C. Roehlkepartain, et al. (eds), *The Handbook of Spiritual Development in Childhood and Adolescence* (Thousand Oaks, CA: Sage, 2006).
[27] David Hay, Helmut K. Reich, and Michael Utsch, "Spiritual Development: Intersections and Divergence with Religious Development", in Eugene C. Roehlkepartain et al. (eds), *The Handbook of Spiritual Development in Childhood and Adolescence* (Thousand Oaks, CA: Sage, 2006), 50.
[28] James W. Fowler, *Stages of Faith* (New York: Harper and Row, 1981).
[29] Robert Coles, *The Spiritual Life of Children* (Boston, MA: Houghton Mifflin, 1990).

foundation for David Hay and Rebecca Nye's concept of spirituality defined as relational consciousness that will be used to evaluate Spirit empowerment in the lives of children at risk.[30]

James Fowler

In the area of religious and spiritual education, Fowler's research provided a shift away from the study of the development of religious concepts to the study of faith development. His work integrated theories of psychosocial, cognitive, and moral development to identify six stages of faith development that span a person's lifetime.[31]

Faith development theory defines faith in both a functional and structural way that includes many faith traditions as well as secular ideologies.[32] Faith is understood in an inclusive sense and is qualified as the foundation for beliefs, values, and meaning, which provides an essential centring process giving direction to human beings, assisting them as they relate in community, and empowering them to deal with the challenges of life and death.[33]

Robert Coles

Coles avoided paradigms and labels as his research evolved and he listened to children's stories, noting an innate spirituality that promoted a resiliency among children living in challenging circumstances. Rather than assessing what a child could understand regarding spiritual matters based on their capacities within a structured situation, Coles spoke directly to children and allowed them to lead the flow of many of the conversations. Coles assumed that all human beings possess awareness or consciousness and, through language, people – children and adults alike – attempt to understand and express what they learn to others.[34] Coles also noted a connection that children drew between meaning and spirituality. He observed that children draw upon religious experience and their spiritual values to understand what is happening to them and why.[35]

---

[30] Hay and Nye, *Spirit of the Child*, 109.
[31] Fowler's stages of faith development are (1) intuitive-projective (toddlerhood and early childhood), (2) mythical-literal (middle childhood and beyond), (3) synthetic-conventional (adolescence and beyond), (4) individuative-reflective, (5) conjunctive faith, and (6) universalising faith.
[32] J.W. Fowler and M.L. Del, "Stages of Faith from Infancy through Adolescence: Reflection on Three Decades of Faith Development Theory" ,in E.C. Roehlkepartain et al., *Handbook*, 43.
[33] Fowler and Del, "Stages of Faith", 36.
[34] Coles, *Spiritual Life of Children*, 22.
[35] Coles, *Spiritual Life of Children*, 100.

David Hay and Rebecca Nye

The work of Hay and Nye has identified the core of children's spirituality as the construct of relational consciousness. According to their research, the simple basis of children's spirituality seems to lie in a relational consciousness from which arise religious experiences that are aesthetic and meaningful, providing personal responses to the mystery of the world around them, and inspiring moral insight.[36]

Spirituality in this sense refers to the consciousness a child expresses always within the context of a relationship. The spirituality of children presents itself as a profound and detailed thought process that can be termed *consciousness* all the while confined within a clearly relational realm.[37]

Hay and Nye identify three categories of spiritual sensitivity that provide a foundation to the study of spirituality and that they believe are part of any person's spiritual experience – awareness-sensing, mystery-sensing, and value-sensing.[38] Awareness-sensing is more than involuntary alertness or focus of attention. It also entails a reflexive process in which the child is aware of what they are experiencing.[39] Awareness-sensing of children's spirituality is seen in the ability to become lost in an experience and to be in touch with the felt sense of reality. Mystery-sensing is the transcendent aspect of spirituality. It refers to the awareness of incomprehensible experiences in the person's life.[40] In the expression of spirituality in children, mystery-sensing is seen in the constructs of wonder, awe, and imagination. Value-sensing, a term first coined by Margaret Donaldson in 1992, is the third category of spiritual sensitivity. It refers to the moral expression of children's spirituality. Value-sensing is conveyed through delight and despair, ultimate goodness, and meaning. These qualities of relational consciousness, as defined by Hay and Nye, inform our discussion of Spirit empowerment for children at risk.

The three-fold expression of spirituality as relational consciousness – awareness-sensing, mystery-sensing, and value-sensing – sets the stage for the Spirit empowerment experienced by children at risk. Children at risk often feel alone. Many are actually alone for much of their time. Others experience a deep sense of loneliness because the adults around them are not caring for them. As these children experience the Holy Spirit, they become conscious of the ongoing presence of the Spirit in their daily lives. They tune in with what the Spirit is doing in their lives, become acutely aware and open to the miraculous, and have a sense of moral values.

---

[36] Hay and Nye, *Spirit of the Child*, 109.
[37] Hay and Nye, *Spirit of the Child*, 109.
[38] Hay and Nye, *Spirit of the Child*, 65.
[39] Hay and Nye, *Spirit of the Child*, 109.
[40] Hay and Nye, *Spirit of the Child*, 75.

Coraíma's story illustrates what this relational consciousness looks like in the day-to-day life of a child at risk.[41] Coraíma lived in a marginalised *barrio* in Caracas, Venezuela. Her neighbourhood was known for gangs, drugs, and violence. After school one day, second grader Coraíma, caring for her special needs sister, returned home to find her mother was not there. Her father was in the house with other men, and they were drinking. Coraíma soon realised the men wanted to molest her and her sister, and she felt threatened. However, she did not feel alone. She knew God's Holy Spirit was with her, so she prayed to Jesus to help her and her sister. When she shared the story the next day to her spiritual mentor, she recognised the miraculous in the event and declared, "Jesus helped hide me and my sister from those men."[42]

The scientific data provided by Hay and Nye's research supports the view that spirituality is entirely natural and grows out of a biological disposition. Although spirituality is innate in the biology of human beings, it can be dimmed or enhanced by culture.[43] Spirituality is essential to culture, providing the foundation for individual and societal contentment. Children have a rich capacity for spirituality that is merited to their psychological qualities and biological make-up. Spirituality naturally flows through the life of children whether they can define it or not. Their understanding of spirituality and experience is not based on religious knowledge or the moral rules that they have been taught.[44] Additionally, Hay and Nye's research demonstrates the importance of a child being aware of themselves as a subject in order to encourage the interpretation of the world in relational terms.[45]

While the culture of communities of high vulnerability can dim the spirituality of children at risk, the culture of a Pentecostal community can enhance it and help children to flourish. Children receive comfort knowing that the Holy Spirit is a constant companion. The Spirit in a child's life also guides them toward good decisions to help them achieve their goals. Mostly, the empowerment of the Spirit gives the child the agency and internal strength to be able to achieve their goals.

Conclusion

All children are created in God's image with great possibility. God intends each child, even those born in a vulnerable state, to grow in a loving and healthy environment. Sadly, many children live in difficult circumstances and are at risk of not fulfilling the potential with which God created them. While alleviation of

---

[41] Coraíma, personal communication with Mary Mahon, personal meeting in June 2008, Caracas, Venezuela. Note: I have chosen not to provide her last name here.
[42] Coraíma, personal communication.
[43] Hay and Nye, *Spirit of the Child*, 141.
[44] Hay and Nye, *Spirit of the Child*, 93.
[45] Hay and Nye, *Spirit of the Child*, 109.

risk factors remains crucial in ministry with children at risk, the internal development of agency is what empowers a child to make decisions and take actions for their own life. With such empowerment, a child can have hope and move toward goals for a better future.[46]

Children are created with an innate capacity for spirituality that is expressed through relational consciousness. Children quite naturally receive an experience with the Holy Spirit. In our ministry with children, we must trust the Spirit to move in their lives. In the same way, we must trust the child's individual spirituality and ability to connect with God on a personal level.

A personal Pentecost can prove transformational for a child at risk, empowering them to overcome the difficulties in their day-to-day life and to envisage a better future. Dr Danny remembers his childhood experiences with the Spirit:

> I remember those moments as a child in chapel as transcendental moments, where the Holy Spirit touched my heart. It was where I cried in the presence of the Lord, where I could feel the fullness of the Holy Spirit, and where the Holy Spirit took away the anguish, fear, and sadness because of family situations. It was about one hour a week when we were exposed to the Holy Spirit, and the Holy Spirit ministered to our hearts, bringing inner healing, bringing freedom, and transforming us in our minds.[47]

Experiences such as these make a significant difference in the life of a child at risk. As the Pentecostal community provides opportunities for children to experience the Holy Spirit, lives will be transformed. Children who live their daily lives with the presence of the Spirit will never be alone; they will have divine guidance to lead them toward good decision making, and the empowerment of the Spirit will foster the agency needed to help them fulfil their God-given potential.

Bibliography

Primary Sources

Coraíma. Personal communication with Mary Mahon, Fuente de Vida School, Caracas, Venezuela, June 2008.

Gonzalez, Danny. Personal communication with Mary Mahon, WhatsApp audio, 31st August 2023.

Gonzalez, Luis. Personal communication with Mary Mahon, in person interview in Los Guido, Costa Rica, 27th May 2022. Follow up conversation on Facebook Messenger 30th August 2023.

---

[46] Chris R. Snyder, "Measuring Hope in Children", in Kristin A. Moore and Laura H. Lippman (eds), *What Do Children Need To Flourish?: Conceptualizing and Measuring Indicators of Positive Development* (New York: Springer, 2005), 61.

[47] Danny Gonzalez, personal communication.

Meza, María. Personal communication with Mary Mahon, WhatsApp audio, 10th September 2023.

Secondary Sources

Bruner, Jerome S. *Acts of Meaning*. Cambridge, MA: Harvard University Press, 1990.

——. *The Culture of Education*. Cambridge, MA: Harvard University Press, 1996.

Christian, Jayakumar. *God of the Empty Handed: Poverty, Power and the Kingdom of God*. Monrovia, CA: MARC, 1999.

Cleary, Edward L. "Latin American Pentecostalism", In Murray W. Dempster, Byron D. Klaus, and Douglas Petersen, Eds. *The Globalization of Pentecostalism: A Religion Made to Travel*. Oxford: Regnum, 1999: 131-150.

Coles, Robert. *The Spiritual Life of Children*. Boston, MA: Houghton Mifflin, 1990.

Cox, Harvey. *Fire from Heaven: The Rise of Pentecostal Spirituality and the Reshaping of Religion in the Twenty-First Century*. Reading, MA: Addison-Wesley, 1995.

Dempster, Murray W., Byron D. Klaus, and Douglas Petersen, Eds. *The Globalization of Pentecostalism: A Religion Made to Travel*. Oxford: Regnum, 1999.

Fowler, James W. *Stages of Faith*. New York: Harper and Row, 1981.

Fowler, J.W., and M.L. Del. "Stages of Faith from Infancy through Adolescence: Reflection on Three Decades of Faith Development Theory", In Eugene C. Roehlkepartain, Pamela Ebstyne King, Linda Wagener, and Peter L. Benson, Eds. *The Handbook of Spiritual Development in Childhood and Adolescence*. Thousand Oaks, CA: Sage, 2006: 34-45.

Harter, Susan. *The Construction of the Self: Developmental and Sociocultural Foundations*. 2nd ed. New York: Guilford, 2013.

Hay, David, and Rebecca Nye. *The Spirit of the Child*. Rev. ed. London: Jessica Kingsley, 2006.

Hay, David. Helmut K. Reich, and Michael Utsch. "Spiritual Development: Intersections and Divergence with Religious Development", In Eugene C. Roehlkepartain, Pamela Ebstyne King, Linda Wagener, and Peter L. Benson, Eds. *The Handbook of Spiritual Development in Childhood and Adolescence*. Thousand Oaks, CA: Sage, 2006: 46-59.

Lausanne Consultation on Children at Risk. "Who are Children-at-Risk: A Missional Definition." Quito, Ecuador: Lausanne Movement, 2015. [Available at: https://lausanne.org/content/statement/children-at-risk-missional-definition#:~:text=Children%2Dat%2Drisk%20are%20persons,fulfilling%20their%20God%2Dgiven%20potential] [Last accessed: 23rd April 2024].

Macchia, Frank D. "The Struggle for Global Witness: Shifting Paradigms in Pentecostal Theology", In Murray W. Dempster, Byron D. Klaus, and

Douglas Petersen, Eds. *The Globalization of Pentecostalism: A Religion Made to Travel*. Oxford: Regnum, 1999: 8-29.

Ratcliff, Donald, Ed. *Children's Spirituality: Christian Perspectives, Research and Applications*. Eugene, OR: Cascade, 2006.

Roehlkepartain, Eugene C., Pamela Ebstyne King, Linda Wagener, and Peter L. Benson, Eds. *The Handbook of Spiritual Development in Childhood and Adolescence*. Thousand Oaks, CA: Sage, 2006.

Ryan, Richard M., and Edward L. Deci. "On Assimilating Identities to the Self: A Self-Determination Theory Perspective on Internalization and Integrity within Cultures", In Mark R. Leary and June Price, Eds. *Handbook of Self and Identity*. New York: Guilford, 2003: 253-272.

Segura-April, Desiree, Susan Hayes Greener, Dave Scott, Nicolas Panotto, and Menchit Wong. "Mission with Children at Risk", Lausanne Occasional Paper 66. [Available at: https://lausanne.org/content/lop/mission-children-risk-lop-66] [Last accessed: 23rd April 2024].

Snyder, Chris R. "Measuring Hope in Children", In Kristin A. Moore and Laura H. Lippman, Eds. *What do Children Need to Flourish?: Conceptualizing and Measuring Indicators of Positive Development*. New York: Springer, 2005: 61-73.

Stern, Daniel N. *The Interpersonal World of the Infant*. New York: Basic, 1985.

Wilson, Everett A. "They Crossed the Red Sea, Didn't They? Critical History and Pentecostal Beginnings", In Murray W. Dempster, Byron D. Klaus, and Douglas Petersen, Eds. *The Globalization of Pentecostalism: A Religion Made to Travel*. Oxford: Regnum, 1999: 85-115.

17. Megachurches and Public Life: How Megachurch Congregants See Life as a Whole and Live Out Their Faith in Public Life

Joel Tejedo

Abbreviations

CCF	Christ's Commission Fellowship
CHC	City Harvest Church
GCQ	New General Community Quarantine
GS	Global South
HIRR	Hartford Institute for Religion Research
JIL	Jesus Is Lord Church
JTF	John Templeton Foundation
LGBTQ	Lesbian, Gay, Bisexual, Transgender, Queer/Questioning
QOS	Qualtrics Online Survey
RT	Ritual Theory
SC	Spiritual Capital
SR	Sociology of Religion
TMCP	Templeton Mega-Church Project
VCF	Victory Christian Fellowship

Introduction

Megachurches are undergoing a massive transition and transformation influenced by the recent global health crisis, wars, and geo-political conflicts on various continents. While it is still in its infancy, the study of megachurches in the Global South will continue to evolve and be forged by global challenges as the twenty-first century unfolds. How megachurch congregants approach lived religion and play their role in public life are questions worth noting in our times. Drawing our attention from perspectives of megachurch congregants, fresh from the results of the empirical research conducted by the research team of Templeton Megachurch Project of John Templeton Foundation, this chapter unpacks the collective voices of church congregants as to how they live out and translate that faith in public life. Using the Qualtrics Online Surveys, we surveyed megachurch congregants from all walks of life about faith and life, politics, socio-economic issues, cultural values, social media, and the COVID-19 pandemic to make important and meaningful discoveries that can shape the global study of religion and the forging of public policy toward religion.

Conceptual Mapping of the Role of Megachurches in the Urban Life of Metro Manila

Even before megachurches developed in Metro Manila, Christian churches had been recognised as prominent markers with an important role in shaping the city's public life. Despite the increasing influence of secularisation and modernisation, Christian churches in the Philippines remain change agents for social and political transformation. Alan Delotavo's analysis of the church's role in the Philippines points out that the church "remains at the forefront of moral empowerment, an agent of political change, a political refuge, and the most influential opposition against corruption".[1] In addition, Delotavo notes that "the church with its interrelated relationship with the state was instrumental for nurturing life and as a therapeutic institution that has a repository of transcendent values that heal an ill nation."[2] Megachurches as an urban face of Christianity resonate well to the flourishing of life providing a strong deposit of belief, spirituality, and moral life of urban centres in Metro Manila, Philippines. In the studies of Jayeel S. Cornelio and Manuel Victor Sapitula on the sociology of religion in the Philippines, three essential observations emerged as to why Christian religiosity in the Philippines is steadily vibrant, regardless of the decline of attendance at Catholic churches. First, the "missionising zeal of Evangelical churches"[3] promotes a "communal and highly experiential mode of spirituality available to other Christian churches."[4] This attracts the Catholic youth to transfer their religious affiliation. Second, religious vibrancy is fuelled by charismatic renewal movements in Catholic and Evangelical churches as they open up religious spaces for Filipinos to find personal meaning that affects spiritual discipline and the betterment of life.[5] Third, Cornelio and Sapitula observe that megachurches have begun to showcase their successes and religious sites as a "grand global appeal" to demonstrate the gravitational shift of Christian mission from the West to the Global South. A case in point is the establishment of El Shaddai's International House of Prayer in Parañaque.[6]

---

[1] Alan J. Delotavo, "Ethical Considerations of Ecclesio-Political Involvement: A People Power Case", *The Asia Journal of Theology* 20(2) (October 2006), 225.
[2] Delotavo, "Ethical Considerations", 226. See also O. Elisha, "Moral Ambitions of Grace: The Paradox of Compassion and Accountability in Evangelical Faith-Based Activism", *Cultural Anthropology* 23(1) (2008), 154.
[3] Jayeel S. Cornelio and Manuel Victor Sapitula, "Are We Losing Faith? An Invitation to the Sociology of Religion in the Philippines", *Philippine Sociological Society*, 20th November 2014 [Available at: https://socialstudiescorner.wordpress.com/tag/philippine-Catholicism] [Last accessed: 24th April 2024].
[4] Cornelio and Sapitula, "Are We Losing Faith?" 1.
[5] Cornelio and Sapitula, "Are We Losing Faith?" 2-3.
[6] Cornelio and Sapitula, "Are We Losing Faith?" 2-3; see also Jayeel S. Cornelio, "Jesus Is Lord: The Indigenization of Megachurch Christianity in the Philippines", in T. Chong (ed), *Pentecostal Megachurches in Southeast Asia: Negotiating Class, Consumption, and the Nation* (Singapore: ISEAS, 2018), 1.

Cornelio's study of the Jesus Is Lord Church (JIL) headed by Eddie Villanueva shows that megachurches like JIL are prime players at the forefront of indigenising Christianity and have "political leverage" in Philippine society. Although they experienced political harassment and an assassination attempt initially, JIL stood as a megachurch with a strong political voice in the Philippines.[7] Cornelio admits this is not always the case for megachurches in the Philippines. His recent study reveals that some megachurches are branded as "apolitical" for failing to take a stand on what is morally right. According to this study, megachurches acknowledge that, although they have an important voice in the social space, they have failed to take a position on crucial political and moral issues. A case in point is President Duterte's "war on drugs," where they failed "to recognise the structural causes and consequences of substance abuse in the country".[8] Cornelio criticises these megachurches because of their ambivalent position when it comes to religious position about protecting the dignity of human life.

Megachurches in the Philippines have significantly changed the congregational life of their members. These megachurches own campuses and multi-site fellowship meetings. They have shifted from using TV media to web pages, Facebook, YouTube videos, and live streams at a fraction of the previous cost. Although they still adhere to mother organisations, they are becoming autonomous in branding, tailoring their programmes, and avoiding bureaucratic delays. On-the-job training is more valued than seminary training.[9] Worship services are contemporary with creative worship styles. Some megachurches are designed like shopping malls to attract and accommodate large crowds. A critique of megachurches indicates that this rationale is anthropologically rather than theologically based.[10]

Another striking observation about megachurches is that they are like therapeutic, spiritual pharmacies for individuals. James K. Wellman Jr., Katie E. Corcoran, and Kate Stockly-Meyerdirk's 2014 study of twelve megachurches in the US from the perspective of ritual theory shows that megachurches produce positive emotional energy. Membership symbols are charged with emotional significance, feelings of morality, and a heightened sense of spirituality. Contrary to the criticism that megachurches are "superficial sources of entertainment that do not produce the significant feeling of belonging, moral responsibility, or spirituality," megachurches are perceived as good drugs that

---

[7] Cornelio, "Jesus Is Lord", 130-38.
[8] Jayeel S. Cornelio and Ian Marañon, "A 'Righteous Intervention': Megachurch Christianity and Duterte's War on Drugs in the Philippines", *International Journal of Asian Christianity* 2(2) (2019), 224, 227 [Available at: https://doi.org/10.1163/25424246-00202005] [Last accessed: 24th April 2024].
[9] John Dart, "Trends of Bigger Churches: Going Mega", *Christian Century*, 27th July 2010: 21-23.
[10] Laceye Warner, "Mega Churches: A New Ecclesiology or Ecclesial Evangelism?" *Review and Expositor* 107(1) (2010), 26.

provide spiritual prescriptions for the betterment of life.[11] Ethnographic observations and interviews among members of megachurches in the US by David Snow et al. show that megachurches attract and appeal to the masses for two reasons: at the personal level, megachurches provide a fine-tuning of a wide array of emotional problems and issues. At the organisational level, megachurches are significant players in a self-help market economy.[12]

The critiques of social scientists and marketing theoreticians also confirm that the megachurch phenomenon successfully markets its witness, power, and influence in the business centres. Joy Chin writes that megachurches like City Harvest Church (CHC) in Singapore "display a striking similarity in their rationalisation of production and consumption to those mass-production corporations of which McDonald's is the epitome".[13] Drawing from George Ritzer and Elizabeth Cook, Chin further argues that through this McDonaldisation of megachurches, they "grow in size in a short period and acquire their unique identities and influences in the society".[14] Joseph Daniels and Marc von der Ruhr, who critique megachurches from an economic perspective, argue that they are attractive and successful because they "assert their ability as consumers of religious products to engage in religious switching."[15] That is to say that megachurches attract religious refugees because they "provide low cost and low commitment at the start, but the moment the attendees perceive a good fit in the church, they increase expectations and commitments".[16]

Similarly, megachurches can create bonding and bridging capital that connects to their influence in the public sphere and transnational networks.

---

[11] James K. Wellman Jr., Katie E. Corcoran, and Kate Stockly-Meyerdirk, "God Is Like a Drug…: Explaining Interaction Ritual Chains in American Megachurches", *Sociological Forum*, 26th August 2014, pp. 650-651. [Available at: https://doi.org/10.1111/socf.12108] [Last accessed: 24th April 2024].

[12] David A. Snow et al., "A Team Field Study of the Appeal of Megachurches: Identifying, Framing, and Solving Personal Issues", *Ethnography* 11(1) (2010), 165 [Available at: https://doi.org/10.1177/1466138109347006] [Last accessed: 24th April 2024].

[13] Joy Tong Kooi Chin, "McDonaldization and Megachurches: A Case Study of City Harvest Church, Singapore", in Pattana Kitiarsa (ed), *Religious Commodifications in Asia: Marketing Gods* (Abingdon: Routledge, 2007), 1.

[14] Chin, "McDonaldization", 2. See Elizabeth Cook, "Would You Like Your Jesus Upsized? McDonaldization and the Mega Church," Senior Thesis Projects, 1993-2002, Knoxville: University of Tennessee, 2002 [Available at: https://trace.tennessee.edu/utk_interstp2/85] [Last accessed: 24th April 2024]; and George Ritzer, *The McDonaldization of Society* (Newbury Park, CA: Pine Forge, 1993).

[15] Joseph P. Daniels and Marc von der Ruhr, "Examining Megachurch Growth: Free Riding, Fit, and Faith", *International Journal of Social Economics* 39(5) (March 2012), 357, 253, 372. [Available at: https://epublications.marquette.edu/econ_fac/139] [Last accessed: 24th April 2024].

[16] Daniels and von der Ruhr, "Examining Megachurch Growth", 372.

Terence Chong, an astute sociologist in Singapore, observes that the rise of megachurches in Asia was due to the influx of Protestant churches that detached themselves from the control of mother organizations for greater freedom of innovating and branding their worship.[17] He observes that the theology of the prosperity gospel and openness to charismata are associated with megachurches because of the upward mobility lifestyle of the middle classes. In addition, megachurches teach the integration of "sacred" and "secular" as a social space of Christian witness to encourage members to become change agents in society.[18] Chong also points out that the development of megachurches in Asia is a by-product of a growing "transnational" relationship with their Western counterparts. Although he acknowledges that some megachurches have an indigenous origin, the influence of international co-operation and globalisation has opened an immense network between these megachurches. They share information, knowledge, resources, and leadership models to maintain their religious status as megachurches.[19]

A study by Cartledge *et al.* on megachurches in London in 2017 shows a variety of activities of social engagement. These include work with children and youth, older people, people experiencing homelessness, families, couples, people with physical and health needs, the widowed and bereaved, and community development such as educational projects and social campaigning against human trafficking.[20] According to this study, megachurches are galvanising civic engagement that positively impacts the lives of the city and its citizens and are working for real change in the communities they seek to serve.[21] Some essential findings from this study resonate with policymakers and social innovators to encourage collaboration between religious groups and civil society. While megachurch pastors, leaders, and congregants value beliefs, rituals, and values, the principal reason for their social engagement is their inherent personal and vibrant relationship with God. Megachurch members engage in social concerns because a relationship with God is the heart of their motivation.[22] The social engagement of megachurches is not primarily motivated by an agenda of proselytisation and evangelism. Still, it is a product of a solid interpersonal

---

[17] Terrence Chong, "Introduction", in Terence Chong (ed), *Pentecostal Megachurches in Southeast Asia: Negotiating Class, Consumption and the Nation* (Singapore: ISEAS, 2018), 407.
[18] Terrence Chong, "Introduction", 408.
[19] Terrence Chong, "Introduction", 411; see also Rene E. Mendoza, "Religion and Secularization in the Philippines and Other Asian Countries", *Institute for Japanese Culture and Classics*, Kokugakuin University, 1999 [Available at: https://www2.kokugakuin.ac.jp/ijcc/wp/cimac/mendoza.html] [Last accessed: 24th April 2024].
[20] Mark J. Cartledge et al., *Megachurches and Social Engagement: Public Theology in Practice* (Leiden: Brill, 2019), 1.
[21] Cartledge et al., *Megachurches and Social Engagement*, 1.
[22] Cartledge et al., *Megachurches and Social Engagement*, 2.

relationship within the faith community and with other partners.[23] As a result, Church social engagement provides a substantial deposit of spiritual and social capital to their members and the broader networks of the community.[24] According to this study, the diversity of forms of social engagement in these megachurches is based on each church's distinctive calling and conviction. There is no uniformity of social engagement but rather a diversity of expressions of Christian faith in the public sphere.[25]

Methodology

The research team who conducted this study made a series of field visits and communications to our pilot projects, secured a research agreement with megachurches' leadership, and observed research protocols by communicating clearly what the research project intended to do.[26] While doing this process, we examined and watched hundreds of online sermon videos, TV interviews of megachurch leaderships, and testimonials of members of CCF and VCF. In addition, we joined the various social media platforms of CCF and VCF to receive and continually update each church's published videos. Finally, while the COVID-19 pandemic restricted us in so many ways from attending the physical services, we participated in the online services of both churches almost every Saturday and Sunday.

The survey instruments used for this study was from the 2015 Survey of North American Megachurches of Hartford Institute for Religion Research designed

---

[23] Cartledge et al., *Megachurches and Social Engagement*, 3.
[24] Cartledge et al., *Megachurches and Social Engagement*, 5.
[25] Cartledge et al., *Megachurches and Social Engagement*, 5-6.
[26] This research project is funded by the generosity of John Templeton Foundation under the "Templeton Megachurch Project in the Global South" of Canisius College in New York, USA. I am pleased to acknowledge the contributions of many people who immensely contributed for the making of this project in the Philippines. To Prudencio Coz, Joseph Antolin, Karlo Timenia, Marichu Soliven Dulay, Ethel Giesbrecht, Lawrence Panaguiton, my research staff who helped me in so many ways to translate, implement, gather data and interview leaders of CCF and VCF. Larry Uy (Executive Secretary of VCF) has tremendously assisted us in promoting and distributing the survey flyer to the pastors and congregations of VCF; Pauline Abegail Matute (Executive Secretary of Peter Tan-chi) has helped us tremendously to communicate the project to the pastors, from securing the research agreement to reviewing our survey questionnaires to the leadership of CCF. Pauline Matute served as a "point person" and communication staff to us so that we could communicate with the church's leadership. J.P. Masakayan (Administrative Pastor of CCF, Georgetown University, USA) has helped us to endorse our research project to Pastor Peter Tan-chi. Pastor Masakayan linked us to the leadership during the formation of the research project in 2020. Ricky Sarthou (Executive pastor of CCF) has equally assisted us in promoting the surveys to CC members.

by Scott Thumma and Warren Bird[27] revised by Timothy Wadkins and the International team of researchers for the study of megachurches in the Global South.[28] The research team of the Global South spent one year of online Zoom meetings to revise, enhance, and add essential variables of the Congregational Survey Instrument to appropriate the instrument in the GS context. Important variables added were engagement with the world, theological questions, and COVID-19 questions. In addition, we used the Qualtrics Online Survey and Google Form Online Survey to collect samples from CCF and VCF. The survey was conducted by the Philippine Regional Team with the partnership of the leadership of CCF and VCF. We crafted three long, short, and abridged survey versions and made the study available in Qualtrics and Google Forms. We also published and printed hard copies of the instruments to make them available on all fronts. Since the data collection's success lies in the endorsement and recommendation of megachurch leadership, we sent the draft to CCF and VCF for review after pretesting the survey instruments. We requested implementation of the survey for the pastors and congregants. We sent emails to the leadership of both churches and charted the plan to implement the surveys. Methodological predicaments encountered during the research process involved meeting the expectations of megachurch leaders. There is reluctance and scepticism from VCF regarding whether data collection can be successful due to the New General Community Quarantine (GCQ) imposed by the national government in Metro Manila, Philippines. The pandemic gravely affected church attendance and the implementation and collection of data on time.

There were at least three phases to collecting data from our target projects. First, we formally requested the leaderships of CCF and VCF to roll out the surveys to their members to ensure we would meet the target number of data we intended to collect. As a result, the online surveys were sent to their pastors in the main churches and then to different satellite churches in the Philippines and overseas. Second, we formed a team of surveyors to promote, send, and distribute the surveys to the congregants attending the CCF and VCF, recruiting and inviting their adherents from various social media platforms to participate. Third, to attract the congregants to join the survey, we created the "Join and Grab" flyer as a research strategy to provide a grab meal to encourage participants to join the survey. While this strategy has proven effective for participants living in Metro Manila, it was only sometimes the case in other provinces of the Philippines and overseas.

---

[27] Scott Thumma and Warren Bird, "Megafaith for the Megacity: The Global Megachurch Phenomenon", in Stanley D. Brunn (ed), *The Changing World Religion Map: Sacred Place, Identities, Practices and Politics* (Dordrecht, Netherlands: Springer, 2015); first online 20th November 2014 [Available at: https://doi.org/10.1007/978-94-017-9376-6_123] [Last accessed: 24th April 2024].

[28] Timothy Wadkins, "Modernization, Megachurches and the Urban Face of Christianity in the Global South", *An Approved Project Proposal for the John Templeton Foundation,* 1st January 2020.

Summary of the Demographic Portraits

Respondents to our surveys were taken from the two prominent evangelical churches yet consider themselves non-denominational with Pentecostal branding concerning their worship styles and ways of worship. Although there were 1,029 total respondents from CCF and VCF, only 880 completed the survey. Four hundred-eight individuals (46.36%) attend Victory Christian Fellowship, and 472 (53.64%) come from Christ Commission Fellowship. Qualtrics extracted 149 participants due to the significant items that these survey respondents did not answer. This section describes the following demography of the respondents.

Q5.1: In what year were you born?

1933-1945	4	Silent Generation
1945-1964	114	Baby Boomer
1965-1980	252	Generation X
1981-2000	432	Millennial
2001-	31	Generation Z
Unknown	47*	No given year

Most congregant survey participants, 432 individuals (49.09%), came from millennials born between 1981 and 2000, followed by Generation X with 252 individuals (26.63% born between 1954 and 1980). Third in rank is the baby boomers, with 114 individuals (12.95%) and 31 individuals (3.52%) coming from Generation Z. Data also show that only four individuals (0.45%) are from the silent generation. Forty-four individuals (5%) did not consent or give the year when they were born. Regarding gender, 340 individuals (38.68%) are male and 537 (61.09%) are female. Two individuals (0.23%) identified as non-binary or third gender. While there were a proportionate number of male participants, the majority of participants were female congregants. Regarding marital status of participants, 464 individuals (52.73%) indicated married, 345 (39.20%) indicated single, 15 individuals (1.70%) said they live with a partner, 26 individuals (2.95%) indicated divorced or separated, and 30 individuals (3.41%) indicated widowed.

With regard to whether the participant's spouse or partner join them in the church, 421 individuals (88.08%) said they attend the same church, 26 (5.44%) attend a different church, 22 (4.60%) individuals said they adhere to a different religious faith, and 9 (1.88%) said they do not adhere to any faith at all. Four hundred and two individuals (45.68%) neither said they have a partner or have a status of single.

When it comes to the work status of participants, 450 individuals (51.25%) work as employees with a salary, 123 individuals (14.01%) said they are a business owner with employees or owners of small businesses, and 84 individuals (9.57%) said that they work as a housewife. Data shows that three groups of participants consider themselves to have no work status. Forty-nine individuals (5.58%) said they are pensioners, retirees, or living with savings. In contrast, 47 individuals (5.35%) are still students, and 44 (5.01%) are unemployed. The data also shows that four participants (.46%) consider themselves living at the pyramid of poverty in the Philippines. Eight individuals (0.91%) consider themselves daily wage labourers, four individuals (0.46%) said they are small farm owners, and three individuals (0.34%) said they are living on welfare and charity. Only one individual (0.11%) said they are a wage earner in the agricultural sector. The data shows, however, that 65 individuals (7.40%) were not included in the bracket. These people serve as missionaries, self-employed/freelancers, or own home businesses.

Number	Percentage	Occupation
450	51.25	Employees with salary
123	14.01	Business owner with employees or owners of small businesses
84	9.57	Housewife
49	5.58	Pensioners, retirees, or living with savings
47	5.35	Students
44	5.01	Unemployed
4	.46	Living at the Pyramid of Poverty
8	.91	Daily Wage Labourer
4	.46	Small Farm Owner
3	.34	Living on Welfare and Charity
1	.11	Wage earner in the Agricultural Sector
65	7.40	Missionaries, self-employed/Freelancers, or Own Home Businesses

Table 1. Work Status of Participants

When it comes to how participants describe their class position in society, 445 individuals (50.63%) say they are middle class, 339 individuals (38.57%) say they belong to the working class, and 73 individuals (8.30%) say they consider themselves lower class. Data shows that 22 individuals (2.50%) say they belong to the upper class. Regarding educational background and achievement, most participants, 468 individuals (53.36%), said they hold graduate and postgraduate degrees, and 216 individuals (24.63%) hold postsecondary and undergraduate degrees. One hundred twenty-one individuals (13.80%) completed diploma, certificate, and vocation courses, while 61 (6.96%) completed their secondary studies. Almost equally, five individuals (0.57%) and six individuals (0.68%) said they completed their elementary education or have some schooling but did not complete their elementary education. Most megachurch congregants are highly educated people with graduate and postgraduate degrees.

Christian Life

Megachurches are believed to be the spiritual capital centres that teach doctrines and beliefs so they know how to behave and act in society. This section of the survey examined the opinions of megachurch congregants relative to different Christian beliefs taught by their pastors. When it comes to the Bible, whether congregants believe that the Bible gives a clear answer about good and evil, 863 individuals (98.97%) said they agree. Asked whether they think that God punishes those who engage in fornication and adultery, the survey revealed that about 819 individuals (94.25%) agreed. When asked about whether God will punish homosexual activity, about 798 individuals (92.25%) agreed. Regarding Christian evangelistic responsibility to share the good news with other religions, 863 individuals (98.97%) said they agreed Christians should do this. Regarding the responsibility of Christians to work for justice for the poor, 755 individuals (86.58%) agreed Christians should do this work, With regard to whether Christians have to help the disadvantaged in society with no expectation that they will convert or join the church, 800 individuals (93.13%) agreed. Regarding giving support and donations to the church, 806 (94.16%) of the congregants agreed that Christians should support the church financially. With regard to paying tithes, 765 (88.63%) agreed Christians should tithe, 69 (7.94%) disagreed this statement.

Regarding spiritual warfare, most megachurch members believe Christians are at war with Satan and his forces in our sin-warped, broken world. 823 individuals (95.03%) highly subscribe to the belief that Christians are involved with satanic forces. Megachurch congregants believe in healing but they do not like associating themselves with faith healers or tele-evangelists who use a medium of instrument for economic exchange and aggrandisement. When it comes to speaking in tongues as the only evidence of Spirit baptism, 155 individuals (17.94%) agreed, 630 individuals (72.92%) disagreed, and 79 individuals (9.14%) felt doubtful about the statement. The survey showed that while minimal agreement exists among members regarding speaking in tongues as the only physical evidence of Spirit baptism, the overall tone of the megachurch congregants was to reject this idea as they are still determining whether tongues serve as the only evidence of Spirit baptism. Regarding the continuity of miracles today, 784 individuals (90.95%) agree and believe in the occurrence and continuity of miracles today, as in biblical times.

Regarding the doctrine of eschatology and last events, 848 individuals (97.47%) say that Jesus is Saviour and Lord and the only way to be saved from eternal damnation and 831 individuals (95.85%) said Jesus will return soon. Regarding the timing of the last days and the Church's rapture, megachurch congregants agree that the religious faithful will be saved and taken up to heaven in what is called the rapture of the Church: 698 individuals (81.45%), and 78 individuals (9.10%) disagreed. Another 81 individuals (9.45%) were doubtful relative to this statement.

A public perception exists of megachurches as the habitat of the prosperity gospel, known as "health and wealth" theology. The "redemption and lift" and upward mobility mentality of the members sometimes fuel congregant attraction to the prosperity gospel. The survey examined whether this holds true within megachurches in the Philippines.

The survey revealed that 452 individuals (52.13%) agreed that God will grant wealth and success to all believers who have true faith, 349 individuals (40.25%) disagreed, and 66 individuals (7.61%) felt doubtful of the statement. When it comes to health, 445 individuals (51.39%) agreed that God will grant good health and relief from sickness to believers who have true faith, 359 individuals (41.45%) disagreed, and 62 individuals (7.16%) felt doubtful about that statement. The data reveals intriguing observations about the belief in health and wealth among megachurch congregants. While a slight majority (52.13% and 51.39%) of both questions show that megachurch congregants believe that God grants wealth and health, these theological stances are faced with a high degree of disagreement (40.25% and 41.45%) among members of megachurches. More than 7% of participants felt doubtful and unsure about the questions. In other words, a theological "tension" of belief is emerging within megachurch congregants about the doctrinal issues of health and wealth theology.

Megachurches are populated primarily by middle-class and working people who are driven by upward mobility and economic success. Although diverse in their opinions about wealth and prosperity, megachurch congregants in the survey clarified what important factors affect personal economic success. This study has enumerated economic indicators for economic success. Regarding hard work, this study found that 804 individuals (92.52%) agreed that hard work is very important, 858 individuals (98.73%) indicated that they see God's will as very important, people's parents' economic situation, 362 individuals (41.85%) regard it as very important, while 424 individuals (49.02%) said they see it as somewhat important. Furthermore, 615 individuals (71.18%) see pastor's prayer and guidance as very important. When it comes to the importance of faith in God, 845 individuals (97.58%) said they see it as very important. When it comes to their perspective on government policies on economics, 503 (58.02%) said that it is very important and 336 individuals (38.75%) said it is somewhat important. Regarding the importance of social capital, 413 individuals (47.58%) think it is crucial, 347 individuals (39.98%) said they regarded it as very important, and another 108 individuals (12.44%) said they see it as unimportant. Regarding obedience to the Bible, 835 individuals (96.53%) said they regard it as an important indicator of economic success. Regarding education, 662 individuals (76.62%) said they believe financial literacy is important while moral character, like integrity and honesty, 815 individuals (94.11%) said is imperative. Regarding the role of the Holy Spirit, 851 individuals (98.04%) said the Holy Spirit is very important while 652 individuals (75.55%) regard fate and luck as not important at all. When it comes to the perceptions of megachurch congregants about the Philippine economy, when asked whether this country is being left behind in terms of economic development, 483 individuals (55.58%)

agreed, 459 individuals (52.82%) say that they agreed the economy is improving, 339 individuals (38.97%) said that it is in the right direction, and 327 individuals (37.54%) said they felt neutral and unsure whether this country is respected in the world.

Political Life

John Choo, Evelyn Tan, and P.S. Goh write that megachurches in the Philippines have begun expanding their political influence by "endorsing political candidates" to their adherents through their church-based political movement, "influencing their middle-class members to be a 'salt and light' in the bureaucracy through fielding political offices," and "galvanising the grassroots by sending their members out of the streets for political causes"[29] These qualitative observations, however, have never been tested empirically and quantitatively. We asked members a series of questions on political issues to see the faces of political engagement of megachurches, 761 individuals (86.97%) said they do not have any political affiliations whatsoever. However, when asked the name of their political affiliations, although restrictive with their responses, the Liberal Party, represented by Leni and Kiko Pangilinan during the past election, is the representative voice of megachurch members. Although some identify as the political party of Uniteam, Manny Pacquiao, and the Christian Values movement of CCF – or some identify themselves as Independent, Republican, or Conservative, the most identified political party of megachurch congregants is the Liberal Party.

Our survey indicated that megachurch congregants remain apolitical and do not want to identify with any political party in the Philippines. Although emerging political movements now exist that voice out the beliefs, values, and choices of megachurches, it appears that information about these political movements owned by megachurches has not been communicated well to the congregants, or perhaps these political choices endorsed by megachurch leadership are politically coerced by their members for personal political choices. The survey shared four noticeable and dominating choices of megachurch congregants about electing a leader of the country: a person who is a Christian (84.00%), a candidate who supports democracy (80.83%), an authoritative leader (72.70%), and a member of the church (69.21%). Our survey also shows that a female candidate (26.74%) and a member of another religious faith (10.53%) are the secondary choice candidates that megachurch congregants will vote for. Candidates who are members or advocates of the LGBTQ community (3.35%) and those with an atheistic belief (1.74%) are the less likely choice candidates of megachurch members. Most of the members always participate in local and national elections. Although the percentage varies, megachurch congregants

---

[29] John Choo, Evelyn Tan, and P.S. Goh, "Christian Megachurches and Politics in the Philippines", *Perspective ISEAS Yusof Ishak Institute* 62 (2020), 1-4.

Chapter 17   269

participate slightly more at the national level (74.02%) than at the local level (68.69%).

When responding to the most controversial social issues in society today, megachurch congregants are staunch in their positions on these social issues. Mainly, when it comes to claiming state benefits to which you are not legally entitled, 694 individuals (79.68%) said they are never justified in receiving them. With regard to cheating on taxes, 819 individuals (93.81%) said it is never justified. When it comes to using illegal drugs such as marijuana or cocaine, 795 individuals (91.07%) said it is never justified. With regard to whether someone is giving or accepting a bribe in the course of their duties, 810 individuals (92.78%) said doing so was never justified.

With regard to homosexuality, 765 individuals (87.93%) said it is never justified, with regard to abortion, 757 individuals (86.91%) said it is never justified. Regarding divorce, the legal separation of a couple, 630 individuals (72.33%) said it is never justified. Our survey also suggested that the biblical prohibition and illegality of the matter in the Philippines likely influenced this perception. Concerning euthanasia or terminating the life of a terminally ill person, 613 individuals (70.62%) said it is never justified. However, when it comes to suicide, 790 individuals (90.29%) said it is never justified. When it comes to pre-marital sex, 815 individuals (93.57%) said it is never justified. With regard to avoiding a fare on public transport, 782 individuals (89.68%) said it is never justified. Regarding prostitution and the buying and selling of sex, 822 individuals (94.37%) said it is never justified. Our survey shows that most megachurch congregants reject and resist any form of sexual promiscuity contrary to the Holy Scriptures.

Concerning artificial insemination or in vitro fertilisation, 364 individuals (41.79%) said it is never justified, and another 421 (48.34%) said it depends upon the situation. While less than half of the participants (41.79%) reject the justification of in vitro fertilisation, an increasing acceptance and justification of artificial insemination or in vitro fertilisation exists among members of megachurches in the Philippines.

When it comes to protesting an unjust government, 679 individuals (77.96%) said it is never justified, 526 individuals (60.60%) said death penalty is never justified. When it comes to carrying a gun for self-protection, 67 individuals (7.68%) said it is justified, but 464 individuals (53.12%) said it is never justified, while 341 individuals (39.11%) said it depends upon the situation. With regard to gay marriage, only 25 individuals (2.86%) said it is always justified, but 808 individuals (92.45%) said it is never justified, while 41 individuals (4.69%) said that it depends. At the same time, a small percentage of acceptance and ambiguousness of the issue exists.

Q9.14: Please indicate whether you agree or disagree with the following statements about government actions and policies.

When it comes to the attitudes of megachurch congregants on government policies and actions, 558 individuals (64.06%) agreed with policies, 148 individuals (16.99%) disagreed with them, and 147 (16.88%) felt neutral. Only 18 individuals (2.07%) preferred not to say that those who earn more should pay higher taxes. Concerning shelter and food, 697 individuals (80.21%) of church congregants agreed that the government should guarantee every citizen food and shelter. Only 63 individuals (7.25%) disagreed, 103 individuals (11.85%) felt neutral, and six individuals (0.69%) preferred not to say their responses.

With regard to whether the government should be tough on crime, corruption, and rebels, 828 individuals (95.28%) agreed, 18 individuals (2.07%) disagreed, 103 individuals (11.85%) felt neutral, and only six individuals (0.69%) preferred not to say their response. Most megachurch congregants highly support the government's tough decisions and actions on crime, corruption, and rebels.

However, regarding the government's aggressiveness to prosecute crime harshly, even at the risk of violating human rights, 305 individuals (35.18%) agreed with that aggressiveness, but 467 individuals (53.86%) disagreed. In comparison, 82 individuals (9.46%) felt neutral, and only 13 individuals (1.50%) preferred not to share their responses. Most megachurch congregants reject the government's actions to prosecute crimes if they violate human rights.

Regarding protecting the environment as a priority, even if it causes slower economic growth and some loss of jobs, 585 individuals (67.71%) agreed with that policy. However, only 67 individuals (7.75%) disagreed, while 200 individuals (23.15%) felt neutral, and 12 individuals (1.39%) preferred not to respond. Most church congregants support the government priority of protecting the environment even if it causes slower economic growth and some loss of jobs.

When it comes to the provision of good health care for all, 839 individuals (97.44%) agreed with providing good health care for all, and only six individuals (0.70%) disagreed, while 14 individuals (1.63%) felt neutral. Two individuals (0.23%) preferred not to say. The survey indicated that among the social issues asked, megachurch congregants highly support the statement that the government should provide good health care for all its citizens. The high responses of the megachurch congregants about healthcare are fuelled by the urgency of this government's actions to the negative impact of COVID-19 on Filipino citizens.

Cultural Issues

Q10.1: How often do you engage in the following activities?
This section of the survey sought to discover the faces and forms of cultural values of megachurch congregants and how modernisation and urbanisation has affected or influenced them. We measured the cultural values of megachurch congregants and how often they go shopping, on vacation, what proportion of their time they spend on entertainment, etc. When it comes to shopping, only 29 individuals (3.34%) never go shopping, but 288 individuals (33.14%) seldomly shop, and 476 individuals (54.78%) occasionally shop. In comparison, 76 individuals (8.75%) said they frequently go shopping. While 33.13% of

Chapter 17

megachurch congregants seldom go shopping, data show that most occasionally go shopping.

When it comes to going on vacation during holidays, 34 individuals (3.9%) never go on vacation during holidays, 397 individuals (45.68%) seldomly have a vacation, while 399 individuals (45.9%) occasionally go for vacation during holidays. Only 39 individuals (4.49%) say the frequently go on vacations during holidays. The majority of responses from megachurch congregants indicate they seldom or occasionally go for vacation during holidays.

With regard to attitudes toward entertainment, such as movies, sports, performances, and concert clubs, only 41 individuals (4.71%) never go to those activities, 422 individuals (48.45%) seldomly attend these activities, and 329 individuals (37.77%) occasionally hang out at these entertainment activities. Only 79 individuals (9.07%) frequently go for these activities. The majority of megachurch members seldom attend locations associated with the entertainment industry.

When it comes to dining out at restaurants or cafes, only 21 individuals (2.41%) said they never go out to restaurants and cafes, 173 individuals (19.89%) seldom go to these places, 493 individuals (56.67%) occasionally dine out, and 183 individuals (21.03%) frequently go to these places. Megachurch congregants are more occasional than frequent in their dining out at restaurants and cafes.

Concerning health and wellness, such as going to the gym, spa, or hiking in nature, only 76 individuals (8.75%) said they do not go to these places, yet 427 individuals (49.14%) seldomly go. In comparison, 275 individuals (31.65%) occasionally attend these fitness areas. Ninety-one individuals (10.47%) said they frequently visit these wholesome places.

When it comes to hobbies such as reading or crafts, only 28 individuals (3.23%) never have hobbies like reading or crafts. However, 291 individuals (33.56%) seldomly read and do crafts, and 321 individuals (37.02%) occasionally read a book and do crafts, while 227 individuals (26.18%) frequently do reading and crafts. The majority of church congregants occasionally have hobbies like reading and doing crafts.

With regard to playing sports, 113 individuals (13.02%) said they never play sports; however, 416 individuals (47.93%) said they seldomly play sports, and 254 individuals (29.26%) occasionally play sports, while 85 individuals (9.79%) frequently play sports. The majority of the megachurch congregants seldom play sports.

When it comes to volunteering, only 39 individuals (4.49%) said they never volunteer, 167 individuals (19.22%) seldomly volunteer, 393 individuals (45.22%) occasionally volunteer, while 270 individuals (31.07%) frequently volunteer. The majority of megachurch congregants occasionally volunteer.

With regard to dating, 292 individuals (33.68%) said they do not date others, yet 290 individuals (33.45%) said they seldom date others, while 209 individuals (24.11%) acknowledged they date others. Seventy-six individuals (8.77%) said they frequently do date other people.

Regarding socialising with friends, 17 individuals (1.95%) said they never socialise with friends, while 143 individuals (16.40%) said they seldomly socialise with their friends. However, 439 individuals (50.34%) acknowledged that they occasionally socialise with friends, and another 273 individuals (31.31%) said they frequently socialise with friends. Megachurch congregants occasionally and frequently socialise with their friends.

Q10.13: On average, how many hours per day do you spend doing the following?

When it comes to time spent using social media, only eight individuals (0.92%) said they spent zero or no time using social media, 177 individuals (20.25%) said they spend one hour or less, but 342 individuals (39.13%) said they spent 1-3 hours, while another 222 individuals (25.40%) believe they spend 3-6 hours, and 125 individuals (14.30%) say it is more than six hours. The time spent on social media among megachurch congregants varies. However, the most obvious observation is that most church congregants spend between 1-3 hours and 3-6 hours on social media.

However, when it comes to using the Internet for their jobs or paid work, 127 individuals (14.65%) said they use it zero or no hours, 80 individuals (9.23%) said one hour or less, 143 individuals (16.49%) said between 1-3 hours, 198 individuals (22.84%) said between 3-6 hours, and 319 individuals (36.79%) said they use it more than six hours. The data clearly shows megachurch congregants are regular users of the Internet for their jobs and paid work.

With regard to text messaging with friends and family, only 34 individuals (3.91%) said they spend zero or no hours text messaging with friends and family, but 439 individuals (50.46%) said they text one hour or less per day, 269 individuals (30.92%) said between 1-3 hours per day, 83 individuals (9.54%) said between 3-6 hours per day, and 45 individuals (5.17%) said they text more than six hours per day. Megachurch congregants are regular users of cell phones and smart phones for communication with 81.38% using these devices between 0-3 hours daily.

In the same way, when it comes to talking on the phone with friends and family, only 68 individuals (7.83%) said they talk on the phone zero to no hours, but 530 individuals (60.99%) said one hour or less, 212 individuals (24.40%) said between 1-3 hours, and 48 individuals (5.52%) said between 3-6 hours. In comparison, 11 individuals (1.27%) said they talk on the phone more than six hours per day. Most church congregants talk on the phone with friends for an hour or less.

When it comes to watching "secular" TV, movies, or videos (including cable and streaming services), only 68 individuals (7.82%) said they watch for zero or no hours, 279 individuals (32.07%) said one hour or less, 401 individuals (46.09%) said between 1-3 hours, and 91 individuals (10.46%) said between 3-6 hours. In comparison, 31 individuals (3.56%) said they watch it for more than six hours. Most megachurch congregants spend time watching secular TV, movies, or videos for 1-3 hours per day.

When it comes to watching or listening to Christian programming such as sermons, talk shows, podcasts, or drama, only 25 individuals (2.87%) said they watch it for zero or no hours, 299 individuals (34.29%) said an hour or less, but 432 individuals (49.54%) said between 1-3 hours, and 99 individuals (11.35%) said between 3-6 hours, and only 17 individuals (1.95%) said they watch Christian programming for more than six hours. Most megachurch congregants spend 1-3 hours per day listening to Christian programming.

Regarding listening to Christian music, either via the radio, CDs, streaming on the Internet, or downloading, only 3.21% said they listen for zero hours per day, but 344 individuals (39.49%) said they listen for an hour or less. In comparison, another 350 individuals (40.18%) said they listen 1-3 hours per day. One hundred and three individuals (11.83%) said they listen between 3-6 hours, while 46 individuals (5.28%) said they listen more than six hours per day. Most megachurch congregants listen to Christian music on radio, CDs, or online sources for under 3 hours per day.

When it comes to playing games online, 495 individuals (60.89%) said they play for zero hours, 181 individuals (22.26%) said for an hour or less, while 10 individuals (12.79%) said between 1-3 hours. Only 23 individuals (2.83%) said they play online games for 3-6 hours per day, while ten individuals (1.23%) said they play for more than six hours per day. While some congregants play online games, the majority do not.

Q10.14: For what church-related purposes do you use social media? (Select all that apply.)

Regarding the use of social media in the context of church affairs, church congregants gave various responses for various reasons: 14.93% want to find out about the events of the church, 14.82% want to be connected with friends from the church, 15.24% want to be in touch with small groups or church organisations, 14.93% want to get communications from the church, 13.14% want to participate in services remotely, and 13.64% want to attend Bible study or other church programmes.

Regarding buying church products, only 3.01% say that they want to purchase church products, and another 9.92% said they want to donate or pay their tithes. Aside from other reasons, 14 individuals (0.29%) said they want to minister virtually, send Bible passages and prayer, attend Zoom meetings, find inspirational and doctrinal sermons for difficulties in life, watch and share sermons, facilitate small groups and Dgroups (discipleship groups), and attend book studies.

Reponses to the COVID-19 Pandemic October 2022

Q11.1: Have you had COVID-19?

While the COVID-19 pandemic continues to ravage and disrupt millions of individuals and families, creating economic and social turmoil globally, Oliwia

Kowalczyk, Krzysztof Roszkowski, and Anna Bajek's study on the role of religion during the global pandemic perceived that "Religion has always played the role of balm for the soul and that churches are like hospitals of the soul."[30] Recent studies by the Pew Research Center in the US show that the COVID-19 pandemic has boosted the faith of believers and bolstered the bonding of family relationships.[31] Religious activities became less expensive and increasingly democratised due to social media platforms and online activities.

Regarding whether the COVID-19 pandemic has infected participants, 544 individuals (62.60%) said no, and 325 individuals (37.40%) said yes. Most had not gotten it themselves although it affected many.

Q11.4: Have you received the COVID-19 vaccine?

Regarding receiving the COVID-19 vaccines, 829 individuals (95.18%) received vaccinations while only 42 individuals (4.82%) said no. There is an overwhelming indication that megachurch people believe in the interplay of faith and fact in dealing with the COVID-19 pandemic. Survey responses indicated that megachurch congregants, while believing in God, also believe in the modern discoveries of medical sciences.

Q11.8: How were you impacted personally by the global COVID-19 pandemic? (Select all that apply.)

Regarding the impact of COVID-19 on personal life, 20.07% said they grew closer to their immediate family, and 20.14% said they were locked down at home mostly. In addition, 13.10% experienced anxiety, depression, and mental fatigue; 12.22% lost a friend through separation or death; and 11.10% were separated from family and friends. Also, 7.11% lost their family income, about 6.06% became ill, about 4.77% lost a family member, and 3.55% lost their regular job. Only 1.90% were not impacted in any way by the global pandemic.

Q11.9: Which of the following occurred in your church life due to the COVID-19 pandemic? (Select all that apply.)

Regarding the result of COVID-19 on church life after the pandemic, 31.34% attended church by watching streaming or pre-recorded services, 26.57% were

---

[30] Oliwia Kowalczyk, Krzystof Roszkowski, Xavier Montane, Wojciech Pawliszak, Bartosz Tylkowski, and Anna Bajek, "Religion and Faith Perception in a Pandemic of COVID-19", *Journal of Religious Health* 59(6) (2020), 2671 [Available at: https://www.ncbi.nlm.nih.gov/pmc/articles/PMC7549332/] [Last accessed: 24th April 2024].

[31] Pew Research Center Religion and Public Life, "More Americans Than People in Other Advanced Economies Say COVID-19 Has Strengthened Religious Faith", *Pew Research Center*, 27th January 2021 [Available at: https://www.pewresearch.org/religion/2021/01/27/more-americans-than-people-in-other-advanced-economies-say-covid-19-has-strengthened-religious-faith] [Last accessed: 24th April 2024].

comforted by God's love, 23.08% missed in-person church attendance, and 10.38% felt closer to their fellow members. However, 6.48% could not financially support the church because of the decline of their financial position, and 1.49% could not participate in church worship services because they lacked the Internet or the necessary technology. With other reasons, 0.66% said that discipleship became more challenging, so they became inactive as a cell group leader. One respondent said, "My fiancée disengaged in her commitment vows and abandoned our relationship due to [our] long distance relationship and her lack of faith. She chose the system and the needs of this world rather than God's purpose for us in Christ's ministry." Although some felt disappointed that the church remained closed, they grew in their relationship with God through worship and served in different capacities than before COVID-19. Some became more active and followed God's calling after they recovered and healed from COVID-19. Thus, they continued to attend their online Zoom meetings. These members realised many important lessons they had learned from the pandemic.

Q11.10: How has your church responded, currently or in the past, to the COVID-19 pandemic? (Select all that apply.)

Regarding how megachurches responded to the effect of COVID-19 on the lives of their people and communities, 19.06% said they shifted from physical services to online worship services, 18.82% immediately distributed food and other supplies to needy people, 18.35% urged everyone to comply with the safety protocols such as wearing masks and maintaining social distancing through media outlets, 15.08% shut down all in-person services and activities, and another 15.00% said that collecting tithes and offerings was done electronically. Other 12.15% opened the church building to people who were sick or health care providers.

As to some other activities undertaken by megachurches, some participants said they have topics in their online classes that deal with the effects of COVID-19, such as anxiety, trusting God, and the like. These churches are more committed to online evangelism and discipleship training, organising daily devotions through Zoom meetings, and supporting people through online efforts and counselling who have difficulty coping emotionally and mentally. The church also distributed COVID-19 aid kits and spiritual support to people during the pandemic.

As to the adverse reactions of congregants, 0.29% said they protested against or resisted the government shutting down church services and the mask mandate and requirement for social distancing, 0.15% just downplayed the impact of the virus and saw it as part of a conspiracy theory, and another 0.05% denied the virus's existence.

Q11.11: In your opinion, the COVID-19 pandemic is... (Select all that apply.)

When asked their opinions about COVID-19, 34.97% of the megachurch congregants surveyed said it was a test of humanity, while 21.18% said it was a sign of the end times. Additionally, 17.53% said it was a natural event not directly caused by God. However, 10.28% said it was a human-made biological weapon.

Regarding the question of whether the virus is a God-induced plague, as in biblical times, 8.89% said it is not, and another 7.16% saw it as a punishment for humanity's sin.

Q11.12: What has been the impact of the COVID-19 pandemic on your faith?

With regard to the impact of the COVID-19 pandemic on their faith, 795 individuals (92.01%) said it has strengthened their faith, 42 individuals (4.86%) said it has not affected it, while 27 individuals (3.13%) said it weakened their faith. Most megachurch congregants claimed that the global pandemic strengthened their faith.

Q11.13: What has been the COVID-19 pandemic's impact on your church attendance, whether in person or virtual? (Select all that apply.)

Regarding the impact of COVID-19 on church attendance, whether in person or virtual, 19.64% attend worship services more, the same percentage of 19.64% now attend online and in-person sometimes, 18.98% said their church attendance has remained the same, while 13.51% said they have attended other churches online. Additionally, 12.23% now only attend online. Moreover, 6.20% have attended less since the pandemic, and 5.67% have just returned to the church. Furthermore, 2.70% say they started attending only after the pandemic began, while 1.32% say they just decided to switch churches.

Q11.14: The COVID-19 pandemic has taught me that... (Select all that apply.)

Regarding the lessons COVID-19 taught congregants, 16.16% say they believe that God is still in control of the situation and not humanity, and 13.07% say the pandemic has encouraged them to live life more responsibly and not take anything for granted. In comparison, another 13.03% recognised the church community as vital during times of crisis. Regarding stewardship, 11.28% see the importance of being better stewards of the earth, and another 11.09% say we also need to change our priorities to focus on family. About 10.46% also believe that in modern human life, despite so much advancement in science and technology, our lives remain fragile. Regarding government responses, 7.92% believe the government is ineffective in providing medical, economic, and social assistance in a crisis. Last but not least, 7.88% said God's judgement over human sin is real.

Summary and Conclusion

The face of megachurches in the Global South, particularly in the Philippines, has changed the face of urban Christianity in the metropolitan cities of Metro Manila. Evidence from the survey indicates that the demographic of these megachurches is mainly multi-generational, primarily millennials and Gen Z –

the new generations shaped and driven by upward mobility. While most congregants are female, married with their spouses and children, an almost equal percentage of single congregants participate in megachurch life operations. Our finding reveals that most church congregants come from middle-class families and are socially elite people with businesses and employees who do not depend much on foreign remittances of their loved ones but sustain themselves by hard work, industry, and innovative business acumen. These people, with their parents, are highly educated and motivated people with college, graduate, and post-graduate degrees from private and public universities. While megachurches are becoming a melting pot of all cultures with multi-ethnic people, megachurches like CCF and VCF are still dominated by Filipino or Filipino Chinese Christians with single citizenship, who are bilingual and trilingual people who can speak their ethnic, national, and international languages, and who are born and are living in the urban cities of Metro Manila.

Second, megachurch congregants appear to have a genuine conversion to Christianity that occurred within the ministry of these megachurches due to intentional discipleship and Bible studies. As a result, megachurch congregants display a tremendous loyalty to what they believe at present by not subscribing to other religious beliefs. The result of the study shows that although most of them come from the three major Christian traditions – Catholic, Protestant, and Evangelical Christianity. Because they felt dissatisfied with their former churches, they have changed their church affiliations multiple times and find megachurches more satisfying to their religious taste and branding.[32] The study also indicated that when it comes to Christian faith and practices, megachurch congregants identify as Christians who adhere to the beliefs and practices of Evangelical and Pentecostal Christianity. This conversion experience to Christianity within megachurches occurred when they were in their teens or early career periods. Most of the megachurch congregants read the Bible daily or every week. While most people in megachurches have never seen physical displays of the Spirit such as laughing, dancing, shaking, and being "slain in the Spirit," many sometimes and frequently see manifestations of charisms within the megachurch services.

Third, when it comes to what they believe, megachurch congregants strongly believe that the Bible stands as an absolute truth that prescribes moral ethics that shape their values and behaviour in society. Congregants take seriously the moral teaching of the Bible as a source of their ethical behaviour. This is evidenced by

---

[32] Jayeel Cornelio, *Being Catholic in Contemporary Philippines: Young People Reinterpreting Religion* (New York: Routledge, 2016), 184-85. See also Cornelio and Sapitula, "Are We Losing Faith?"; J.A. Bautista and P.J. Braunlein, "Ethnography as an Act of Witnessing: Doing Fieldwork on Passion Rituals in the Philippines", *Philippine Studies: Historical and Ethnographic Viewpoints* 62 (2014), 501-528.; David S. Lim, "Consolidating Democracy: Role of Evangelicals in Deepening Democracy in the Philippines from 1986-1998", in David H. Lumsdaine (ed), *Evangelical Christianity and Democracy in Asia* (Oxford: Oxford University Press, 2009), 235-284.

the fact that although there is a slight degree of resistance and rejection about fornication, adultery, and homosexuality, most megachurch congregants show their high regard for teaching what the Bible says against sexual promiscuity. The survey indicated that megachurch congregants are highly motivated people to evangelize, they work for justice, they provide financial support and tithe for the cause of the church. While a certain degree of resistance to support the church exists, the overarching mindset of megachurch congregants is that they willingly invest their money and resources for religious purposes and missions endeavours.

Fourth, although most megachurch congregants do not belong to political parties, most participate in the national and local elections and believe that the political sphere can be an excellent platform to make a difference. Therefore, when we ask who to vote for, the overwhelming response is a Christian (preferably male) political leader who supports democracy but is solid and authoritative, especially if he is a member of their church. While our data show that our country is left behind regarding economic development, half of our respondents believe we are now improving and going in the right direction, but the other half are neutral and unsure about it.

As the data shows, we also do know that, like other Filipinos living in urban centres of Metro Manila, the cultural lifestyle of megachurch congregants are manifested by occasionally dining out with families and friends at restaurant and cafes, shopping, socialising with friends, and volunteerism, etc. Our data shows that the scope of friends of these members extends to other members of other Christian churches or other religions, no religion at all, and even extend to members of the LGBTQ community. These interpersonal relations can extend even to acknowledging having relatives and friends in over five countries. However, when asked about trusting other people, our data shows that megachurch congregants trust their fellow members in the church more than outside of their church. Therefore, when they asked whether they are happy people, our data shows most as more than happy and pretty happy attending their current church.

Our data also reveals that people of faith in megachurches are highly technological and digitalised people with the Internet and personal gadgets like smartphones, computers, laptops, or tablets. These gadgets are used for an average of three to six hours per day but more than six hours at work. Regarding church activities, we now know that megachurch congregants use these gadgets to stay in touch with small groups and church-related events and programmes, to connect with friends in the church, and/or to participate in an online Bible study or services. Our data also shows that megachurches have Facebook, YouTube, Instagram, WhatsApp, Twitter, and TikTok accounts.

Finally, our data shows that, while COVID-19 did not infect most megachurch congregants, most took the vaccines and see them as a modern discovery of medical science to fight the virus. Our data also shows that almost all were in lockdown at home and experienced anxiety, depression, and mental fatigue due to the virus aggravated by the loss of income and livelihood; loss of loved ones, relatives, and friends; and prolonged separation from the people they loved. However, most congregants acknowledged becoming closer to their immediate family members. Our data reveals that while our respondents missed the physical worship services by watching streaming or pre-recorded services, most believed that God comforted them. We now also know that, although megachurches stopped their physical services and moved to online services, the megachurch congregants contributed to the rule of law by observing public measures like wearing masks and observing social distances. These churches were instrumental in distributing food supplies and medical kits to people in need. As to how they collected financial support from their congregants during the pandemic, our data also shows they collected tithes and offerings from their members through electronic banking and other online outlets.

Regarding their opinion about COVID-19, the overwhelming response of megachurch congregants from our data reveals that COVID-19 was a test of humanity's faith, an indicator of the end times, and a natural event not directly caused by God. Some saw it as a biochemical weapon. While the impact of COVID-19 on individuals has strengthened their faith, megachurch congregants have democratised their participation in megachurch life by attending both physical and online worship services. Overall, our data also reveals that megachurch congregants learned vital lessons that God – not humanity – is still in control, that the church remains essential in times of global crisis, and that we should live a responsible life and not take everything for granted.

This project was made possible through the support of a grant from the John Templeton Foundation. The opinions expressed in this publication are those of the author(s) and do not necessarily reflect the views of the John Templeton Foundation.

Bibliography

Bautista, J.A., and P.J. Braunlein. "Ethnography as an Act of Witnessing: Doing Fieldwork on Passion Rituals in the Philippines", *Philippine Studies: Historical and Ethnographic Viewpoints* 62 (2014), 501-528.

Cartledge, Mark J., Sarah L.B. Dunlop, Heather Buckingham, and Sophie Bremner. *Megachurches and Social Engagement: Public Theology in Practice.* Leiden: Brill, 2019.

Chin, Joy Tong Kooi. "McDonaldization and Megachurches: A Case Study of City Harvest Church, Singapore", In Pattana Kitiarsa, Ed. *Religious Commodifications in Asia: Marketing Gods.* Abingdon: Routledge, 2007: 563-583.

Chong, Terence. "The Introduction", In Terence Chong, Ed. *Pentecostal Megachurches in Southeast Asia: Negotiating Class, Consumption and the Nation.* Singapore: ISEAS, 2018.

Choo, John, Evelyn Tan, and P.S. Goh. "Christian Megachurches and Politics in the Philippines", *Perspective ISEAS Yusof Ishak Institute* 62 (2020), 1-4.

Cook, Elizabeth. "Would You Like Your Jesus Upsized? McDonaldization and the Mega Church", Senior Thesis Projects, 1993-2002. Knoxville, TN: University of Tennessee, 2002. [Available at: https://trace.tennessee.edu/utk_interstp2/85] [Last accessed: 24th April 2024].

Cornelio, Jayeel. *Being Catholic in Contemporary Philippines: Young People Reinterpreting Religion.* Routledge, NY, 2016.

──. "Jesus Is Lord: The Indigenization of Megachurch Christianity in the Philippines", In Terence Chong, Ed. *Pentecostal Megachurches in Southeast Asia: Negotiating Class, Consumption, and the Nation.* Singapore: ISEAS, 2018: 127-55.

Cornelio, Jayeel S., and Ia Marañon. "A 'Righteous Intervention': Megachurch Christianity and Duterte's War on Drugs in the Philippines", *International Journal of Asian Christianity* 2(2), (2019), 211-30. [Available at: https://doi.org/10.1163/25424246-00202005] [Last accessed: 24th April 2024].

Cornelio, Jayeel S., and Manuel Victor Sapitula. "Are We Losing Faith? An Invitation to the Sociology of Religion in the Philippines", *Philippine Sociological Society.* 20th November 2014. [Available at: https://socialstudiescorner.wordpress.com/tag/philippine-Catholicism/] [Last accessed: 24th April 2024].

Daniels, Joseph P. and Marc von der Ruhr. "Examining Megachurch Growth: Free Riding, Fit, and Faith", *International Journal of Social Economics* 39(5), (March 2012), 357-72. [Available at: https://epublications.marquette.edu/econ_fac/139] [Last accessed: 24th April 2024].

Dart, John. "Trends of Bigger Churches: Going Mega", *Christian Century.* 27th July 2010.

Delotavo, Alan J. "Ethical Considerations of Ecclesio-Political Involvement: A People Power Case", *The Asia Journal of Theology* 20(2), (1st October 2016), 221-229.

Elisha, O. "Moral Ambitions of Grace: The Paradox of Compassion and Accountability in Evangelical Faith-Based Activism", *Cultural Anthropology* 23(1), (2008), 154-89.

Kowalczyk, Oliwia, Krzystof Roszkowski, Xavier Montane, Wojciech Pawliszak, Bartosz Tylkowski, and Anna Bajek. "Religion and Faith Perception in a Pandemic of COVID-19", *Journal of Religious Health* 59(6), (2020), 2671. [Available at: https://www.ncbi.nlm.nih.gov/pmc/articles/PMC7549332/] [Last accessed: 24th April 2024].

Lim, David S. "Consolidating Democracy: Role of Evangelicals in Deepening Democracy in the Philippines from 1986-1998", In David H. Lumsdaine, Ed. *Evangelical Christianity and Democracy in Asia.* Oxford: Oxford University Press, 2009: 235-284.

Ma, Julie. "The Growing Church in Manila: An Analysis", *The Asia Journal of Theology* 11(2), (1997), 324-342.

Mendoza, Rene E. "Religion and Secularization in the Philippines and Other Asian Countries", *Institute for Japanese Culture and Classics*, Kokugakuin University. 1999. [Available at: https://www2.kokugakuin.ac.jp/ijcc/wp/cimac/mendoza.html] [Last accessed: 24th April 2024].

Pew Research Center Religion and Public Life. "More Americans Than People in Other Advanced Economies Say COVID-19 Has Strengthened Religious Faith", *Pew Research Centre,* 27th January 2021. [Available at: https://www.pewresearch.org/religion/2021/01/27/more-americans-than-people-in-other-advanced-economies-say-covid-19-has-strengthened-religious-faith] [Last accessed: 24th April 2024].

Ritzer, George. *The McDonaldization of Society.* Newbury Park, CA: Pine Forge, 1993.

Snow, David A., James A. Bany, Michelle Peria, and James E. Stobaugh. "A Team Field Study of the Appeal of Megachurches: Identifying, Framing, and Solving Personal Issues", *Ethnography* 11(1), (2010), 165-88. [Available at: https://doi.org/10.1177/1466138109347006] [Last accessed: 24th April 2024].

Thumma, Scott, and Warren Bird. "Megafaith for the Megacity: The Global Megachurch Phenomenon", In Stanley D. Brunn, Ed. *The Changing World Religion Map: Sacred Place, Identities, Practices and Politics*. Dordrecht, Netherlands: Springer, 2015: 2331–2352. First online: 20th November 2014. [Available at: https://doi.org/10.1007/978-94-017-9376-6_123] [Last accessed: 24th April 2024].

Wadkins, Timothy. "Modernization, Megachurches and the Urban Face of Christianity in the Global South", *An Approved Project Proposal for the John Templeton Foundation*, 1st January 2020.

Warner, Laceye. "Mega Churches: A New Ecclesiology or Ecclesial Evangelism?" *Review and Expositor* 107(1), (2010), 21-31.

Wellman, James K. Jr., Katie E. Corcoran, and Kate Stockly-Meyerdirk. "God Is Like a Drug...: Explaining Interaction Ritual Chains in American Megachurches", *Sociological Forum*. 26th August 2014. pp. 650-72. [Available at: https://doi.org/10.1111/socf.12108] [Last accessed: 24th April 2024].

18. Digital Pneumatology: Presence and Power of the Holy Spirit in the Metaverse

Guichun Jun

Introduction

One distinctive feature that has influenced the ministry and mission of the church since the second half of the twentieth century is digitalisation – the revolution that began with the invention of computers and accelerated with the Internet. On the one hand, some theologically conservative Christians feel anxious about the rapid development of digital devices and their negative influences on spirituality due to the dichotomic view of secular and sacred things. On the other hand, some churches actively use various digital devices and mass media (radio, television, and the Internet) not only for effective evangelism and ministry to spread the gospel but also for charismatic ministries, such as faith healing by touching the screen when televangelists pray.[1]

At the beginning of the second decade of the twenty-first century, the fourth industrial revolution began to bring a fundamental change in all aspects of human life and work, including religious practices. Recently, during the COVID-19 pandemic and its aftermath, churches have actively used various digital platforms such as YouTube and Zoom to conduct online worship services and prayer meetings and to communicate with their members. According to a survey, approximately 72 percent of respondents reported that the pandemic changed the way they practice their faith, with many adopting new private religious practices in the home or joining services online.[2] A report by the Hartford Institute for Religion Research indicated that 80 percent of US churches in November 2021 utilised a hybrid worship service in which congregants simultaneously gather in person and online.[3]

---

[1] Shane Denson, "Faith in Technology: Televangelism and the Mediation of Immediate Experience", *Phenomenology & Practice* 5(2) (2011), 94 [Available at: https://shanedenson.com/articles/Denson_Faith_in_Technology.pdf] [Last accessed: 25th April 2024].
[2] Manmit Bhambra and Austin Tiffany, "From the Sanctuary to the Sofa: What Covid-19 Has Taught us about Sacred Space", *LSE Research Online,* last modified 10th October 2021 [Available at: http://eprints.lse.ac.uk/id/eprint/110575] [Last accessed: 4th May 2024].
[3] Hartford Institute for Religion Research, "Navigating the Pandemic: A First Look at Congregational Responses", *Exploring the Pandemic Impact on Congregations: Innovation Amidst and Beyond COVID-19,* last modified 14th December 2021

One notable trend in religious practice in this contemporary digital age is the launch and development of churches in the metaverse. The first metaverse church (VR Church: www.vrchurch.org) was established in 2016. Since then, many metachurches in virtual space launched in order to reach more people by transcending time and distance. The concept of the death of distance[4] by technological revolution is fulfilled not only in business and communication but also in religious practices. Digital technologies converged into the metaverse enable the church to function anywhere at any time with anyone. As a church in the metaverse exists as a fully virtual reality church, every user participates through their avatars in religious activities, such as Sunday worship, small groups, Bible studies or prayer meetings. Due to the nature of avatar-mediated interactions, some believers feel concerned that religious experiences in virtual spaces cannot be replaceable with the ones in the traditional Christian community. Nevertheless, it is undeniable that believers have been increasingly participating in various religious activities in the metaverse since the pandemic.[5] D.J. Soto, founder of VR Church, intimates that a radical shift in terms of theological understanding of the nature of the church and the characteristics of its ministry is coming in the age of digitalisation.[6] Despite these rapid changes in religious practices and phenomena triggered by technological advancement, there has been little theological reflection on them. In particular, not enough attention has been paid to digital pneumatology to understand the person and the role of the Holy Spirit in the intersection of theology and technology.[7] Therefore,

---

[Available at: https://www.covidreligionresearch.org/wp-content/uploads/2021/11/Navigating-the-Pandemic_A-First-Look-at-Congregational-Responses_Nov-2021.pdf] [Last accessed: 4th May 2024].

[4] Frances Cairncross, *The Death of Distance 2.0: How the Communications Revolution will Change Our Lives* (London: Texere, 2001), 2.

[5] Luis Anders Henao and the Associated Press, "Religious People are Increasingly Attending Worship Service in the Metaverse", *Fortune*, last modified 31st January 2022 [Available at: https://fortune.com/2022/01/31/virtual-worshipping-services-religion-metaverse/] [Last accessed: 4th May 2024].

[6] Luis Henao, "Faith in the metaverse: A VR quest for community, fellowship", Religion News Service (January 31, 2022). Available at https://religionnews.com/2022/01/31/faith-in-the-metaverse-a-vr-quest-for-community-fellowship/

[7] Recently, Chris Green and Steven Félix-Jäger edited a book, *The Spirit and the Screen: Pneumatological Reflections on Contemporary Cinema*, which examines contemporary films through the lens of Pneumatology to understand how the concepts of the Spirit shed light on filmmaking. The contributors identify "Spirit figures" in movies (showcasing characters moved by the Spirit) and uncover implicit and explicit representations of the Spirit in popular culture. This book aims to explain the nature of film and filmmaking from the Pentecostal perspective and introduce cultural hermeneutics to connect the person and work of the Spirit to popular cultural symbols. However, the inclusion of this book in the category of digital pneumatology is

this chapter intends to explore the theological possibility of digital pneumatology to understand that the Holy Spirit can present and work in digital spaces in reference to the metaverse.

Digital Pneumatology

Digital pneumatology is a new field of study for the theological exploration of the presence and power of the Holy Spirit in digital spaces. It seeks to understand how the Holy Spirit is presented in digital spaces and how believers experience the work and the power of the Holy Spirit through advanced technology. As there has not been a significant amount of academic writing in this particular field yet, digital pneumatology is currently based on the theological presupposition that the Holy Spirit can be present and demonstrate his power and attributes in digital spaces in the same way that he is present and active in physical spaces. It is theologically legitimate to speculate that the presence or manifestation of the Holy Spirit is not limited by physical boundaries, and that his power can be perceptibly experienced in any space, including digital spaces. COVID-19 has played a significant role in developing this theological speculation into a form of digital pneumatology that the classical understanding of the presence and the power of the Holy Spirit can be extended to digital spaces. Churches and mission agencies have used various digital platforms to spread the gospel and form digital communities for worship and fellowship. Robert Wuthnow[8] and Nancy Ammerman,[9] prominent sociologists of religion, and Heidi Campbell,[10] an outstanding scholar in religion and digital culture, commonly say that digital technologies can create online and virtual platforms not only for complementing traditional practices and accessing religious resources but also for providing new opportunities for enhancing religiosity (or spirituality) in digital spaces. Nicky Gumbel, founder of Alpha Course, mentions his theological belief that the Holy Spirit can be present and work through virtual platforms like Zoom. He states in an interview with Premier Christianity, "The Holy Spirit is not limited by the technology that we use. The Holy Spirit can work through a Zoom call, just as

---

somewhat strained as it lacks a robust conversation about the person and role of the Spirit at the junction of theology and technology.

[8] See Robert Wuthnow, *The Restructuring of American Religion: Society and Faith Since World War II* (Princeton, NJ: Princeton University Press, 1989), 268-96.

[9] See Nancy Tatom Ammerman, *Sacred Stories, Spiritual Tribes: Finding Religion in Everyday Life* (Oxford: Oxford University Press, 2014), 288-304.

[10] See Heidi Campbell, *When Religion Meets New Media: Media, Religion and Culture* (Hoboken, NY: Taylor & Francis, 2010), 41-63. Heidi Campbell, *Digital Religion: Understanding Religious Practice in Digital Media* (Abingdon: Routledge, 2022), 1-22. Heidi Campbell, *Exploring Religious Community Online: We are One in the Network* (New York: Lang, 2010), 53-74.

much as he can work through a live meeting."[11] This perspective highlights a growing recognition among religious leaders that virtual spaces can serve as platforms for spiritual experiences, transcending physical limitations traditionally associated with religious gatherings.

Many church leaders and mission agencies have the same belief as Gumbel that digital platforms will be continually used for their ministries, such as virtual worship services, prayer meetings, and other spiritual practices. Therefore, it is time to deepen our understanding of the evolving relationship between digital technologies and Christian spirituality from the Pentecostal perspective. Early in 2023, a great spiritual awakening took place at Asbury University in Wilmore, Kentucky. Spiritually hungry Gen Z students seeking transforming power from above experienced an outpouring of the Holy Spirit. The occurrence gained widespread popularity on the Internet, particularly on the social media platform TikTok, where the hashtag #asburyrevival garnered over 100 million views.[12] The university campus could not accommodate the huge influx of more than 15,000 worshipers daily.[13] As a consequence, the University allowed several YouTube channels to do live streaming of the worship services after several days. One of the channels was SermonIndex.net. Over 150,000 people from all over the world joined the live-streaming services for several days and testified by leaving comments that they also experienced the presence and the power of the Holy Spirit while watching them online in their own physical spaces.[14]

On the one hand, one can legitimately raise concerns about the potential risks and dangers of relying on digital technology for spiritual experiences. Some may argue that digital platforms diminish the authentic sense of community and fellowship in the physical spaces and increase the sense of spiritual superficiality and religious consumerism only by accessing online content without physical interactions with other believers in the traditional church contexts. On the other hand, as a counterargument, digital technology has been used to foster spiritual

---

[11] The Economist, "Your Own Personal Jesus: Online Services Swell the Church of England's Congregations", *Economist Website,* last modified 4th June 2020 [Available at: https://www.economist.com/britain/2020/06/04/online-services-swell-the-church-of-englands-congregations] [Last accessed: 4th May 2024].

[12] Thomas Lyons, "When a Christian Revival Goes Viral: At Asbury University, in Kentucky, A Student Chapel Service Turned into a Revival That Has Captivated TikTok", *The Atlantic,* last modified 23rd February 2023 [Available at: https://www.theatlantic.com/ideas/archive/2023/02/asbury-kentucky-university-christian-revival/673176/] [Last accessed: 4th May 2024].

[13] Heather Preston, "Asbury Relocates Revival off Campus, Following Overcrowding", *Premier Christian News,* last modified 21st February 2023 [Available at: https://premierchristian.news/en/news/article/asbury-relocates-revival-off-campus-following-overcrowding] [Last accessed: 4th May 2024].

[14] YouTube Video, "Asbury University Revival Live 2023 – Feb 15, 2023 (Worship – Part 1)", *YouTube,* Channel: SermonIndex.Net, 16th [Available at: https://www.youtube.com/watch?v=_FpKv5O2wMI&ab_channel=SermonIndex.net] [Last accessed: 4th May 2024].

experiences and growth for decades. From the viewpoints of religious phenomenology and empiricism, technology contributed to enhancing and deepening spiritual experiences and growth to a certain degree,[15] although theological challenges and practical limitations remain in the intersection between digital technologies and spirituality. This debate has opened up a new avenue for theologians and practitioners to move forward from religious phenomenology to digital theology – in particular, digital pneumatology – to reimagine the future possibility of Pentecostal theology and ministries in the metaverse for Gen Z and beyond.

Presence of the Holy Spirit in the Metaverse

Grace Rose raises a thought-provoking question: "Will the metaverse leave God and His congregations in the past or will it be an extension of God's creation and support His church beyond our wildest imaginations?"[16] Ozan Sönmez rightly points out that many Christians remain trapped in the dualistic Christian belief that separates physical spaces and virtual spaces concerning the presence of God, while large numbers of believers have already utilised technological advancement to form their spiritual communities and interact with the Spirit of God in digital spaces.[17] The metaverse already has become a new way of life in all aspects, including religious practices in all religions. For example, Muslims can participate in the pilgrimage (*Hajj*) to holy Mecca through a digital platform in the metaverse called "Experience Makkah" since 2015.[18] Jewish believers can pray and place a slip of prayer in the Western Wall through the metaverse.[19] These unprecedented digital opportunities have opened a new door for religious people not only to satisfy their religious hunger and promote their religiosity but

---

[15] Don Iannone, "The Two Faces of Digital Spirituality: Contrasting Motives for Digital Spirituality", *KOSMOS: Journal for Global Transformation*, last modified February 2023 [Available at: https://www.kosmosjournal.org/kj_article/the-two-faces-of-digital-spirituality/] [Last accessed: 4th May 2024].

[16] Grace Rose, "How Will God and the Church Fit into the Metaverse?" *Comm-entary* 18(1) (2022), 4.

[17] Ozan Sönmez, "Context before Technology: The Possible Utopian/Dystopian Elements of the Metaverse with Examples from Great Literature", in Enis Karaarslan, Ömer Aydin, Ümit Cali, and Moharram Challenger (eds), *Digital Twin Driven Intelligent Systems and Emerging Metaverse* (Singapore: Springer, 2023), 299.

[18] Lara Katharina Schneider, "Religious Acts in Metaverse: Catholic Christianity", *GRIN*, last modified 15th March 2023 [Available at: https://www.grin.com/document/1338328#:~:text=A%20metaverse%20makes%20sacred%20sites,confessions%20and%20other%20religious%20rituals] [Last accessed: 4th May 2024].

[19] Luis Andres Henao, "From the Western Wall to Mecca: VR Lets Virtual Pilgrims Explore World's Holy Sites", *The Times of Israel*, last modified 8th August 2022 [Available at: https://www.timesofisrael.com/from-the-western-wall-to-mecca-vr-lets-virtual-pilgrims-explore-worlds-holy-sites/] [Last accessed: 4th May 2024].

also to experience their gods in immersive virtual spaces.[20] As the empirical approach of the sociology of religion and religious phenomenology informs that God is already in cyberspace through his Spirit and people encounter him,[21] it is meaningless to ask questions, such as "Does God exist in the metaverse?" or "Has God entered into the metaverse?"[22] The aforementioned phenomenological human experiences of the presence of the Holy Spirit in the metaverse require further theological reflection to develop a digital pneumatology.

Omnipresence of the Holy Spirit

From a biblical and theological standpoint, it is acknowledged that all things were created by God, and nothing was created without him, as stated in John 1. This understanding affirms that virtual spaces are not a product of human creativity but a part of God's creation. Therefore, one can reasonably claim that virtual spaces, such as the metaverse, exist within the universe God created and sustains.[23] This origin of the virtual spaces enables us to have a theological inference for God's presence in the metaverse through the concept of the omnipresence of God. In other words, the concept of God's omnipresence extends beyond the limitations of time and space, allowing him to exist in all corners of the universe and beyond. As the third person of the Trinity, the Holy Spirit is similarly present in all places, reflecting the divine essence of God. This understanding of God's presence in all locations logically extends to the virtual realm, including the metaverse, where the Holy Spirit also can be present. Jeff Reed,[24] founder of Thechurch.digital, uses the principle of Henry Blackaby,

---

[20] Seiji Kumagi, "Development of Buddhist AI, AR, and VR toward the Establishment of Buddhist Metaverse", *Kuensel*, last modified 10th October 2022 [Available at: https://kuenselonline.com/development-of-buddhist-ai-ar-and-vr-toward-the-establishment-of-buddhist-metaverse-tera-verse/] [Last accessed: 4th May 2024].

[21] Lavinia Byrne, "God in Cyberspace: Media and Theology Project Public Lectures", *Cambridge Theological Federation*, 2000 [Available at: https://www.ed.ac.uk/files/imports/fileManager/god%20in%20cyberspace.pdf] [Last accessed: 4th May 2024].

[22] Euronews and AP, "God Has Entered the Metaverse – and Faith in the Virtual World is Flourishing", *Euronews.next*, last modified 3rd February 2022 [Available at: https://www.euronews.com/next/2022/02/01/god-has-entered-the-metaverse-and-worship-in-virtual-worlds-is-booming] [Last accessed: 4th May 2024].

[23] Guichun Jun, "Virtual Reality Church as a New Mission Frontier in the Metaverse: Exploring Theological Controversies and Missional Potential of Virtual Reality Church", *Transformation* 37(4) (2020), 300 [Available at: https://doi.org/10.1177/0265378820963155] [Last accessed: 4th May 2024].

[24] Jeff Reed has written two books concerning mission in the metaverse: Jeff Reed, *VR & The Metaverse Church: How God is Moving in this Virtual, Yet Quite Real, Reality* (London: Leadership Network, 2022). Jeff Reed and John Harris, *Sharing Jesus Online: Helping Everyday Believers Become Digital & Metaverse Missionaries* (London: Exponential, 2023).

author *Experiencing God*, to argue that God is always at work around us through his Spirit, even in virtual realms.[25] Therefore, the aforementioned empirical experiences of a divine encounter in the metaverse prove possible if the omnipresent God is present there through his Spirit.

Transcendence of the Holy Spirit

One common feature found in the intersection between pneumatology and the metaverse is that both involve the idea of transcendence. Pneumatology aligns the Holy Spirit with transcendence, the ability to go beyond human understanding. Similarly, the metaverse enables individuals to surpass physical barriers and experience what may be impossible in the physical world. The Holy Spirit's transcendence implies that he exceeds the limits of physical realities, operating on a transcendent level beyond physical reality. The metaverse's transcendent nature allows individuals to explore new dimensions and realities beyond their physical senses, offering unique ways of encountering and connecting with God. Consequently, the metaverse provides a way to transcend limited understanding of the Holy Spirit's presence and power beyond the physical world, similar to how pneumatology associates the Holy Spirit with transcending human understanding. This new perspective of digital pneumatology in light of the transcendence of the Holy Spirit may enable believers to experience God in ways that were previously impossible in the physical world.

Immanence of the Holy Spirit

The Holy Spirit is not only transcendental but also immanent in all his creations. On the one hand, the Holy Spirit is beyond humanity's full experience and perception of both his attributes and power. On the other hand, his presence and power permeate humanity's mundane so that he is knowable and graspable. In particular, since the outpouring of the Holy Spirit on the Day of Pentecost in Acts 2, the indwelling of the Holy Spirit in believers' lives is promised with empirical evidence as he guides, teaches, rebukes, and loves his people with his wisdom, power, and authority. This nonphysical sense of immanence and indwelling of the Holy Spirit in believers may be extended to the metaverse through the embodied relation between humans and their created avatars.

Don Ihde, a philosopher of science and technology, proposes four types of human and technology relations. One of them is embodied relations, which can serve as an appropriate theoretical approach to explain how one can empirically

---

[25] Jeff Reed, "Blackaby's Experiencing God: Metaverse Edition", *TheChurch.Digital*, last modified 15th March 2022 [Available at: https://be.thechurch.digital/blog/can-we-experience-god-in-the-metaverse-what-does-henry-blackaby-think] [Last accessed: 4th May 2024].

experience the presence of the Holy Spirit in the metaverse through one's avatar. Through its immersive nature, the metaverse plays a significant role in mediating human users' sensory experiences in embodied relations with their avatars. In Ihde's theory, avatars are not only representatives of their human users through digital anthropomorphism but also the virtual presence of the users through the digital embodiment by the technology merging of the physical world and virtual world. This immersive nature of interconnectedness between human users and their avatars not only enables the users' cognitive functions to perceive things in the metaverse but also enhances the sense of homogeneity through psychological, emotional, and spiritual intimacy.[26] In particular, this sense of homogeneity between the self and avatars helps believers to have empirical experiences of the presence of the Holy Spirit when they engage in collective religious activities, such as worship services or prayer meetings in virtual communities.[27]

Spiritual Communion and Community of Believers

The three aforementioned theological presuppositions grant a legitimate reason for building spiritual communities to worship and fellowship among believers in the metaverse. The promise of Jesus saying, "Where two or three are gathered together in my name, I am there among them" (Mt. 18:20), is also valid and applicable in the metaverse. This carries significant theological implications. First, from the ecclesiological perspective, churches in digital spaces are equally valid with the traditional churches in physical spaces in terms of their nature and functions. This does not mean that virtual churches can completely replace the value of real-life relationships and the richness of physical interactions among believers in traditional church contexts. However, virtual churches can prove efficacious in building missional communities and enhancing spiritual experiences collectively when believers together seek God who is present in virtual spaces. In particular, the idea of fostering communities and engaging in spiritual activities in virtual spaces in the same way we do in physical spaces can be an inclusive act of practising communion of Gen Z believers who are digital natives seeking different ways of believing and belonging and those who are housebound when physical proximity is not possible.

Second, from the perspective of pneumatology, the Spirit of God plays the role of fostering communion and community among believers in both physical

---

[26] Anthony Steed, Ye Pan, Fiona Zisch, and William Steptoe, "The Impact of a Self-Avatar on Cognitive Load in Immersive Virtual Reality", *IEEE Virtual Reality (VR)* (2016), 67-76 [Available at: https://doi.org/10.1109/VR.2016.7504689] [Last accessed: 4th May 2024].

[27] Robby I. Chandra and Noh I. Boiliu, "The Metaverse's Potential Impacts on the God-Centred Life and Togetherness of Indonesian Christians", *Theologia Viatorum* 46(1) (2022) [Available at: https://doi.org/10.4102/tv.v46i1.157] [Last accessed: 4th May 2024].

and virtual churches. For example, 1 Corinthians 12:13 states that all believers are baptised by one Spirit into one body. Based on this verse, communion and unity among believers can be achieved and maintained through the indwelling of the Holy Spirit among believers. This pneumatological understanding of communion and unity can be extended to virtual churches in the metaverse as believers gather, worship, and fellowship together in God's presence.

Power of the Holy Spirit

God's omni-attributes remain inseparable. If God is omnipresent, he is also omnipotent. If God is present in the metaverse, it logically follows that he can also operate his power in the metaverse. It means that, as the Holy Spirit is present and operates his power in physical spaces, the same holds true for virtual spaces. The power of the Holy Spirit for transformation, sanctification, impartation, and restoration is not constrained by the boundary between physical and virtual spaces.

Then, how does the Holy Spirit operate his power in the metaverse, and where are the impacts of his power effectively and evidently demonstrated? We need to revisit Ihde's mediation theory to find answers to these questions. The embodied relation between the human and the avatar provides a framework for understanding the spiritual interplay between the Holy Spirit and human beings through their avatars in the metaverse. The psychological and emotional intimacy between the human and the avatar can also apply to their spiritual interconnectedness. It means that the spiritual integration and unity between the human and the avatar are indivisible as they are considered as one entity within the virtual environment and homogeneous as a strong sense of alignment exists between the human's real identity and the anthropomorphic avatar reflecting the human user's appearance, characteristics, and cultural behaviours in interactions with others in the metaverse.

Due to this profound sense of inseparable and homogeneous interconnectivity, the power of the Holy Spirit can impact the lives of believers in physical spaces as they interact with him through their avatars in virtual spaces. It is important to remember that the ultimate purpose of the power of the Holy Spirit working in the metaverse by interacting with the avatars is to transform, sanctify, and restore individual believers to sincerely follow Christ as his disciples in the physical world.

Transformative Power for Regeneration

The Holy Spirit is the sole agent of salvation. In other words, without the inward work of the Holy Spirit, all the human efforts to save a soul can never be effective.[28] The ultimate purpose of the Father is to redeem us, and the Son has accomplished the Father's redemption plan for fallen humanity. This divine gift of salvation cannot be accomplished, however, without the agency of the Holy Spirit. As salvation is not understood as an event but a process, the Holy Spirit plays several important roles in the process of salvation. First, the Holy Spirit convinces individuals of their sinfulness and convinces them of the need for forgiveness through Christ. Second, the Holy Spirit brings a spiritual new birth to truly repentant individuals, enabling them to begin a personal relationship with God. Finally, the Holy Spirit indwells believers' lives and seals them to secure their salvation as eternal inheritance. D.J. Soto confirms that the Holy Spirit's transformative power for spiritual conviction, regeneration, and preservation works in the metaverse in the same way that he does in physical spaces.[29] The metaverse has become a new harvest field for modern missions as digital natives who formerly experienced a deep sense of emptiness and even identified as atheists have testified that they encountered God and were saved by hearing the gospel through the work of the Holy Spirit in virtual spaces.[30] In other words, biblically and theologically authentic conversion experience has happened to people in their physical lives while they participated in various activities of churches through their avatars in the metaverse. Through the embodied relation between human and avatar in the immersive virtual environment, the power of the Spirit of God works in the minds and hearts of human users for spiritual conviction of their sins and the need for forgiveness. This conversion experience through the immersive metaverse environment will continually impact their spiritual desire to grow as disciples of Christ in their daily lives in the physical world.

Empowerment for Sanctification

The Holy Spirit empowers believers. Generally, the empowerment of the Holy Spirit is understood as receiving power for mission and evangelism.[31] Certain

---

[28] Yuzo Adhinarta, *The Doctrine of the Holy Spirit in the Major Reformed Confessions and Catechisms of the Sixteenth and Seventeenth Centuries* (Carlisle, UK: Langham Monographs, 2012), 69.
[29] D.J. Soto, "4 Lessons from a Metaverse Pastor", *The Future of the Church is the Metaverse*, last modified 30th September 2022 [Available at: https://vrchurch.substack.com/p/4-lessons-from-a-metaverse-pastor] [Last accessed: 4th May 2024].
[30] Jeremy Lukens, "The Metaverse Is a New Harvest Field for Modern Missions", *Indigitous*, 8th June 2022, last modified 12th July 2023 [Available at: https://indigitous.org/article/the-metaverse-is-a-new-harvest-field-for-modern-missions/] [Last accessed: 4th May 2024].
[31] Amos Yong, *In the Days of Caesar: Pentecostalism and Political Theology* (Grand Rapids, MI: W.B. Eerdmans, 2010), 171.

contemporary Pentecostal scholars, exemplified by Bradley Truman Noel[32] and Vinson Synan,[33] maintain adherence to classical Pentecostal doctrines, notably advocating for the distinct delineation between sanctification and empowerment as separate outcomes arising from the baptism of the Holy Spirit. However, Donald Gee, a prominent British Pentecostal theologian in the early to mid-twentieth century, believed that the ultimate purpose of empowerment of the Holy Spirit was to sanctify believers to live a holy life.[34] Gee's Pentecostal theology always emphasised the importance of the empowerment of the Holy Spirit in light of sanctification. In this regard, the power of the Holy Spirit strengthens and enables believers to overcome the power of temptation and sin and to live consecrated lives to experience progressive transformation into the likeness of Christ. If the metaverse is part of God's creation, and God is present there, his Spirit must play a crucial role in empowering his believers to live holy and righteous lives in virtual spaces.

Neal Stephenson wrote *Snow Crash*, in which he introduced the metaverse as a utopia.[35] After thirty years, his imagination of the metaverse has been realised through the convergence of digital technologies and the Internet. However, the metaverse is far from the concept of utopia at present. In reality, all sorts of cyber-crimes take place in the metaverse, so an urgent need exists for meta jurisdiction to create safe virtual environments.[36] This is the reason why the empowerment of the Holy Spirit for believers' sanctification in the metaverse is so significant – to make the metaverse a safer and better place by demonstrating Christ-like characters and attitudes.

Impartation for Service

God desires to impart not only his power but also his life, wisdom, and all good gifts to his people. This nature of God's impartation is well-demonstrated throughout the Bible, especially in the history of God's redemption. For example, the self-impartation of the Son in the Incarnation and the Cross to obey the Father's will effectively shows the divine desire to bestow his grace and love to restore the fallen humanity into his image. Ten days after the Son ascended to heaven, the Father and the Son imparted the Holy Spirit to believers fervently

---

[32] Bradley T. Noel, "From Wesley to Azusa: The Historical Journey of the 'Second Work' Doctrine", in Scott A. Dunham (ed), *Full of the Holy Spirit and Faith* (Wolfville, Nova Scotia: Gaspereau Press, 1997), 52-53.
[33] Vinson Synan, *Century of the Holy Spirit 100 Years of Pentecostal and Charismatic Renewal, 1901-2001* (Nashville, TN: Thomas Nelson, 2001), 338, ePub.
[34] Donald Gee, *Wind and Flame* (Southampton, UK: The Revival Library, 2013), 32, ePub.
[35] Neal Stephenson, *Snow Crash* (New York: Bantam, 1992), 37.
[36] Guichun Jun, "Mission in the Age of Digitalization: Metaverse, Metamodernism and Metanarratives", in Risto Jukko (ed), *Together in the Mission of God* (Geneva: WCC Publications, 2022), 244-45.

seeking power from above on the Day of Pentecost. Afterwards, the Holy Spirit imparted his gifts to believers to give them spiritual abilities to fulfil their functions or callings for God's mission.[37]

Notwithstanding the critical contention from cessationists, the transformative bestowal of spiritual gifts by the Holy Spirit continues to exert a profound influence on the spiritual lives of individuals and their theological perspectives. For example, Jack Deere, a former professor at Dallas Theological Seminary, used to be a cessationist, but he has become a continuationist after personally experiencing the Holy Spirit imparting spiritual gifts unto him.[38] Gordon Fee affirms that the Holy Spirit works ceaselessly to impart his spiritual gifts to believers to serve God and his Kingdom.[39] This stimulates our theological speculation to understand whether this continual impartation of the Holy Spirit in the physical world is also available in the metaverse as believers seek spiritual gifts and power. If the transcendental nature of the presence and work of the Holy Spirit is possible in the metaverse, the digital impartation of the Holy Spirit is also possible because God cannot violate his divine nature of imparting all the good gifts to his people where he is present and operates his power whether in physical spaces or virtual spaces. Furthermore, digital impartation may include the transmission of spiritual gifts or knowledge between believers willing to give and receive spiritual blessings from one another through the mediation of the Holy Spirit in a similar way that the Apostle Paul wanted to impart some spiritual gift to the church in Rome as stated in Romans 1. This theological notion of digital impartation posits the crucial function of digital platforms in facilitating spiritual experiences and practices that foster a sense of community among believers enabling them to acquire the spiritual endowments of the Holy Spirit for their service to God in both physical and virtual worlds.

Healing for Restoration

Mediatisation, a process involved in the influence and changing role of the mass media in a variety of social and cultural spheres,[40] has impacted various aspects of Christian ministries and missions to evangelise unbelievers and promote Christian faith; in particular, divine healing ministry has taken advantage of it

---

[37] Jim Wainscott, *Eleventh-Hour Overcomers: In Pursuit of the Ultimate Prize* (Bloomington, IN: Westbow, 2013), 205.
[38] Jack Deere, *Why I Am Still Surprised by the Power of the Spirit: Discovering How God Speaks and Heals Today* (Grand Rapids, MI: Zondervan, 2020), 48.
[39] Gordon Fee, *God's Empowering Presence: The Holy Spirit in the Letters of Paul* (Grand Rapids, MI: Baker Academic, 2011), 607.
[40] Stig Hjarvard, "Mediatization and Cultural and Social Change: An Institutional Perspective", in Knut Lundby (ed), *Mediatization of Communication* (Berlin, Boston: De Gruyter Mouton, 2014), 204.

over decades.[41] Media-mediated divine healing raises a question to understand how the divine healing power of the Holy Spirit can interplay with human faith through media. Although media itself does not have the power of healing, it is certainly used as a channel of healing. God transmitted his power through objects in the Bible, such as the mantle of Elijah to empower Elisha (2 Kgs. 2:13-14), the hem of Jesus' garment (Luke 8:40-48) and the Apostle Paul's handkerchief or apron to heal the sick (Acts 19:12). Even Peter's shadow could be a divine means of healing for the sick (Acts 5:15-16).

As technology has continually advanced, the trend of Christian ministries based on technology has shifted from mediatisation to digitalisation. Mobile applications for divine healing have been developed for believers, such as "The Healing App,"[42] which provides Bible verses concerning healing and the users' testimonies of healing. The metaverse is also used for various medical purposes, such as supporting patients with mental health issues or elderly people with cognitive decline.[43] Research shows that socially anxious individuals benefited substantially from social skills training sessions in the metaverse since the programmes allowed them to engage and acquire skills in communication that boosted their self-esteem.[44]

The metaverse has more than 400 million active users every month,[45] and behind 400 million avatars are real people with various kinds of pain in all dimensions. As believers participate in worship services or prayer meetings in the metaverse, the Spirit of God can heal their physical, emotional, and spiritual diseases through their embodied relations with their avatars. According to J. Kwabena Asamoah-Gyadu, a lot of modern Pentecostals hold the belief that the Holy Spirit is present and active in virtual platforms, and they claim to have experienced divine healing of illnesses while taking part in online spiritual

---

[41] Sonny E. Zaluchu, "The Impact of Mediatisation in the Healing Ministry of African Preachers", *Verbum et Ecclesia* 42(1) (2021) [Available at: https://doi.org/10.4102/ve.v42i1.2198] [Last accessed: 4th May 2024].

[42] "The Healing App," Apple Store Preview [Available at: https://apps.apple.com/us/app/the-healing-app/id1293927143] [Last accessed: 4th May 2024].

[43] Dominikus David Biondi Situmorang, "Will Metaverse Become a More Exciting Place to Listen to Music Streaming for Mental Health?" *Journal of Public Health* 45(2) (2023), 363-64. Defu Zhou, Yi Jin, and Ying Chen, "The Application Scenarios Study on the Intervention of Cognitive Decline in Elderly Population Using Metaverse Technology", *Chengdu: Sichuan Society for Biomedical Engineering [Sheng Wu Yi Xue Gong Cheng Xue Za Zhi]* 40(3) (2023), 571.

[44] Suji Kim and Eunjoo Kim, "The Use of Virtual Reality in Psychiatry: A Review", *Journal of the Korean Academy of Child and Adolescent Psychiatry* 31(1) (2023), 26-32 [Available at: https://doi.org/10.5765/jkacap.190037] [Last accessed: 4th May 2024].

[45] Geri Mileva, "48 Metaverse Statistics: Market Size and Growth (2023)", *Influencer MarketingHub*, last modified 20th July 2023 [Available at: https://influencermarketinghub.com/metaverse-stats/] [Last accessed: 4th May 2024].

activities, like healing services or Holy Communion.[46] Although divine healing is granted by the power of the Holy Spirit, it often takes place in communal settings as believers gather to support one another. The metaverse can provide opportunities to form support groups for people with various issues, such as mental health, grief, addiction, social phobia, or trauma. By creating a virtually safe environment where people can share experiences and receive advice, fostering a culture of care, and building a sense of belonging, these virtual support groups can contribute to healing and restoration through the presence and power of the Holy Spirit.

Conclusion

The emergence of the metaverse has opened a new avenue for contemporary mission and church ministry. As Mark Zuckerberg says, "Metaverse isn't a thing a company builds. It's the next chapter of the internet overall."[47] Reimagining pneumatology and Pentecostal ministries in the age of digitalisation is an option Pentecostals may not consider but the necessary direction to pursue with a professional understanding of technology and theology.

All sectors of our society fervently explore opportunities to maximise the effectiveness of their work in the metaverse. As aforementioned, the health sector has been developing programmes to reduce pain or cure disease by using the benefits of the metaverse. Education is another sector using the metaverse to overcome the failed promises of the current pedagogy taking place within the traditional classroom setting and to provide children with access to the relevant, creative, collaborative, and challenging learning environments they need to succeed.[48]

There is no need for further noteworthy descriptions regarding the remarkable progression in the utilisation of the metaverse across the domains of gaming, entertainment, business, and social networking. It seems that various sectors in our society are giving serious consideration to the importance of reimagining their visions and missions in virtual spaces. This shift is necessary to overcome the limitations imposed by traditional concepts and practices that have been developed and maintained in physical spaces for a significant amount of time. Fortunately, there are discussions and writings in various fields of theology related to the metaverse. For example, the book, *Ecclesiology for a Digital*

---

[46] J. Kwabena Asamoah-Gyadu, "Locked Down but Not Locked Out: An African Perspective on Pentecostalism and Media in a Pandemic Era", in Heidi Campbell and John Dyer (ed), *Ecclesiology for a Digital Church: Theological Reflections on a New Normal* (London: SCM, 2022), 88-9.
[47] Mileva, "48 Metaverse Statistics".
[48] John D. Couch and Jason Towne, *Rewiring Education: How Technology Can Unlock Every Student's Potential* (Dallas, TX: BenBella, 2018), 148.

Church, has compiled articles on profound theological reflections on challenges and opportunities in the age of digitalisation.[49]

It is time for Pentecostal scholars and practitioners to delve deeper into theological discussions for developing digital pneumatology and ministry possibilities in the metaverse. As I theologically speculated and argued above, the presence and power of the Holy Spirit are not confined to physical spaces but permeate all corners of the created universe, including the metaverse. Religious phenomenology and sociology of religion already have embarked on research to explain human spiritual experiences in digital spaces and theorise them. In this significant transition time, digital pneumatology will play a crucial role not only in developing digital ministries for regeneration, transformation, impartation, and restoration in virtual spaces but also in laying the foundation of digital Pentecostalism to deepen and widen our understanding of the person and power of the Holy Spirit in this digital age.

Bibliography

Adhinarta, Yuzo. *The Doctrine of the Holy Spirit in the Major Reformed Confessions and Catechisms of the Sixteenth and Seventeenth Centuries*. Carlisle, UK: Langham Monographs, 2012.

Asamoah-Gyadu, J. Kwabena. "Locked Down but Not Locked Out: An African Perspective on Pentecostalism and Media in a Pandemic Era", In Heidi Campbell and John Dyer, Eds. *Ecclesiology for a Digital Church: Theological Reflections on a New Normal*. London: SCM Press, 2022: 86-100. eBook.

Bhambra, Manmit, and Austin Tiffany. "From the Sanctuary to the Sofa: What Covid-19 Has Taught us about Sacred Space". *LSE Research Online*. Last modified 10th October 2021. [Available at: http://eprints.lse.ac.uk/id/eprint/110575] [Last accessed: 4th May 2024].

Biondi Situmorang, Dominikus David. "Will Metaverse Become a More Exciting Place to Listen to Music Streaming for Mental Health?" *Journal of Public Health* 45(2), (2023), 363-64.

Byrne, Lavinia. "God in Cyberspace: Media and Theology Project Public Lectures." 2000, *Cambridge Theological Federation*. [Available at: https://www.ed.ac.uk/files/imports/fileManager/god%20in%20cyberspace.pdf] [Last accessed: 4th May 2024].

Cairncross, Frances. *The Death of Distance 2.0: How the Communications Revolution will Change Our Lives*. London: Texere, 2001.

Campbell, Heidi. *Digital Religion: Understanding Religious Practice in Digital Media*. Abingdon: Routledge, 2022.

---

[49] Heidi Campbell and John Dyer, *Ecclesiology for a Digital Church: Theological Reflections on a New Normal* (London: SCM, 2022).

——. *Exploring Religious Community Online: We are One in the Network*. New York: Lang, 2010.
——. *When Religion Meets New Media: Media, Religion and Culture*. Hoboken, NY: Taylor & Francis, 2010.
Campbell, Heidi, and John Dyer. *Ecclesiology for a Digital Church: Theological Reflections on a New Normal*. London: SCM Press, 2022.
Chandra, Robby I., and Noh I. Boiliu. "The Metaverse's Potential Impacts on the God-Centred Life and Togetherness of Indonesian Christians", *Theologia Viatorum* 46(1), (2022), n.p. [Available at: https://doi.org/10.4102/tv.v46i1.157] [Last accessed: 4th May 2024].
Couch, John D., and Jason Towne. *Rewiring Education: How Technology Can Unlock Every Student's Potential*. Dallas, TX: BenBella Books, 2018.
Deere, Jack. *Why I Am Still Surprised by the Power of the Spirit: Discovering How God Speaks and Heals Today*. Grand Rapids, MI: Zondervan, 2020.
Denson, Shane. "Faith in Technology: Televangelism and the Mediation of Immediate Experience", *Phenomenology & Practice* 5(2), (2011), 93-119. [Available at: https://shanedenson.com/articles/Denson_Faith_in_Technology.pdf] [Last accessed: 4th May 2024].
The Economist. "Your Own Personal Jesus: Online Services Swell the Church of England's Congregations", *Economist Website*, 4th June 2020. [Available at: https://www.economist.com/britain/2020/06/04/online-services-swell-the-church-of-englands-congregations] [Last accessed: 4th May 2024].
Euronews and AP. "God Has Entered the Metaverse – and Faith in the Virtual World is Flourishing", *Euronews.next*. 1st February 2022, Last modified 3rd February 2022. [Available at: https://www.euronews.com/next/2022/02/01/god-has-entered-the-metaverse-and-worship-in-virtual-worlds-is-booming] [Last accessed: 4th May 2024].
Fee, Gordon. *God's Empowering Presence: The Holy Spirit in the Letters of Paul*. Grand Rapids, MI: Baker Academic, 2011.
Gee, Donald. *Wind and Flame*. Southampton, UK: The Revival Library, 2013. ePub.
Green, Chris, and Steven Félix-Jäger, Eds. *The Spirit and the Screen: Pneumatological Reflections on Contemporary Cinema*. Lanham, MD: Lexington, 2023.
Hartford Institute for Religion Research. "Navigating the Pandemic: A First Look at Congregational Responses", *Exploring the Pandemic Impact on Congregations: Innovation Amidst and Beyond COVID-19*, Last modified December 14, 2021. [Available at: https://www.covidreligionresearch.org/wp-content/uploads/2021/11/Navigating-the-Pandemic_A-First-Look-at-Congregational-Responses_Nov-2021.pdf] [Last accessed: 4th May 2024].

"The Healing App", Apple Store Preview. [Available at: https://apps.apple.com/us/app/the-healing-app/id1293927143] [Last accessed: 4th May 2024].

Henao, Luis Andres. "From the Western Wall to Mecca: VR Lets Virtual Pilgrims Explore World's Holy Sites", *The Times of Israel*. Last modified 8th August 2022. [Available at: https://www.timesofisrael.com/from-the-western-wall-to-mecca-vr-lets-virtual-pilgrims-explore-worlds-holy-sites] [Last accessed: 4th May 2024]/.

Henao, Luis Anders, and the Associated Press. "Religious People are Increasingly Attending Worship Service in the Metaverse", *Fortune*. 31st January 2022. [Available at: https://fortune.com/2022/01/31/virtual-worshipping-services-religion-metaverse/] [Last accessed: 4th May 2024].

Henao, Luis Anders, "Faith in the metaverse: A VR quest for community, fellowship", *Religion News Service*. 31st January, 2022} {Available at https://religionnews.com/2022/01/31/faith-in-the-metaverse-a-vr-quest-for-community-fellowship/

Hjavard, Stig. "Mediatization and Cultural and Social Change: An Institutional Perspective", In Knut Lundby, Ed. *Mediatization of Communication*. Berlin; Boston: De Gruyter Mouton, 2014: 199-226. [Available at: https://doi.org/10.1515/9783110272215.199] [Last accessed: 4th May 2024]

Iannone, Don. "The Two Faces of Digital Spirituality: Contrasting Motives for Digital Spirituality", *KOSMOS: Journal for Global Transformation*. Last modified February 2023. [Available at: https://www.kosmosjournal.org/kj_article/the-two-faces-of-digital-spirituality/] [Last accessed: 4th May 2024].

Jun, Guichun. "Mission in the Age of Digitalization: Metaverse, Metamodernism and Metanarratives", In Risto Jukko, Ed. *Together in the Mission of God*. Geneva: WCC Publications, 2022: 247-260.

——. "Virtual Reality Church as a New Mission Frontier in the Metaverse: Exploring Theological Controversies and Missional Potential of Virtual Reality Church", *Transformation* 37(4), (2020), 297-305. [Available at: https://doi.org/10.1177/0265378820963155] [Last accessed: 4th May 2024].

Kim, Suji, and Eunjoo Kim. "The Use of Virtual Reality in Psychiatry: A Review", *Journal of the Korean Academy of Child and Adolescent Psychiatry* 31(1), (2023), 26-32. [Available at: https://doi.org/10.5765/jkacap.190037] [Last accessed: 4th May 2024].

Kumagi, Seiji. "Development of Buddhist AI, AR, and VR toward the Establishment of Buddhist Metaverse", *Kuensel*. Last modified 10th October 2022. [Available at: https://kuenselonline.com/development-of-buddhist-ai-ar-and-vr-toward-the-establishment-of-buddhist-metaverse-tera-verse] [Last accessed: 4th May 2024].

Lukens, Jeremy. "The Metaverse Is a New Harvest Field for Modern Missions", *Indigitous*. Last modified 12th July 2023. [Available at: https://indigitous.org/article/the-metaverse-is-a-new-harvest-field-for-modern-missions/] [Last accessed: 4th May 2024].

Lyons, Thomas. "When a Christian Revival Goes Viral: At Asbury University, in Kentucky, A Student Chapel Service Turned into a Revival That Has Captivated TikTok", *The Atlantic*. Last modified 23rd February 2023. [Available at: https://www.theatlantic.com/ideas/archive/2023/02/asbury-kentucky-university-christian-revival/673176/] [Last accessed: 4th May 2024].

Mileva, Geri. "48 Metaverse Statistics: Market Size and Growth (2023)", *Influencer MarketingHub*. Last modified 20th July 2023. [Available at: https://influencermarketinghub.com/metaverse-stats/] [Last accessed: 4th May 2024].

Noel, Bradley Truman. "From Wesley to Azusa: The Historical Journey of the 'Second Work' Doctrine", In Scott A. Dunham, *Full of the Holy Spirit and Faith*. Wolfville, Nova Scotia: Gaspereau Press, 1997: 41-62.

Preston, Heather. "Asbury Relocates Revival off Campus, Following Overcrowding", *Premier Christian News*. Last modified 21st February 2023. [Available at: https://premierchristian.news/en/news/article/asbury-relocates-revival-off-campus-following-overcrowding] [Last accessed: 4th May 2024].

Reed, Jeff. "Blackaby's Experiencing God: Metaverse Edition", *Leadership Network*. Last modified 15th March 2022. [Available at: https://www.leadnet.org/blackabys-experiencing-god-metaverse-edition] [Last accessed: 4th May 2024].

——. *VR & The Metaverse Church: How God is Moving in this Virtual, Yet Quite Real, Reality*. London: Leadership Network, 2022.

Reed, Jeff, and John Harris. *Sharing Jesus Online: Helping Everyday Believers Become Digital & Metaverse Missionaries*. London: Exponential, 2023.

Rose, Grace. "How Will God and the Church Fit into the Metaverse?" *Commentary* 18(1), (2022), 4.

Schneider, Lara Katharina. "Religious Acts in Metaverse: Catholic Christianity", *GRIN*. Last modified 15th March 2023. [Available at: https://www.grin.com/document/1338328#:~:text=A%20metaverse%20makes%20sacred%20sites,confessions%20and%20other%20religious%20rituals] [Last accessed: 4th May 2024].

SermonIndex.net. "Asbury University Revival Live 2023 – Feb 15, 2023 (Worship – Part 1)", YouTube Video. Channel: SermonIndex.Net, 16th Feb 2023 [Available at: https://www.youtube.com/watch?v=_FpKv5O2wMI&ab_channel=SermonIndex.net] [Last accessed: 4th May 2024].

Sönmez, Ozan. "Context before Technology: The Possible Utopian/Dystopian Elements of the Metaverse with Examples from Great Literature", In Enis Karaarslan, Ömer Aydin, Ümit Cali, and Moharram Challenger, Eds. *Digital Twin Driven Intelligent Systems and Emerging Metaverse*. Singapore: Springer, 2023: 197-316.

Soto, D.J. "4 Lessons from a Metaverse Pastor", *The Future of the Church is the Metaverse*. Last modified 30th September 2022. [Available at:

https://vrchurch.substack.com/p/4-lessons-from-a-metaverse-pastor] [Last accessed: 4th May 2024].

Steed, Anthony, Ye Pan, Fiona Zisch, and William Steptoe. "The Impact of a Self-Avatar on Cognitive Load in Immersive Virtual Reality", *IEEE Virtual Reality (VR)* (2016), 67-76. [Available at: https://doi.org/10.1109/VR.2016.7504689] [Last accessed: 4th May 2024].

Stephenson, Neal. *Snow Crash*. New York: Bantam, 1992.

Synan, Vinson. *Century of the Holy Spirit 100 Years of Pentecostal and Charismatic Renewal, 1901-2001*. Nashville, TN: Thomas Nelson, 2001. ePub.

Tatom Ammerman, Nancy. *Sacred Stories, Spiritual Tribes: Finding Religion in Everyday Life*. Oxford: Oxford University Press, 2014.

Wainscott, Jim. *Eleventh-Hour Overcomers: In Pursuit of the Ultimate Prize*. Bloomington, IN: Westbow, 2013.

Wuthnow, Robert. *The Restructuring of American Religion: Society and Faith Since World War II*. Princeton: Princeton University Press, 1989.

Yong, Amos. *In the Days of Caesar: Pentecostalism and Political Theology*. Grand Rapids, MI: Eerdmans, 2010.

Zaluchu, Sonny E. "The Impact of Mediatisation in the Healing Ministry of African Preachers." *Verbum et Ecclesia* 42(1), (2021), n.p. [Available at: https://doi.org/10.4102/ve.v42i1.2198] [Last accessed: 4th May 2024]

Zhou, Defu, Yi Jin, and Ying Chen. "The Application Scenarios Study on the Intervention of Cognitive Decline in Elderly Population Using Metaverse Technology". *Chengdu: Sichuan Society for Biomedical Engineering [Sheng Wu Yi Xue Gong Cheng Xue Za Zhi]* 40(3), (2023), 573-581.

19. Global Christianity and Gen Z: What is the Hope for the Future of Faith?

Antipas Harris

Introduction

This study offers a global perspective on how Generation Z engages with Christianity. Gen Z is often defined as comprising of those individuals born between 1996 and 2012 and is identified as the most disengaged from religion in modern history. This global observation necessitates further investigation, beyond the scope of this chapter, to comprehend the diverse racial, cultural, and contextual settings that shape their generational characteristics. On the one hand, this generation is religiously disaffiliated. On the other hand, this study reveals that Gen Z possess a deep spiritual hunger amid fast-paced societal changes.

As Spirit-filled people of God, it is important to remain aware of cultural and contextual realities while acknowledging spirituality as a unique gift to society. Clinically speaking, spirituality has to do with one's hunger for supernatural agency for meaning and purpose. The Holy Spirit offers meaning and purpose to a generation in such a quest.

This chapter explores four significant concerns in this generation's search for meaning: spiritual, technological, social-psychological, and personal-communal, including the family. The role the church plays as the agency of the Holy Spirit to "serve this present age" (*a la* Charles Wesley) requires a revised approach to faith to address Gen Z's needs. This study proposes five suggestions: normalise advanced technology as part of congregational life, develop communities of meaning, commit to diligent prayer, involve young people in rethinking the way we do church, and connect faith to relevant needs in everyday life.

There are dynamics pertinent to generational examination. The next section outlines the precautions. In summary, several dynamics play a role in sociological realities. Also, generations do not exist in neat and distinct categories. With these dynamics in mind, all living generations in varying ways participate in the current religious landscape to be discussed in subsequent sections in this chapter.

Five Precautions

Pew Research Center's president, Michael Dimock, offers five important precautions in generational study[1] apropos to this discourse on global Christianity and Gen Z. The first is that generational categories are not scientifically defined and thereby remain imprecise.[2] Second, categories can lead to over-generalisations and stereotyping. Groupings violate the fullness of human personhood and diversity.[3] Third, categorising generational differences tends to get more attention than generational commonalities, i.e., millennials are like this, and Gen Zs are like that.[4] Therefore, comparisons are false methods of assessment. Fourth, generational research is often "skewed toward the experiences of the upper middle class."[5] Some of the research does not capture a full picture of socio-economic, racial/ethnic, and perhaps gender diversity. Lastly, people change over time. Dimock aptly notes, "Young adults have always faced a different environment than their parents, and it's common for their elders to express some degree of concern or alarm."[6] Categorising people based on their generation demarcates human behaviour with oblivion to similar behaviour in previous generations.

Issues of a Changing World Affect All Generations, With Gen Z in the Vanguard

From the digital revolution to changing views on sexual morality; from climate change to war and terrorism; from the uptick in violent behaviour to post-pandemic stress and more, the world is rapidly changing. Many adverse experiences result from a fast-moving world where people have little time to process before other adverse experiences occur. Psychologists observe trauma amid unprocessed personal and societal adversity. Some of the changes such as with digital technology advance society as a whole. Others like climate change, the threat of nuclear and biological war, and the sexual revolution raise philosophical, theological, and anthropological questions of identity, the meaning of life and death, the role of spirituality, and hope. At the same time, faith is not the obvious resource to quench the thirst of this generation. While all

---

[1] Michael Dimock, "5 Things to Keep in Mind When You Hear about Gen Z, Millennials, Boomers and Other Generations", Pew Research Center, 22nd May 2023 [Available at: https://www.pewresearch.org/short-reads/2023/05/22/5-things-to-keep-in-mind-when-you-hear-about-gen-z-millennials-boomers-and-other-generations/] [Last accessed: 7th May 2024].
[2] Dimock, "5 Things".
[3] Dimock, "5 Things".
[4] Dimock, "5 Things".
[5] Dimock, "5 Things".
[6] Dimock, "5 Things".

living generations are affected by these many issues, the younger generation experiences the brunt of it.

To consider the future of faith in the face of so many global issues, this chapter analyses the situation of faith and Gen Z from a position of concern about the future of the Church. American millennials came of age at the peak of American secularism. Because of this, Pew labels millennials as drivers of religious disaffiliation.[7] They are tagged "the generation of 'nones,'" popularising "spiritual but not religious".[8] Gen Z scholar, Ryan P. Burge,[9] Christian historian, Dale M. Coulter,[10] and others point to several attributes for the stark decline of faith affiliation. Some have to do with political ideology, a more bold confession of disaffiliation, growing multiple secularisms,[11] and demographic issues such as increased formal education, challenging questions about Christianity's participation in racial histories, racialised nationalisms, marital status, sexuality, and matters related to gender. Moreover, some of the reasons are not merely cynicism about Christianity as much a slow, long-term shift of priorities more crystalised in this generation. Therefore, such concerns must not be discussed

---

[7] Michael Lipka and Claire Gecewicz, "More Americans Now Say They're Spiritual but Not Religious", *Pew Research Center*, 6th September 2017 [Available: https://www.pewresearch.org/short-reads/2017/09/06/more-americans-now-say-theyre-spiritual-but-not-religious/] [Last accessed: 7th May 2024].

[8] Lipka and Gecewicz, "More Americans."

[9] See Ryan P. Burg, *The Nones: Where They Came From, Who They Are, and Where They Are Going* (Minneapolis, MN: Fortress, 2021). See Daniel A. Cox, "Generation Z and the Future of Faith in America", *Survey Center on American Life*, 24th March 2022 [Available at: https://www.americansurveycenter.org/research/generation-z-future-of-faith/] [Last accessed: 7th May 2024].

[10] See Dale M. Coulter, "Thoughts on the Future of American Christianity", *Firebrand*, 3rd October 2023. [Available at: https://firebrandmag.com/articles/thoughts-on-the-future-of-american-christianity-firebrand-big-read?fbclid=IwAR3azTAmv3axMdffq9uQJ277a9Ppe0-yAo_Uozj1C3ukx0HpXw8PdA-0_h8] [Last accessed: 7th May 2024].

[11] The academic conversation has moved beyond European secularism that compartmentalises religion as non-essential in public discourse. Post-secularism and post-liberalism consider religion important for private life but not public discourse. However, my usage of secularisms seeks to capture Jose Casanova's insights of local challenges with religion rather than an import of European long-known secularism. Also, this chapter's reference to secularisms pushes Casanova's views towards new insights into how this generation separates institutional religion from spirituality. This contemporary lived reality seeks to break down the secular-sacred divide while also distancing from traditional forms of religion. The new form of religion (*a la* spirituality) is more fluid, syncretic, ever-changing, connects divine love as affirmation of human-centred interests, and is less concerned about religious routines unless they are mysterious (other worldly), meaningful (feels personal), and practical (adds positivity to how one feels about themselves and the world). See Clayton Crockett, "What is Postsecularism?" *American Book Review* 39(5) (2018), 6-14 [Available at: https://doi.org/10.1353/abr.2018.0062] [Last accessed: 7th May 2024].

independently of living generations such as baby boomers, Gen Xers, and millennials.

When making value comparisons between generations, however, we must note that times are changing more than generational comparisons reveal. *All* generations participate in and are impacted by the changes. Thus, comparisons are more fluctuant than static. As Dimock aptly notes:

> [G]enerational thinking can help us understand how societies change over time. The eras in which we come of age can leave a signature of common experiences and perspectives. Similarly, historical advances like desegregation, effective birth control, the invention of the internet, and the arrival of artificial intelligence can fundamentally change how people live their lives, and the youngest generations are often in the vanguard.[12]

Sociology observes emerging trends in human behaviour incalculable to hard science. This means that one must not take a hard stance such as, this generation is about this, and that generation is about that. All generations are experiencing shifts at the same time, even if one generation behaves differently than another when they were *this* or *that* age.

As we consider Gen Z, we find ourselves saying, "That's not really unique to Gen Z!" Or, "We were kind of like that in my day," as if our "day" no longer exists. Actually, there are probably more youth trends across generations than not. Yet, paradoxically, generational attributes contribute to the lived reality and views of faith. Much of what impacts Gen Z are ripple effects from previous generations. At the same time, studies show evidence of discontinuities in which one generation moves in the opposite direction of another.[13]

An Ipsos Global Advisor study revealed some surprising twists regarding generational religious affiliation. Researchers surveyed twenty-six countries[14] and found that overall, younger people are less likely than older adults to identify as Christian, especially Catholic. Religious young people are more likely to identify as Muslim or other religions.[15] The same study indicated an even more notable shift – the difference in religious affiliation among boomers in comparison to Gen Zers.[16] While in nearly all countries at least one-third of all adults believe in God as described in holy Scriptures, Gen Zers are the ones less

---

[12] Dimock, "5 Things."
[13] "Global Religion 2023: Religious Beliefs across the World", *Ipsos*, 11th May 2023, 2 [1-39]. [Available at: https://www.ipsos.com/sites/default/files/ct/news/documents/2023-05/Ipsos%20Global%20Advisor%20-%20Religion%202023%20Report%20-%2026%20countries.pdf] [Last accessed: 7th May 2024].
[14] Nicolas Boyon, "Two Global Religious Divides: Geographic and Generational", *Ipsos Global Advisor* [Available at: https://www.ipsos.com/en-us/two-global-religious-divides-geographic-and-generational] [Last accessed: 7th May 2024].
[15] Boyon, "Two Global Religious Divides".
[16] "Global Religion 2023".

likely than boomers to hold such beliefs.[17] However, that trend is reversed in less religious countries. Gen Zers tend to gravitate toward faith in countries where older adults are less religious.[18] In countries where religious practice is low, young people tend to have higher participation rates.[19]

Critical Factors Impacting Gen Zs' Faith Participation

Several crucial factors currently impact the global Christian situation: (1) elements of secularisms mixed with non-religious spirituality, (2) continued decline in traditional family systems, (3) modern technology, and (4) social isolationism. While these crucial elements are listed separately, they are interwoven.

Secularisms Mixed with Non-Religious Spirituality

First, the decline in religious affiliation in Gen Z exists as a by-product of multiple generational shifts away from holding church affiliation as essential to faith formation. A three-hundred-year-rise of multiple iterations of secularism, post-secularism, and the resurgence of secularism is coming to a head, impacting a diverse world in multiple ways. The resurgence of secularism is complex. On the one hand, it comprises a variety of secularisms rather than the traditional Western one. On the other hand, contemporary secularisms are unique because they are not absent of spirituality but rather integrate non-traditional spiritualities. Thus, calling this a resurgence of "secularism" proves problematic.

However, the new secularisms are hard to define. For the sake of discussion, I will mention a few perspectives. White South African scholar, B.J. van der Walt, defines secularism in the following manner:

> Secularism, born from the atheistic notions of three centuries, is a subjectivist, relativist and utilitarian view – as well as the resulting state of affairs – according to which [hu]man[kind] is so-called free, independent and having come of age. Because of the part the particular powers which [human beings] ha[ve] at [their] disposal [humanity] has taken the place of God, who in [their] view has become superfluous, so that [human beings] can now live solely out of, by and toward this life which is closed off in itself.[20]

---

[17] "Global Religion 2023". Also, see Samantha Saad, "Where Boomer Faith in God Is Low, Gen Z Belief Is Up", *Christianity Today*, 24th July 2023 [Available at: https://www.christianitytoday.com/news/2023/july/ipsos-global-religion-survey-boomer-gen-z-belief.html] [Last accessed: 7th May 2024].
[18] Saad, "Where Boomer Faith in God Is Low".
[19] Saad, "Where Boomer Faith in God Is Low".
[20] B.J. Van der Walt, *Transforming Power: Challenging Contemporary Secular Society* (Potchefstroom, South Africa: ICCA, 2007), 298, quoted in T. Derrick Mashau, "A Reformed Missional Perspective on Secularism and Pluralism in Africa: Their Impact on African Christianity and the Revival of Traditional Religion", *CJT*, 44 (2009), 108–

While van der Walt provides insights into an anti-religious, anti-God version of secularism, other scholars argue for a more nuanced view, pointing out many secularisms as opposed to a single Western version.

Another definition of secularism hails from The Center for Inquiry. This definition bootstraps secularism with humanism in the following manner: "Secular humanism is a nonreligious worldview rooted in science, philosophical naturalism, and humanist ethics. Instead of relying on faith, doctrine, or mysticism, secular humanists use compassion, critical thinking, and human experience to find solutions to human problems."[21] An attempt to define many approaches to secularity is evident in this definition.

The research is a mixed bag. Some secular humanisms are anti-religious and anti-God. Others are not concerned about God so much as they are with understanding the human situation. The human-focused secularists may be where many "nones" are. They are neither atheists nor religious. Many expressions of secularism emerge from contextual social struggles. Jose Casanova explores this from a global-comparative perspective: "[M]ore importantly [than a European comparative analysis] the further recognition that with the world-historical process of globalisation initiated by the European colonial expansion, all these processes [of secularisation] everywhere are dynamically interrelated and mutually constituted.[22] Although there are variations of secularisms, they maintain a common focus on responding to the human condition. They tend to account for highly diverse experiences, globalisation, social environments, and human history in all its complexity.[23] This means that secularism is not all a reaction to religion or God per se. Some secularisms even critique Western ideals and how religion has wielded oppression, privileging some human persons over others. In this sense, any reasonable religious person would laud global secularity for its needed critique of historical Western religious overreach and abuse.

---

126. 110 [Available at: https://www.calvin.edu/library/database/crcpi/fulltext/ctj/2009-441-108.pdf] [Last accessed: 7th May 2024].
[21] "What is Secular Humanism?" *Center for Inquiry* [Available at: https://centerforinquiry.org/definitions/what-is-secular-humanism/#:~:text=Secular%20humanism%20is%20a%20nonreligious,find%20solutions%20to%20human%20problems] [Last accessed: 7th May 2024].
[22] José Casanova, "Rethinking Secularization", *Hedgehog Review* 8(1-2) (Spring/Summer 2006), 11 [Available at: https://hedgehogreview.com/issues/after-secularization-special-double-issue/articles/rethinking-secularization] [Last accessed: 7th May 2024]. Also, see Aprilfaye T. Manalang, "Generation Z, Minority Millennials and Disaffiliation from Religious Communities: Not Belonging and the Cultural Cost of Unbelief", *Interdisciplinary Journal of Research on Religion* 17 (Article 2) (2021), 2 [1-24] [Available at: https://www.religjournal.com/articles/article_view.php?id=159] [Last accessed: 7th May 2024].
[23] Casanova, "Rethinking Secularization", 1-2.

Decline in Traditional Family Systems and Values

The second factor impacting the global Christian situation as pertaining to Gen Z is the continued decline in traditional family systems and values. Failing systems include the disintegrating family nucleus (father, mother, and children). Declining values refers to regular family time playing games, talking about life and faith, sharing family dinners, taking trips with, and going to church as a family. A report from the Survey Center on American Life of the American Enterprise indicates that previous generations produce more religious detachment in the next generation. The detachment may also be described as a break from the secular-sacred divide while also detaching from traditional forms of religion. The new form of religion (*a la* spirituality) is more fluid, culturally syncretic, ever-changing, employs divine love as affirmation of human-centred interests, and less concerned about traditional religious routines unless they are mysterious (other worldly), meaningful (shedding light on personal inklings and affectivity), and practical (adding positivity to how one feels about themselves and the world).

The evolution of religious engagement, detachment, and new forms of engagement is an incremental process from one generation to the next. It often appears reasonable, empowering, and harmless. Examples are as follows. Busyness has pushed family meals down the priority list. They are no longer centrepieces for family life with prayer being part of the daily or even weekly family table fellowship. The Survey Center on American Life reports that

> For as long as we have been able to measure religious commitments, childhood religious experiences have strongly predicted adult religiosity. They still do. If someone had robust religious experiences growing up, they are likely to maintain those beliefs and practices into adulthood. Without robust religious experiences to draw on, Americans feel less connected to the traditions and beliefs of their parents' faith.[24]

The trajectory is set. Without another societal Great Awakening, the future will continue in the direction of secularism and church disaffiliation. Sunday school is almost obsolete. There is often a justifiable reason to choose work, leisure, or sports over regular church attendance. The separation between church and state has construed a false notion of divided human consciousness when we are in fact holistic beings. Like everyone else, Christians are just trying to keep up in a fast-paced world. Subsequently, they participate in *secularisation* while also rejecting *secularism*. As a result, young generations are moving further away from fidelity to faith or affiliation with the church.

---

[24] Daniel A. Cox, "Emerging Trends and Enduring Patterns in American Family Life", *Survey Center on American Life*, 9th February 2022 [Available at: https://www.americansurveycenter.org/research/emerging-trends-and-enduring-patterns-in-american-family-life/] [Last accessed: 7th May 2024].

Modern Technology and Social Isolationism

Third, while modern technology is an asset in many ways – enhancing the spread of the Christian message through digital means (apps, YouTube, GodTube, streaming technology, and social media outlets) –the digital age has, nevertheless, challenged the role of faith in contemporary times. A world made smaller through technology amidst social isolationism is a perfect storm for mental health challenges and to stifle communal formation in a generation that is hungry for community and belonging.

In Jean M. Twenge's book, *iGen,* she notes that the problem of loneliness is much deeper than merely a popular desire for belonging or seasonal depression. She says that "More young people are experiencing not just symptoms of depression, and not just feelings of anxiety, but clinically diagnosable major depression."[25] That depression has led to a growing epidemic of self-injury such as cutting and even suicidality. Twenge highlights comments from New York psychiatrist, Fadi Haddad, in *Time Magazine* where Haddad laments, "Every single week we have a girl who comes to the ER after some social-media rumour or incident that upset her."[26] Those ER visits are almost always caused by girls cutting themselves. According to a report from the Centers for Disease Control, "[P]oor mental and health remains a substantial public health problem, particularly among adolescent females."[27] Twenge points out, "Many parents have no idea what their children are doing on social media, and many feel helpless."[28] Particularly, girls often cry out for help in subtle ways, even on social media.

In an article in *The Gospel Coalition,* Sarah Eekhoff Zylstra points out that Gen Z, often called iGen,[29] is anxiously digital.[30] Twenge asserts that Matt Carmichael, *Advertising Age's* former director of data strategy, asserts that more than "Gen Z," this generation is more accurately described as "iGen."[31] They

---

[25] Jean M. Twenge, *iGen: Why Today's Super-Connected Kids Are Growing up Less Rebellious, More Tolerant, Less Happy – and Completely Unprepared for Adulthood* (New York: Atria, 2017), 108.

[26] Twenge, *iGen,* 109.

[27] Centers for Disease Control and Prevention, "Emergency Department Visits Involving Mental Health Conditions, Suicide-Related Behaviors, and Drug Overdoses among Adolescents – United States, January 2019–February 2023", *Morbidity and Mortality Weekly Report* 72(19) (2023), 502-12, CDC, 12th May 2023 [Available at: https://www.cdc.gov/mmwr/volumes/72/wr/mm7219a1.htm?s_cid=mm7219a1_w] [Last accessed: 7th May 2024].

[28] Twenge, *iGen,* 109.

[29] Twenge, *iGen,* 7.

[30] Sarah Eekhoff Zylstra, "6 Things Christians Should Know about Gen Z", *The Gospel Coalition* [Available at: https://www.thegospelcoalition.org/article/gen-z/] [Last accessed: 7th May 2024].

[31] Twenge, *iGen,* 7. Twenge explains: "The prominent magazine *Advertising Age* has backed iGen as the best name for the post-Millennials. 'We think it's the name that best

seek approval and validation, and they express their opinions and cry for help in digital spaces. Zylstra explains: "Part of the problem is that every social media platform is like a stage on which Gen Zers both perform and compare themselves to others."[32] They create social media pages and soon delete them. Or they create multiple pages and make them private for select friends in each one. Twenge points out that New York psychiatrist Haddad reports, "One mother found that her self-harming daughter had seventeen Facebook accounts, which the mother promptly shut down. 'But what good does that do?' asked Haddad. 'There will be an eighteenth.'"[33] Or they create public pages, post photos, and soon delete the pictures and start over.[34] Image insecurity is blatant in a culture of bullying and a generation with an unprecedented desire for peer acceptance. Zylstra quotes from her interview with Malisa Ellis who has worked in various parts of the world with a youth ministry called Cru: "The level of panic is high. Everything is out there all the time on social media [...]. As this generation leans into that, their anxiety goes up. But as they disengage from it, they feel like they're missing out. They're constantly battling back and forth between deleting and reinstalling their social media."[35] One might conclude that in this way, Gen Zers have a love-hate relationship with digital resources.

The current digital age offers many assets, but at a time when social isolation and anxiety are at an all-time high, what once was a source of human progress is adding to social ills. For example, on the one hand, the Bible app is conveniently available for the smartphone as are many preaching videos and opportunities for virtual community. Most Christians would say that is a great thing. On the other hand, so too are negative things immediately and freely available such as anti-religious thought, porn, and damaging misinformation. The virtual good, bad, holy, profane, and propaganda all flood the digital natives at the click of a button. A world ravenous for more and more vices, more and more success, and more and more attention is overwhelming Gen Z. So, they engage a bit and then want to pull back for self-preservation.

Selected Global Cases

The following four global cases – the Netherlands, the US, Ghana, and Singapore – shed light on Gen Z and its potential to lead a revolution of faith. Admittedly, these cases do not reflect all the continents and are thus an inadequate representation of a global context. Notwithstanding, they demonstrate the urgent

---

fits and will best lead to understanding of this generation,' Matt Carmichael, *Advertising Age's* former director of data strategy, told *USA Today*."
[32] Zylstra, "6 Things".
[33] Twenge, *iGen*, 109.
[34] Zylstra, "6 Things".
[35] Zylstra, "6 Things".

need for a more robust conversation to examine faith's relevance in a global context, revealing both the challenges and the potential for a revival of faith.

The Netherlands

For centuries, a Euro-secularism matured across Europe and influenced other parts of the world. In 2002, Dutch scholars, Manfred Te Grotenhuis and Peer Scheepers, studied why, since 1937, the Netherlands is one of the most secular countries in the world.[36] Most Dutch people do not attend church regularly, and most of the population does not affiliate with any church. They found that people are introduced to rationalisation at a young age. As people deepen their analysis of life with logical reasoning as the primary tool, the role of faith in their lives fades into shadow. Religious disaffiliation did not suddenly drop in the millennial and Gen Z generations. As structures of logical reasoning have taken centre stage, the role of faith has been pushed to the margins. This process has been underway for decades.[37]

Ipsos Global Advisor's study, mentioned earlier, offers a glimmer of hope. In mostly religious countries where baby boomers are more religious, younger generations tend to be less religious. But, where older generations are less religious, younger people are more likely drawn to religion. With this trend in view, the Netherlands may be positioned for revival. As the current generation is largely secular, Gen Z may be the key to a forthcoming Great Awakening in the Netherlands!

The United States of America

The United States is also experiencing an ongoing faith erosion. As in the Netherlands, it did not start with millennials but accelerated among them and continues in Gen Z. Christian historian, Dale Coulter, points out that "The tag 'none' has been used since the 1960s as shorthand for those who consider themselves 'spiritual but not religious'".[38] Pew Research Center reports that in 2017, 27 percent of cross-generational adults (boomers, Gen Xers, millennials, and older Gen Zers) said they are "spiritual but not religious" – an 8 percent increase over five years.[39] The arc is sharply bent toward increased religious disaffiliation in this generation, including women and men; whites, blacks, and Hispanics; varying educational levels; and a mixture of political affiliations. Much could be said about what happened in preceding generations that

---

[36] See Manfred Te Grotenhuis and Peer Scheepers, "Churches in Dutch: Causes of Religious Disaffiliation in The Netherlands, 1937-1995", *Journal for the Scientific Study of Religion* 40(4) (2001), 591-606, JSTOR [Available at: https://www.jstor.org/stable/1387654] [Last accessed: 7th May 2024].
[37] Te Grotenhuis and Scheepers, "Churches in Dutch", 591-606.
[38] Coulter, "Thoughts on the Future of American Christianity".
[39] Lipka and Gecewicz, "More Americans".

facilitated this.[40] Notably, older adults cultivate the environment for Gen Zers. They are the parents, leaders, teachers, and influencers.

Norfolk State University sociologist of religion, Aprilfaye T. Manalang, explains: "Although Gen Z and minority millennials feel ambivalent about their relationship to the church, they do not regard unbelief as either atheistic or religious per se, but a more nuanced negotiation in their daily lives."[41] They respect religion and would likely say they believe in God. This stems from their sense of loyalty to family. In communities of colour, integration of faith and God-talk remain part of the cultural fabric that binds parents, children, grandparents, grandchildren, etc.

The spread of spiritual exploration intermingled with elements of secularism accelerates through the virtual halls of high-speed Internet. One observes emerging challenges related to the digital revolution in Gen Z. For example, Sarah Eekhoff Zylstra, shares an article in *The Gospel Coalition* entitled, "6 Things Christians Should Know About Gen Z." Concerning the "Anxiously Digital" generation, Zylstra quotes her interview with Craig Millard, College Ministry pastor at Redeemer Church in New York, saying:

> When we announce we're doing a 24-hour ministry-wide fast, they immediately think of fasting from social media. When I first started, I thought that was an easy way out of fasting from food. But now I can see how hard it is for them […]. Students are more aware of how damaging it is to be constantly online, but it's so wrapped up in how they think of the world.[42]

In other words, Gen Z has a love-hate relationship with the digital age. Food is not the source of Gen Z's most serious gluttony. Social media is! It keeps them up at night. As Twenge observes,

> Smartphone use may have decreased teens' sleep time: more teens now sleep less than seven hours most nights. Sleep experts says that teens should get about nine hours of sleep a night, so a teen who is getting less than seven hours a night is significantly sleep deprived. Fifty-seven percent more teens were sleep deprived in 2015 than in 1991. In just the three years between 2012 and 2015, 22% more teens failed to get seven hours of sleep.[43]

Differently than reading a traditional book or watching TV, electronic devices and social media are addictive. Twenge explains that "[t]he allure of the smartphone, its blue light glowing in the dark, is often too much to resist."[44] As part of Gen Z's everyday life, digital technology is both an asset and a challenge.

---

[40] Racism, misogyny, and Christian nationalism – to name a few.
[41] Manalang, "Generation Z", 1-24. Manalang examines faith disaffiliation and unbelief among Gen Zers and Millennials in American communities of colour, specifically, Filipino Americans (the second-largest Asian-American group), African Americans, and Hispanic Americans.
[42] Zylstra, "6 Things".
[43] Twenge, *iGen*, 114.
[44] Twenge, *iGen*, 115.

The world acknowledges the digital age as a gift in human advancement. However, more attention must be given to the impact of modern technology on Gen Zer's mental health.

A similar observation exists related to digital media and worship. Many Gen Zers have greater attraction to cathedrals and traditional worship space than to worship spaces inundated with digital screens and flashing lights. Notwithstanding, the complexity is that Gen Z is not completely averse to all digital assets.

Millard's point above is that, while Gen Zers seem lost in the crevice of the worst fractures in the structures of faith, they are crying out for a better way. To say this is an "anxious" generation is an understatement. A current mental health crisis exists, exacerbated by the aftermath of the COVID-19 pandemic. Gen Z is in search of spiritual and mental better-ness. Yet, better is not a return to some previous generation's way. It is a search for a way forward that includes the digital age but with more guidance and temperance. It is a search for holistic treatment of mental, spiritual, and physical wellness. Christian spirituality has internal norms to satisfy this thirst if only the church rethinks the role of the Holy Spirit in the everyday life of the believer with Gen Z's interests in mind.

Ghana

Countries like Ghana, where Christians make up 71.2 percent of the country,[45] boast more Gen Z religious affiliation than many countries. Ghanaian scholar and pastor, Mensa Otabil, explains two important factors in strong faith participation: (1) family and (2) the African spiritual culture. First, Otabil says Ghanaian parents continue to heavily influence young people's faith practices.[46] The central role of faith incubated in the home cannot be overstated. The influence and authority of the family remain strong in Ghana and other African countries. Second, Otabil points out, "Even the most secular African is also spiritual."[47] So, a Ghanaian Gen Zer may be less likely to say, "I am spiritual and not religious," since spirituality is inherent to the persisting pan-African culture. Notwithstanding, one wonders what the future of faith will look like for Africa. Certainly, they struggle with forms of secularism and even the infiltration of Western versions of secularism as indicated above in South Africa. However, Ghanaian Gen Zers, for example, do not seem to have significantly wavered amid the global resurgence of secularisms.

It is not surprising that Spirit-filled Christianity fans the flames of young African spiritual excitement. Pentecostal expressions of the faith find home amid

---

[45] The World Factbook, "Introduction: Africa, Ghana", *Ghana Statistical Service* [Available at: https://statsghana.gov.gh/docs/countrypdf_gh.pdf] [Last accessed: 7th May 2024].
[46] Mensa Otabil (Pastor of International Central Gospel Church) conversation with Antipas Harris, 21st September 2023.
[47] Otabil, conversation.

cultural spirituality. So, while family nurtures faith in children, Ghanaian theologian J. Kwabena Asamoah-Gyadu observes that when they come of age, they make their faith commitment in Christian high schools and post-secondary schools.[48] That is when they often deepen their faith commitment and experience the baptism of the Holy Spirit. Because the younger generation feels excited about their experience of the baptism of the Spirit, Pentecostal spirituality permeates many denominations as well as Catholicism.

Christianity in the Global South does not seem to be tapering off any time soon. However, Asamoah-Gyadu points out a brewing rift between older generations and Gen Z on the basis of what he calls "denominational uprootedness."[49] Gen Zers pull away from traditional denominational approaches in search of church experiences more aligned with contemporary culture, which is largely informed by normalised high-speed Internet, new forms of music, Western influence on dress, as well as personal and societal trauma and victories. Nigerian business leader, Tunji Adegbite, aptly notes:

> Gen Zs [sic] were born during the dot com era and were raised on technology. They witnessed the election of Barack Obama, rise of gender equality, sexual orientation equality, shared family responsibilities, and collective volunteerisms. However, they were born into a deeply troubled system, a time of worldwide terrorism attacks, Arab uprisings, effects of climate change and a great recession. This generation (c.32% of world's population) have come of age to shape policies and open doors they were locked out of.[50]

Fast-paced technological advancements stimulate excitement for innovation and hope for material success. Ghanaian and other churches must keep reimagining ways to bridge faith with Gen Z where they are – socially, spiritually, aspirationally, etc. The global trend is that young people tend to lose interest in faith that they deem disconnected from their complex experience of self and the world at large. Churches in countries like Ghana, parts of Nigeria, and other places where Gen Z remains highly connected must invest more in hearing their voices and ideas as well as including them in leadership roles.

Singapore

Singapore is experiencing shifts amidst the maturing digital revolution and other related cultural shifts. A version of Western-like secularism is affecting Singaporean views about self, life, family, morality, sexuality, and faith, with Gen Zers raised in both a far less religious world and a society resistant to

---

[48] J. Kwabena Asamoah-Gyadu (President of Trinity Theological Seminary), conversation with Antipas Harris, 15th September 2023.
[49] J. Kwabena Asamoah-Gyadu (President of Trinity Theological Seminary), conversation with Antipas Harris, 3rd November 2023.
[50] Tunji Adegbite, "Tapping into the Chutzpah of Nigeria's Generation Z", *This Day Live* [Available at: https://www.thisdaylive.com/index.php/2020/10/18/tapping-into-the-chutzpah-of-nigerias-generation-z] [Last accessed: 7th May 2024].

traditional values. The challenge presents itself not only in Christian families but also in other religions and non-religious families.

Reflecting on Gen Z and the church in a *Christianity Today* article, Pearlyn Koh writes, "Many young people's views on issues like sexuality or what comprises a family unit are no longer defined by Asian societal norms."[51] She points out that a 2020 census revealed that a growing number of Gen Zers have joined the Western "nones" – from 21 percent in 2010 to 24 percent in 2020.[52] Pew reports that the rise of "nones' in Singapore is "uniquely high" along with other countries.[53] This in part results from the influence of the Western world. Parents encourage education and new experiences, not gauging how they might lure youth away from tradition. It is, however, not surprising that Gen Z has benefitted from exposure to cultural and ideological diversity. Also, Gen Z has also been impacted by varying parental decisions about faith and church attendance, changing family systems, modern technology, and an isolationism compounded by COVID-19 and more.

Opportunities

Many opportunities exist to engage the younger generation. The first, education, is such a shaper of culture. There is a need for more Pentecostal scholarship and Christian education, which must engage the whole person. When considering human beings, there really is no separation of *secular* and *sacred*. Pentecostal-sponsored education must show concern about the mind, soul, body, and spirit.

The second opportunity has to do with leadership. Gen Z is a generation of leaders. Empowering young people to lead through experiential learning is key to capturing their faith interest. Koh points out that Heart of God Church in Singapore has "succeeded in attracting a hard-to-capture demographic: the average age of its congregants has remained steady at 22 years old."[54] They employ an effective strategy to host Gen Z-led main services. The Church's co-founding pastor, Cecilia Chan, explains: "Youths need to be invited, included

---

[51] Pearlyn Koh, "To Keep Gen Z in the Pews, One Singapore Church Lets Them Run the Service", *Christianity Today*, 10th February 2023 [Available at: https://www.christianitytoday.com/ct/2023/february-web-only/singapore-youth-church-gen-z-ministry.html] [Last accessed: 7th May 2024].
[52] Koh, "To Keep Gen Z in the Pews."
[53] William Miner, "In Singapore, Religious Diversity and Tolerance Go Hand in Hand", *Pew Research Center*, 6th October 2023 [Available at: https://www.pewresearch.org/short-reads/2023/10/06/in-singapore-religious-diversity-and-tolerance-go-hand-in-hand/] [Last accessed: 7th May 2024]. "Among Singaporean adults, 26% identify as Buddhist, 18% as Muslim, 17% as Christian, 8% as Hindu, 6% as a follower of Chinese traditional religions like Taoism or Confucianism, and 4% as some other religion, including Indigenous religions. Another 22% do not identify with any religion."
[54] Koh, "To Keep Gen Z in the Pews".

[and] involved, before they can be influenced and impacted."[55] This also suggests that to capture the innovation and spiritual energy of this generation is to centralise space for experiential congregational leadership and experiential spirituality.

As in many other contexts, ministries in Singapore struggle to adjust to a generation where change is their new norm. Change challenges traditional forms of normalising communal practices. Yet, to reach this generation effectively, creating new norms of change remains crucial for the future of faith. Cru Singapore published an article called the "Future of Youth Ministry" by Deborah Ng, who sums up an interview with a Singaporean youth leader who observed that "one of the main weaknesses highlighted by youth leaders [...] seemed to be a resistance to change. That ministry was 'running in the same way when the culture is changing', and 'just struggling to hold on to certain forms of discipleship, certain programmes.'"[56] The same report explains a similar issue in varying proportions globally: "Young people are thinking about questions like meaning, purpose, identity, and sexuality. These questions are not new, but in a post-truth world where they've been told to think with their feelings, they are facing more uncertainty in dealing with these questions than ever before."[57] The relationship between Christianity and everyday life is in question. Ministries in Singapore must continue to learn and creatively adjust approaches to ministry to capture the imagination of this generation while remaining faithful to the core tenets of faith. This is no small task. Yet, we have hope!

Ng quotes Max Jeganathan, Director of Thinking Faith, who says, "It makes sense to me, why issues like anxiety and loneliness are at an all-time high among young people."[58] From the article, it is not altogether clear why Jeganathan draws such a conclusion. However, reading between the lines, it seems that his conclusion is based on what he perceives as a gap between this generation of digital natives and previous generations. The digital age coupled with the social isolation effects of COVID-19 pandemic have created the perfect storm for anxiety and loneliness for everyone, particularly Gen Z. Moreover, Ng understands Max to believe that conditions are ripe to respond to Gen Z's search with a gospel belonging, community, meaning, and purpose. Singaporean youth need a renewed presentation of the person of Jesus Christ whose life and teachings have more relevance to them.[59] When the church's vision of Christ is renewed, the faithful are more authentically equipped to extend a relevant Jesus in this generation. Revisioning is necessary for the future of the church.

---

[55] Koh, "To Keep Gen Z in the Pews".
[56] Deborah Ng, "The Future of Youth Ministry in Singapore", *Cru: Christian Stories about Helping Others* [Available at: https://www.cru.org/sg/en/stories/helping-others-grow/the-future-of-youth-ministry-in-singapore.html] [Last accessed: 7th May 2024].
[57] Ng, "Future of Youth Ministry in Singapore".
[58] Ng, "Future of Youth Ministry in Singapore".
[59] Ng, "Future of Youth Ministry in Singapore".

Conclusions

This chapter provides only a snapshot of the complexities related to the current crisis of faith. There are no quick fixes. There remains insufficient research to capture all contemporary nuances pertinent to a survey of Christianity and Gen Z. Yet, this birds-eye view ponders important characteristics to begin that study.

Importantly, Gen Z are growing up as "nones" but are searching for spiritual awareness. I teach many of them in my "Life, Death, and Meaning" course at Old Dominion University. One of the gifts of teaching in a secular university is that students are often either not affiliated or loosely affiliated with a religious tradition. When I lecture on religion, it is as if I have them in the palm of my hands. A student recently asked me to start a podcast. Another student commented, "It will be very popular!" Every week, I rediscover a hunger for meaning and identity formation. Students have questions about life and death and wonder whether faith can give sufficient answers. Podcasts and YouTube are the new pulpits. Millennials as well as Gen Zers look for answers there rather than at church. It might also be argued that they bring their search to the classrooms, whether online or in-person.

Gen Z and the Non-Faith Based Spiritual Search

Often, my students share their admiration for their grandparents' religion and are curious to learn more. Some don't see the point of going to church but do believe in God. Others grew up in church and are questioning whether a church is the best expression of God in the world. Yet others believe in something out there but are not sure whether "God" is the best way to describe that "something". Some are exploring other faiths like Wicca, indigenous religions, science of consciousness, and expanded consciousness. Some agnostics question the validity that there is a "God" or "something out there" altogether. Then, there are those holding on to their faith but weary with questions about faith and life that the church does not answer adequately. They are exploring how to follow Jesus differently than traditional approaches. They want a Jesus who cares about the things they care about and who navigates the world the way they do. That Jesus is down for their cause. In short, he attends to brokenness in the world, affirms love in whatever forms people claim it, includes everyone, and incorporates digital reality and social media as the social and religious norm.

Notwithstanding, the same bout with faith manifests itself in the neighbourhood. Gen Zers everywhere are asking the same questions. I was pleasantly surprised when I visited Barnes and Noble. Young people's heads were buried in books. There is no denying their hunger for truth and deeper understanding. A closer examination observes an unprecedented spiritual search. This means the search for truth is no longer purely a scientific one. Gen Z may be dubbed a generation of creativity – not because previous generations were not – but because they are most unrestrained by the rules of what's right and wrong, appropriate, and inappropriate. So, even in their spiritual search, there are no rules; nothing is off-limits. They are more creative, more "in-touch" with today's times, it seems. Integration is premium, even the integration of religious thought, signs, and symbols with scientific ones.

Gen Zers are looking for something scientifically supported but that also brings peace, joy, love, identity, community, and a sense of belonging. This means that affectivity is just as sacred as anything else. Feelings, motivation, emotions, and belief systems must exist in tandem with that which is cause-driven, affirming, non-discriminatory, and non-sectarian. They care about social evolution – why should things remain the way they've always been? They also value art, science, ecology, climate change, peace over war, fairness, and a type of community that both affirms and includes each person's gifts.

These salient theological anthropological questions sum it all up:
- Who am I?
- Why am I here?
- Is there a power greater than me?
- Does that ultimate being care about what's going on in the world?
- Can life be better for me?

These are complex queries. The answers must not be cookie cutter but contextual and must include Gen Z in the discovery of truth. Importantly, such complex questions require deeper analysis of the questions. Where are they coming from? Why are the questions important to you, and why now? Understanding where the questions are coming from sheds light on ways to arrive at the answers in a meaningful and inviting manner. Many times, probing questions reveal abuses and trauma embedded in the life of the questions. All of this is important to reimaging faith and local church ministry for greater engagement with Gen Z – and any other generation for that matter.

What Should Churches Do about the Gen Z Crisis of Faith?

Churches attuned to what's important to Gen Z are best positioned to attract and cultivate a faith environment to produce a Great Awakening amidst a generation of spiritually hungry, spiritual but not religious, unchurched young people. Thom Rainer offers helpful observations for pastors around the world interested in evangelising and retaining Gen Zers:

1. Churches who are negative and fight often will not even be considered by Gen Z. "Gen Z will quickly walk away from churches fighting over such trivia as times of worship services, styles of music, and facility preferences. They hate the divisiveness and pettiness they see when church members complain about their pastors. They've had enough negativity! They are wondering if any church members really remember the gospel is good news!"[60]

2. Gen Z will strongly prefer churches that are focused and simple. "They detest activity-driven churches. They will not hang around long if you ask them to

---

[60] Thom Rainer, "3 Significant Issues for Churches to Reach Gen Z, Teenagers", *The Pentecost*, 5th October 2021 [Available at: https://thepentecost.ng/2019/12/3-significant-issues-for-churches-to-reach-gen-z-teenagers] [Last accessed: 7th May 2024].

attend a plethora of events and activities that make no sense to them. The simple church will be the church of choice."[61]

3. Change-resistant churches will not attract Gen Z. This generation is not stuck in a rut of "it's always been this way." "This is a generation of digital natives. They understand constant change. They live in a world of technological disruption. Change is their norm. Gen Zers, therefore, have no concept of the pettiness of many church issues."[62]

4. Additionally, churches that invite Gen Zers into worship and administrative leadership roles are more likely to attract and retain them. This is a generation of innovators accustomed to navigating life more independently.

The search for community amidst an epidemic of isolation, the desire for meaning, the hunger for spiritual awareness within a generational religious draught – all these must not be taken lightly. The atmosphere is set. The harvest is ripe. We must pray to the Lord of the harvest to send labourers like the children of Issachar who understand the times. A Great Awakening is just beyond the horizon!

Glimmers of Hope

Pockets of Gen Zers are rekindling the flames of revival, providing glimmers of hope. Globally, Pentecostal, or Charismatic-type Christian spirituality is leading the charge. As a recent article in the Washington Examiner asserts:

> Younger generations of Christians are particularly drawn to the charismatic experience today. So it is with Holy Spirit-led churches each week around the world. The Asbury Revival and others like it embody a universal desire to experience the more supernatural, metaphysical faith that has been absent in many of the churches that are haemorrhaging members. Headlines often declare the loss of religion in the United States, a notable trend toward those who identify as "nones." That shift, however, is being slowed dramatically by the rise of charismatic movements found partially in the influx of immigrants from Latin America, Africa, and Asia to the U.S.[63]

Congregations unafraid to engage in ongoing re-imaginative ministry remain on the cutting edge of youth attraction. Some examples are referenced above; examples are the Ghanaian prayer gatherings in secondary and post-secondary schools and the sparks of congregational enthusiasm at Heart of God Church in Singapore.

---

[61] Rainer, "3 Significant Issues".
[62] Rainer, "3 Significant Issues".
[63] Ericka Andersen, "Charismatic Christian Movements Offer Hope for Gen Z", *Washington Examiner*, 12th April 2023 [Available at: https://www.washingtonexaminer.com/opinion/charismatic-christian-movements-offer-hope-for-gen-z] [Last accessed: 7th May 2024].

Another example is the 2023 Asbury University Outpouring,[64] sparked during a chapel service that lasted twenty-four hours, seven days a week, for a few weeks. Local news in Louisville, Kentucky reported that approximately 50,000 to 70,000 people from around the world gathered at Asbury University to attend a worship service that started at 10 a.m. on Wednesday, 8th February 2023, and continued uninterrupted[65] until 24th February 2023, when the university officials ended it. Notably, the revival was at a Christian university and not a secular one. As stated earlier, Pew Research Center reports Gen Z as the highest generation of "nones." Most Gen Zers attracted to the Asbury experience – on campus and beyond – seem to have been among the declining remnant of Gen Z Christians. Not many of the testimonies were from people who converted from being a "none" to the faith. For example, Anneli White is a student at the University of Kentucky and a member of Immanuel Baptist Church. She journeyed to Asbury for the revival experience and commented, "The Holy Spirit was tangible in the room. Chains were broken, confession happened, and God was praised as holy, holy, holy."[66] While White and others touched by the revival were already Christians, their experiences represent the need for a fresh wind of the Holy Spirit among the remnant of believing Gen Zers. The hope is concealed in their renewed excitement about the faith. Their congregational participation and leadership inspire new ways of communicating the relevance of faith in their generation.

Churches worldwide that include young people in the ongoing work of theological reimagination – bridging faith, higher education, business, care for the environment, community formation, and technology – prove more effective in attracting and retaining young people most affected by secularism. Faith integration in the pursuit of meaning in everyday life produces fresh religious excitement in this generation.

---

[64] Asbury University, "What Happened at Asbury University?" *Asbury University* [Available at: https://www.asbury.edu/outpouring/] [Last accessed: 7th May 2024].
[65] WDRB, "Asbury University Student Uses Map to Track Worshipers Who Came to 'Revival' Services", *WDRB*, 24th February 2023 [Available at: https://www.wdrb.com/news/asbury-university-student-uses-map-to-track-worshipers-who-came-to-revival-services/article_a5e03506-b459-11ed-b30e-474a6ca5ff8b.html#:~:text=Over%20the%20past%20couple%20of,for%20more%20than%20a%20week] [Last accessed: 7th May 2024].
[66] Mark Maynard and Hannah Julian, "All Eyes Focus on (Another?) Asbury Revival", *Kentucky Today*, 13th February 2023 [Available at: https://www.kentuckytoday.com/baptist_life/all-eyes-focus-on-another-asbury-revival/article_6994621a-a9b0-11ed-9cf7-67c841f9b6a3.html?fbclid=IwAR1tq3P_4dntYTur7ipKOPbi7w3zGoBLB_-t2ishqBEjSQRdzB2OUxOT6dg] [Last accessed: 7th May 2024].

Bibliography

Primary Sources

Asamoah-Gyadu, J. Kwabena. Conversation with Antipas Harris, 15th September 2023.

——. Conversation with Antipas Harris, 3rd November 2023.

Otabil, Mensa. Conversation with Antipas Harris, 21st September 2023.

Secondary Sources

Adegbite, Tunji. "Tapping into the Chutzpah of Nigeria's Generation Z", *This Day Live*. 18th October 2020. [Available at: https://www.thisdaylive.com/index.php/2020/10/18/tapping-into-the-chutzpah-of-nigerias-generation-z] [Last accessed: 7th May 2024].

Andersen, Ericka. "Charismatic Christian Movements Offer Hope for Gen Z", *Washington Examiner*. 12th April 2023. [Available at: https://www.washingtonexaminer.com/opinion/charismatic-christian-movements-offer-hope-for-gen-z] [Last accessed: 7th May 2024].

Asbury University. "What Happened at Asbury University?" *Asbury University*. [Available at: https://www.asbury.edu/outpouring/] [Last accessed: 7th May 2024].

Boyon, Nicolas. "Two Global Religious Divides: Geographic and Generational", *Ipsos Global Advisor*. 11th May 2023. [Available at: https://www.ipsos.com/en-us/two-global-religious-divides-geographic-and-generational] [Last accessed: 7th May 2024].

Burg, Ryan P. *The Nones: Where They Came From, Who They Are, and Where They Are Going*. Minneapolis, MN: Fortress, 2021.

Casanova, José. "Rethinking Secularization", *Hedgehog Review* 8(1-2), (Spring/Summer 2006), 7-22. [Available at: https://hedgehogreview.com/issues/after-secularization-special-double-issue/articles/rethinking-secularization] [Last accessed: 7th May 2024].

Center for Inquiry. "What is Secular Humanism?" *Center for Inquiry*. [Available at: https://centerforinquiry.org/definitions/what-is-secular-humanism/#:~:text=Secular%20humanism%20is%20a%20nonreligious,find%20solutions%20to%20human%20problems] [Last accessed: 7th May 2024].

Centers for Disease Control and Prevention. "Emergency Department Visits Involving Mental Health Conditions, Suicide-Related Behaviors, and Drug Overdoses among Adolescents – United States, January 2019–February 2023", *Morbidity and Mortality Weekly Report* 72(19), (2023), 502-12. CDC. 12th May 2023. [Available at: https://www.cdc.gov/mmwr/volumes/72/wr/mm7219a1.htm?s_cid=mm7219a1_w] [Last accessed: 7th May 2024].

Coulter, Dale M. "Thoughts on the Future of American Christianity", *Firebrand*. 3rd October 2023. [Available at: https://firebrandmag.com/articles/thoughts-on-the-future-of-american-christianity-firebrand-big-read?fbclid=IwAR3azTAmv3axMdffq9uQJ277a9Ppe0-yAo_Uozj1C3ukx0HpXw8PdA-0_h8] [Last accessed: 7th May 2024].

Cox, Daniel A. "Emerging Trends and Enduring Patterns in American Family Life", *Survey Center on American Life*. 9th February 2022. [Available at: https://www.americansurveycenter.org/research/emerging-trends-and-enduring-patterns-in-american-family-life/] [Last accessed: 7th May 2024].

——. "Generation Z and the Future of Faith in America", *Survey Center on American Life*. 24th March 2022. [Available at: https://www.americansurveycenter.org/research/generation-z-future-of-faith/] [Last accessed: 7th May 2024].

Crockett, Clayton. "What is Postsecularism?" *American Book Review* 39(5), (2018), 6-14. [Available at: https://doi.org/10.1353/abr.2018.0062] [Last accessed: 7th May 2024].

Dimock, Michael. "5 Things to Keep in Mind When You Hear about Gen Z, Millennials, Boomers and Other Generations", *Pew Research Center*. 22nd May 2023. [Available at: https://www.pewresearch.org/short-reads/2023/05/22/5-things-to-keep-in-mind-when-you-hear-about-gen-z-millennials-boomers-and-other-generations/] [Last accessed: 7th May 2024].

Ipsos. "Global Religion 2023: Religious Beliefs across the World", *Ipsos*. 11th May 2023. [Available at: https://www.ipsos.com/sites/default/files/ct/news/documents/2023-05/Ipsos%20Global%20Advisor%20-%20Religion%202023%20Report%20-%2026%20countries.pdf] [Last accessed: 7th May 2024].

Koh, Pearlyn. "To Keep Gen Z in the Pews, One Singapore Church Lets Them Run the Service", *Christianity Today*. 10th February 2023. [Available at: https://www.christianitytoday.com/ct/2023/february-web-only/singapore-youth-church-gen-z-ministry.html] [Last accessed: 7th May 2024].

Lipka, Michael, and Claire Gecewicz. "More Americans Now Say They're Spiritual but Not Religious", *Pew Research Center*. 6th September 2017. [Available at: https://www.pewresearch.org/short-reads/2017/09/06/more-americans-now-say-theyre-spiritual-but-not-religious/] [Last accessed: 7th May 2024].

Manalang, Aprilfaye T. "Generation Z, Minority Millennials and Disaffiliation from Religious Communities: Not Belonging and the Cultural Cost of Unbelief", *Interdisciplinary Journal of Research on Religion* 17 (article 2) (2021), 1-24. [Available at: https://www.religjournal.com/articles/article_view.php?id=159] [Last accessed: 7th May 2024].

Mashau, T. Derrick. "A Reformed Missional Perspective on Secularism and Pluralism in Africa: Their Impact on African Christianity and the Revival of Traditional Religion", *CJT*, 44 (2009), 108-126. Calvin University. [Available at: https://www.calvin.edu/library/database/crcpi/fulltext/ctj/2009-441-108.pdf] [Last accessed: 7th May 2024].

Maynard, Mark, and Hannah Julian. "All Eyes Focus on (Another?) Asbury Revival", *Kentucky Today*, 13th February 2023. [Available at: https://www.kentuckytoday.com/baptist_life/all-eyes-focus-on-another-asbury-revival/] [Last accessed: 7th May 2024].

Miner, William. "In Singapore, Religious Diversity and Tolerance Go Hand in Hand", *Pew Research Center*. 6th October 2023. [Available at: https://www.pewresearch.org/short-reads/2023/10/06/in-singapore-religious-diversity-and-tolerance-go-hand-in-hand/] [Last accessed: 7th May 2024].

Ng, Deborah. "The Future of Youth Ministry in Singapore", *Cru: Christian Stories about Helping Others*. [Available at: https://www.cru.org/sg/en/stories/helping-others-grow/the-future-of-youth-ministry-in-singapore.html/] [Last accessed: 7th May 2024].

Rainer, Thom. "3 Significant Issues for Churches to Reach Gen Z, Teenagers", *The Pentecost*. 5th October 2021. [Available at: https://thepentecost.ng/2019/12/3-significant-issues-for-churches-to-reach-gen-z-teenagers/] [Last accessed: 7th May 2024].

Saad, Samantha. "Where Boomer Faith in God Is Low, Gen Z Belief Is Up", *Christianity Today*, 24th July 2023. [Available at: https://www.christianitytoday.com/news/2023/july/ipsos-global-religion-survey-boomer-gen-z-belief.html] [Last accessed: 7th May 2024].

Te Grotenhuis, Manfred, and Peer Scheepers. "Churches in Dutch: Causes of Religious Disaffiliation in The Netherlands, 1937-1995", *Journal for the Scientific Study of Religion* 40(4), (2001), 591-606. JSTOR. [Available at: https://www.jstor.org/stable/1387654] [Last accessed: 7th May 2024].

Twenge, Jean M. *iGen: Why Today's Super-Connected Kids Are Growing up Less Rebellious, More Tolerant, Less Happy – and Completely Unprepared for Adulthood*. New York: Atria, 2017.

Van der Walt, B.J. *Transforming Power: Challenging Contemporary Secular Society*. Potchefstroom, South Africa: ICCA, 2007.

WDRB. "Asbury University Student Uses Map to Track Worshipers Who Came to 'Revival' Services", *WDRB*. 24th February 2023. [Available at: https://www.wdrb.com/news/asbury-university-student-uses-map-to-track-worshipers-who-came-to-revival-services/article_a5e03506-b459-11ed-b30e-474a6ca5ff8b.html#:~:text=Over%20the%20past%20couple%20of,for%20more%20than%20a%20week] [Last accessed: 7th May 2024].

The World Factbook. "Introduction: Africa, Ghana". *Ghana Statistical Service Website*. [Available at: https://statsghana.gov.gh/docs/countrypdf_gh.pdfhttps://www.thegospelcoalition.org/article/gen-z/] [Last accessed: 7th May 2024].

Zylstra, Sarah Eekhoff. "6 Things Christians Should Know about Gen Z", *The Gospel Coalition*. 15th February 2022. [Available at: https://www.thegospelcoalition.org/article/gen-z/] [Last accessed: 7th May 2024].

Contributors

Editors

Kong Hee
Co-founder and Lead Pastor, City Harvest Church, Singapore
MA Theology Vanguard University
Doctoral studies Bangor University

Byron D Klaus
President, Assemblies of God Theological Seminary (1999-2015)
Chair, Board of Directors, The In Trust Center for Theological Schools
DMin Fuller Theological Seminary

Douglas Petersen
Margaret S Smith Distinguished Professor of World Mission and Intercultural Studies (Emeritus), Vanguard University
Distinguished Professor of Social Theology, School of Theology City Harvest Church, Singapore
PhD Oxford Centre for Mission Studies

Contributors

Kwabena Asamoah-Gyadu
President and Baeta-Grau Professor of African Christianity and Pentecostal/Charismatic Theology at Trinity Theological Seminary (Ghana)
PhD University of Birmingham

Paul Bendor-Samuel
Executive Director-Oxford Centre for Mission Studies
MBBCH (Cardiff) MRCGP (London) CDRS (Cambridge)
MBE awarded for medical services in Tunisia (2000)

Juan Angel Castro
Senior Pastor, Centro Evangelistico, San Salvador, El Salvador
MA Vanguard University

Kim-Kwong Chan
Honorary Research Fellow at International Centre for Law and Religion-University Centre for China Studies at the Chinese University of Hong Kong
PhD University of Ottawa
D Th Pontifical St. Paul University

Jacqui Grey
Professor of Biblical Studies, Alpha Crucis University College (Australia)
PhD Charles Sturt University

Jennifer and Karl Hargestam
Jennifer Hargestam is co-founder of Mission One Eleven. MALS Vanguard University; Doctor of Global Leadership (Cand.) Fuller Theological Seminary. Karl is founder of the Joshua Campaign and serves as Executive Director of City Serve and former director of Missions for the Swedish Pentecostal Church.

Antipas Harris
Founder/President of Urban Renewal Center – Norfolk, Virginia
Founding President of Jakes Divinity School Dallas, Texas
D Min Boston University School of Theology
PhD St Thomas University

Young Hoon Lee
Senior Pastor, Yoido Full Gospel Church Seoul, South Korea
PhD Temple University

Julie Ma
Professor of Missions and Intercultural Studies, Undergraduate College of Theology and Ministry. Oral Roberts University
PhD Fuller Theological Seminary

Wonsuk Ma
Executive Director, ORU Center for Spirit-Empowered Research-Distinguished Professor of Global Christianity Oral Roberts University
PhD Fuller Theological Seminary

Frank Macchia
Professor of Christian Theology, Vanguard University
Associate Director of the Centre for Pentecostal and Charismatic Studies, Bangor University (UK)
DTheol University of Basel

Mary K Mahon
President and Executive Director of ChildHope
PhD Biola University

Ivan Satyavrata
Chair, Board of Directors, World Vision International
Pastor Emeritus, The Assembly of God Church, Kolkata, India
PhD Oxford Centre for Mission Studies

Brian Stiller
Global Ambassador for the World Evangelical Alliance
President Emeritus at Tyndale University College and Seminary
DMin Gordon Conwell Theological Seminary

Joel Tejedo
Director of Asia Pacific Research Centre at Asia Pacific Theological Seminary
DMin Asia Pacific Theological Seminary

Gani Wiyono
Academic Deam, Satayabhaki Advanced School of Theology (Indonesia)
ThM Asia Pacific Theological Seminary